£3.00

TRADITION AND TRUTH

David Edwards has been a Fellow of All Souls College, Oxford, and Dean of King's College, Cambridge, and his work on church history includes *Christian England*, a history from the Romans to 1914 revised in one volume in 1989. But he is mainly known as a priest of the Church of England, now Provost of Southwark Cathedral in London, who has for many years presented and assessed the work of contemporary theologians. He was a publisher as Editor of the SCM Press 1958–66 and since then has been an almost weekly book-reviewer in the *Church Times*.

His recent books include *The Futures of Christianity* (1987). 'A most impressive book marked by keen perception, intelligent analysis and acute judgment, combined with an attractive style seasoned with aphorism' (*Expository Times*). 'Readable, accurate and enlightening on many issues, imparting a global perspective. And who else would have had the courage to write it?' (*The Tablet*). 'Fascinating and rewarding reading, it stands out as a masterpiece' (*Ecumenical Review*). In *Essentials: A Liberal-Evangelical Dialogue* (1988) he conducted a dialogue with the Evangelical leader John Stott. 'Edwards and Stott are admirably qualified for the task. Both have immense experience, theological skill, facility with words, and a profound respect for each other and each other's faith. If anyone can succeed in this undertaking, surely they can' (*Theology*). Now he attempts a dialogue with theologians at the opposite end of the spectrum from doctrinally conservative Evangelicalism.

TRADITION AND TRUTH

The Challenge of England's
Radical Theologians 1962–1989

David L. Edwards

with responses from
John Bowden, Don Cupitt, John Hick,
Dennis Nineham and Maurice Wiles

HODDER AND STOUGHTON
LONDON   SYDNEY   AUCKLAND   TORONTO

The quotation from J. S. Bezzant on pp. 20–2 is reproduced by permission of Constable and Co.

British Library Cataloguing in Publication Data

Edwards, David L. (David Lawrence), *1929–*
  Tradition and truth.
  1. Jesus Christ
  I. Title
  230

  ISBN 0-340-51452-3

CONTENTS

Preface		7
1	These Turbulent Priests: Objections to traditional beliefs	9
2	John Robinson and the Images of God: Is God only the depth of what is obviously real?	30
3	Don Cupitt and the Reality of God: Is religion only human?	68
4	Maurice Wiles and the Activity of God: Does God intervene after creation?	98
5	Geoffrey Lampe and the Incarnation of God: Was Jesus only a man filled by the Spirit of God?	125
6	John Bowden and the Facts about Jesus: What do we know about the man behind the gospels?	169
7	Dennis Nineham and the Relevance of Jesus: If revelation is culture-bound, is it authoritative?	191
8	John Hick and the Uniqueness of Jesus: Is Jesus of Nazareth the world's only Saviour?	212
9	What, Then, Should We Believe?	254
	Responses	283
	Don Cupitt	283
	Maurice Wiles	286
	John Bowden	291
	Dennis Nineham	296
	John Hick	306
	Bibliography	311
	Index	320

PREFACE

I have had the privilege of being involved in a movement in English theology which since 1962 has gained widespread attention because it has offered radical, and often constructive, criticisms of traditional Christian beliefs. I have the feeling that despite the backlash against it the movement has done much of what it set out to do. So I have attempted to sum it up and assess it, deliberately courting the criticism that I have been too selective in the subjects covered and too subjective in the opinions offered, too favourable at some points and too hostile at others. The attempt was really beyond my powers but has educated me. It has meant thinking out where I believe the movement spoke truths of lasting importance and where (as is the fate of all theological movements) it fell short of perfection. I have tried to write for a public far wider than the circle of academic specialists in theology – a public which these radicals addressed with a remarkable success. The response to the debate has shown that there are large numbers of people who ask themselves whether traditional Christianity is true – and who are ready to think hard, provided that technical terms are explained.

I, too, am an amateur. By inclination and some training I prefer history to theology. But from 1958 to 1966 I was Editor and Managing Director of the SCM Press, Britain's leading theological publishing house, which has made available many of the most significant books in this debate, and I am grateful to my successor, Dr John Bowden, for his co-operation in the present project. Not long after leaving the SCM Press I became a regular reviewer for the *Church Times*, the Church of England's leading newspaper. Its editor, Dr Bernard Palmer, who retired in 1989, gave me this opportunity and responsibility almost every week for some twenty years, and I thank him for permission to reprint some of my reviews. I dedicate this book to him with affection. I have shortened the reviews slightly in order to reduce what was clumsy, ephemeral or repetitious, and I hope that with all their inadequacies they will preserve something of the flavour of a long debate. I also offer some more mature reflections.

Hodder and Stoughton have encouraged me by publishing my own recent attempts to do theology: *The Futures of Christianity*, a study of the dialogues between churches and cultures in the contemporary world (1987), and *Essentials*, a dialogue with the Evangelical leader John Stott (1988). I thank David Wavre for his suggestion that I should write a sequel to *Essentials* and for his ready agreement with the idea that this should be a dialogue with theologians at the opposite end of the spectrum from doctrinally conservative Evangelicalism. In *Essentials* I attempted to discuss some subjects which I scarcely touch here – the authority of the Bible, the atonement, miracles, Christian ethics, human destiny.

I am grateful to the distinguished theologians who have found time to comment on my chapters which discuss their writings. I changed any detail in my own drafts which they wished to see changed because it misrepresented them, and I am glad to be able to print responses in this book from five of them. With a couple of exceptions, they saw only the chapters to which they refer. I could have reviewed these reviews of my reviews, and I should have enjoyed exploring the question why they are sometimes more acid than Dr Stott was in his responses to my criticisms of his theology, but it seemed more useful to leave the verdict to the reader. At least I hope that some will see a bit more clearly what the issues are. Of course I regret that John Robinson and Geoffrey Lampe died some time before this book was begun, but I believe that they now know the answers to the questions which theologians ask.

Finally I repeat from previous books my gratitude to David Mackinder, who lavished care on the final editing of my text; to colleagues in Southwark Cathedral, who have released me from much of the work of a busy London church in order that I might read and write; and to my wife Sybil, whose support is vital.

D.L.E.

1

THESE TURBULENT PRIESTS:
Objections to traditional beliefs

It began in Cambridge University in the autumn of 1962. My predecessor as Dean of King's College, Alec Vidler, edited a volume of essays called *Soundings* which called for, and inaugurated, a radically new movement in Christian theology. In the next term he gave one of four lectures addressed to non-theologians in the university. That outspoken series protesting against complacency in the Church was published as *Objections to Christian Belief*. Both *Soundings* and *Objections* were bought and discussed eagerly inside and outside Cambridge, and the lectures were crowded with audiences of about fifteen hundred. It was the beginning of public attention and controversy which were often to surround the protests of England's radical theologians.

In many spheres of life, and in many countries, the 1960s were a decade of protest and innovation, and in many parts of international Christianity the Church and its theology were being renewed. It was, for example, the time of the *aggiornamento* around the Second Vatican Council, and many Catholic theologians, from Hans Küng downwards, were to be more boldly radical than that brave but often two-faced council itself. The World Council of Churches was the centre of many brave hopes for Christian reunion, and was a platform for more radical anti-colonialism from the Third World. In America the most eminent figure among Protestant theologians engaging in an intellectual dialogue with the modern world, Paul Tillich, was to die in 1965, but other theologians, less subtle than Tillich, were to announce the 'death of God'. The 1960s were to show that, whether or not God was dead, Christians certainly were not, for in the churches there was to be a storm of radical activism in support of 'civil rights' and other political and ethical causes. The ferment was to transform the previously conservative religious scene in the

Netherlands (for example), and of course German theologians were to be neither silent nor shallow. But it can be argued that nowhere has the intellectual debate about objections to traditional Christian beliefs been more public, or more sustained, than in England, and it is interesting to ask why that may be true about a country not famous for a passionate interest in theology.

A part of the explanation is that England is a comparatively small and fairly well-educated country, where journalism, TV and bookshops can communicate the thought of the universities to a fairly wide non-academic public if that thought is reckoned to be news. In the 1960s a number of factors encouraged this communication: the country was full of energy not all of which was due to the cheapness of oil, the universities and colleges were expanding in order to educate the post-war baby boom, the paperback revolution was a fairly recent phenomenon in the bookshops, and TV programmes included some fairly serious discussions, partly in order to show that this new medium was respectable. What seemed discussable had to be new, but quite often 'radical' theology *was* news, partly because of the spectacle of clergymen criticising Christianity. The attention given to these theologians has also been a factor of England's basic traditionalism. This both stimulates and protects, for modernisers feel the need to rebel against tradition for the sake of truth but their adherence to tradition does give them some prestige and security, whether or not their adherence goes deep. (In British politics the radical modernisers have gained by calling themselves the Conservative Party.) In Cambridge although much of the university is secular the traditional arrangements have survived which provide for a substantial department of theology ('Divinity Faculty') in the university and for 'deans' (senior chaplains) in the colleges. In the rest of England the tradition of taking some interest in religion survives more widely than the habit of churchgoing. And one of the English traditions is the maintenance of free speech. This tradition makes sure that the Church of England, for example, nowadays never takes legal action against any of its members who may seem to be heretical. There is a feeling of freedom. Germans have been known to complain that too much English theology has been written within the sound of church bells. But at least it has not been written within the sound of gallows being erected by an Inquisition.

All these and other factors helped to provide a local and national audience for the Cambridge theologians when they pleaded that the time had come for the public airing of fundamental questions about the Christian Church's traditional doctrines. 'We've got a very big leeway to make up,' said Alec Vidler on TV, 'because there's been so much suppression of real, deep thought and intellectual alertness and integrity in the Church.'

Naturally there was a reaction from traditionalists who were thus rebuked. There was anger. Henry II is said to have sent the knights to Canterbury with the question: 'Who will rid me of this turbulent priest?' Since most of the Cambridge theologians who created this disturbance were priests of the Church of England, week by week the *Church Times* was filled with protests at their disloyalty. In *Objections to Christian Belief* are preserved Professor MacKinnon's counter-attacking references to the 'unbridled venom . . . cosy acquiescence in conventional ways of thought . . . [and] Philistine anti-intellectualism of the *Church Times*' (p. 22). But if the conservatives barked, they did not bite. By commissioning the murder of an archbishop in Canterbury Cathedral Henry II made Thomas Becket a martyr, and the lesson has been thoroughly learnt in the modern Church of England's tradition of free speech and toleration.

A pat on the back, however, may be more deadly than a sword, since this policy of toleration has often turned out to be an effective way of marginalising and discouraging subversives, who become not martyrs but nonentities. That might have been the fate of England's radical theologians. For the strength of the English tradition of taking an interest in religion should not be exaggerated. When the word 'theology' is used in common speech it is often intended to suggest that here is a debate which never ends and never matters much. In the days when Harold Wilson wished to divert the electorate's attention from the traditional commitment of Britain's Labour Party to take the means of production into common ownership, he used to deride the discussion about Clause 4 of the Labour Party's constitution (where that aim is still enshrined) as 'theology'. Even in England's churches theologians usually carry little weight. All the emphasis is practical and positive – on lay life, the pastoral work of the clergy, evangelism, running the churches as organisations, contributing to the good causes in the surrounding society. And theologians can react to the churches' dismissive treatment of them and their concerns by becoming even more negative towards the churches and distant from them, increasing the impression that a dialogue is impossible. In an issue of the journal *Theology* (1986) honouring one radical theologian, Professor Dennis Nineham, another, Professor Leslie

Houlden, expressed in his editorial 'A Wilderness Voice' a mood
of some bitterness. 'The fact is', he wrote,

> that during this period the links between the Church and all but
> the more conservative elements in the world of formal theology
> have grown weaker and weaker, and the 'churchy' among
> theologians have become more and more distinguishable from
> the theological community in general, just as they have become
> more and more of a minority (p. 340).

In contrast, Houlden was under the impression that the anonymous writer of wide-ranging Prefaces in *Crockford's Clerical
Directory* 'has clear ideas on how theologians should behave. They
should fortify the Church as it is and serve its needs; they should be
edifying in a practical and prosy way; and they should not push
novelties in our faces or provoke churchpeople to too much
self-scrutiny' (p. 339). I was then the Preface-writer.

In England, however, radical theology was neither completely
martyred by its enemies nor completely suffocated by apathy. One
reason for its survival was that the movement which was started in
Cambridge in 1962–3 was made irreversibly public by two boldly
provocative theologians with a rare gift for words and with personalities as interesting as they were puzzling – John Robinson,
who spent some time away from Cambridge as Bishop of Woolwich and became the author of a bestseller, and Don Cupitt, who
remained in Cambridge and from that base attracted attention and
controversy through TV and a series of books. Both were called
atheists, in one case accurately. I shall devote my next two chapters
to those two turbulent priests. Other theologians attracted publicity when journalists spotted the word 'myth' in their book titles,
and towards the end of the period which I cover remarks on TV by
David Jenkins, Bishop of Durham, stirred up controversy.

But there was another reason for the survival of the questions
asked by England's radical theologians. These questions could not
be silenced either by anger or by a bored toleration, and could not
be forgotten when no longer 'news', because they really do matter
to thoughtful Christians. They often trouble those who are in their
own eyes the guardians of orthodoxy. They are asked not only by
professional theologians but also by millions of people whose
attention to religious subjects is far more spasmodic. They probe
the claim of Christianity to be true. Is God best pictured not as a
Daddy in the sky but as the depth of what is obviously real? Or does
that lead to atheism? Is religion 'only human' – not in any way a

meeting with God? Does God interfere after creation, for example by miracles? Was Jesus a man filled by the Spirit of God – and no more? What do we know about the man behind the gospels? If the revelation of God through Jesus Christ is 'culture-bound' – shaped by the society which deals with it in any one period – is it meaningful or in any sense authoritative for all people and all time? And when we put him alongside the other great religious teachers of humanity, can we truthfully say that Jesus of Nazareth is the world's only Saviour? How are such questions best answered if at the heart of the Christian tradition is the awe expressed in the Book of Common Prayer's translation of Psalm 51:6, 'Lo, thou requirest truth in the inward parts'?

As I look back on the explosion of radical theology in the early 1960s I am struck by the fact that these questions had not been discussed very seriously by most theologians in England or elsewhere during the 1930s, 1940s and 1950s. In this and many other countries almost the whole Church had become anchored to a static orthodoxy – as orthodoxy had been expressed by repeating the language of the Bible and of the Fathers and councils in the first five Christian centuries, supplemented in the case of Roman Catholicism by the decrees of the Vatican and of the First Vatican Council. Such adhesion to an old orthodoxy is to be understood and respected in the setting of world history. It had been the age of resistance to Hitler and Stalin, and of the reconstruction of Europe after total war: an age of self-sacrifice and much idealism (associated in England with the creation of the Welfare State). And although secularisation had been advancing beneath the surface of society, English Christianity had seemed to be fairly secure as the established, respectable, public philosophy. In the war men had been told that they ought to be prepared to fight and die for 'Christian values' or 'Christian civilisation' – and had often agreed. In peacetime the vast majority of the public refused to tell investigators conducting public opinion polls that it was sure there was no God. Most people, according to what they told public opinion polls, believed in a 'personal' God, and most of the rest in Something. There were few secular funerals (a situation which has lasted to the end of the 1980s). The doctrines of Christianity, if not precisely believed in, had appeared to be stable and to offer stability in the background of society. Queen Elizabeth II had been crowned in Westminster Abbey amid public delight in the gorgeously traditional ceremony; religious education had been provided by Parliament in all the State's schools; religious

programmes occupied much time on radio and TV, specially on
Sundays. For believing Christians, the prevailing conservatism had
been articulated in the teachings of Pope Pius XII, or of the Church
of England's own C. S. Lewis, who articulated the churchgoing
laity's impatience with questioning theologians.

Alec Vidler, for a time the key figure in the new movement, was
editor of *Theology*, then published monthly, from 1939 to 1964.
When I worked through the back numbers of that journal in order
to write an article on '*Theology* under Dr Vidler' to mark his
retirement, I observed that these fundamental questions had not
been debated there with any great interest. Subjects such as the
significance of baptism or of bishops had got the controversies
going. There had been much hopeful support for the ecumenical
movement for Christian unity and much confidence that 'biblical
theology' would provide an adequate consensus for unity. 'Biblical
theology' tended to mean that a single, coherent 'biblical view' of a
subject was thought to be both discoverable and authoritative.
There was an emphasis on the unity of the Bible and on the
superiority of Israel and the Church to surrounding cultures.
Accordingly the 'Hebrew understanding' would be preferred to
the 'Greek'. The Bible was often called 'the book of the Church'
and was said to have been written 'from faith to faith'. What people
might make of the Bible if they did not share the Church's
traditional faith was not a topic much considered. Liturgical renewal had indeed brought some enthusiasm and even revision into
the worship in the churches, but at the heart of this renewal had
been the Eucharist (Holy Communion, the Mass), a rite very
strange to those not accustomed to its language about body and
blood; and the liturgical movement had been far more concerned to
get back to the pattern of worship in the early Christian centuries
than to express beliefs arising in the age of science. In the Church
of England the Book of Common Prayer had remained the
only fully official way of worship, and the energy of the Church
Assembly had been absorbed in the revision of the regulations
called canon law and of the system of ecclesiastical courts to
enforce them. Geoffrey Fisher, Archbishop of Canterbury from
1945 to 1961, described this enormous undertaking to his
biographer William Purcell as

> the most absorbing and all-embracing topic of my whole archi-
> episcopate . . . With the instincts of a headmaster I knew that it
> was absolutely essential to the well-ordering and self-respect of

the Church of England to have canons which could and should be obeyed. The lack of order had become quite dreadful (Purcell, *Fisher of Lambeth*, 1969, pp. 206–7).

The mood in the Church of England – as in England's other denominations – had been one in which the truth of traditional Christianity had been largely taken for granted and the concentration had been on tidying up the life of the Christian community with only minor modernisation.

However, these Cambridge theologians did not live in the ivory tower where they were stationed by the imaginations of many of their enraged critics. It is true that university teachers can be sheltered from some human problems. But it is a feature of life in a number of English universities, most notably 'Oxbridge', that those who teach theology rub shoulders with those who teach very different subjects because they all belong to colleges where they eat, chat, do business and care for students together. When I followed Alec Vidler as Dean of King's College I experienced the oddity that a famously beautiful chapel which looks like a large medieval cathedral belongs to a college pursuing its own concerns which are far from medieval; and I think that Vidler coped with this oddity better than I did. (Vidler's predecessor, the most sensitive of us three, took his own life.) The senior members of Oxbridge and many other English universities are also encouraged to take an interest in subjects other than their own, and in those studying them, with involvements even more varied than the life of a college. A university is not a monastery.

So the contributors to *Soundings* showed a sensitive awareness of the cultural situation around them. Howard Root, then Dean of Emmanuel College, had suggested the book, and he now started it with a chapter called 'Beginning All Over Again'. He wrote:

> The great problem of the Church (and therefore of its theologians) is to establish or re-establish some kind of vital contact with that enormous majority of human beings for whom the Christian faith is not so much unlikely as irrelevant and uninteresting. The greatest intellectual challenge to faith is simply that thoroughly secularized intelligence which is now the rule rather than the exception, whether it expresses itself in science or philosophy or politics or the arts. It is by no means clear that anything like Christian faith in the form we know it will ever again be able to come alive for people of our own time or of such future time as we can imagine. It is just as uncertain that

Christian ideas and ways of thought, as we know them, will be able to re-engage an intelligence and imagination now so far separated from them (pp. 6–7).

In *Soundings* John Habgood, a young theologian who had been a Research Fellow of King's College in science, rejoiced that science had 'built up a stable and, for the most part, universally accepted body of knowledge by its slow, cautious, piece-meal approach to practical problems which can actually be solved' (p. 28). In contrast theology was in danger of ceasing to matter (pp. 27–8). George Woods, then Dean of Downing College, began his essay with a quotation from Professor R. W. Hepburn: 'The language of "transcendence", the thought of God as a personal being, wholly other to man, dwelling apart in majesty – this talk may well collapse into meaninglessness, in the last analysis. And yet to sacrifice it seems at once to take one quite outside Christianity' (p. 45).

In such a climate of opinion these theologians were dissatisfied with what Root called 'the fashionable biblical theology, which never sees need to go beyond the words and concepts of Scripture' (p. 5). 'The fashionable biblical theology', wrote J. N. Sanders, then Dean of Peterhouse, '. . . is self-contained and self-consistent, but out of touch with experience' (p. 130). Equally these radical theologians rejected Archbishop Fisher's emphasis on the Church's organisation. Vidler wrote:

> The fact is that religion is a form of human activity which readily lends itself to the ambitions of organizers, and organizers are always with us to fasten upon it . . .
> [But] . . . many of the religious elements in historic Christianity and much that has gone under the name of religion may . . . be outgrown, or survive chiefly as venerable archaisms or as fairy stories for children, and we cannot tell in advance how they will be replaced or which of them will need to be replaced (pp. 251, 254).

Vidler quoted F. D. Maurice, a theologian prominent in Victorian Cambridge: 'we have been dosing our people with religion when what they want is not this but the Living God' (p. 243). But how is God to be known to be alive? The appeal to 'revelation' is not enough by itself. Two essays by Woods explored the human experiences of encountering 'the transcendent' and of being under moral 'obligation', pointing out that a 'natural' (in distinction from a 'revealed') theology is necessary. Otherwise 'there is no reasonable belief in a God who may choose to reveal himself' (p. 46). But how is the transcendent, or moral obligation, experienced in our time? 'The best text-books for contemporary natural theologians', Root urged,

> are not the second-hand theological treatises but the living works of artists who are in touch with the springs of creative imagination . . . We shall have to contemplate and absorb the disturbing visions of human nature which find expression in serious modern literature. We shall have to come to terms with a world in which old patterns of morality no longer direct or inspire because they no longer have life (pp. 18, 19).

Openly siding with those who rejected old patterns, some contributors argued that the appeal to 'authority' in the approach to God may be very dangerously misleading. Harry Williams, then Dean of Chapel of Trinity College, contributed a deeply felt essay on the danger of a poisonous image of God being taught by authority. He criticised the Prayer Book which was then used as the standard of the Church of England's worship and doctrine:

> The God . . . of the Book of Common Prayer seems sometimes to be a merciless egocentric tyrant, incapable of love, and thus having to be manipulated or cajoled into receiving his children . . . It is inevitable that what looks like Cranmer's deep lack of faith in God's mercy should communicate itself to many who use his liturgy, and should produce in them that spirit of bondage again unto fear from which Christ came to deliver us (p. 79).

And Geoffrey Lampe, then Ely Professor of Divinity, attacked the teaching of the Church of England's Thirty-nine Articles that Christ 'truly suffered, was crucified, dead and buried, to reconcile his Father to us, and to be a sacrifice, not only for original guilt, but also for all actual sins of men'. This, he declared, 'is not the gospel of the free love of God' (p. 180). The 'disastrous translation of personal reconciliation with the Father through the acceptance of free justification into terms of debit and credit has gone far to reverse the true meaning of Christ's death' (p. 182) – which is 'the supreme expression of the love of God' (p. 190).

John Burnaby, then Regius Professor of Divinity, contributed an essay on prayer which on the surface seemed fairly conventional. This was partly because of frequent references to the Book of Common Prayer. But a closer inspection showed that the professor had a concept of prayer which denied that it could influence God to take direct action in the affairs of the world: 'the power of God's love takes effect in human history in no other way than through the wills and actions of men in whom that love has come to dwell' (pp. 232–3). How, then, did God act in Christ, if miracles are impossible? Hugh Montefiore, then Dean of Gonville and Caius College, pleaded for the translation of the orthodoxy about the divine and human natures of Christ into 'a language more comprehensible today' (p. 172). He proposed instead that Christians should be content to say that 'God works in a personal way' (p. 166) and that 'in Jesus the divine activity was fully present so far as is possible in human personality' (p. 171). And in a challenge to the complacency which had assumed that Christ was the only religious teacher worth deeply serious attention, Ninian Smart, then a professor in Birmingham, pleaded that Christians should learn about, and from, the great non-Christian faiths.

As I try to assess *Soundings* almost thirty years after its publication, I notice of course that it is dated. Some omissions are glaring and some silences deafening when one looks back over subsequent Christian concerns and debates, for there was nothing in this book about the crisis of the poor nations, or the threats to the environment, or the nuclear peril, or the protests against racism and male chauvinism, or the call to the Church to be a model society embodying the kingdom of God. Harry Williams, so far from predicting the rise of feminism, assured his readers that the 'devotion to the Motherhood of God' encouraged by St Anselm among others in the Middle Ages 'had no future and was quickly forgotten. It had nothing in human experience on which to fasten' (p. 100). George Woods in his essay on Christian moral judgements mentioned cigarette smoking without criticising that drug (p. 198). And Alec Vidler ended the book by recommending for 'the time being' the continuation of the establishment of the Church of England by the State, including the appointment of bishops by the Prime Minister, in order to lessen the danger of reducing the National Church to a sect.

But the relevance of *Soundings* is, I believe, far more important than its failure to cover some subjects which were to become prominent in later Christian discussion and action. Challenges to care about the survival of the human race, or the liberation of its poor majority, or the dignity of its feminine half, are (of course) the proper concern of Christians, but those subjects have been high on the agenda of many bodies and individuals for many years. The

World Council of Churches, for example, has made this emphasis. Popes have not kept their convictions secret. More than one Evangelical conference has added its voice. Such international bodies have rightly concentrated on the practical problems which can be a matter of life and death, and such leadership has stimulated liberationists, liberals and conservatives alike. However, intellectual questions about traditional Christian beliefs are also bothersome, at least in some minds which have been freed from the necessity of concentration on urgent physical challenges, and bodies such as the World Council of Churches or the papacy or an international assembly of Evangelicals have found them too difficult to handle with openness and rigour. I conclude that it is the vocation of some theologians to ask these awkward questions out loud and to struggle to find honest and convincing answers.

If one grants the legitimacy and importance of these limited aims of the *Soundings* group, one sees (I think) that its foresight is more remarkable than its datedness. The pleas of Root for more imaginative Christian communication with a secular society, of Habgood for more sensitivity in the relationship between religion and science, of Woods for more discernment of the presence of God outside his explicit revelation, have not been entirely disappointed in the last quarter-century. Warnings such as those of Williams and Lampe against images of God which deny his love have been heeded by almost all Christians, and Montefiore's point that orthodoxy about Christ must be translated from old philosophical language has been generally granted. In the spiritual life many Christians have been willing to appreciate the strengths of non-Christian religions, in particular understanding prayer as the contemplation, not the manipulation, of God: thus the essays of Smart and Burnaby appeal. And some of the contributors to *Soundings* have gone on to steer the ship of the Church through stormy seas. Although Alec Vidler began a long retirement in 1967 and death has cut short the work of Burnaby, Lampe, Sanders and Woods, John Habgood became Archbishop of York, Hugh Montefiore Bishop of Birmingham and Howard Root a professor and then Director of the Anglican Centre in Rome, while Harry Williams and Ninian Smart became prolific writers with a big influence. I review one of Professor Smart's books later (pp. 248–50), and have also welcomed his large and large-hearted presentations of *The Religious Experience of Mankind* (1969) and *The World's Religions* (1989).

I had the minor honour of naming the movement which began

with *Soundings*. At least that is my claim, and I base it on what Alec Vidler wrote in his *Twentieth Century Defenders of the Faith* (1965): 'I have taken the title "Christian Radicalism" from the essay by Mr David Edwards on "A New Stirring in English Christianity" in *The Honest to God Debate*' (p. 101). But Vidler rightly used the title 'only as a convenient way of indicating a variety of trends or tendencies', and with approval he quoted me as advocating in 1963 'not a premature theological synthesis, and even more certainly not the organisation of a new religious party, but a host of other experiments in thought and life' (p. 117). I am writing the present book with a conviction that in the history of the movement since then much has gone wrong. I believe that this can and should be said by one who is profoundly grateful for all the experiments that have gone right.

I certainly do not think that what has subsequently gone wrong proves that the radicals were wrong to embark on their voyage. Errors could not be avoided, since theology is a human enterprise and to be human is to be fallible. Humanly speaking it was inevitable that in *Soundings* insights which have so far stood the test of time should be mixed with remarks which with hindsight seem liable to develop into mistakes. It was, I believe, right to decide that the old orthodoxy was no longer a fit harbour for the ship of Christianity. But as the ship left harbour there were rocks ahead.

I can, I hope, illustrate both the wisdom of embarkation on a new voyage and the dangers of rocks. For I can refer to a book which was much less cautious than *Soundings* – the lectures published as *Objections to Christian Belief.*

In his lecture J. S. Bezzant, then Dean of St John's College, denounced the old orthodoxy fiercely and at length. His most effective passage, however, demolished the credibility of the old system of dogmas simply by stating what it would mean to be orthodox in that style. He said:

Traditional Christianity had what was known as the scheme of salvation. It was based on Scripture regarded as the verbally inspired record of Divine revelation; and the scheme as a whole, but by no means all included in it, stands or falls with that view of the Bible. The Pauline teaching on sin and salvation was elaborated into a scheme containing elements of Aristotelian science and the theology of St Augustine. It began with an alleged rebellion of Satan against God in which angels fell. By direct acts of God, Adam and Eve were created, apparently as adults, not only innocent but fully righteous. Their descendants were intended to restore the number of the angels depleted by the heavenly revolt. Moved by envy, Satan persuaded our first parents to disobey one absolute command of God, that they were not to obtain knowledge, and so brought about their fall from original righteousness, in consequence of which they transmitted to all their offspring, by natural generation, a corrupted nature wholly inclined to evil, an enfeebled will, and also the guilt of their sin. Thus all mankind lay under the curse of sin both original and actual, justly the object of Divine wrath and destined to damnation.

In order to restore his thwarted purpose God sent his Son who, assuming human nature, was born on earth, whereon was wrought the drama of his death and resurrection. Jesus, pure from all defect of original and actual sin, alone fulfilled the conditions of a perfect sacrifice for human sin. By this God's legitimate anger with guilty mankind was appeased and his honour satisfied; he was graciously pleased to accept his Son's sacrifice, enabled to forgive sin, and man was potentially redeemed. The Christian church, a Divine corporation, came into being; those baptized into it who by grace persevered in the fulfilment of its commands would be secure in the life to come. From the supernatural life of the church, the world and history derived their meaning and without it would at a last day perish by fire. This would happen when the unknown number of souls required to replace the fallen angels was complete. The Anglican Prayer-book office for the burial of the dead still prays that God may be pleased shortly to accomplish the number of the elect and to hasten his kingdom. The dead would be raised from their graves in their bodies, despite St Paul's clear assertion that flesh and blood cannot inherit the kingdom of God nor corruption incorruption. The saved were predestined to their salvation by an inscrutable decree of God, not for any merits of their own, but solely for those of Christ. As to the fate of the rest, there were differences of opinion, but it was generally held that they would suffer endless torment in the flames of a hell, by which climax not only would God's power and justice be finally vindicated but heaven's bliss intensified.

This outline has been so shattered that the bare recital of it has the aspect of a malicious travesty. Known facts of astronomy, geology, biological evolution, anthropology, the comparative study of religions, race and genetical and analytic psychology, the literary and historical criticism of the Bible, with the teaching of Jesus and the moral conscience of mankind, have banished this scheme beyond the range of credibility. But though it can no longer be taken seriously, certain doctrines vital in the Christian gospel of salvation are still taught in forms which derive from the vanished scheme and from nothing else; and this hinders the effective presentation of Christianity today (pp. 82–4).

Bezzant made it clear that he did not object to that form of traditional Christianity simply because it was a faith. He said:

There is not, nor is there ever likely to be, any view of the meaning, purpose, value and destiny of human life, not even the view that it has none, that is not in a greater or less degree founded upon faith, for neither the negative nor the positive belief is demonstrable, i.e., capable of proof (p. 81).

But he warned against any idea that facts and experiences known to Christians can be interpreted only 'in relation to the mythical world-pictures . . . whether Jewish or Hellenistic', or only on the basis of 'abstract nouns treated as actualities' when describing Christ (pp. 85–6), or only after the interpretation of Christ's work by a doctrine about the ingrained and inherited depravity of human nature (pp. 92–9). Holding that 'truth' is 'the correspondence of mind with fact' (p. 109), he insisted that the revelation of God is not by propositions which deserve to be believed although they contradict known facts. The mind must rebel against such dogmatism, and must not be deterred when traditionalists appeal to 'religious experiences' which are ranked higher than the known facts. 'Human understanding and assimilation are involved in asserting the trueness of any proposition whatsoever' (p. 101) and 'it is only by reference to a wider range of experience and knowledge than purely religious experiences that reasonable men can find *grounds*, as well as *causes*, for religious beliefs that can claim truth' (p. 106).

But the effective presentation of Christianity today can also be hindered by the errors of radicals, and I have come to think that *Objections to Christian Belief* included two tendencies where the ship was heading for the rocks.

The first was a tendency to identify Christianity with the acceptance of our natures, not emphasising the transformation of our natures in a new life lived in the Christian community and in a humble dependence on God the Father, on Jesus as Saviour and on the Holy Spirit. Conformity to nature became prominent; conversion to Christ became obscure or suspect. This tendency was an understandable reaction against the tradition that Christianity condemns and rejects humanity's natural instincts and all human beings who follow their instincts. These Cambridge theologians as they lived among young people agreed that the gospel teaches that God loves, accepts and uses us as we are, not as we think we ought to be. Professor Donald MacKinnon eloquently denounced a negative legalism, particularly directed against sexuality, which had perverted the Church's moral teaching. For example:

> It is impossible to escape the impression that, to certain sorts of clergy, the effective exclusion from sacramental communion of divorced persons who have remarried is the highest form of the Church's moral witness. The cynic might well be tempted to say that the heartless zeal frequently displayed in the bearing of this particular testimony, is a way in which ecclesiastics compensate for their unwillingness to engage with other besetting moral issues of our age, for instance the moral permissibility of nuclear weapons (p. 14).

MacKinnon also denounced a false passivity which had counselled Christians to accept intolerable evils 'when revolt rather than acceptance is a plain human duty' (p. 32) for people living 'in an age that is at once one of unprecedented excitement and unprecedented fear' (p. 22). In such attacks on the Church's record in ethics were to be heard the beginnings of the healthy protest which was to explode later in the 1960s and which was to be voiced in the slogan 'make love not war'.

But it was, as I now see things, a pity (although inevitable) that the second lecture in this series, by Harry Williams, was noticed chiefly for its exposition of the need to accept some physical expressions of sexuality outside marriage. In *Soundings* Williams had praised two films where sexual hang-ups were cured by generously loving partners who were not spouses (pp. 81–2). Now he produced further instances of honesty, love and liberation in such unconventional settings, and further criticism of the Church which 'bludgeons' us into submission to its mistaken morality by 'inflating the feelings of guilt which lie latent in us all' (p. 50). As he tells us in his frank autobiography, *Some Day I'll Find You* (1982), this emphasis on fulfilment was inspired by his gratitude for liberation, through psychoanalysis and much personal suffering and courage, from a sexual code which had been false to what he had learnt to accept as his God-given nature, homosexuality. And as I have learnt from personal and pastoral experience, much in the old code of Christian sexual ethics did indeed deserve to be abandoned. A liberation that was good and of God came when this code was no longer enforced by the law or by public opinion. But many evils also came: divorce as an epidemic, homosexual practices attracting the bisexual because put on the same level as marriage, the rise in illegitimate births, the diseases and heartbreaks resulting from sex without the bond of responsible love. People, and specially the young people most exposed to these evils, were going to look at Christianity for moral guidance, rather than for the tame approval of moral chaos, if they were going to look in that direction at all. They were going to want guidance more realistic than Victorian morality but also more realistic than the simplistic blessings on sexual liberation heard in the early 1960s – and they were going to be in fear of AIDS. The liberated scene was to appear cruel and sordid, and words such as 'discipleship' and even 'discipline' were often to be spoken with confidence and were sometimes to be heard with gladness. And it was to be known that a distinctively Christian lifestyle, the life of a disciple, makes sense only if a distinctively Christian faith in God – which is more than trusting and following ambiguous 'nature' – is true. So questions about behaviour were to make questions about belief inescapable. In a number of passages in his 1963 lecture Harry Williams guarded himself against leaving the impression that he was advocating the abandonment of all restraint or the naive yielding to everything that can be called 'natural'. More telling still was his decision, on leaving Cambridge, to become a monk in the Community of the Resurrection – a decision in keeping with the deep spirituality to be seen in his books, most notably in his Cambridge writing on *The True Wilderness* (1965) and *True Resurrection* (1972). But it can now be seen, I suggest, that there were rocks ahead in the course he was advocating. The author of books which have become spiritual classics, helping many people to accept themselves and Christ, could be misunderstood as a hippy guru preaching sensuality.

The second dangerous tendency in *Objections to Christian Belief* can be seen, as I now think, in Alec Vidler's lecture on 'historical objections'. This repeated current questions about the Christian Church's traditional attitudes to Jesus without seriously attempting to deal with the problems one by one. Writers who 'considered that Christian belief ought to be about the teaching, not the person, of Jesus' (p. 60) were quoted and sympathy was expressed for the view that 'it is the *practical* implications of Christian belief which are of decisive importance . . . and not the historical origins or the *speculative* implications' (p. 62). Without going into specific problems of New Testament scholarship – a strange omission, surely? – Vidler stressed that beliefs about history 'can never have more than a very high degree of probability' (p. 65) and that 'those who have made themselves competent to form an opinion of their own . . . differ very widely in their conclusions' (p. 67). He affirmed that 'the authentic personality of Jesus does still make its impact', but this was quickly balanced by the remark that 'I often find myself more in sympathy or *en rapport* with non-Christians who have a sense of the strangeness and incertitude of our world and of the duty of a large measure of agnosticism than I do with Christians who are cocksure about their beliefs' (p. 77).

None of these statements seems to me objectionable in itself. When radical theologians say that such-and-such a fact about Jesus (or about God) cannot be proved, that negative statement usually cannot be proved wrong. But unless I am mistaken, an impression was conveyed by Vidler, however unintentionally, of some aloofness from the commanding claims which Jesus makes in the gospels and which have pumped the lifeblood into Christianity. It may have been part of a veteran's rather weary mood expressed in the 1967 sermon printed in Vidler's autobiography, *Scenes from a Clerical Life* (1977): 'for the present I do not find myself being carried away, or being particularly excited, by the contemporary apologists for, or critics of, the Christian faith' (p. 169). Some later radicals were to say something more definite and more negative than this – that God cannot be known, that Jesus cannot be known. But for most Christians the mood was to be very different in the years ahead. In fairly large numbers Christians reacting against the evils and confusions of the age were to be fascinated by the person of Jesus, were to feel challenged by his demand for their personal allegiance, and were to be interested in particular by his revelation of God. Quite often the new mood was to revive a theological conservatism. For others, conversions in the Catholic or Evangelical (or other orthodox) tradition could be combined with a reluctance to be dogmatic about history or metaphysics. In that sense it could be said that many definite Christians were to some degree theological 'liberals', and I should like to be included in that group myself. However, at one point there was to be agreement among almost all of those identifying themselves as Christians, whether conservatives or liberals. For the purposes of life it was to be thought crucially important to reach a working, life-changing, answer to the insistent questions 'What was Jesus?' and 'Who is Christ for us today?' There was to be less interest in any attempt to construct a version of Christianity which avoided personal decisions for or against 'the Man from Nazareth and the Exalted Lord' (to use the sub-title of Eduard Schweizer's book of 1989) and for or against his God.

As a reminder of the issues at stake, I reprint an article which I wrote twenty-one years after *Soundings*, about a priest and a New Testament scholar who was overwhelmed by the objections to any kind of belief in God – and who had the courage to accept the logic of his new convictions. Dr Michael Goulder had been a lecturer in the 'extra-mural' (adult education) department of Birmingham University. At a conference organised by his department he was in dialogue with Professor John Hick, a theologian whose teaching we shall be studying later. The two men tackled the greatest of all human questions.

Review of *Why Believe in God?* by Michael Goulder and John Hick (1983)

While the contributions by Professor John Hick to this book are a useful summary of his theology, the chapters by Michael Goulder inevitably hold the centre of the reader's attention because this Anglican scholar-priest has resigned his holy orders on becoming fully – and, as he thinks, finally – unable to believe in the reality of the God whom the Christian Church worships. Here he gives the reasons why he has felt compelled to be an atheist and to face the consequences.

The reasons are mainly reasons of the heart; psychology has been more decisive than philosophy. That is almost inevitable. We believe, or do not believe, with our whole selves – selves in which the intellect is only the tip of the iceberg. Save for rare spirits, a person's religious or irreligious history is for the most part a social history and a history of instincts, habits and emotions. And in Goulder's case the key emotional factor has been that he feels he has never experienced God. 'This unbroken aridity raises a rather stark dilemma, to which I have now given my uncomfortable answer,' he writes:

Either I have a sort of spiritual tone-deafness, whether innate or from continuing sinfulness; or all of the church's saints and devotional writers, and some of my most admired Christian friends, have been deceived, or perhaps are even guilty of something approaching a confidence trick. Naturally at first I preferred the former option, that the fault lay in me (pp. 3–4).

It is, I am afraid, the natural inclination of those of us who do believe in God to insist that it was Goulder's fault – or, at least, his tragedy in not meeting the 'right' Christians or Christian books. But the concise autobiography which he unveils in this book will, I hope, show us all that it will not do to dismiss his atheism with the pitying comment that he was unfortunate. For he was, in fact, highly privileged in his Christian experience. 'Between the ages of eighteen and fifty I rarely spent less than half-an-hour each day in prayer: between twenty-three and thirty-nine it was commonly an hour and a half' (p. 4). No one should presume to 'answer' this atheist without a comparable track-record in the struggle to find and obey the Eternal. And no one should presume to say that Goulder's experiences are too narrow. He is an academic now and was a scholarship boy from an early stage; but, unless he is dishonest in what he writes here (and why should we think that?), he enjoyed serving 'ordinary' people in his spells as a parish priest in Hong Kong and Manchester. Certainly he is no dry-as-dust don now. If he had been more purely the don, he would not have bothered to resign as a priest because he would not have been aware of the reactions of 'ordinary' people to the spectacle of an atheist priest.

Did he have the wrong sort of teacher in the faith? Possibly. He was at Eton; and he remembers the Provost, Lord Quickswood, referring to 'boring duties like cleaning your teeth and saying your prayers'. But in Hong Kong he was the protégé of one of the undoubted saints of twentieth-century Anglicanism, Bishop R. O. Hall. Hall even had the wild idea that Goulder ought to be the next Bishop of Hong Kong. In Oxford he was a favourite pupil of Austin Farrer – another saint who was also often reckoned a bit of a genius. Still to this day, when Goulder writes about a 'red-blooded' belief in the divine providence as a belief he can no longer pretend to share, it is Farrer's teaching on this topic that he immediately recalls. It is not easy, after reading such an autobiography, to hold that all would have been well if only he had come across X, Y or Z.

Indeed, if any contemporary theologian is academically and

temperamentally equipped to commend belief in God, it is John Hick; and here the author of *Evil and the God of Love* (1966) and of other much-appreciated works of religious philosophy does his best. He insists both how widespread and deep is religious experience and how necessary it is to abandon some beliefs about God which, however time-honoured, nowadays seem to be incompatible with our general experience and knowledge.

God, Hick grants, cannot be pinned down in a set of propositions such as a creed. Much religious belief is culturally evolved; much religious language is symbolic rather than literal; and, because of what we know from other sources to be true, it is right to reject 'the pre-modern idea of God as omnipotently determining the course of events constituting the world, and as occasionally issuing special commands and performing special favours in the form of miraculous answers to prayer' (p. 106). Yet, despite these and other difficulties which surround propositions about God, Hick argues that the atheist vision of the existence of human animals as 'a transient form of life on the surface of one of the planets of a minor star on the periphery of a small galaxy' in a universe completely governed by blind chance also runs contrary to experience. And supreme among those who have experienced God, and who have communicated that experience, is Jesus. No wonder, Hick says, that the attempted disproofs of God's existence have, like the attempted proofs, not proved to be generally convincing!

That is the outline of the kind of apologia for religious belief which many thoughtful believers would offer in our time. But Goulder is able to reply that the concessions which Hick makes are in truth nothing less than preliminaries to the total abandonment of belief in God. When religious language is reduced to culturally conditioned symbolism, where is the authority of the saints – indeed, of Jesus? When miraculous healings are reduced to telepathy, where is the God who does things? Why, Goulder asks, should we love the God that is left in John Hick's sophisticated theology? 'John's God never leaves a bunch of roses, or washes our shirt when we are not looking' (p. 50). That God, says Goulder, 'acts only by willing our good; and this action becomes effective only as we respond to his impressive presence.' And Goulder has never found God's presence deeply impressive – although there was a time when he thought he had undergone an Evangelical conversion as a student.

In reply, Hick defends himself against the charge that he is an eighteenth-century Deist believing in a God who long ago set the world process in motion and decided to leave it alone. 'On the contrary, [God] is creatively present at every moment of time and every point in space, so that it is in principle possible for human beings to be consciously related to him in any phase or region of human history' (p. 98).

I have been left with three reflections after studying this dialogue in which the cleverness and the integrity of both the atheist and the believer shine out beyond dispute. The first is that Goulder was right and brave to cease to function as a priest, while Hick is profoundly a Christian theologian. The second is that neither side in this great debate can wield knock-down arguments. Religious or semi-religious experience is widespread, and there is a deep feeling in most men and women that they are here to serve a higher purpose; but religious spokesmen often sound too cocksure. And my third reflection is that, as John Bowden puts it in his Preface, there is 'no neutral ground' and 'one has to respond personally to the reality that is perceived'. One person will respond with belief arising as, so to speak, the scent thrown off by experience; another person will respond with no belief because there has been no experience, or at least no acknowledged experience.

What accounts for the difference? It is a question which must puzzle sociologists and psychologists alike, for the divide separates citizen from citizen, brother from brother, hearty from hearty, neurotic from neurotic, professor from professor. For the believer the ultimate explanation may lie in the mysterious predestination of God, who has given to some but not to all the privilege of feeling him near before they die.

2

JOHN ROBINSON AND THE IMAGES OF GOD:

Is God only the depth of what is obviously real?

When *Soundings* and *Objections to Christian Belief* were being planned in Cambridge as the 1950s became the 1960s, one very remarkable man was missing. The theologian who was Dean of Clare College and was soon to achieve a world-wide fame for his eloquent radicalism was not invited to join in creating the ferment. John Robinson was thought to be too conservative. And that misunderstanding was to be typical of a general puzzlement about a man who could be criticised, sometimes bitterly, both as an 'atheist bishop' and as an excessively conservative scholar. Most bishops are content to preach about an omnipotent but fatherly God and are encouraged to do so by their own powerful but benign status in a hierarchy which is also a self-supporting club. That was not true of Bishop Robinson. And most scholars are content to be professional, cool, cautious, critical, sceptical, and are encouraged to be so by the guarded approval of their fellow scholars. That was not the case with Dr Robinson. He was himself.

I was often puzzled. On 19 March 1963 the SCM Press, of which I was editor, published his highly controversial and (as it often seemed) profoundly radical paperback, *Honest to God*. 'English religion in the 1960s', writes Adrian Hastings in his *History of English Christianity 1920–1985* (1986, p. 536), 'will always remain more associated with *Honest to God* than with any other book.' But I did not expect a much wider readership for it than for Robinson's previous books, and we had already published for a limited public many of the theological books which it quoted. We had, for example, brought out *Beyond Religion* by Daniel Jenkins in the previous year as a study of 'The Truth and Error in "Religionless Christianity,"' which had become a familiar idea in our circle. So we printed 6,000 copies of *Honest to God* for the

British market and 2,000 for the American publisher. But the book sold about a million copies in its first three years and so far as I know no one has disputed my boast that no book in the history of serious theology in the world has ever had a larger sale. I subsequently edited *The Honest to God Debate*, a collection of favourable or hostile reviews with readers' letters selected from those that poured in during the first three months of excitement. I wrote an introductory chapter welcoming 'A New Stirring in English Christianity' but in all honesty I could not say that *Honest to God* was itself more than an experiment, for after working through all this material I remained puzzled about Robinson's basic position. My puzzlement did not diminish much when I ceased to be a publisher and became the reviewer responsible for introducing his later literary output to readers of the *Church Times*. (It was a change from the days when the paper had led the hostile reaction to the Cambridge radicals and *Honest to God*.) He thought my reviews 'sympathetic and civilised' although not uncritical, and said so in a letter printed in the paper; and I had the privilege of preaching at the last Evensong over which he presided at the end of his return to Cambridge University after his period as Bishop of Woolwich. We had a further link when I was appointed to serve the cathedral of the diocese which he had served as a bishop and where he is still remembered with pride and affection. But I never felt that as a thinker or a man he was easy to understand.

The circumstances which gave him his fame or notoriety were a part of this surrounding atmosphere of puzzlement. *Honest to God* was drawn to public attention because of an article which Robinson wrote for the *Observer* summing it up on the eve of publication, and particularly because of the headline added by the paper, 'Our Image of God Must Go.' The Archbishop of Canterbury, Michael Ramsey, in a public address to representatives of the clergy complained of 'much damage', knowing that many of the clergy felt that the bishop had decided that *any* image of God 'must go'. But it was not long before the archbishop, a truly great because humble man of God, wrote a far more sympathetic pamphlet, and in later years he more than once apologised for his hasty overreaction in 1963. Towards the end of their lives, the theologies of Ramsey and Robinson were not far apart. The decisive thought for Ramsey was this:

As a Church we need to be grappling with the questions and trials of belief in the modern world. Since the war our Church has been too inclined to be concerned with the organizing of its own life, perhaps assuming too easily that the faith may be taken for granted and needs only to be stated and commended. But we state and commend the faith only in so far as we go out and put ourselves with loving sympathy inside the doubts of the doubting, the questions of the questioners, and the loneliness of those who have lost their way (*Image Old and New*, 1963, p. 14).

A Baptist theologian, Keith Clements, wrote a quarter of a century later: 'This statement . . . marked a kind of Rubicon-crossing, however reluctant, by the leadership of the Church of England' (*Lovers of Discord*, 1988, p. 200). After Robinson's death his theological library was taken to Lambeth Palace for the use of another archbishop, Robert Runcie, and his successors – which may show that Clements was right.

In 1963 journalists whose attention was drawn by the *Observer* article had already noticed Robinson, who had appeared as a witness for the defence when Penguin Books had been prosecuted little more than a year before for publishing an allegedly obscene novel by D. H. Lawrence, *Lady Chatterley's Lover*. During the trial the young bishop had testified that the sex vividly described by Lawrence (and resulting in rapid sales more than three times larger than the success of *Honest to God*) was 'in a real sense something sacred, in a real sense an act of holy communion'. It was also adultery. So was Robinson only defending a novel of great integrity and some literary merit by a major figure in twentieth-century English literature, when under unsuccessful attack under a soon to be changed anti-obscenity law? Or was he glorifying sex outside marriage, as an advocate of what was already an accelerating revolution in morality, speeded up about that time by the novelty of the contraceptive pill? Had Robinson become 'a stumbling block and cause of offence to many ordinary Christians', as the then Archbishop of Canterbury (Geoffrey Fisher) maintained in a public rebuke?

The biography by Robinson's literary executor Eric James, *A Life of Bishop John A. T. Robinson: Scholar, Pastor, Prophet* (1987), was admirably honest. It modestly avoided any close analysis of the theology and concentrated on the life, which, however, had its own paradoxes. It recorded that the bishop was indeed a hard-working scholar, a pastor tender to those who consulted him and a prophet ahead of the Church in his time. But it also showed that people around him often did not feel close to him.

He was awkwardly shy and could be clumsy in personal relationships. He could seem self-centred: he had a serious writer's preoccupation with his current literary project, together with the delight in publicity which was natural in a man who had expected to be obscure. Many of his fellow clergy suspected him because he was such an unconventional bishop, yet made much of being a bishop. He was a prophet without much local honour during the years when he was back in Cambridge as Dean of Chapel in Trinity College. And many people who valued him highly found it hard to place him.

It was not only that he had an unusually agile and well-stocked mind and a habit of enthusiasm about books which he had recently been reading. Even when he simplified his teaching so that it could be intelligible to a non-theological or non-intellectual audience (as he did in the popular articles collected as *But That I Can't Believe!* in 1967), he could puzzle more conventional people. On which side of a fence did he really mean to come down? And those who had the ability and the patience to examine his teaching with care could still be puzzled. His *The Human Face of God* (1973) was reviewed by Colin Gunton as 'an eclectic and slippery book' because 'so often . . . it takes away with the left hand what has only just been given with the right' (*Theology*, 1973, p. 486). His theology has been studied as a whole, sometimes with conclusions different from my own, by Dr Alistair Kee of the University of Edinburgh under the title *The Roots of Christian Freedom* (1988). Kee has impeccable credentials as a radical, one of his books being entitled *The Way of Transcendence: Christian Faith without Belief in God* (1965). He now called himself one of those who 'scarcely knew John Robinson' and 'have always been puzzled' by the ambiguity of his work (p. vii). He thought that 'if there is one thing above all that will become clear' about Robinson it is that he 'was not a liberal' (p. 5). But also 'he cannot be understood either as a conservative or a radical, in the conventional usages of these terms' (p. 4), for he is 'more critical than critical scholarship, but reaches conclusions often more traditional than conservative scholarship' (p. 19). A puzzle indeed!

Robinson is not likely to be forgotten in any future assessment of these English radical theologians. But there is a danger that this apparently unclassifiable man who puzzled both critics and admirers, both the public and the experts, may in the end not be taken very seriously. He may seem to have been a perpetually bright undergraduate or *enfant terrible*, always anxious to shock the Establishment, arguing a case like a clever barrister but not putting his heart into it, as Adrian Hastings puts it: 'at heart not unconservative yet with a penchant for appearing a little naughtily radical' (p. 537).

His biggest book, *Redating the New Testament* (1976), was an attempt to show that the whole of the New Testament might have been written before AD 70. It began, we are told, as 'little more than a theological joke' (p. 10), and although as it grew it included many detailed arguments intended to refute the prevailing consensus it did not leave a final impression of being totally and exclusively concerned to get at the historical truth or probability. By comments, or the absence of them, the scholarly world dismissed the book. The Master of Trinity College (Lord Butler) quipped in an after-dinner speech that Robinson had tried to prove that the New Testament was written considerably before the birth of Christ. More solemnly a fellow scholar teaching the New Testament in Cambridge, John Sturdy, offered a 'definitely adverse judgment' in a review in the *Journal of Theological Studies* (1979, pp. 255–62). He complained that Robinson was fighting 'a rearguard action against the change in the emphasis of British scholarship which has come about in his lifetime, which he has never come to terms with, and which has left him stranded in the company of the Conservative Evangelicals'. Only 'by sleight of hand' could Robinson avoid the 'clear implications' of passages in the gospels which seemed to refer to the fall of Jerusalem in AD 70. Sturdy ridiculed the claim that a document such as 2 Peter, which announced that it is 'from Simeon Peter' but classes the letters of Paul among 'the other scriptures', was authentically 'approved' by Peter during Paul's lifetime although actually written by Jude, a brother of Jesus. He declared that Robinson was 'certainly wrong' in his suggestions about the relationships between the gospels and in his reliance on details in the Acts of the Apostles. Robinson, he judged,

> onesidedly ignores difficulties for his views, steamrollers the evidence, again and again advances from an improbable possibility into a certainty. He ignores his own remark that every statement must be taken as a question, and so reaches a conclusion which is unevidenced and intrinsically absurd.

If readers were less stern than Sturdy, Robinson's insistence on independence might be thought to be teasing. An article about the birth of Jesus which he had written in 1948 was reprinted and expanded in a collection which he prepared for publication after his death. He did not regard the stories about the virgin birth told by Matthew and Luke as 'gynaecological fact', but he still insisted on accepting their evidence that the birth was unusual. 'The first and most indisputable fact about the birth of Jesus', he wrote, 'is that it occurred out of wedlock. The one option for which there is no evidence is that Jesus was the lawful son of Joseph and Mary. The only choice open to us is between a virgin birth and an illegitimate birth' (*Twelve More New Testament Studies*, 1984, pp. 3–4). He agreed neither with those who hold that the resurrection of Jesus must have involved the transformation of his corpse nor with those who hold that the appearances after the resurrection must have been psychic or visionary. On the one hand the Christian must be free to say that 'the bones of Jesus may still be lying about somewhere in Palestine' after a possible removal of the body from the original tomb (pp. 7–8). On the other hand, 'the finding of the grave empty was simply part of what was indelibly remembered to have been discovered that morning' (*Can We Trust the New Testament?*, 1977, p. 123). The shroud in Turin which after Robinson's own death was proved to be a medieval fake was taken seriously as possible evidence (as in *Twelve More New Testament Studies*, 1984, pp. 81–94). And there was a suggestion that the Church gathered after the resurrection was at its core almost a family firm, including in its small ranks the mother, four brothers, an aunt, an uncle, an aunt by marriage and five cousins of Jesus (pp. 95–111). He also permitted himself a brief reference to a question asked at a conference in Canada: 'When the woman wiped Jesus' feet with her hair, she performed a highly sexual action. Did Jesus at that moment experience an erection?' Robinson commented: '*Of course* there is no answer. The gospels are not there to answer such questions. It *is*, however, a good question to ask *ourselves*, to test our reaction' (*The Human Face of God*, 1973, p. 64). He seemed to be testing his readers' reactions too often for those reactions to be entirely in keeping with the gravity of the subjects which were his deepest concern. Even his last book, much of which was written when he knew he was dying, all of which was intended to be taken seriously by students of the gospels, had a title which was a tease: *The Priority of John* (1985).

He came to think that his first book, *In the End God* (1950), was too conservative, and in 1957 he said so. It 'makes the assumption . . . that it is possible to accept the New Testament teaching about the Second Coming more or less as it stands and then to build up on it' (*Jesus and His Coming*, 1957, p. 11). But when *In the End God* was reissued in 1968, he introduced the new edition with these words: 'In one sense, I could never write it now. In another I found I wanted to alter remarkably little' (p. 1). Such words represented a frequent attitude of semi-detachment from his work. Looking back over his books shortly before his death, he mused: 'Wouldn't want to un-say anything I've written, but wouldn't want to say it like that now' (*Where Three Ways Meet*, 1987, p. ix).

He disappointed those who had hoped that he would become an authority on the New Testament and a trusted leader of the Church like the Victorians who had gone from Trinity College, Cambridge, to become Bishops of Durham, Lightfoot and Westcott – men to whom he often referred in admiration. After such hopes the apparent lack of gravity and judgement was dismaying, and in *God's Truth*, a collection of essays marking the twenty-fifth anniversary of *Honest to God* in 1988, a Cambridge colleague, J. C. O'Neill, recalled that 'he was the more highly regarded the further from Cambridge he travelled' (p. 165). But other essayists remembered the disappointment of the radicals that Robinson had not systematically developed the new insights of *Honest to God*, becoming the standard-bearer, if not the general, of a crusade to transform Christianity. For example, John Bowden complained that thoroughgoing radicals 'discovered, meeting John Robinson face to face, that in temperament he really was an Anglican bishop and was in no way prepared to abandon his biblical theology'. He parried 'just about every question' with 'I think that we must remain open on that point'. Bowden commented that 'what can be expected if you put everything into a melting pot which is open on all sides took place: it ran away into the sand' (p. 45). So for academics, churchmen and radicals alike, Robinson was the lost leader.

Despite all my own puzzlement, however, I sensed during his life, and saw more fully after his death, that he was a thoroughly Anglican radical. That is a clue if not a classification. It made him a conservative in many ways, for his heart was in the tradition, in what he loved to call his 'roots'. Lecturing in New Zealand in 1979 he gave a long exposition of this loyalty, beginning 'I was born and bred under the shadow of Canterbury Cathedral' (*The Roots of a Radical*, 1980, p. 10). 'I have never really doubted the fundamental truth of the Christian faith,' he declared in *Honest to God* (p. 27), 'although I have constantly found myself questioning its expression.' He also said that as an adolescent or adult he had never seriously doubted that he ought to be a priest. Many Roman Catholics sympathised with him, and an American theologian, Richard McBrien, wrote an admiring study of *The Church in the Thought of Bishop John Robinson* (1966), based on a doctoral dissertation at the Gregorian University in Rome. Many Evangelicals admired his devotion to Christ and his love and intimate knowledge of the New Testament.

This background of security in the Established Church of England also helped him to be willing to pronounce on a wide range of subjects, even when he reached unconventional conclusions. Thus successive chapters in *The Roots of a Radical* offered his opinions on the legal age of consent for sexual relations and on 'nuclear power options'. As a commissioned teacher of Church and State, he expected a hearing even when he was not teaching theology. And partly because Church and State were far from distinct in his own background, his constant tendency was to merge the Christian with the human. In his ethical teaching he gave little attention to the possibility that Christians as such might have a vocation to be a distinct minority and to shine as lights in a dark world. They were, instead, to show the same love that non-Christians also acknowledged as 'reality'. In his theology God was not pictured as the Lord and Judge who is 'holy, holy, holy', and Jesus was not pictured as the Holy One surrounded by sinners. In 1982 he delivered a lecture in Ontario which summed up what he had been saying for many years. Jesus, he said, 'offers the best clue we inhabitants of planet earth have been given to what Blake called "the human form divine", or Tennyson "the Christ that is to be"'. He also said:

> Let me state the only sense in which I would want to defend the uniqueness of Christ. This is that Jesus is unique because he alone of all mankind of whom we have any external evidence or internal experience was truly normal. He was *the* son of man, *the* son of God, the Proper Man, who lived in a relationship to God and to his fellow men in which we are all called to live but fail to live (*Where Three Ways Meet*, pp. 11, 17).

Thus Robinson found encouragement in the Anglican tradition to venture on his radical 'explorations'. He often said that he knew of no institution which would have given him such freedom as the Church of England had done. It was his home and he knew he would never be thrown out of it. He inherited from his parents a love of Psalm 16:7 in the Prayer Book version: 'The lot is fallen unto me in a fair ground: yea, I have a goodly heritage.'

What made him special among Anglican radicals was that he had a rare courage based on a rare self-confidence, a rare intellectual energy and a rare gift for making memorable phrases, so that he was able to use with a rare effectiveness the fame given to him by *Lady Chatterley's Lover* and *Honest to God*, reaching out beyond the closed circles of theology and church life. Whatever subject he touched, he displayed the combination of traditionalism ('roots') and open-mindedness ('explorations') which has been characteristic of many Anglicans, but the display was noticed far more widely than usual because it was his. The impression formed might well be unfavourable, concluding that here was a muddle-headed amateur or a naughty adolescent. But with this character he attracted many: here was the honest bishop, the independent scholar. And whether or not they admired, all agreed that he was always bravely, publicly, irrepressibly, debatably, himself.

A Biblical Theologian

His early books are manifestly the work of a man who is in love with his wife, his Bible, his Church and his God, and who wants to share his enthusiasms with an evangelist's conviction, clarity and power. When he reissued *In the End God* he retained a self-revealing passage:

> We have known what it is to be confronted by a love too strong to resist . . . And how wonderful that moment of surrender was! We felt that that was the moment for which we had been waiting in order to become ourselves; we knew then that we had been born for just such an act as this. And yet, as the weeks passed, there still seemed so much of us that was not bound over and committed, so much that we would far rather surrender to the other's keeping but with which we could not bring ourselves to part . . . What ground was there for supposing that the complete surrender for which we yearned would ever be made possible to us? . . .
>
> And then we seemed to hear a voice, which told us we need have no fear. It spoke of another love, which, though we knew it not, had all the while been meeting us in that love we knew . . . We knew this love, that it was none other than the infinite love of

God. And we laughed that we had ever allowed ourselves to think that there might not be a power without us great enough to conquer those last shreds of our pride and independence (pp. 123–4).

This vision, he explained,

has deliberately been put in terms of personal experience and not of argued statement. For it is only from the point of view of the subject in actual personal relation with God and other people that these things make sense. This is simply another way of saying with Kierkegaard that 'truth is subjectivity', or with Buber that reality is found only in the *I-Thou* relationship of meeting. Directly one begins to consider the matter objectively, with the eye of the scientist or the spectator, the truth eludes one. Brunner himself has shown in his brilliant little book, *Truth as Encounter*, what shipwreck has been made in theology by trying to express in 'objective' terms what is revealed and known only to the subject-in-meeting (p. 125).

Those last few sentences summarise the argument of the long dissertation entitled *Thou Who Art* with which Robinson had won his Cambridge PhD in 1945. He had been working on this project before he met his wife Ruth (a fellow student), but his theoretical personalism had then lacked much personal experience. The son of a canon of Canterbury and of another canon's daughter, the nephew of a Dean of Westminster who was an outstanding scholar, he had been educated in the Latin and Greek classics at Marlborough, a public school founded for the sons of the clergy, and exempted from military service. His early years had been very bookish (partly because his father died when he was aged nine), and his contemporaries had mostly, it seems, thought of him as a rather conceited intellectual, so that the strength of his wish to 'surrender' in a personal relationship can be understood. One can also understand that with a heritage that was richly Christian his deepest surrender was to the revealed God as 'Thou'. An 'I-It' relationship to God as an object was totally inadequate – as was any understanding of God as three 'persons' in the modern sense of that word (a subject also covered in *Thou Who Art*).

Thou Who Art has never been published. In his book on Robinson Alistair Kee regrets this because he believes that the theology outlined in *Honest to God* would have been seen to be coherent and mature had readers been pointed to this systematic work in the philosophy of religion. But Robinson was himself never prepared to revise the work for publication: he had 'moved on'. After the award of the doctorate with high praise his experience was enriched by encountering social problems as a curate in Bristol, where he also met the power of 'liturgy' with its centre in the Parish Communion. To make an impact on the world, he now saw that the Church must be a body. When he was able to resume academic work on the staff of Wells Theological College, he took these fresh 'social' insights into a closer study of the New Testament, eventually resulting in the first of his biblical books, *The Body: A Study in Pauline Theology* (1952).

It was a brilliant short book, often reprinted. It developed the argument of *In the End God* that the New Testament's great 'myths' about the end of history should be seen as truths. They were

> first and foremost descriptions of *present* realities within the life of the New Age. The Second Coming has happened in the return of Christ in the Spirit; the Resurrection of the Body has occurred in the putting on of the new man in the Body of Christ; the Millennium has been inaugurated in the reign of Christ in his Church on earth; the Antichrist is a present reality wherever final refusal meets the Christian preaching; the Messianic Banquet is celebrated whenever the wine is drunk new in the kingdom of God; Satan falls from heaven as each man decides for the Gospel, and in the finished work of Christ the Prince of this world has been judged; the Last Judgment is being wrought out in every moment of choice and decision; Christ is all in all, since all things *have been* reconciled in him (p. 77).

Robinson, who was to appear in much of his work a great individualist, began *The Body* by announcing that 'the age of individualism is over' (p. 7). This moderniser who was to be famous for his welcome to humanity's 'coming of age' in the modern world here celebrated the 'Hebrew' idea of the personality as 'an animated body' given life by relationships with God and the neighbour. The treatment of the Old Testament was not entirely successful; it was to be criticised by the more expert James Barr in the course of his lethal onslaught on the facile generalisations of 'biblical theology' (*The Semantics of Biblical Language*, 1961). But the point for the young Robinson was that in the Old Testament – or much of it – death is the near-complete weakening of life because these life-giving relationships are severed; and so St Paul, a

'Hebrew of the Hebrews', is haunted by the vision of humanity as alienated from God and therefore nothing more than the 'body of death'. But another body has appeared on the human scene! For Paul, it appeared when on the road to Damascus he was arrested by the vision of Jesus as the one who was being persecuted in the persecution of the Christians. 'It is almost impossible to exaggerate the materialism and crudity of Paul's doctrine of the Church as literally now the resurrection *body* of Christ' (p. 51). 'The appearance on which Paul's whole faith and apostleship was founded was the revelation of the resurrection body of Christ, not as an individual, but as the Christian Community' (p. 58). 'The singularity of Christ's resurrection body is taken for granted, just as it was by those who saw it on Easter morning. It is the fact that it can consist of a number of persons that really calls for explanation' (pp. 58–9). But these persons are the Christians, who have been baptised and who partake of the Eucharist. Incorporated into the body of Christ by these sacraments, they are the 'first fruits' of a creation which is all to be 'redeemed', for the Church's function is 'to extend throughout Christ's redeemed universe the acknowledgment of His victory' (p. 71) and thus 'the Church is at once the witness to the world of its true nature and the pledge and instrument of its destiny' (p. 83). No wonder that from a Roman Catholic point of view Richard McBrien could describe *The Body* as 'quite comfortably "orthodox"' (p. 43)!

Robinson returned to Cambridge in 1951 as the dean of a particularly beautiful college in an atmosphere which encouraged the life of the chapel and the teaching of theology despite the secular tendencies already present. These tendencies were strong enough to strengthen the Christians' sense of identity, but not strong enough to discourage. When he proceeded to make his heritage distinctively his own, it was with confidence. For example, he was the youngest member of the group translating the New Testament for the New English Bible.

The emphasis was on the corporate character of the Eucharist in the college chapel. As he recalled in *Liturgy Coming to Life* (1960):

I arrived in a boom period in Cambridge religion, when the college chapels had never been fuller, into one of the most friendly and united colleges in the university, with a governing body which allowed us an almost entirely free hand, with a compact congregation of as lively and intelligent young men as could be found in the country, with no money to be raised and two ordained colleagues (p. 18).

It was also a time when the Church of England seemed to be united, with 'the traditional party lines yearly becoming more obsolete' (p. 13). The words of the Book of Common Prayer were retained, as was the traditional hour of 8 a.m., but sermons and a 'Communion manual' explained the service carefully. As much as possible was said together, the priest faced the congregation instead of turning his back, there was an offertory procession where laymen brought up ordinary bread and wine, worship was followed by breakfast together, and there were many weekday meetings in the rooms of dons or undergraduates. It was all a part of the Parish Communion movement which at this time was transforming the Sunday morning worship of the Church of England. Although the Alternative Service Book which eventually appeared in 1980 after long experiments has been criticised because the words are too conservative, it is only fair to note that in the 1950s Robinson had been happy to keep the Prayer Book unchanged. Later on he advocated only a conservative revision of formal, public worship. He felt to the end that here a combination of a human togetherness with a dignified sense of mystery and continuity was what was wanted, although he encouraged bold experiments in informal, private groups.

He would have had mixed feelings, I think, about Dennis Nineham's comment in *God's Truth* (p. 156) that 'perhaps silence is best' when the Alternative Service Book has the congregation making the acclamations:

> Christ has died
> Christ is risen
> Christ will come again.

For Robinson never ceased to regard the cross and resurrection of Jesus as the centre of history – and his other way of making his heritage his own during the 1950s was further study of the New Testament's 'myths' about the end of history. He had many hesitations about the phrase 'second coming'. It was not biblical and it might suggest the present absence of Jesus. The New Testament Greek word which it translated, *parousia*, meant 'presence'. But he put great emphasis on the hope that Jesus would be fully vindicated and the Father completely triumphant – the hope which was expressed in the term 'second coming' and in the apocalyptic imagery of the New Testament itself.

Jesus and His Coming (1957) was in many ways on the level, and in the mood, of *The Body*. It was based on lectures delivered in

Harvard University, and Bishop Stephen Neill welcomed it in the
Church of England Newspaper:

> It is encouraging to find such evident vitality in the Cambridge
> school of New Testament theology, with its traditional virtues of
> patient attention to detail, exact understanding of the meaning
> of words, openness to new light, and a steady maintenance of the
> connection between theological understanding and the living
> experiences of faith.

But by 1957 the 'new light' in Robinson's developing mind had
made him realise more fully that the passages in the New Testament which predicted Christ's second coming had lost much of
their credibility owing to the long delay, and anyway could not be
taken literally as an accurate picture of the 'last things'. He
therefore had to face the question whether Jesus himself had
shared the enthusiastic illusions which are expertly called 'apocalyptic'. In his new book he argued that Jesus had indeed expected
his vindication when he went to the Father, but had *not* taught that
there would be a return from the Father, a future coming from
heaven to earth in manifest and final glory. Robinson had to admit
that this teaching 'forms the distinctively Christian centre of the
New Testament hope' (p. 18). He had to grant that it is prominent
in the letters of Paul written before the gospels, that the men who
compiled the gospels shared this hope (although St John marginalised it), and that the gospels as they stand represent Jesus as having
shared it. But he attempted to show that the passages in the gospels
which teach this apocalyptic hope are either additions to the
teaching of Jesus made by the evangelists or else edited accounts of
authentic teaching which originally referred to the one and only
coming. His own conviction was that 'there is but one coming,
begun at Christmas, perfected on the Cross, and continuing till all
are included in it' (p. 185).

The book did not cause a public controversy. Its arguments were
criticised by almost all of the New Testament scholars who reviewed it, but it was an exercise within the closed world of biblical
theology. It acknowledged that Paul and other writers of the New
Testament had made a mistake in expecting the imminent end of
history but insisted that Jesus had not done so. I shall return to this
problem, which has been at the centre of debate about the historical Jesus. All that needs to be said here is that most scholars have
accepted some arguments which Robinson stated. They have
agreed that the most important issue for Christian faith is not the

claim that the future can be known in advance, but the experience
of the present 'Lordship' of Christ. And they have agreed that for
the historical Jesus the experience of the present Lordship of the
Father, creating an urgent offer and challenge, far outweighed in
importance any particular hopes for the future. But most scholars
are agreed that it is unlikely – and certainly cannot be demonstrated – that Jesus had no hopes beyond those which were fulfilled
by the vindication glimpsed in the New Testament as his 'resurrection', 'ascension' or 'exaltation'. The parables and sayings of Jesus
as we have them have no doubt been edited, and probably they
have quite often been made to refer to the future coming when
originally they called for a response to Jesus in his lifetime. But
Jesus seems to have taught that a decision for or against him was
also a decision for or against the coming 'kingdom of God' – which
for him meant the transformation of history into an age when the
will of God is done 'on earth as in heaven'. The 'Son of Man' would
be designated by God the Father as the judge of all at that supreme
crisis, and it is almost certain that Jesus identified himself with this
Son of Man. Even the Old Testament passage about 'a son of man'
being vindicated by 'the Ancient of Days' which Robinson interpreted as a basis for Jesus' hope of a vindication in heaven seems to
refer to a judgement on earth and certainly ends with the bestowal
of 'sovereign power' over 'all peoples, nations and men of every
language' (Dan. 7:9–14). It seems improbable that all these references to a future vindication on earth misrepresent the mind of
Jesus, although it is equally improbable that a man so submissive to
the Father made his entire mission depend on the validity of his
hope that the end of 'the world' would come soon. The report that
he did not know 'the hour' seems far more likely because far more
in character. If he hoped – something different from knowing – and
was too hopeful, a Christian who accepts his Lordship because of
his life taken as a whole is entitled to say that his optimism
demonstrated his humanity. To be human is to hope – and to be
sometimes too hopeful.

The reconstruction of the message of Jesus which I have outlined
seems to be a way of fitting together the various texts which have
been debated in the voluminous literature. But such a solution to
the problem did not commend itself to Robinson. He offered a
solution which, he hoped, preserved the authority of the teaching
of Jesus as traditionally received while frankly abandoning the
traditional view of the authority of the rest of the New Testament.
He made his ardent faith in 'Jesus and his coming' absolutely plain

but perhaps did not pause to examine with enough sympathy the faith in the second coming vividly pictured in the New Testament and in the Church's hymns. Had he been more patient in his treatment of this Christian tradition he could still have taught that the apocalyptic imagery of the biblical pictures is indeed mythological, so that a modern Christian is under no obligation to 'believe' it literally. But he could have interpreted with more sympathy than was shown in *Jesus and His Coming* the passion with which the imaginations of people who were cruelly oppressed or persecuted in the first century AD developed this imagery of a glorious future. (His posthumous collection of essays, *Where Three Ways Meet*, was to include a sympathetic interpretation of the book of Revelation in the New Testament.) And he could have felt free to acknowledge more fully than he did in *Jesus and His Coming* that it was no disgrace if Jesus did share the widespread longing and prayer for the kingdom of God to come gloriously and soon.

Robinson himself hoped for a kind of second coming, for he hoped for a time – or an eternity – when 'all will be included' in the kingdom of God inaugurated by the coming of Jesus, and he believed that the 'Christ' who would be revealed in this triumph would be larger than Jesus of Nazareth because the final 'Christ' would include Christians and (as he proposed in later books) many non-Christians too. Thus there were at least two stages in his 'eschatology' (doctrine of the last things). However, as the 1960s began what interested him most was not argument about the beliefs of the first century, or speculation about the end of history, but the relevance of the first 'coming' to the immediate hopes and fears, faith or unbelief, of humanity. In a lecture of 1959 printed in *On Being the Church in the World* (1960) he discussed how to preach the 'second coming'. He said that 'to see the *Parousia* as a single datable event of future history' (p. 149), and in particular to clothe that expectation in the imagery of a hymn such as 'Lo! he comes with clouds descending . . .', was to make it seem 'utterly remote and fantastic' (p. 154). The real purpose of the doctrine, he insisted, was to say that 'Christ comes in' – and 'that part of Christian doctrine whose specific purpose is to insist that Christ comes into everything should not surely be the most difficult to make relevant' (p. 158).

His essays collected in *On Being the Church in the World* breathed the confidence of the 1950s in the Church's message and mission. Introducing the new edition for 1977 he wrote: 'Looking back on that decade, historians of Christian thought will see in it, I suspect, a temporary period of relative self-confidence'. But at the time his confidence was great. He quoted – not for the last time – a passage in the *Epistle to Diognetus* from the second century, translated by Bishop J. B. Lightfoot: '. . . what the soul is in a body, this the Christians are in the world' (p. 17). It was a world viewed from within the Church and the Bible; indeed, the meaning of 'world' and 'body', 'matter' and 'power', was expounded at length on the basis of the Bible. The innovations urged here were ecclesiastical and intended to display the corporate nature of the Church. The unity of the Spirit-filled Church ought to transcend not only individualism and racism but also the dominance over the laity by the clergy and the lack of communion between Anglicans and Free Churchmen. And page after page clearly implied that, empowered by the Spirit, the Church could be a model to the world.

An Honest Bishop

In 1958 Robinson accepted a suggestion initiated by the Bishop of Southwark, Mervyn Stockwood, that he should become Bishop of Woolwich in that diocese. The suggestion was opposed by the then Archbishop of Canterbury (Geoffrey Fisher) and by colleagues in Cambridge who hoped for further work as a New Testament scholar before a call to church leadership at a maturer age, but Stockwood had been Robinson's vicar and intimate friend in Bristol (perhaps even a father-figure) before becoming the success-ful vicar of the university church in Cambridge. So this invitation prevailed over cautious counsels. It was a challenge because the diocese of Southwark covers South London and its adjoining towns and villages. The area is a mixture of poverty and affluence, suburban homes and rootless 'bedsitter-land', but in general in the 1950s church attendance was not high and was about to fall dramatically. One problem for the clergy is that in this area the Church of England does not have a traditionally prominent and privileged position. The diocese was formed as recently (by English standards) as 1905. But the basic reason for the secular-isation in the area must be that general tendencies in England and Europe are accentuated in the nation's capital. The religious position in the ancient diocese of London, north of the Thames, is similar.

The national situation was analysed in, for example, *The Need for Certainty: A Sociological Study of Conventional Religion* (1984) by Robert Towler. That book was based on an examination of about four thousand letters written to Robinson after *Honest to God*, mostly from people who had either not read the book or had not understood, or cared about, enough of it to discuss it carefully. They told the 'honest bishop' what they themselves believed or did not believe. Most of them did not regard the Church as a spiritual home, and when Robinson organised a couple of conferences for his correspondents he was taken aback by the vehemence of their criticisms of the Church. Towler quoted (p. 3) an American sociologist, Thomas Luckmann, as suggesting that 'What are usually taken as symptoms of the decline of Christianity may be symptoms of a more revolutionary change: the replacement of the institutional specialization of religion by a new social form of religion' – a form called by him *The Invisible Religion* in a book of 1967. In this religion no church seems to be needed because the traditional Church's doctrines about the supernatural are rejected, Jesus being regarded as an example to, and of, humanity. Or else no church is needed because the interest is in what Towler calls a modern 'Gnosticism', stressing life after death, spiritual influences on this life and the unreality of evil in comparison with the spiritual. Even when there is a popular belief in God ('theism'), bringing good out of evil, it is not usually thought that any church has much to contribute. In sharp contrast, the religious situation also contains what Towler calls 'conversionism'. This refers to the emphasis on a definite break between the secular environment and commitment to a congregation, usually adhering to 'traditionalism'. In the political jargon of the 1980s, there is a conservative backlash. So Towler emphasises the confusion in the public. But he observes that all these different opinions share one characteristic. Many people seem to want certainty in religion because they want order and meaning in life. To have a faith which includes much doubt is not reassuring enough.

Honest to God had in its background a quite widespread attempt in the diocese of Southwark, and in the Church of England as a whole, to bridge the gap between churchgoers and their neighbours at home and colleagues at work. The concerns of the world, including politics, were given priority over the interests of organised religion, often called 'the ecclesiastical machine'. A new slogan was heard in the Church: 'The world writes the agenda.' New attitudes and practices in the Church were developed in the hope that 'the world' would feel more at home there. For example, new hymns were sung, sometimes using the words of *Honest to God*. But that book went deeper theologically than any other experiment of the time. It was written while Robinson had to rest because of back trouble, not long after moving to this complex scene in South London. Books were read to him as he lay immobilised by a slipped disc, and he had time to reflect on his early experiences of a secular city in connection with his previous immersion in biblical theology. By then he had become aware of the size of the problems. He had not always been aware. His first sermon preached as a bishop to Confirmation candidates had assured them: 'You are coming into active membership of the Church when great things are afoot. I believe that in England we may be at a turning of the tide. Indeed, in Cambridge, where I have recently come from, I am convinced that the tide has already turned.' He had been so busy with a bishop's routine work that he could have largely ignored the problems in the background. But he was too honest to ignore them as he lay on his back and thought.

The book which he wrote in about three months (and later revised a little) fascinated because it was ambiguous. It was full of unresolved contradictions and unanswered questions. Yet it was also full of faith. And the mixture was what made it special.

Passages in the book pleased Christians converted into traditionalist congregations. The Preface began: 'It belongs to the office of a bishop in the Church to be a guardian and defender of its doctrine' (p. 7). The image of God that is questioned in the book is, he tells us, the author's. 'It is the God of our own upbringing and conversation, the God of our Fathers and of our religion, who is under attack' (p. 14). Even after the attack, the New Testament's witness is accepted that 'if one looked at Jesus, one saw God . . . Through him, as through no one else, God spoke and God acted: when one met him one was met – and saved and judged – by God . . . Here was more than just a man: here was a window into God at work' (p. 71).

At no stage of his life did Robinson withdraw these great Christian affirmations. But other passages gave rise to the verdict of an able philosopher deeply interested in religion, Alasdair MacIntyre, in *The Honest to God Debate*: 'What is striking about Dr Robinson's book is first and foremost that he is an atheist' (p. 215). In part this impression was conveyed by the dismissals in *Honest to God* of popular images of the Father and the Saviour – 'the Old Man in the sky' (p. 17) and 'God dressed up – like Father Christmas' (p. 66). And in part Robinson now seemed very heretical because he seemed to be abandoning the use by the New Testament writers, when describing Christ, of 'the "mythological" language of pre-existence, incarnation, ascent and descent, miraculous intervention, cosmic catastrophe, and so on, which according to Bultmann, make sense only on a now completely antiquated world-view' (p. 24). Robinson was attacked by some spokesmen for orthodoxy for caricaturing their beliefs as ridiculously naive. It was pointed out forcefully that the Christian tradition contained, in addition to these vivid pictures of the Father and the Saviour, a more philosophical or mystical attitude which stressed that they were only pictures to help understanding and devotion, God himself being the *ens realissimum* ('most real entity'), great beyond all pictures. St Anselm defined God as 'Something than which nothing greater can be thought.' St Thomas Aquinas called God 'the ocean of infinite substance'. Another great medieval theologian, John the Scot, named God 'He who is more than being.' But there can also be no doubt that the reception given to *Honest to God* showed that many Christians took the pictures more or less literally and felt that their entire faith depended on them. For example, the rich imagery of Christmas was not often – or at least not often publicly – acknowledged to be poetic rather than straightforwardly historical. So this paperback, and the discussion around it, played a part in the education of the public in the nature of religious language, where the poetry of 'myth' has a place.

Sophisticated students of twentieth-century theology accustomed to proposals to 'demythologise' the birth and infancy narratives and the rest of the gospels for the sake of communication with the age of science were more interested in something more novel – the apparent rejection of all pictures and ideas of God 'up there' or 'out there'. 'Statements about God', Robinson wrote,

> are acknowledgements of the transcendent, unconditional element in all our relationships, and supremely in our relationships with other persons . . . To assert that 'God is love' is to believe that in love one comes into touch with the most fundamental reality in the universe, that Being itself ultimately has this character (pp. 52–3).

Chapter 2 was called 'The End of Theism?' The short chapter on Jesus was entitled 'The Man for Others', because the love of Jesus for his fellow men shows that he is 'the one in whom love has completely taken over, the one who is utterly open to, and united

with, the Ground of his being' (p. 76). And 'the only way in which
Christ can be met, whether in acceptance or rejection, is through
"the least of his brethren"' (p. 61). Moreover, these theological
(or antitheological?) points were reinforced by chapters which
presented the holy as 'the "depth" of the common' (p. 87), which
interpreted prayer in a 'non-religious' manner ('to open oneself to
another *unconditionally* in love *is* to be with him in the presence of
God', p. 99), and which understood morality as working out the
implications of love (so that 'nothing can of itself always be labelled
as "wrong"', p. 118). In the history of modern theology what was
new in *Honest to God* was the linking of Rudolf Bultmann's
proposals for 'demythologising' with these wider ideas, expressed
in vivid quotations from two difficult writers, Paul Tillich and
Dietrich Bonhoeffer. For readers who had never before come
across Bultmann, Tillich or Bonhoeffer, the effect was stunning.
English theology now paid the price for its previous insularity and
the English churches were punished for their previous skill
in shielding churchgoers from the international debate of the
theologians.

It has to be asked why Robinson, previously an apostle of
biblical theology, had got himself in a position where, as he wrote,
'the line runs right through the middle of myself, although as time
goes on I find there is less and less of me left, as it were, to the right
of it' (p. 8) and 'it will doubtless seem to some that I have by
implication abandoned the Christian faith and practice altogether'
(p. 123). It seems to me, after reflection which has covered more
than a quarter of a century on and off, that his main motive arose
out of his discovery that 'for all their apparent difficulty and
Teutonic origin' theologians such as those he quoted 'so evidently
spoke not only to intelligent non-theologians but to those in closest
touch with the unchurched masses of our modern urban and
industrial civilisation' (p. 25). And when confronted by the secularisation of South London he was himself helped by them as he
was not helped by his former understanding of biblical theology.
While troubled by the apparent irrelevance of his tradition to most
of the life around him, and by the triviality of much in that
tradition, he reflected that he had learnt to love, in his marriage
and in his relationships within a small Christian community. Unchurched people also loved – and (as Towler's book was to stress)
they often believed in the good if not in God, and in the spiritual if
not in the Church. Their delight in family and friends meant all the
more if their urban environment was – as it often was in South

London – impersonal and unlovely. Surely it would make sense to them if he asked them to probe the depths of what they already experienced, to ask themselves what they believed to be the 'ultimate reality'? So far from being an atheist, he had never known what it is to think that there is no God and that phrases such as 'ultimate reality' are meaningless in a universe which is indifferent to human prayers and sentiments.

'One cannot argue whether ultimate reality *exists*,' he wrote.

> One can only ask what ultimate reality is like – whether, for instance, what lies at the heart of things and governs their working is to be described in personal or impersonal categories. Thus, the fundamental theological question consists not in establishing the 'existence' of God as a separate entity but in pressing through in ultimate concern to what Tillich calls 'the ground of our being' (p. 29).

He acknowledged that 'we are here on very dangerous ground' (p. 50), and repeatedly denied that he was teaching that 'love is God'. But at this stage he seemed to be attracted by a way of thinking that has no room for God conceived as 'a supreme Person, a self-existent subject of infinite goodness and power, who enters into a relationship with us comparable with that of one human personality with another' (p. 48). Instead, he was attracted by Tillich's talk about the 'God above the God of theism' and by the whole vast tradition behind Tillich which taught that the image of God as a person was only an image. He tried to combine the impersonal and personal images of God by saying that 'to say that "God is personal" is to say that "reality at its very deepest level is personal", that personality is of *ultimate* significance in the constitution of the universe, that in personal relationships we touch the final meaning of existence as nowhere else', so that 'theological statements are not a description of "the highest Being" but an analysis of the depths of personal relationships – or, rather, an analysis of the depths of *all* experience "interpreted by love"' (pp. 48–9).

In the end he came back to Christ and Christianity – as Tillich taught and practised prayer addressed to God personally, as Bonhoeffer approached death in frequent prayer based on the Bible and Lutheran hymns, as mystics such as Eckhart contemplated *deitas* but prayed to the personal *Deus*. He wrote:

> The Christian affirmation is not simply that love *ought to be* the last word about life, but that, despite all appearances, it *is* . . .

And that takes an almost impossible amount of believing. It is frankly incredible *unless* the love revealed in Jesus is indeed the nature of ultimate reality, unless he is the window through the surface of things into *God* (p. 128).

But he hoped that he had been shown a way towards this conclusion that could be trodden by the secular, or at least unchurched, people around him. And the response made it clear that such people, and many churchgoers, do indeed find a new reality in religion when they see it as the 'depth' of their daily experience and when they learn that they can meet God there, not merely in church or in heaven. Countless people felt liberated and grateful when, either by trying to understand *Honest to God* or by hearing reports about it, they discovered that a scholarly bishop was recommending this way – which during and since the 1960s has been recommended by many other spiritual teachers. The trouble was, and always has been, that mortals cannot avoid the decision for or against the claim that God remains real when our personal relationships have been ended by alienation or death. It is a decision which demands a response of faith or unbelief, assured knowledge being impossible. For Christianity, the decision has its focus in the response to Jesus. And the decision is not likely to be easy for those whose experience of human love has been less thoroughly Christian than Robinson's.

Sequels appeared which tried to answer some of the many questions left open by *Honest to God*. In *The New Reformation?* (1965) Robinson wrote that

I have not the least desire to weaken or deny the distinctive affirmations of the Christian faith. Among these I should certainly wish to assert: (1) The centrality of the confession 'Jesus is Lord', in the full New Testament sense that 'in him all things cohere' and 'in him the whole fulness of the deity dwells bodily'; and (2) the centrality of the utterly *personal* relationship of communion with God summed up in Jesus' address '*Abba*, Father!' (p. 13).

But he also repeated his conviction that in our time a theologian is called 'not to relevance in any slick sense but to exposure, to compassion, sensitivity, awareness and integrity' (p. 75). He reprinted a lecture in which he faced the question 'Can a truly contemporary person *not* be an atheist?' His answer showed that he was indeed sensitive to the widespread contemporary feelings that God is intellectually superfluous when understanding the world scientifically, that he is emotionally dispensable ('the call of atheism is . . . to move out of the shadow of the Father-figure', p. 110), and that he is morally intolerable ('A Being who "sends" the worst into the lives of individuals or who stands aside to "permit" it is a God who must die', p. 121). In its life within a largely secular society the Church must be ready to welcome the 'Christ incognito' far from its own customs – and must be ready to abandon many of its old institutions in order to travel light. Robinson urged the development of a 'genuinely lay' theology, starting with the life of the laity and breaking down the 'clergy line' which had so disastrously put so much of the initiative in church life into the hands of the ordained.

A shrewd reviewer of *The New Reformation?*, J. S. Bezzant, wrote that

> charges that the Bishop is an atheist are absurdly false, but his manner of writing does afford some measure of excuse for them to readers who do not know him. What he should do if he wishes to be more truly helpful either to believers or unbelievers is to show *how* he passes from his more negative statements to the orthodoxy which he sincerely professes (*Theology*, 1965, p. 449).

Seeking to answer this sort of challenge, Robinson wrote *Exploration into God* (1967), which turned out to be his last published excursion into the Western philosophy of the spiritual life. It was not a fully satisfactory answer, but the contrast was striking between its exploration and (for example) *Radical Theology and the Death of God*, an obituary by Thomas Altizer and William Hamilton (1966).

He offered no apology for *Honest to God*. It had made 'God' news; 'hardly a week passes without articles and interviews in the secular journals and the mass media' (p. 30). And 'to say that this was atheistic because it questioned traditional theism's image of a supreme Being was surely absurd' (p. 23). That always was his attitude. He could not see how Christians not prepared to use any God language 'can be Christians at all' (p. 57). He knew that when he used Tillich's language about God as 'the Ground of Being' he used it in order to express his own profound faith in God – and because its imagery was non-personal 'in fact, I have since found myself using it less and less' (p. 23). 'It is entirely natural', he wrote, that the reality of God should be *expressed as* the grace and claim of another Person. As a myth, as a projection, the description of God as a *Person*, encountered and addressed in prayer, is an entirely legitimate way of putting it. It is the simplest possible aid to the human imagination. Indeed, for most people most of the time (at any rate in the West) it is impossible to conceive of prayer except as talking to an invisible Person (p. 114).

But he valued impersonal language about God as a way of reaching those who wrongly considered themselves godless, holding that what is essential is 'the conviction that reality is reliable, not merely in a rock-like way, but in the kind of way in which a person can be trusted'. This belief, he still maintained, is what is 'transposed into belief in an ultimate divine Person', as in the proposition that 'God is a Being who loves' (p. 135).

The book contained many quotations from spiritual and mystical writers who had found God within the world; the most quoted were Bonhoeffer and Teilhard de Chardin. But it did not make it entirely clear whether the perception of reality 'in the kind of way in which a person can be trusted' without belief in 'an ultimate divine Person' was essentially the same experience as the experience which was the source of belief in God as personal. Many nature-mystics (for example Richard Jefferies, also extensively quoted) would say that there *is* a contrast between nature-mysticism and theistic mysticism. Nor did the book explain why Robinson, who was manifestly sincere in his worship of 'the Thou at the heart of all things', repeatedly insisted that the Thou need not be imagined as a Person and that 'Love as the Ultimate Reality' need not involve any image of a Lover. He of course taught that God is not a person in the same way as human beings are persons, and he of course saw value in contemplating the mystery of God in non-personal categories; but then, all thoughtful Christians teach or believe both those points. He also retained the belief that God is more properly prayed to than described; and this belief, too, is common to Christians. But he was so anxious to help people who preferred non-personal categories to reach his own experience of faith and worship that he was prepared to exaggerate the existing common ground. And what he learnt from the non-personalists was a breadth of vision. Through their scorn he escaped from the belief that God can be relied on to send favours to his favourites and suffering to his enemies. Through their eyes he saw that the whole world is 'charged with the grandeur of God'

(p. 85). In particular he had been moved by the novelists Nikos Kazantzakis and Petru Dumitriu, with their vivid sense of the presence of God everywhere. What he could finally accept from this vision which he called 'panentheism' was the belief that God, while greater than everything, is in everything. And for him 'panentheism' was more than an interesting philosophical position. In the coming years he was to quote Dumitriu's words more than once, and in the end they were to comfort his dying: 'God is everything. He is also composed of volcanoes, cancerous growths and tapeworms' (p. 90).

In 1970 Robinson collected shorter pieces written during a busy decade and called them *Christian Freedom in a Permissive Society*. They included the text of a broadcast 'On Being a Radical', made a month before the publication of *Honest to God*, defining the 'radical' as the one who 'goes to the roots' of a tradition, in distinction from the revolutionary who simply abolishes it and the reformist who tinkers with it. For example, 'the radical believes in "the ethic of the situation", with nothing prescribed – *except love*, in the New Testament sense of intense personal care and concern' (p. 5). Later essays worked out this insight in relation to current questions about premarital sex, contraception, abortion, divorce and the crime of obscenity – all questions which were answered more permissively by the law or by public opinion during the 1960s. In each case the new answer alarmed many conservatives, but in each case it won Robinson's approval. He was accused of encouraging promiscuity and took the advice of friends to delete a long passage in *The New Reformation?* which might be misunderstood, but actually his position was far from wild. If asked about premarital sex, for example, his blessing was very guarded: everything depended on the deeply loving intentions of the couple, not on a young man's passing fancy. In practice his own lifestyle (like that of Dietrich Bonhoeffer, whose advocacy of a 'religionless' Christianity fascinated him) was a model of propriety and piety.

Other essays in the 1970 collection gave glimpses of the politics of a churchman, who, 'brought up an unthinking Tory' (p. 89), had left the Conservative Party in disgust at Churchill's electioneering denunciation of Labour and had left the Labour Party for the Liberals in disgust at Wilson's electioneering refusal of immigration rights to Asians expelled from Kenya. Together the essays left the impression of a man who had practised what he had preached in an article written for *The Times* on ceasing to be

Bishop of Woolwich: 'The bishop's role is to lead in setting men free. And that means allowing them, for a start, really to see that the Church has a greater investment in integrity than in orthodoxy' (p. 224).

A Conservative Scholar

As he looked forward to a return to the academic world in 1969, he hoped that freedom from the routine of a bishop's work would enable him to think deeply and to roam widely. 'I wish', he said, 'to witness in the name of the Church (and that by remaining actively a bishop, as I shall do) to the subordination of the Church to God-in-the-world and to the world-in-God, which is what the New Testament means by the Kingdom' (p. 237). And he seemed to have found a new stability from which to prophesy when he delivered lectures on *The Difference in Being a Christian Today* in 1971 and published them as another successful paperback. He welcomed Cambridge's gift of leisure and libraries, and his first personal project was the writing of his book on Christology, which I shall discuss later (pages 135–8). But he had been appointed by Trinity College in order to teach students of theology, to be a pastor to other students and to preside over the college chapel. These things he did over fourteen years. Inevitably now that he was out of the limelight he was asked less often for his opinions about current affairs and articles to fill the religious slots in the media. Aspects of the routine of university life now irked him and his wife. She decided to spend her whole time in homes in Surrey and (later) Yorkshire, where he joined her as soon as term was over. He was not given back the university lectureship which he had resigned in 1959, and was never made a professor, a diocesan bishop or the dean of a cathedral, although he had some dreams in all those directions. His voice was not now heard on any of the central bodies in the life of the Church of England. What he achieved was a series of books, often encouraged by invitations to lecture outside Cambridge. Those on the New Testament were, as I have already mentioned, ill received by most scholars although the reviews which I am about to reprint record my welcome to them in a place which surprised him, the *Church Times*, concentrating more on what they implied about John Robinson than on what they proved about the New Testament. An impressive book, *Truth is Two-*

eyed, arose out of a visit to India and I shall later reprint my review of it (pp. 245–8).

His encounter with Hinduism showed, more clearly than his encounter with Western secularism had done so far, that while he was eager to appreciate another tradition his mind was decisively Christian because his heart was. As he put it in his last contribution to *Theology* (1982, p. 338), his final position was that Jesus was 'a man shaping and embodying in its fulness the self-expressive activity of God from the beginning'. In a dialogue in 1982 with a more extreme radical who was then a rising star, Don Cupitt, he was asked whether his way of doing theology was 'a sort of fixing religious labels to moral virtues'. 'No,' he replied, 'I think it is trying to be articulate about things that I find will not let me go.' He contrasted this with Cupitt's view of God as 'the personification of our ideal' (*Where Three Ways Meet*, pp. 27, 29).

In some ways he relaxed while back in Cambridge. He missed the excitement of the 1960s and was hostile to many aspects of the new conservatism (specially in Mrs Thatcher's politics), but on the whole he was hopeful. He told Cupitt that he was 'not sure that the gap between secular and Christian ways of thinking is widening. On science and religion, even on sexual morals, I would say that they were probably closer' (p. 26). And he became happier to be somewhat conventional in the expression of his belief in the God of the Christians. His *Wrestling with Romans* (1979) was a straightforward exposition of St Paul's religion. His sermons in Trinity College Chapel were not so close to personal anguish as those of his predecessor, Harry Williams, and were unusual mainly in that each was a little masterpiece. The question of God, he now said, is

> the question within, that comes nevertheless from without, of the Beyond *in* the midst. We can know this spiritual reality only as a dimension of our being. But it would be absurd to say that God was merely a dimension of human existence, that without us he would not be: just the opposite (p. 133).

One of his favourite quotations was from Gerard Manley Hopkins:

> Thou mastering me
> God! giver of breath and bread . . .
> Over again I feel thy finger and find thee.

This calmer faith in God was accompanied by a stronger belief that God had provided a New Testament which was, on the whole, reliable as a record of what Jesus and his apostles had taught and done. In 1977 he published another popular paperback, *Can We Trust the New Testament?*. The general answer was that we could. This biblical conservatism dismayed many radicals in the Church and most New Testament scholars in the academic world, but if it was mistaken it deserves to be understood as something very human – a last expression of a long love of the Bible. In 1974 he preached a sermon which based on the New Testament a response to the ravages of cancer or an earthquake. Some religious or mystical interpretations of such things accept them as the terrible faces of God – the God who creates or sends evil as well as good, who is 'beyond good and evil' as well as beyond personality. And sometimes Robinson seemed very attracted by such ideas, as when he quoted Dumitriu's 'God is composed of volcanoes . . .' But in the final analysis his belief was not that such things should be worshipped. It was that such things can be used. They are

> processes which in themselves are random and sub-personal – usually neutral but often anti-personal in their effects. Yet God is to be found in them rather than turning away from them. Love is there to be met, responded to, and created through them and out of them. Meaning can be wrested from them, even at the cost of crucifixion. Literally everything can be taken up and transformed rather than allowed to build up into dark patches of loveless resentment and senseless futility. This is the saving grace: God is not outside evil any more than he is outside anything else, and the promise to which the men of the New Testament held as a result of what they had seen in Christ is that he 'will be all in all' *as love*. Over most of the processes of what Teilhard de Chardin dared to call this 'personalizing' universe it is still waste and void and dark. But, for the Christian, a light has shone in the darkness, in the face of Jesus Christ, which the darkness cannot quench (p. 137).

It may seem that Robinson was merely returning to the confidently biblical theology of his earlier period in Cambridge. But the confidence had now been tested, deepened, purified; and out of the fire had come gold. Nine years after preaching the sermon just quoted he stood in the same chapel saying that he had an inoperable cancer – and he repeated this confidence (*Where Three Ways Meet*, 1987, pp. 189–94). He vigorously attacked the popular beliefs that cancer is the great unmentionable but that somehow 'God sends it'. To be told that he had six months to live had been 'a stunning shock' (p. 190). But he assured his congregation (perhaps the most attentive and appreciative that he ever had) that he had learnt from cancer to prepare for death and to reflect that for the living 'health means wholeness. It is concerned not simply with cure but with healing of the whole person in all his or her relationships' (p. 194). He had said that before, but now in the autumn of 1983 he said it as a dying man, with two months left. He said that cancer-sufferers swing from optimism to pessimism, 'but the Christian takes his stand not on optimism but on hope' (p. 194). Finally he quoted St Paul's prayer that 'always the greatness of Christ will shine out clearly in my person, whether through my life or through my death. For to me life is Christ, and death gain . . .' 'According to my chronology he lived nearly ten years after writing those words,' he added; 'others would say it was shorter. But how little does it matter! He had passed beyond time and its calculations. He had risen with Christ' (p. 194).

The memorial service in this chapel included a sentence which he had selected from John Donne: 'Whom God loves, he loves to the end: and not to their end, and to their death, but to his end, and his end is that he might love them more'.

Review of *The Difference in Being a Christian Today* by John A. T. Robinson (1971)

He has very genuine sympathy with the older generation because the rate of change requires us to live several lifetimes in one. He knows that there are traditional congregations and parish churches which are deeply and transformingly successful – and that not merely in the superficial, worldly sense of that term. He is himself a bishop very much involved in organised religion; and one of the reasons why he is glad to be ordained is that what is purchased by setting priests free from other employment is time – time for persons. But he thanks God that in movements such as Marriage Guidance, Shelter, Oxfam and Amnesty International – movements centred not on the clergy or on church buildings but on human problems – the initiative and membership are disproportionately Christian. And, when he thinks about Christian laymen at work in the world, he knows that being a Christian is something different from the everyday. It is a mysterious kind of citizenship, of belonging yet not belonging. The Christian may well give his life for this world, but he will not give his life to it.

Changes will be involved in the traditional categories of layman and priest, but these changes will amount to a return to the original basis of Christianity. In the New Testament the two words *cleros* and *laos* are both used to designate the whole people of God. He is himself constantly grateful for his rootage in the past, but he finds the current revolution in the life of the people of God exciting rather than bewildering. He quotes St Paul about never ceasing to be confident.

Who is this bishop who is so good at expressing ideas which are fast becoming commonplaces? Why, it's John Robinson! Almost every word in this review so far has been taken from his new paperback, which is based on university sermons in Cambridge and on lectures at the Union Theological Seminary, Buenos Aires.

To be sure, he joins in the current questioning of the value of sermons in church. But look how he does it! '"Sermon" comes from the Latin word for conversation, not monologue.' That is the scholarly tone he adopts throughout. And he makes that particular remark after giving us four of the longest, most impressive and most endearingly characteristic monologues to be preached in modern times! Why, then, did he ever gather a redder-than-red reputation? Perhaps part of the sensation around him was due to his simultaneous seriousness and liveliness: some other church leaders escape controversy by never touching on a real problem, or if they do, by leaving few people awake when they have finished. But partly the trouble came from his teaching method. It is as if, while preaching, he is trying to conceal the impression of delivering a monologue by carrying on a debate with himself.

Many teachers, specially officials holding responsible positions, think that duty demands a balance in every sentence. According to this formula one ought to write, if one can keep awake oneself while doing it: 'While many sincere people are convinced that many hands make light work, others who are no less sincere, and with whom I have no desire to quarrel, hold that too many cooks spoil the broth.' This is not Robinson's method. On the contrary, he goes all out to reach an audience. He usually writes short sentences. Each reveals a part of his mind, thrown into the conversation with no time to hesitate. Sometimes it contains an exaggeration meant to startle. Sometimes it may be an exaggeration from another writer without any safeguarding qualification. Sometimes the sentence is, by itself, teasingly ambiguous, like the very title of this book. That may not be the right style for a bishop, or for a theologian – but it is readable: and gradually, sentence by sentence, Robinson's full mind does emerge. When it emerges, this mind often turns out to be balanced. Once again he here says that the 'crucial divide' in the Church (radical versus conservative) 'cuts across individuals, as I know from myself'. This is what makes the conversation between the different John Robinsons instructive, for what finally comes out is that the truth itself is partly what radicals see and partly what conservatives see.

'The truly human is not one thing for Christians and another thing for non-Christians.' That sharp sentence is typical of Robinson's devices for making us stay awake and think. We can quote it out of context if we like. We can applaud or condemn if we like. We should, however, be foolish to take it as his last word on the subject of Christian ethics, for the rest of this book – short as it is – is packed with reflections on the difference it makes to believe in the transcendent God and to commit oneself to Jesus Christ as Lord. What Robinson really means is best expressed in his quotation from St Paul: 'Let your aims be such as all men count honourable.' And he writes:

> Herein is love: not that we love God – or man – but that he loves us . . . Yet this is frankly incredible. What evidence is there for such an estimate of the cosmos? What indeed, apart from the grace of our Lord Jesus Christ! Christians are distinguished by the conviction that we do here have a window . . . which enables us to trust that at heart being is gracious . . . accepting, forgiving . . . There is ultimately nothing to worry about, nothing you have to be defensive about, nothing you can only secure by clinging (p. 29).

Those who have followed John Robinson's life and work with sympathy will find here little that is new, but this small book is vastly encouraging. It shows that back in Cambridge he is full of eloquent conviction and of reasoned hope. Although he offers the very sensible guess that 'in twenty-five years from now in my own Church priests in secular jobs will outnumber those who are not', the integrity, energy and concern of these pages are likely to make quite a few young men ask: 'Why shouldn't I be a priest?' Even: 'Why shouldn't I be a preacher?'

Review of *Redating the New Testament* by
John A. T. Robinson (1976)

What fun it is to come across a really fascinating book about the Church's chief challenge and treasure – the Bible!

Dr Robinson has let off another bombshell. He argues that the whole of the New Testament was written within forty years of the resurrection of Jesus, the discovery of which took place on 9 April 30. He thus takes his stand against the whole of the scholarly world, where the books of the New Testament are commonly put at various dates between 50 and 110, one (2 Peter) being delayed until about 150. He warns us not to take his conclusions as meaning that he has been converted to fundamentalism. But it is now hard not to call him a conservative in the New Testament field. He often attacks the needless scepticism of many of the recent leaders of New Testament criticism, and accuses them of being influenced more by each other than by a careful and dispassionate examination of the evidence.

The 'first surviving finished document of the Church' is, he thinks, the letter of James the brother of Jesus, written before 50. He attributes the letter of Jude to another brother, about a dozen years later. (In contrast, the most prestigious German introduction to the New Testament, Kümmel's, dates both letters about 100.) He is on more commonly accepted ground when he dates the letters of Paul, beginning with the two to the Thessalonians, in 50–1. But Paul's output becomes all the more astounding when we find Robinson accepting as authentic all the letters traditionally associated with the apostle (except Hebrews) and assigning them all after Thessalonians to the three years 55–8. The production of Romans and ten lesser masterpieces in that period is not incredible. After all, the maximum allowed by the evidence for the public ministry of Jesus is also three years. But it takes the breath away to think of the postman Tychicus setting out from Caesarea one morning in the summer of 58 with three new letters in his bag – to Philemon, to the Colossians and to the Ephesians. And one fears that many letters from Paul were not properly filed.

When Paul finished the last of his surviving letters (2 Timothy), it was autumn 58. According to Robinson, the next few years saw the four surviving gospels take their final shape. Mark was finished first, perhaps by about 60, and was very soon used by Matthew and Luke – but also corrected by them, for sometimes they could draw on older materials. (Kümmel's dates are: Mark about 70, Luke

70–90, Matthew 80–100.) Luke is presented firmly as Paul's travelling companion, even as 'Paul's Boswell'. He wrote up Acts as his second volume from his researches and travel diaries. He ended it two years after Paul's arrival in Rome for the simple reason that the book was written then.

This chronology moves the gospels and Acts much closer to the events recounted than is generally accepted by present-day scholars. On its showing, before Peter and Paul were executed in 65–7 they could have read the three 'synoptic' gospels and Acts. They could also have read the first edition of John's gospel (written in Asia Minor between 50 and 55, it is suggested). And all four gospels were based on stories and sayings collected in the 30s and 40s.

Then came Nero's persecution. In it Peter and Paul were executed along with many fellow Christians. To that fiery ordeal belong, in Robinson's reconstruction, three major books: 1 Peter, Hebrews and (apart from its prologue) Revelation. All were intended to rally the persecuted or the threatened. So Nero, regarded as a minister of God in Romans 13, became the Beast of Revelation. But his tyranny was ended by his suicide in 68, and no near-successor was as brutal an enemy of the Church. The persecution under Domitian in the 90s, which most modern scholars think evoked 1 Peter, Hebrews and Revelation, is here dismissed as a 'non-event' in which 'no Christian was for certain put to death'. Comparative peace came to the Church – 'comparative', for Robinson still has to account for the prologue to Revelation, the letters to the seven churches. These he does date after Nero, 68–70.

Disaster came to Jerusalem with the destruction of city and temple in 70. Robinson, however, argues that the fall of Jerusalem is not reflected anywhere in the New Testament. For the New Testament was complete before it. The gospels do include prophecies of the destruction of the city and temple, and these are thought by many scholars to have been either inspired or coloured by the actual fall in 70; but Robinson is one of those who believe that the expectation of disaster was a real piece of foresight by the historical Jesus – and a not very surprising one, given the circumstances. The vivid details were stock imagery derived from the Old Testament.

Often Robinson seems to be floundering in guesswork. But his aim is to show that the textbooks, too, rest largely on guesses. Or, as he quotes Austin Farrer: 'the datings of all these books are like a line of tipsy revellers walking home arm-in-arm; each is kept in position by the others and none is firmly grounded' (p. 343). He stresses that the first clear quotation from a New Testament book comes when Clement of Rome cites Hebrews; according to most scholars this is about 95, according to Robinson about 70. He acknowledges that no book of the New Testament dates itself beyond dispute from the internal evidence. And the only absolutely firm date in the whole of the New Testament is the proconsulship of Gallio, shown by an inscription to have begun in the early summer of 51 (Acts 18:12–17).

In response to this book's detailed suggestions, probably the only wise course for most of us is to await the outcome of the scholarly debate in the next few years. But the fact is that, because of the fame he acquired during his ten stormy years as Bishop of Woolwich, many who hear of the publication of this book will be more genuinely interested in what it shows about John Robinson than in what it suggests about the apostle John. And firmer answers may be given to that question than to the hundred-and-one scholarly problems now reopened. For this book, so different in content from *Honest to God*, displays the same combination of characteristics: the seriousness half-concealed by impishness; the courage (he fights with academic giants); the freshness of phrasing (he makes chronology interesting, as he previously made Being news); the brilliantly clear teaching at one moment with an equally emphatic, it may be contradictory, sense of mystery at the next; the constant admissions that his mind has changed even while writing this book – admissions which will disarm some and infuriate others.

Review of *The Priority of John* by
John A. T. Robinson (1985)

It is, I find, very moving that John Robinson, who might have wanted to deepen the famous radicalism of his *Honest to God* and similar paperbacks into a coherent theology of his own when he returned to the academic leisure of Cambridge, chose to spend his remaining years on the meticulous study of the New Testament. He hoped to show that it was more reliable historically than is generally thought by his fellow scholars. Now we have his last book, on St John's gospel. It demonstrates, I think, less than he hoped – but at least it proves that he loved this gospel far more than he loved his own ideas.

This was never intended to be a popular book. Here we have a scholar talking with colleagues; mentioning a host of them by name in abundant footnotes; arguing gently about points which interest him; and ignoring other questions which are likely to be of more concern to the public. He nursed the hope that there might be a more popular book as a sequel, but that was not to be. Had he lived he might have tightened this book up, for the footnotes do sprawl and the gaps in the argument are conspicuous. But the editors to whom the manuscript was entrusted when he knew that he must soon die of cancer have rightly felt that it would have been wrong for them to do more than the most obvious little jobs on the text.

In such a book, a lot of the interest lies in detailed points which future commentators or close students will wish to weigh with a similar care. My own contribution is best made by an attempt to see Robinson's position as a whole. It is a more cautious position than would be expected by all who remember his preference for being in a minority, 'refreshing' (one of his great words) the Establishment. He produces many suggestions about the historical basis of the gospel without claiming that they are more than possibilities. He often admits that St John's gospel, from its first word to its last, was written with theological as well as historical motivation. Less plain is another admission, but it is there – the admission that we can never be quite sure whether a sentence in the teaching of the Jesus of John is the very voice of the historical Jesus, or whether a detail in the narrative is sacramental rather than scientific. He expounds the various theories that the gospel was spoken rather than written and was left unpolished or disordered by its author (like this book!), but reaches no firm conclusions.

He thinks that the gospel was written or dictated in Ephesus by John the son of Zebedee, the 'beloved disciple'. He argues for an early date, before the destruction of Jerusalem in AD 70; and this helps his more important argument that the gospel contains much historical information which is an improvement on the information in the other gospels. And he thinks it possible that John's mother was the sister of the mother of Jesus (which may explain why Jesus entrusted Mary to John's care, ignoring her surviving sons) – and that, although he left Jerusalem at an unknown date, John kept up his links with the city to its end.

Robinson therefore considers it worthwhile to explore the geography of Palestine in connection with this gospel. (What a contrast with Rudolf Bultmann, who also wrote a big book on this gospel but never visited the Holy Land or wanted to visit it!) He even reconstructs the chronology of a ministry which took Jesus from his baptism in the spring of 28 to his death on 7 April 30. He grants that the gospel is meditative; that, as Browning said, what others saw as mere 'points' in that universe which was and is Jesus John saw as 'stars'. But he resists the suggestion that the gospel is Gnostic; *gnosis*, knowledge, is not one of its themes, and *Logos*, Word, comes only in the prologue. Nor for him is John anti-Semitic.

The book's title may be misleading. Robinson does not want us to believe that John completed his gospel before Mark – only that the tradition behind the writing in our possession started as close to the historical Jesus as did the Petrine tradition behind Mark. If the tradition sounds a bit like the movement which grew into Gnosticism in the second century, or at least a bit Greek, we must remember that as recent scholars have stressed there was no complete contrast between 'Greek' and 'Jew'. Many devout Jews used Gnostic-sounding phrases like 'darkness versus light'; we know that now from the Dead Sea Scrolls. And many Jews spoke Greek – as did John and probably, Robinson thinks, Jesus himself.

However, this book does not really tackle the biggest puzzle, which is why the teaching in the fourth gospel is so unlike the parables and sayings of Jesus in the other three. What all the gospels have in common is legitimately stressed here – but still the 'I am' of the Jesus of John (expounded in long statements, not parables, and accompanied by fierce attacks on 'the Jews') does not sound like the Jesus of the synoptists, the Jew who told stories but seldom talked about himself. This gospel, so simple and so profoundly illuminating in the spiritual truths which are its business, becomes a riddle when we seek to root it in detailed facts. The reader is told that the grass was plentiful (6:10), that the name of the High Priest's servant was Malchus (18:10), or that the catch of fish was as large as 153 (21:11), presumably because as a matter of fact it was. But, in the course of a prayer to which no one except the Father listened, he is told that 'this is eternal life: to know thee who alone art truly God, and Jesus Christ whom thou hast sent'. If the reader concludes that those last words were added editorially, what is the ground on which he can stand if he is not to think that the 'plentiful grass', 'Malchus' and '153' were also editorial touches, perhaps with some mystic significance which now utterly escapes us?

The secret of the riddle seems to be that John the Evangelist was convinced that Jesus was still alive and speaking in Ephesus (or wherever) thirty years (or whenever) after the crucifixion. He was convinced of this as surely as was John the Prophet who heard what the Living One wanted him to write to the church at Ephesus. So history and experience formed a continuum. A faint analogy is provided by our common practice of saying that a dead teacher is still teaching this or that. It is a practice into which I fell naturally in the course of this little review. As John Robinson points out here, Plato was a pupil of Socrates who nevertheless wrote dialogues in which he made no attempt to distinguish between his own reflection and the voice of his master. It was the common practice in the ancient world to give oneself freedom in this kind of portrait-painting, and it did not show that there was no 'sitter' at all for the portrait. Nor was the practice thought to indicate dishonesty. On the contrary, it suggested a proper humility.

Such was the humility of John Robinson himself. His book ends with an exposition of his understanding of the incarnation. Jesus is the human face of God, the embodiment of the Ground of Being in the Man for Others, although it is unbiblical and indeed impossible to speculate meaningfully about the relationships of Father, Son and Spirit in eternity. But John Robinson did not end his teaching in his own words! He was much more interested in saying that this was what St John meant by the prologue which he added to his gospel (a prologue which, some scholars think, was based on an existing hymn): 'What God was, the Word was . . . So the Word became flesh.' Whether he seemed to be a radical among bishops or a conservative among scholars, that was the testimony of a man of our own confused century named John.

An assessment of John Robinson was made by John Knox in *Theology* (1989, pp. 251–68). This eminent scholar wrote: 'I shall always think of him, not only as an extraordinarily gifted, but also as a very significant, New Testament scholar – and this despite the fact that I disagree with his conclusions more often, perhaps, than I agree' (p. 252).

3

DON CUPITT AND THE REALITY OF GOD:

Is religion only human?

Don Cupitt, Dean of Emmanuel College, Cambridge, and a university lecturer in the philosophy of religion, became in the 1980s both the best known and the most controversial of the Church of England's academic theologians. This was partly because he became the most extreme among the radicals. Is he an atheist? The review which I wrote in the *Church Times* about his *Taking Leave of God* (1980) was entitled *Atheist Priest?*, and that title was also used by the first book to cover his teaching as a whole, the quite short but sympathetic study by Scott Cowdell (1988), but in his book based on a widely acclaimed BBC TV series, *The Sea of Faith* (1984), Cupitt observed that 'atheist' is 'a word which historically has been used as a quasi-political swear-word to brand innovators, including at one time the early Christians' (p. 224). Understandably he prefers to say that his interpretation of Christianity is 'non-realist'.

I reprint from the *Church Times* my review of his first book, almost ten years before *Taking Leave of God*. It shows that I did not always place him among the atheists.

Review of *Christ and the Hiddenness of God* by Don Cupitt (1971)

Don Cupitt has written this book in order to persuade Christians to be more careful in what they tell others about God and Christ. It is not a book that is basically hostile to 'popular' or 'practical' religion – in fact, it balances some contemptuous remarks about muddle, myth and so forth with other passages which recognise the advantage of some vivid, direct simplicity in religion. But essentially it is an austere book. As Cupitt says, 'the simple questions "What do you mean?" and "How do you know?" have tremendous power to prune and purge' (p. 101).

Part of the austerity comes from the fact that the book, based on Stanton Lectures in Cambridge, is addressed primarily to an academic audience. Its readers are expected to find David Hume's *Dialogues concerning Natural Religion* 'familiar' (p. 67), and to be curious about some long-forgotten disputes among English and Irish theologians on the exact status and scope of mankind's alleged 'natural' knowledge of God. Readers outside universities are, however, presumably allowed to skim lightly over the historical references, for Cupitt is not a mere historian; he thinks his own thoughts about the perennial mysteries, and makes a point of stressing that logical arguments are still important in the religious sphere.

His argumentation is rigorous. Cupitt was a student of natural science, and, although he quotes some modern novels (with telling effect), the background still stimulating his mind as a theologian is what he calls a 'developed scientific culture' – an atmosphere where, as he says, the ways in which we think about the universe are shaped by mathematics and technology rather than by personal imagery. His thinking will therefore appeal not only to students of David Hume (who is, after all, a paperbacked author!) but also to others who are aware of Hume-type challenges to popular or practical religion arising from the age of science. This wider public exists far beyond academic circles.

Part One wrestles with some of the difficulties which are inevitable in all human talk about God. 'If theology's basic concepts ever become clear and specific, it is falling into idolatry; if they are refined away, theology falls into vacuity' (p. 67). Although Cupitt is very much on his guard against the former danger, he is also tough with demythologising theologians such as Bultmann who have (he argues) fallen into the alternative pit. For himself he struggles hard to find 'a middle way between anthropomorphism and agnosticism', or rather (as he tells us on p. 91) a way which 'encompasses both'. This part is somewhat enigmatic, and makes one wish that Cupitt would write more constructively and at greater length.

Part Two tackles some basic questions about the specifically Christian form of belief in God – the form where, it is claimed, the dangers which have alarmed us in Part One may be avoided by accepting the personal self-revelation of God in Christ. Alas, we find ourselves, if not out of the frying-pan into the fire, then at least out of the frying-pan into some very hot water. For Cupitt shows us that it is by no means as simple as we might think to 'know' Jesus, who is a first-century teacher but is also our 'Christ', our Lord and God.

What is the right mix of the historical with the existential in our 'knowledge' of Jesus as the Christ? What is the right emphasis on 'event' or on 'faith' in our account of the resurrection of Jesus? On the one hand Cupitt warns us against depending on specific stories about the empty tomb and the resurrection appearances, all of which he apparently regards as legendary. On the other hand, he deplores the tendency to use the word 'Christ' so vaguely that it has little more historical content than has the figure of King Arthur. Part Two is therefore far from sentimental. Truth to tell, it is at points unreasonably negative. But it does put the questions very well, and now and then it mentions an answer.

Here is a teacher who should be exempt from what he calls (p. 60) 'the popular suspicion that the cleverer a theologian the less he believes'; for Cupitt is a very clever man who believes in God through Christ. In books to come he may tell us more fully why, in his own words, 'Christians believe that Jesus is the Christ, and still lives now, and still actively relates men to God', because they 'discern in the narrative of his life and death the epitome of the universal human situation before God' (p. 213) – and why (going beyond this) they also believe in a God who acts.

What will emerge when all the pruning and purging have been done? One clue may be that Cupitt ought to develop further the meaning of personal imagery. Despite mathematics, technology and all that, for almost everyone personal relations matter more than anything else in the universe, although it is often very difficult to argue about them or even to make them public in the sense that Cupitt seems to think is necessary. This preoccupation with the personal exists among scientists, if not in science. To explore its most profound application to religion – in other words, to think hard about prayer to God through the living Jesus Christ – might be a very rewarding exercise for a philosopher of Cupitt's great ability.

The Creed of an Atheist Priest

Since that book and my review appeared, Don Cupitt's teachings have changed greatly. So have my reactions to them. His development has been in the opposite direction to the one I hoped for, so that from thinking him 'a very clever man who believes in God through Christ' I have moved to see him as a very clever man who has clearly become an atheist and who ought to clear the air by ceasing to function as a priest while he holds his present attitude to belief in God.

Why does he feel entitled to remain a priest? I should not feel so entitled myself if I believed as little of traditional Christianity as he does, and I have never forgotten the agony of mind which I went through in Cambridge in 1954 when the time for my ordination drew near and in some moods I thought that I *did* believe as little. In later life I have often found it hard to renew the commitment I made then, which was more than commitment to a job. But as a former dean of a Cambridge college I appreciate that a priest in that position does not have to undertake much of the kind of work that fills the life of a more normal clergyman. And I also appreciate that Cupitt feels, and discharges, a duty to a wider public. I recognise in him a prolonged, although diminishing, fascination with the figure of Jesus and with the Christian movement. I have no reason to doubt his sincerity when he hopes that his godless version of Christianity will turn out to be Christianity's future, as the 'sea of faith' which has ebbed in Europe over the past two hundred years (at least) returns in a floodtide after being purified in this very drastic manner. Cupitt's wish to be counted among the Christians is part of a continuing concentration on the study of major thinkers who discuss the meaning of life – or, as he puts it in his most recent teaching, the 'sea of meanings'. I also recognise in him a strong morality sharing much in common with the best Christians and amounting to what Iris Murdoch (for example) has commended as belief in *The Sovereignty of Good* (1970).

It takes courage for Cupitt to expose himself to criticism of the kind which I and many others offer, when it would have been possible to enjoy the quiet of an academic life, teaching people about the history of religious thought without entering public controversy. He exhibits the 'disinterestedness' that he often praises. To be sure, those who give their blood to save the sick or who pray for the dying or the dead are moving examples of this virtue, as he points out. But some praise should be spared for the 'disinterestedness' of a man with a message who has angered his ecclesiastical superiors by being so heretical so publicly, who has aroused the contempt of fellow philosophers such as Sir Alfred Ayer by still identifying himself as a clergyman, and who has also forfeited the admiration of many fellow academics by being a populariser wide open to expert criticism. When Cupitt wrote of 'Hyperborean faith' in *The World to Come* (1982) he referred to the Greek myth about a people that has somehow found warmth beyond the icy wastes of the North. But he also, it seems to me, obliquely referred to himself. I have the impression that he has suffered considerably by abandoning the warm assurances of traditional religion and the warm support of its adherents. This has struck me when I have watched him on television. The words are dogmatic but the lines of thought and pain are etched upon his face.

I have grown to understand why such a man, although (I fear) largely isolated from his professional colleagues, has attracted many admirers outside ecclesiastical and academic circles. The risk which BBC TV took when it expensively filmed a series of programmes about philosophy and theology as interpreted by him was largely justified by the size of an appreciative audience which was grateful for the energy of a brilliant teacher. A smaller but sufficient audience has supported the publication of a row of books which, because of their intensely serious and often abstract subject matter, cannot be easy reading. Many people who admire his kind of courage and integrity reckon not that he is a disgrace to the priesthood but that he is a rare exception to the rule that parsons are weak-minded fools and fence-sitting cowards. And many people think that his sort of popularisation, based on much hard study, is an admirable use of a post in a university financed by public money. Indeed, many lay people and a few clergy who want to be called Christians share his general attitude that traditional orthodoxy is incredible or unintelligible and that what matters is spirituality or morality. I reckon that Cowdell is right to say that while the sophistication of Cupitt's treatment of theology appeals to a 'relatively small group (historically and geographically) of disaffected Christian intellectuals' there are larger numbers who 'seem to have no difficulty' with his attempt to be a Christian without making Christianity depend on a strong belief in God's reality (p. 73).

Why, then, have I and many others been angry with this turbulent priest? I have to acknowledge that often anger in controversies about the basic religious questions is a symptom of suppressed uncertainty about one's own position. One is liable to react with alarm when someone else brings out into the open a doubt or denial which one has buried in one's own mind for the sake of loyalty or comfort; and one is liable to use 'a quasi-political swear-word'. But if this is one explanation of anger about Don Cupitt, in all honesty I have to say that the tendency to abusiveness does not originate in replies to him. His books are peppered with harsh words about traditional Christian faith and its adherents. He patronises it as 'immature' or 'vulgar' and scorns it as inauthentic. 'Over much of the bourgeois Christian world,' we are assured in *Only Human* (1985), 'faith has become the purest superstition' while theologians display 'a determination to believe against experience' (p. 199).

In *The Long Legged Fly* (1987) he regrets that 'I am fated to be one of the last ecclesiastical theologians' – to be associated with the Church as the 'organisation, power-structure and machinery of control' which 'throughout the classical Christian period' rigorously opposed 'everything that was most innovative, revolutionary and liberating in Christianity', so that 'the objectified God of Christendom had been created by power for power's sake' (pp. 7, 157–8). But the reply rises to the lips that his identification with the Church and with the God of Christendom by being a priest is not fate but his own persistent choice. And it is a choice that is bewildering. He sounds a bit like a member of the royal household who arranges ceremonies at Buckingham Palace while being a fervent republican, or a public speaker who frequently denounces the working class while remaining a Labour politician. So far as I know he has never explained in public how he manages in good conscience to officiate at worship addressed to a God not thought to be real with phrases which he thinks are insults to human dignity and intelligence. He has not even publicly expressed gratitude for the liberty to continue to hold that office. He has pursued a line of conduct that has inevitably exposed him to the hostility often directed at people rightly or wrongly suspected of treachery, but his response to those hurt has been one of contempt rather than sensitivity. However, one possible explanation seems to be that here is a man who is criticising immature religious enthusiasms which nearly trapped him (as he feels) and who is arguing against the continuing power of a deep pull on him as an adult – for his rejection of the Church which exists is not expressed in a calm indifference. On the contrary, it has inspired him to hope that the

Church will be remodelled so that his own version of Christianity becomes its creed (to use an old-fashioned word). He set out this hope in his book on *Radicals and the Future of the Church* (1989), which, however, added no important new point to his theology.

Even if a deep anxiety is the true explanation of the anger in the criticisms and counter-criticisms which have been shouted in the encounter between Cupitt and some of his contemporaries, it is hard to justify his tendency to present great men of God in the past as people who shared his own denial of God's reality.

George Tyrrell famously remarked that a liberal Protestant theologian seeking the 'historical Jesus' was like a man looking down a well and seeing his own face at the bottom. No doubt everyone who looks at Jesus does treat him, to a greater or less extent, as a mirror and our hope must be that the mirror will not too greatly conceal what can be known about the historical Jesus or too sharply reveal what in ourselves is unlike him. But the danger is especially obvious in Cupitt's case, for in his earlier teaching he took exceptional pains to come to terms with what is written in the gospels. He wanted to see the water. That was obvious in *Jesus and the Gospel of God* (1979), where he argued that it was

> necessary to start again from Jesus himself. I believe that the primitive faith is intelligible and defensible where Christendom is not, and that the stock objections that we know too little of Jesus, and that what we do know is too strange to be intelligible today, can be overcome. The old religion is returning. Christianity's first task today is the restoration of its own integrity (p. 9).

And for a summary of the teaching of Jesus, he turned to the Lord's Prayer. 'In successive clauses the prayer expresses the devout man's intimate fellowship with God, the divine transcendence, the longing to see God's reign, faith's utter dependence upon God, the identity of religious and moral categories, and a cry for preservation in the final conflict' (p. 54).

God is transcendent and God's arrival annihilates all else, so that at this stage Cupitt believed that

> only the relation to God matters; its demand overrides all else and simply wipes away all relativities. Ruthless and drastic action becomes imperative . . . Thus Christianity – Jesus's way of salvation – is the final truth, and the society which springs from him, even if it has confused his way, has never wholly lost it (pp. 68, 70).

In an article of 1975 reprinted in *The Leap of Reason* a year later, Cupitt declared that

> no reader of the New Testament can fail to observe that its most fundamental affirmations concern the uniqueness, the sole sufficiency and the finality of what God has done in Jesus Christ . . . That Jesus is God's only Son; that only through him can men be saved; that God acted in him once for all; that world history will be wound up by him; and that he is God's chief executive, seated henceforth at God's right hand: these are some of the forms in which it is expressed (p. 120).

And in his contribution to a Cambridge symposium edited by Stephen Sykes and John Clayton on *Christ, Faith and History* (1972), he explored the theme of 'One Jesus, many Christs?', concluding that Christianity was 'a family of monotheistic faiths which in various ways find in Jesus a key to the relation of man with God . . . Jesus' legacy to mankind is . . . an urgent appeal to each of us to acknowledge above all else the reality of God' (pp. 142–4).

But in *Who Was Jesus?* (1977), based on a BBC TV series and written in collaboration with its producer Peter Armstrong, Cupitt began to offer another interpretation of the message of Jesus. He still showed great confidence that a reliable portrait of the historical Jesus was provided by the New Testament and by such other evidence as exists (within the limits agreed on by most biblical scholars). In agreement with this evidence he said that Jesus called for 'total faith in God' in a message completely 'God-centred' (p. 59). But the message could also be summed up as '*Now*, here in this world and in the present moment, is absolute salvation' (p. 90) and on his last page Cupitt provided a glimpse of his future development by claiming that the proclamation 'The Kingdom of God is at hand!' 'unified all the opposites' including 'the world and God' (p. 92).

In *The Debate about Christ* (1979) the voice of Jesus could still be recovered, if not his exact words, and found to be the voice of God: 'His words are his work, and in his words he still lives and still relates men to God' (p. 138). But by 1982 things were seen differently. In *The World to Come* Jesus was placed as 'a figure from an exotic and pre-modern culture who has left us no writings in his own hand', so that 'we cannot expect to be able to intuit his unique personal individuality without the risk of back-projection and fantasy' (p. 78). Now 'the name of Jesus signifies a moment of religious awakening by the use of irony' (p. 79). 'People who live within a single supernaturally-guaranteed framework naturally see no need for irony' (p. 84), but Jesus was not among them. Using the weapon of irony he delivered us from 'every enduring moral framework' (p. 118) and 'from the consciousness of sin and the self-mutilating psychology of "ever-deepening penitence"' (p. 104). Thus the opposites of sin and holiness have been unified, and 'the true forgiveness of sins is the disappearance of "sin"' (p. 98). Now the voice of Jesus asked merely: 'What will you choose to be and to do when everything passes away and you face the void?' (p. 119). And in later books Cupitt has drawn the logical conclusion that the New Testament's version of the teaching of Jesus about God and man need no longer be considered in any detail. Perhaps in the 1980s he has forgotten his own regret that 'much of modern Christianity, and *especially* orthodoxy, has become a projection of basically secular humanist and personal values' (*The Debate about Christ*, p. 144).

This treatment of the founder of Christianity is matched by over-simplification of the teachings of some modern Christians who are conscripted into the ranks of thinkers such as Lucretius or Feuerbach who have plainly taught that for one reason or another man made God in his image. 'Classical Christianity has now become our Old Testament', we are told (*Taking Leave of God*, p. 135). But just as the study of the Old Testament can be pursued without pretending that the Hebrew heroes were honorary Christians, so (I suggest) Cupitt ought to grant that the teachers of classical Christianity believed in God. Unfortunately he has not always done this. For example, in *The Sea of Faith* he presented the ardent Christian of the seventeenth century, Blaise Pascal, as a man to whom the question whether 'there are real invisible objects out there such as God and Christ . . . presumably does not matter' (p. 52). But in the very same passage he quoted the well-known prayer after a mystical experience in 1654. Pascal prayed to 'God of Abraham, God of Isaac, God of Jacob . . . God of Jesus Christ . . . The world forgotten, and everything except God' – the prayer which Pascal always carried on his person. Cupitt also referred to Pascal's famous comparison of trust in God with betting a life on a wager with an uncertain outcome (p. 54). In a similar manoeuvre, in the most recent of his surveys of modern religious thought (*Life Lines*, 1986), the great theologian Friedrich Schleiermacher, for whom Christianity was essentially the message that 'the Redeemer assumes believers into the power of his God-consciousness', was made to understand faith in God as 'a fundamentally aesthetic and reconciling response to the world as an infinite Whole of which we are a part' (p. 120). That would be pantheism. In fact the task of Schleiermacher's life, with its climax in the writing of *The Christian Faith* at the beginning of the 1820s, was to commend belief in 'the eternal and holy Being that lies beyond the world' to its 'cultured despisers'. He accepted the scientific account of nature in so far as he knew it ('all things are conditioned and determined by the interdependence of nature'). But he insisted that the religious consciousness was awareness of 'the absolute dependence of all finite being on God'. In other words, although feeling the strength of the Romantic movement's rediscovery of God in nature Schleiermacher ended up in the worship of the Christians' God, as did his English contemporaries, Coleridge and Wordsworth. Even Karl Barth, who battled against his theological influence, fully acknowledged this piety.

Another great Christian of the nineteenth century, Søren Kierkegaard, has also been seriously misrepresented. He is held to say that 'God is identical with the awesome challenge and promise of the task of becoming an individual' (*The World to Come*, p. 46) and that faith is 'simply piety, and as such no longer presupposes any truths outside itself' (*Only Human*, p. 14). Yet Kierkegaard expounded (admittedly with many poetic images, paradoxes, exaggerations and obscurities) the life of faith as a passionate and risky encounter with the Other who in Christ has come to meet and save us. The 'infinite qualitative difference' between God and man was to Kierkegaard so absolute that the union in Christ of God and man, eternity and time, infinity and the finite, was 'the absolute paradox' – but the Christian responded to the 'moment' of the encounter with this fact, this Subject, this One. So the Christian life was a very different thing from living aesthetically or ethically, and from conforming to Christendom or to the world. The truly religious life challenged the 'knight of faith' to the 'leap of faith' in fear and trembling through dread and despair, as when Abraham was prepared to sacrifice his only son. Accordingly Cupitt seems to have admitted that his presentation of this passionate Christian as an atheist requires revision. He grants that at times Kierkegaard 'still yearns for eternal happiness and a transcendent God to torment him' (*The New Christian Ethics*, 1988, p. 91).

Cupitt has not only misinterpreted great figures in the history of religion in order to fit them into his schematic summaries. He has also failed to represent realistically the great forces which have from time to time changed that history. Obviously, great minds addressing issues of general interest have had an influence as their teachings filter through the general public, but I suggest that Cupitt exaggerates the influence of philosophers. In *Life Lines*, for example, he retold the spiritual story of modern Europe in terms of the influence of books. He claimed that 'Descartes introduced a new way of thinking' (p. 6) and that 'Nietzsche overthrew various ideas such as the beliefs in progress, in a permanent and objective world-order, and in timeless objective moral values' (p. 220). It would have been more historically accurate to say that for some intellectuals Descartes was a suitable philosopher for an age when scientists were beginning to think about the world and Nietzsche a suitable prophet for an age when Europe had lost self-confidence and moral stability through the misuse of science in a great war. In *The Long Legged Fly* he observed that the modern age 'has become radically post-theistic, in the sense that all the leading thinkers have left traditional metaphysical belief in God far behind' (p. 7), whereas it would surely have been more realistic to mention the secularising influences of industrialisation, communism, consumerism and other non-intellectual forces. Consistently Cupitt has underestimated the social reality of religion and the social factors in a religion's rise or decline. His summary of history is brilliant, but it is not history, because he sees in it more people like himself than were actually there.

After the Death of God

In *Life Lines* this was Cupitt's mature answer to the question 'How does the religious person emerge?': 'The productive life-energy is annulled, and no longer expresses itself in representation at all. For a time out of time, there is total silence and darkness'. But 'the Christian existentialist' goes 'more deeply and trustingly into the Nihil' because 'in search of selflessness' – and 'emerges thinking of all life as pure gift' and 'is an individualist because she thinks each individual must experience the Nihil in order to gain salvation'. The 'productive life-energy spontaneously surges up . . . We are reborn, raised from the dead' (pp. 131–2). However, Cupitt was surely right to think that 'a fully autonomous spirituality' so described 'is very rare' (*Taking Leave of God*, p. 5). The religious person here pictured has an unusual capacity for isolated and abstract thought, an unusual compulsion to take leave of all religious, social and moral conventions, and an unusual belief in spontaneously vanishing and reappearing 'life-energy' as the conclusion of this solitary and terrible pilgrimage. What this passage seems to show is how Cupitt himself experienced the spiritual crisis which Nietzsche in the 1880s called the 'death of God' – and how he moved beyond its desolation.

As Cowdell notes in his book about him, towards the end of the 1980s he has moved to a more 'playful' position which takes far more account of ordinary people's experience – although 'despite relaxing in mid-life, Cupitt is still very serious' (p. 27). However, this new position still seems elitist. Its denial of the reality of 'the world' (as well as of God) would strike most people as lacking in common sense, for most people spend most of their lives dealing with material objects which are real enough to make them tired – and spend most of their emotional energies on relationships with other people who are fascinating in their mysterious physicality. The scope for ideas which may be said to construct a mental 'world' of 'culture' is limited. So a religion which belongs only to that world is not common.

For the great bulk of religious people through the centuries, religion has been mainly a response to what are perceived, rightly or wrongly, as facts which are public property. Initially these facts are given in the teachings of parents, educators and pastors. Later these facts include the conventions of a society to which individuals wish to conform, but behind the pressure from society is the perception of the world taught in a society's religious tradition. Sometimes this tradition may urge the total rejection of the world, but in the history of religion as a whole Cupitt is right to say that 'fundamental confidence in the worth of one's own world is the most elementary form of religious faith. Where it is present, people can and will endure almost anything without complaint' (*Only Human*, p. 21). He is also right to say that religious traditions usually offer the hope that what seems to be evil in this partially good world will be defeated in a 'salvation' accomplished by God or gods or a saviour or one's own enlightenment. So the religious tradition teaches reliance on a reality which is greater than nature – 'supernatural' or 'metaphysical' or divine. In *The Sea of Faith* Cupitt correctly observed that despite their basic confidence, religious people feel 'how frail the human is, how wretched most men's lives and how threatened our happiness is by evil within us and about us', so that 'for 999 people out of every thousand religion has to do with metaphysical yearnings and a desire to be reassured about God's existence and a real life after death, and suchlike' (pp. 32, 221).

For most people religion, although including such 'yearnings', has been mainly a matter-of-fact business. In practice it means participation in religious actions such as prayer and visits to religious buildings such as churches (even if only as seen on a TV set), and it is fed by religious scriptures such as the Bible (even if only through somewhat vague memories). Thus people are encouraged to believe that certain facts of history reveal what is factually there in, but also beyond, nature. This 'revelation' is supplemented by 'religious experience' which is interpreted as pointing in the same direction and by arguments which are said to show that it is reasonable to regard God, the soul, eternity, etc., as facts. So believers are encouraged to have a positive attitude to the facts of life today – the facts which are there to be enjoyed and the facts which are there to be endured in hope. As Cupitt once said:

> It is a mistake to argue that because faith is sometimes defiant of facts it is non-factual. On the contrary, experience could not tell against faith, or put it on trial, unless faith implies assertions about what is really so. The man of faith says, the facts seem to be thus and so, they seem to suggest such and such a picture of the nature of things, but it is intolerable that it should be so, things must really be otherwise (*Christ and the Hiddenness of God*, p. 44).

Cupitt's later thought, however, arises within a society which seems unable to accept any such framework of 'facts' human and divine to surround and support the individual: 'Today we cannot see how the public moral order can be re-established in a form that will stand up to critical questioning' (*The World to Come*, p. 129). So he believes that even genuinely religious people have lost interest, or ought to lose interest, in the question whether God is the greatest fact in a 'frame' which surrounds and supports them. 'Inevitably the question will be put, "Does God exist outside faith's relation to God, or is the concept of God just a convenient heuristic fiction that regulates the religious life?"' Provocatively he adds: 'the crucial point about this often-asked question is that it is of no religious interest' (*Taking Leave of God*, p. 96).

Properly (in my view) in *Christ and the Hiddenness of God* he wrote: 'Religion demands, it lives by, a solid assurance of the reality of God and his promises, and theology, if it is to be true to religion, must seek some way of representing and stating the grounds of this assurance' (p. 47). And properly in recent books he has acknowledged that most religious people still are interested in the question about the reality of God. In *Life Lines* he provided a kind of map of the history of religion. He allocated places on this map to 'mythical realism' ('a form of religious consciousness in which religious objects are apprehended through an unsystematic miscellany of stories, symbols and pictures received from tradition'), 'doctrinal realism' ('a form of religious consciousness in which the "reality" of God consists in the supreme power and authority of his will as the source of a systematic sacred law of belief and conduct for the community') and 'designer realism' ('a form of religious consciousness that is grounded, not in the social sphere, but in a claimed primal, natural and universal response of awe and wonder at the majesty of Nature'). And in his Prologue he appeared to be tolerant of these positions (I have quoted their definitions from his Glossary at the end). 'Live with as much commitment to life as you can, broadly within the framework of our Western and Christian tradition, and you will find yourself passing along a route shown somewhere on the map' (p. 3). But a closer examination of *Life Lines* shows a conviction that all should 'pass' out of belief in the reality of God into Cupitt's own most recent position.

In the 'older tradition', he wrote, those who reflected about God recognised the mystery, the 'dazzling darkness', but 'it was certainly *there*: whereas for us this is no longer the case' and 'ours is a real darkness' (p. 5). 'Most people's thinking remains mythical and they probably do a good deal better than us who for good or ill have become demythologised', but the voluntary acceptance of 'the death of God, and not just of Christ, as a necessary stage in the religious life', has become essential (*Life Lines*, pp. 33, 111). The interpretation that 'salvation must ultimately be sought from above, and would be found only outside this life altogether, beyond death' is, Cupitt says firmly, 'no longer available to us' (p. 164).

Cupitt has written:

If you are a dogmatic realist, then you may stay in that position, and I have no wish or right to push you out of it . . . The only stipulation I can make is that if your dogmatic realism is to be intelligible to others it must have a coherent logic, apparent in both your linguistic and your ethical practice. If you can do it, I envy you. I really do (p. 205).

But as many passages in his recent books show, he thinks that no form of belief that God is real can pass the tests he requires. In *The Long Legged Fly*, for example, although he says that 'each of my books tends to begin from a perceived fault in the one before' (p. 11), he strongly objects to ideas which he once expounded with no less vigour. The 'variety of optional perspectives more or less well-lit and interesting' (p. 29) does not include traditional theism. That is not a 'genuine alternative' (p. 90). It is a road which has simply 'melted away' (p. 102). It must be 'altogether discarded if we are to get on the right path again' (p. 147). And it is suggested that no one seriously taught it:

> If there were ever Christian teachers who taught the unity and integrity of the religious life – and there certainly were – then they *must* have used a deconstructive rhetorical strategy that brought God down to earth, dispersed him into the proximate and the contingent, and then identified his service as the next step (p. 156).

At one stage Cupitt made much of the spiritual capacity of man and of the human response to what spirituality demands, as in *The Nature of Man* (1979); and in 1980 he attempted to fill the God-shaped gap in his version of Christianity by arguing that belief in God is really an acceptance of the discipline of the ethical and spiritual life. He suggested that God's 'immutability' means that the requirement to be good is 'absolute and unchanging'; God's 'aseity' (not depending on any other reality) means that this requirement is 'autonomous and intrinsically authoritative'; God's 'infinity' means that it is 'experienced precisely as a call to break out of the rut'; God's simplicity and eternity mean that 'the more your soul is scattered or dispersed over external objects, worries and desires, the further you are from religion'. In brief, 'the doctrine of God is an encoded set of spiritual directives' (*Taking Leave of God*, pp. 100–1). At this stage God is a symbol representing 'everything that spirituality requires of us and promises to us' (p. 14). 'I continue to speak of God,' Cupitt concluded. 'He is the religious demand and ideal, the pearl of great price and the enshriner of values. He is needed – but as a myth' (p. 166).

This was the position which two other philosophers, Keith Ward and Brian Hebblethwaite, tried to refute in their books of 1982 and 1988, *Holding Fast to God* and *The Ocean of Truth*. In his Foreword to Scott Cowdell's more admiring study of his thought, Cupitt complained that these critics 'were not concerned to ask either how I reached the early-eighties views or why I have since moved away from them' (p. ix). But is that a satisfactory response? Ward and Hebblethwaite attacked Cupitt for his neglect of recent work done by professionals in their common discipline, philosophical theology. They accused him of a consistent failure to reckon with the best that has been thought by Christians in modern times (Hebblethwaite supplies a list of recent books in English) on the subjects with which he deals superficially before reaching atheistic conclusions. These were allegations with which Scott Cowdell (who said 'I like Cupitt and find him immensely challenging') largely agreed (pp. 55–64). They deserve an answer. Cupitt's whole position, in the early 1980s and later, has come to be based on the rejection of traditional theism, and it is of fundamental importance that he can be said to have joined those who, in Hebblethwaite's words, 'make things far too easy for themselves by describing objective theism in such a way as to tie it down to obviously naive, outmoded and untenable conceptual forms' (p. 13). But instead of giving a reasoned answer to Ward and Hebblethwaite Cupitt replied in his Foreword to Cowdell's book: 'the truth is in the movement – and that (by the way) is doubtless why I am so bad at answering criticisms. By the time they have come in I have moved on . . .' (p. ix).

He added a fascinating summary of his theological and post-theological development, showing that although he has not spent time on a dialogue with colleagues he has been to some extent self-critical. In particular he has largely taken leave of *Taking Leave of God*, thus silently agreeing with Ward and Hebblethwaite that its position is untenable. But he has not moved to a position of which they would approve. He recalled in May 1988:

In the late 1960s I hoped to move from grossly inadequate to less inadequate images of God. The trail of broken images would become an arrow pointing towards the transcendent. Then, as objective truth began to pass away and I decided that no dogmatic theology was possible, the arrow pointing up to heaven became, as one might say, internalized. It was an inner pathway of self-transcendence, and a philosophy of the religious life. Later, when even *self*-transcendence became problematic to me, I suggested that in our post-dogmatic century it is precisely our own religious struggles that change us, propelling us along a personal track of spiritual development. Later, the movement became more of a spontaneously-created work of life-art, personal and variable, as I moved towards an aesthetics of religious existence. Finally, and most recently of all, the spiritual movement became the movement of meaning itself, endlessly spilling over sideways. 'I' – the human self – became decentred (*Atheist Priest?*, p. x).

If we ask what have been the sequels to *Taking Leave of God* in Cupitt's own developing thought, we meet changes as great as those which accompanied his rejection of traditional theism.

That book, like those of earlier date, left on me an impression of a man still struggling energetically to find God or a substitute. Indeed, on the title page a medieval mystic, Eckhart, was quoted: 'Man's last and highest parting occurs when, for God's sake, he takes leave of God.' And I could see why this farewell to the old God of Cupitt's earlier thought had become for him intellectually and morally necessary, for to his mind that God's control of events had become an idea so vague as to say 'nothing definite' and God's influence on the spiritual life had become 'altogether unspecifiable' (pp. 6, 13). That God had boiled down to 'traditional culture personified' (p. 20). But something remained. 'The task is *not* to move from an objective and god-centred theology to a man-centred theology as has too often happened', for 'God is both the beginning and the end of the religious life' (pp. 43, 95). In a brief exchange of letters in the journal *Theology* (1981, p. 201) after my review which had asked whether he had now become an atheist, Cupitt protested that his 'account has a hidden Transcendent beyond objectivity, but no objective metaphysical world-ruling individual God'. This seemed to suggest some connection with, for example, the project to discover a 'God beyond God' pursued by Paul Tillich, one of the modern philosophical theologians whom he was said to neglect. Or there might be a connection with the existentialist trust in a mysterious God preached by some New Testament scholars such as Rudolf Bultmann and John Robinson. But Cupitt's account of the 'hidden Transcendent beyond objectivity' was quite soon replaced by a different teaching. 'This has become a *religious* imperative,' he wrote in 1987. He explained:

> We have to *cleanse* ourselves of the old will to downgrade the manifest by looking beyond it to something else that is ranked higher than it. Nothing is hidden, everything is manifest, nothing is wrong with the manifest, faith chooses and embraces the manifest, and all nostalgia for any sort of Elsewhere or other-than-this is to be forgotten. Hidden entities of every sort are

ghosts hungry for blood who want to suck the value out of life (*The Long Legged Fly*, pp. 8, 75).

The appearance of continuity in this priest's teaching has been assisted by the continuing use of religious language and by the continuing sermonic, even dogmatic, tone of his books. Cowdell acutely observes that 'Cupitt believes in religion, though he does not believe in God' (p. 64). He loyally reckons that Cupitt remains 'a rigorous apologist for prophetic monotheism, for Christianity ranked first among the world religions . . .' (p. 84), but in fact Christianity has now been deprived of any specifically Christian content and of any spiritual connection with Jesus of Nazareth. In *The Long Legged Fly* 'the Church is the Christian tradition, which is a river of signs. As they flow through us, we have to take them up and make something fresh of them which will express our desire' (p. 146). The world-view desired has become totally secular:

> We value things insofar as they turn us on, that is, heighten or stimulate the life-impulse in us . . . We must get rid of all ideas of the substantial and the lasting, all fantasies of omnipotence and invulnerability, and accept completely the radical contingency, the fleetingness and transitoriness of our life . . . Human salvation is now understood to consist in the integrity and plentitude of our expression and affirmation of life now, in this fleeting moment. It passes, and we are gone. There are no more guarantees of progress or preservation (pp. 43, 80, 85).

God now 'functions only to remind us that we are out of nothing' (p. 105) and the self is now 'a mere temporary aggregation of processes' (p. 122). Cupitt has more than once claimed an affinity between these views and Buddhism, but it seems better to call them secular, since there is none of Buddhism's concern to avoid life after death by the denial of every element of selfishness which may make the self subject to the penalty of rebirth in future lives. Here the 'life impulse' of the ego is praised, but death automatically brings the end to every ego, with or without self-discipline. The connection with Buddhism seems as tenuous as the connection with Christianity.

The attitude to death implied in the last four sentences quoted was spelt out more fully in 'Good Night', the last chapter of *Life Lines*. There it is said that baptism, traditionally regarded as a sacrament of union with the death and resurrection of Christ, teaches the 'immeasurably simple lesson' that 'you will disappear, vanish, cease to be' (p. 199). But it is indeed hard to see why anyone should think that the mission of Jesus which brought about his own crucifixion was to teach people to abandon the 'fiction' of 'the hope of sovereign, ever-wakeful, invulnerable and indestructible selfhood' and accept the inevitability of death (p. 200). In his varied estimates of the historical Jesus, the earlier Cupitt had always taken his words or 'voice' seriously and had always concluded that in Scott Cowdell's fine phrase 'to be the follower of Jesus is to be his contemporary at the end of the world' (p. 16). But now the only reference to the message of Jesus made at this climax to *Life Lines* was to the cry from the cross, 'My God, my God, why have you forsaken me?' This prayer taken by Jesus from a psalm was interpreted as 'his real acceptance of the world'. Christian language such as 'Life Everlasting' (the title of chapter 15 in *Life Lines*) is being retained as a veneer to cover a secular substance, as a thorough believer in the merits of capitalism might retain Communist language because he had been brought up and was employed in the Soviet Union or China; and implicitly this lack of a solid connection between the Christian language and the secular substance seems to be acknowledged, because in the later books there is no solid attempt to show that the earlier books, with their very different teaching, totally misrepresented the content of Christianity and of its founder's gospel. The conclusion of the matter is that Cupitt has accepted the world as seen through secular, not Christian, eyes.

But as he has contemplated this world, his view has become very different from the secular 'common sense' which tells us that the world is real and that nothing else is. For the world itself now seems to lack substantial reality. In *The Long Legged Fly*, much attention is paid to the French writers Michel Foucault and Jacques Derrida as exponents of a 'post-modern' philosophy, which may loosely be called 'deconstructionism'. As a revolt against the tendency to classify everything in a pattern imposed by religion, metaphysics, Marxism or existentialism, this may be regarded as the Parisian equivalent of English empiricism. But whereas the empiricists have tended to assume that things are real, the deconstructionists come nearer to the 'idealists' in their rejection of that common sense. We are told by Cupitt that

> every aspect of what we call 'reality' is established in and by language . . . The surface play of phenomena – words, signs, meanings, appearances – *is* reality . . . The self, body and feeling

are themselves constructed within language . . . The world just
is the 99.9% of all our beliefs which we are not just at present
disposed to challenge (pp. 18, 20, 35, 88).

Such phrases might be regarded as legitimate (if rhetorical) reflections of an obvious truth, which many philosophers explored
before Foucault and Derrida. The mind usually interprets the
sensations reaching the brain by using images and ideas which do
not exactly correspond with the external reality. We do not usually
take in more than the superficial appearance of things, and often
we use images and ideas, suggested by the surrounding society,
which are very unreal. Even self-awareness is not complete awareness of what is real, and even the advanced study of physics cannot
completely describe, or even understand, the reality of the
elementary particles. But it is not the case that this sort of difficulty
is completely inescapable 'because I have no super-language', as
Cupitt says. Although every language must fail to comprehend and
communicate what is really 'out there', mankind's perceptions of
the environment and of selfhood have been improved over countless centuries by explorations which could be understood and
shared; and over the last three centuries or so scientists have
refined such explorations with considerable effect, using methods
and reaching results which can be verified and in many cases be
seen to work around the world.

It is very striking that Cupitt, who eloquently celebrated the
progress of science in *The Sea of Faith* ('from myths to maths'),
appears to be seeing something very different from the dry land of
common sense and of science now that the old sea has in his view
completely withdrawn from the beach. He wrote a good short
study of *The Worlds of Science and Religion* in 1976, but a dozen
years later seems to have grown bored with both those worlds,
concentrating instead on the appeal of 'abstract' art (which does
not claim to be representational) and of 'deconstructionist' literary
criticism (which does not claim to illuminate the personal and
historical background of a writer). Hebblethwaite writes wisely:

Common sense conviction that the world about us consists of
things and kinds of things that are what they are prior to and
quite apart from any observation or thought, and are discovered
to be what they are by the learned and self-correcting use of
fallible human faculties, is a conviction that for the most part
survives sceptical assault (p. 104).

In *Life Lines* Cupitt chided Professor Richard Swinburne about his closely argued books on *The Coherence of Theism* (1977) and *The Existence of God* (1979). Swinburne was accused of wanting 'an objective and intelligible cosmos out there whose fundamental structure is known to us, so that the actual existence of a rational designer-god may be inferred from *its* existence' (p. 59). In contrast Cupitt asks 'Isn't it obvious?' that 'such big objects as the world, history and our life have only such meaning as we have put into them through our evolving discourse about them – and no more, for everything really is contingent, language, culture, ourselves, our life and our world' (pp. 153–4). What *is* obvious, I submit, is that religion interprets the ultimate meaning of the world, history and individual lives in ways that are open to debate. What is *not* obvious is that common sense and science are unable to establish any reliable and useful truths about an objective and intelligible cosmos. Of course many atheists, along with people with many different religious beliefs, have discovered such truths about reality at that down-to-earth level. Yet in Cupitt's development the loss of faith in God has, it seems, been followed by a loss of confidence in common sense and science. Each person is now the creator of 'the world' and 'the creation myth in effect says "You can do it; here's how"' – or so we are told in *Only Human* (p. 181). But it seems very hard to tell from this account whether one creation of the human will is more truthful than another as a picture of the world which people share in common, for Cupitt seems to have lost interest in what was admired as recently as *The World to Come*: 'the rigorous testing of theories against evidence not under their control, by free critical reason' (p. 143).

Here is a warning about the possible anti-rational consequences of Nietzschean atheism, a warning reinforced by the tragic story of Nietzsche's own bizarre life ending in madness. The 'death of God' seems to be followed by the death of reason. The contrast is great with the history of modern science, which although often misunderstood and resisted by clergymen, arose in a Europe saturated by the Jewish and Christian faith that an objective, intelligible, meaningful and 'good' creation is 'out there' and open to investigation and use by man, himself a rational creature 'made in the image of God'. For a defence of 'critical realism' in scientific, artistic and religious attempts to see and interpret the real world I refer readers to the work of a theologian with wider knowledge than mine, John Bowker (conveniently summarised in his oddly named book, *Licensed Insanities*, 1987).

A loss of confidence in moral argument has also followed the 'death of God' for Cupitt, although of course many atheists are highly (and often conventionally) moral. In *The World to Come* he declared that after the experience of the ultimate truth about life (the Nihil), all previous moralities are 'seen as created by egoism, anxiety and the will to dominate' (p. 137). In *The Long Legged Fly* he outlined

> five styles of moral argument that are incommensurable with each other. They are, first, the argument that we should 'act according to Nature,' a survival from prescientific times; secondly, the appeal to rational consistency and universaliz-ability, left over from the rationalism of the Enlightenment; thirdly, utilitarianism, the ethic of the benign, efficient adminis-trator; fourthly, the appeal to traditional religious authority and God's revealed will; and lastly, the appeal to individual self-realization, left over from the heyday of individualism (pp. 40–41).

Stripped of technical terms and cleansed of the tendency to see life in terms of intellectual fashions, this list can be seen as a series of signposts along a road not to chaos but to maturity as free people try to see what behaviour best corresponds with reality. It is surely all to the good that people hesitating over a course of action should ask themselves whether it is natural, reasonable, such as they would approve in other people, useful in the increase of happiness and likely to help them to fulfil themselves: that is what moral reasoning is about. If they believe in God, people should also try through prayer and study of the Scriptures they hold sacred to think out whether it is the will of God: that is the business of ethics within religion. But Cupitt assumes that 'nobody could accept' all these styles of moral arguments and that the debate between their adherents is 'notoriously bitter and intractable'. So he advises us 'do not look for foundations', because 'there is no anterior or external standpoint from which the whole language – and life complex – can be either praised or blamed' (p. 46).

In *The New Christian Ethics* we are in 1988 and there is no more talk of cashing the term 'God' as 'everything that spirituality requires of us'. Indeed, there is contempt for the whole tradition, associated in the history of philosophy with the influence of Kant, which has put the 'moral imperative' or the 'conscience' at the centre of religion. 'We have rejected and avoided all those accounts of morality, supernatural or heteronomous, that picture the ethical as a hidden super-authoritative demand of which we are intuitively aware' (p. 165). The thorough rejection of any 'super-natural' authority is thought necessary because 'in historic Christianity God arrogated all true creativity to himself and human creativity was denied, not affirmed'. Although individual Christians might be 'robust, . . . strikingly forceful, dramatic and creative', that kind of religion produced 'insipid and mouselike' characters (pp. 14–17). 'I can personally testify that the old terroristic, corrupt, cosmic-protection-racket Christianity was still flourishing in the 1950s, because I was brought up in it' (p. 59). But what is new is the emphasis on public actions which are good at the expense of self-examination and self-purification. Apparently instead of a variety of 'Christian Buddhist' meditation by the individual as recommended in previous books, action to improve the world is urged, for 'everything they thought God had already done for them we are going to have to do for one another' (p. 6). Here is an ethic of work which should be co-operative and creative, but it is combined with an ethic of self-fulfilment which the old Protestant apostles of work would have condemned as self-indulgence. 'A modern Christian ethic can only be bad if we utterly forget pre-Enlightenment Christianity. *Our* ethics will be an ethics of the flesh, an ethics of human feeling, an ethics of libido and being true to the life-energy in us' (p. 41). This ethics certainly is fairly 'new' in the development of Cupitt's thought. What is much harder to see is any sense in which it is specifically 'Christian'. No doubt most or all of the actions which Cupitt would advocate would be admired by many or all Christians, but the Christian tradition of ethics is very seldom mentioned except to be castigated (and caricatured). Now any belief in life after death has become a 'barmy fantasy' and 'just the fact of Christ-and-the-Spirit is the death of God' (pp. 67–70).

Why, then, has Cupitt felt driven to abandon the God of traditional theism, with the subsequent losses – first the loss of belief in the authority of 'spirituality' and the conscience, and then the loss of belief in the reality of the world? Why has he felt driven to a position where he feels compelled to argue that the faith which raised the cathedrals (all different!), and filled the modern world's art galleries with pictures of Christ and his mother, and was the religious background of so many creators of modern world denied human creativity? Why does he say that traditional doctrine called for 'insipid and mouselike' Christians? The explanation is, I suggest, that he is not fair to the traditional account of God.

Cupitt and the Christians' God

Since this reply was directed at me in 1981 I may be forgiven for singling out Cupitt's description of traditional theism's God as 'objective, metaphysical, world-ruling, individual'. But I shall also respond briefly to his later warning, already quoted, that 'dogmatic realism' 'must have a coherent logic, apparent in both your linguistic and your ethical practice' (see above, p. 81). This warning refers of course to the well-known facts that there is much evil in the world said to have been made, and to be governed, by the good God and that there is much evil in the lives of professed worshippers of God.

Evidently there came a stage when the difficulties in thought about God as objective, metaphysical, world-ruling, individual and good overwhelmed Cupitt. That is not surprising. Many people in our time find it very difficult or impossible to believe in any kind of God. Quite often I do. Most people who are aware of the objections to the belief in the God described by Cupitt agree with him that the belief is wrong in many senses. I do. But his colleagues of the calibre of Ward and Hebblethwaite are, as I see it, right to remind Cupitt that traditional theism has not been, and ought not to be, identified with the crudely insensitive use of these adjectives. God's reality is not so easily disproved. I shall refer in particular to Keith Ward's *Holding Fast to God*, for it is the work of a man who 'moved towards a fairly traditional Christian view from a position of complete atheism, while I was teaching philosophy' (p. 151). And it is the work of one who was in critical dialogue with exponents of Cupitt's later positions long before Cupitt moved to them, as was shown by his book on *The Concept of God* (1974). I shall also have in mind many of the essays collected in Cupitt's own *The Leap of Reason* (1976) and *Explorations in Theology* (1979). Those were expositions of what may be called 'critical' mainstream Christianity – the kind of Christianity which has thoughtfully reckoned with objections to faith based on knowledge and experience of the real world. And of course *Christ and the Hiddenness of God* should not be forgotten. But I shall try to put things very plainly.

The thoughtful Christian who regards the divine reality as 'objective' is not saying that the Creator is merely one object among others or that his reality can be apprehended without the involvement of the believer's self. He is saying that God's reality is different from our approach to it. Our approach must be 'self-involving' or 'existential' and therefore 'subjective', but the truth about God is not exhausted when one agrees with Kierkegaard that in heartfelt religion 'truth is subjectivity'. The thoughtful Christian who treats the divine reality as 'supernatural' or 'metaphysical' is not suggesting that God can be known by human beings by direct access. God, if he can be known at all, must be known 'as in a mirror darkly' through humanity's senses as they operate in the only world which humanity knows and as they are interpreted by what Kant called 'practical' (as contrasted with 'pure') reason. '"God"', as Ward has said, 'is that mysterious depth which is mediated in certain symbols and events in our lives; which comes to us as moral challenge, and which can transform us with new vision and power' (*Holding Fast*, p. 21). As Cupitt himself noted in *Taking Leave of God*, 'traditional theism always insisted that we have no knowledge of God as he is in himself, for we know God only as he enters into our experience' (p. 38). But the thoughtful Christian says that the God who is known by his presence and power within the world (as 'immanent') is also greater than the world (he is 'transcendent'). Consequently God is, in Keith Ward's rather startling words, 'a thing which would exist even if no humans existed at all; so he is objective' (p. 2). And Ward is one of the many Christian and other philosophers who have presented reasoned arguments for thinking that there *is* such a very special, utterly unique, thing, although these arguments do not amount to logical proof.

The thoughtful Christian who calls God 'world-ruling' is not saying that God is 'an interfering busybody with unlimited power' (which was Ward's summary of the impression left by Cupitt's denunciations). He is saying that God's power is not limited except by his own will. As he reflects on modern knowledge of nature, evolution and human history, he will add that God has evidently chosen to create life and spirit by means which exclude over-riding the free will of human beings and frequent interferences with the regularities of the creation. These regularities we call, somewhat inappropriately, the 'laws of nature'. In nature creatures feed off each other and their environment can change disastrously, as when earthquakes, floods or changes in the climate wreck human lives; in evolution we observe the 'natural selection' of those who survive and breed most efficiently in relation to their environments; and in history we see the processes which give the advantage to those who combine courage, intelligence and hard work, with force often being decisive. Not all of this cosmic spectacle is attractive to the

Christian believer. We may conclude with Ward that 'the purposes of God are deeply hidden, and so intertwined with the chains of causality and human freedom that they cannot be clearly disentangled and isolated for inspection' (p. 95). And these facts of life teach us that God does not interfere to stop deeds of evil men such as the crucifixion of Jesus or the virtual extermination of European Jewry. In *Taking Leave of God* Cupitt dismisses the immense and agonised wrestle with God's 'absence' or 'silence'. With no detailed reference to the large number of books and conferences that have discussed the question, he complains that 'we are not actually given the sufficient reason for the Holocaust; we are told that there must be a reason and a God who knows it, but as to what it *is* we are none the wiser' (p. 27). But one conclusion of the discussion can be stated very simply. The reason for the Holocaust is human evil, permitted by God (most Christians would add) for the sake of human freedom. And not only in philosophy but supremely in the lives of people who have suffered greatly, Christianity makes *some* sense out of evil. I shall of course be returning in this book to this terrible mystery, and at a more academic level I may mention John Hick's book to be discussed later (pp. 235–7) or Kenneth Surin's presentation of *Theology and the Problem of Evil* (1986). Philosophical theology is both summarised and criticised by Surin. What emerges is the will to endure, and ultimately transcend, evil in the faith inspired by Calvary that God himself endures the sufferings that afflict us.

Christians know that human brains and hands are needed to transform nature and history (an attitude which Cupitt praised in his contributions to the symposium on *Man and Nature*, edited by Hugh Montefiore in 1975). And there is much stress in Christianity on experiencing the power of God not as a domineering control which crushes human freedom but as a 'grace' which helps and which liberates both self and society from bondage to dehumanising habits and structures. Christianity, when it is true to its Founder and so to itself in this matter, does not advocate blind, robot-like obedience to God or an infantile dependence on God's power. There is nothing profoundly Christian about the kind of assault on human dignity and autonomy that makes Cupitt write that we must reject the God who 'imposes the religious demand' and that 'today obedience is sin' (*Taking Leave of God*, pp. 85, 94). Least of all does Christianity offer what Cupitt cynically calls 'the old bargain: Accept absolute domination over your inmost self, and you will find that in and through the acceptance you will be given a like power over others' (*The World to Come*, p. 7). The obedience and dependence which Christianity praises are more like the loving relationship between a good father and a son with a mind of his own (as in the parables of Jesus) or between a husband and a wife (as often in Christian mysticism). As Ward says, 'Christians are supposed to wonder what God's will really is; they are supposed to have to apply it to particular new cases themselves; they are required to follow their own consciences, as a primary duty' (p. 43). They feel free – free to love God and to work with God. In the service of such a God they find perfect freedom and complete adulthood, although that takes time and eternity.

The thoughtful Christian who thinks of God as 'personal' (a word much more often used in this connection than Cupitt's word 'individual') is not pretending that God is a man or a woman, with or without a long white beard. He is affirming out of the Christian community's experience and his own that when God is prayed to there is a response which, however mysterious it may be, is somewhat like the response of a person to a person, disclosing something like a character, a will and a love. And the thoughtful Christian who calls God 'good' does not forget the colossal problem of evil. He makes an affirmation or a cry in awe, fear and trembling, amid many tears. He says that God's purpose, including his decision to make and to accept human free will and the regularities of the creation, is good and will ultimately, with great patience as well as power, achieve the best *possible* outcome. As Ward puts it in his critique of Cupitt, God may still be called perfectly good if he brings into being a world in which 'every instance of suffering or evil . . . is either a necessary condition or a necessary consequence of some vastly overwhelming good for the creature concerned' (p. 107). Of course such a philosophical proposition can seem wickedly aloof from the real world of suffering and evil. It can seem damnably smug to argue that the loss of life in an earthquake or hurricane is necessary if the earth and the weather are to be what we enjoy, or that the killing of a child by cancer is necessary if the human body is to be what it is, or that a Holocaust must be possible if men are to be allowed to be wicked. But this challenge may be answered if Christians are not smug and if God himself is not held to be altogether exempt from suffering. The cross of Jesus has often been understood as a declaration of God's willingness to suffer. At any rate the centrality of this picture of suffering characterises the whole of Christian thought and art, and Ward is typical when he says that 'the true God is seen on the cross, a love as strong as death, invincible in endurance' (p. 145). And the cross ought to be a sufficient reminder that Christian hope is not facile optimism.

It may be wrong for the thoughtful Christian to say these things, because they may not correspond with the reality of an ugly world. If he does say these things in faith, he must always use images and words which have been developed in order to describe what is not divine and which therefore must be unsatisfactory tools in this attempt, both one by one and even when taken and used together (as they should be). But all attempts to speak about subjects other than the material particulars of mathematics and science must use metaphors and other analogies. Cupitt's attempts do copiously, both before and after his loss of faith in God's reality. Although human images and ideas are always open to correction in the light of knowledge and experience, religious believers need not be ashamed of the poetry in their language. When thinking about the mystery that surrounds life we cannot do without symbolism. To call upon the later Cupitt to make 'more of symbolism and of the appeal to mystery' is not necessarily to call for 'more obscurantism', despite the cynical allegation which he makes at the end of *Only Human* (p. 199). The general denial of realism in *The Long Legged Fly* was spectacular in its lavish use of symbolism and in its richly mysterious rhetoric, beginning with the title. He ought to show greater understanding of religious language when it is used by people less original or less eloquent.

Like every other supremely worthwhile human endeavour, religion is fraught with difficulties and dangers. Most of these are moral. In the intellectual sphere many of the difficulties and dangers of modern Christian religion were presented by Cupitt in *The Sea of Faith*. He rightly criticised some Christians for defending doctrines 'as a matter of obedience and communal loyalty' (p. 14), without care for the truth. He rightly attacked some historic Christian attitudes 'to the Jews, to women, to children, to sexual behaviour and so on' while noting that they have been 'criticised and dispelled' (p. 13). This was a summary of his critique in *Crisis of Moral Authority* (1972, reissued in 1985). In *The Sea of Faith*, looking back on his own early experience as a hospital chaplain he rightly rejected beliefs that God simply causes the birth of a deformed child or the death of a victim of cancer, or adjusts someone's eternal destiny to the presence or absence of deathbed prayers. He was entirely justified in lamenting the insistence of Roman Catholic (and Protestant) authorities on the picture of an

earth-centred, small and short-lived universe which science corrected. He correctly denounced the resistance to the literary and
historical 'criticism' of the Bible; the reluctance to accept evolution
as the means of the creation of more complex forms of life; the
clergy's frequent identification with the interests of the landowners
and the capitalists; the failure to admit that many ideas used to
think about God are derived from our experience of human
parents. He told the stories of Strauss, Darwin, Marx and Freud,
who often had truth as well as genius on their side. But he gave too
little emphasis to the fact that the painful lessons have been learnt
by millions of modern Christians including almost all of his fellow
theologians.

Fundamentalism persists, but the Christian alternative to it is
not as empty as Cupitt alleges. It was an unfair parody of recent
Christian thought to allege that in it

> God has become no more than the expression of a diffuse cosmic
> optimism, a 'fundamental trust' that deep down and despite
> appearances, the universe is friendly to us, a pious hope that
> since human beings are the most complex objects in the uni-
> verse, and love is the supreme human value, then the universe
> itself or the 'ground of all being' must itself be in a mysterious
> way also loving. So ambiguous, so destitute of real explanatory
> value, and so utterly lacking in living religious power is such
> language that it is evident that there is today a looming crisis
> of belief in God even within the churches (*The Sea of Faith*,
> pp. 15–16).

What has happened to Cupitt, it seems to me, is something like a
Victorian clergyman's 'loss of faith'. I say this although he differs
from the Victorian 'doubting' clergy who felt obliged to leave the
priesthood at considerable cost to themselves. Reading him I am
often reminded of the seriously post-Christian Victorians, and in
particular of Matthew Arnold's haunting poetry. 'I can't live with it
and I can't live without it', the verdict on traditional religious belief
which begins *Taking Leave of God*, is a very Victorian emotion and
for me a very moving one. But more can be said than Cupitt says,
and he is right to mock the tendency of Hegel and Marx to claim
that 'the final truth of things is just coming into flower in their own
thinking' (*The Long Legged Fly*, p. 31). The final truth on most of
the subjects he handles can probably never be said. My criticism of
him is not that he has often changed his mind. As the Victorians
were told by Newman, 'to live is to change'. I criticise him because

at the various stages of his pilgrimage he has made a habit of condemning other people's positions with always clever but often unjust phrases. He has not allowed himself time or space in which to absorb or expound the subtleties of religious attitudes which he has come to reject. In particular he has abused traditional Christianity as if the tradition had never been revised since the early days of the Victorian Age. And so I see no reason to regard him as intellectually or morally superior to those who while becoming Victorian or modern or post-modern in response to the challenges of the knowledge and thought of their time have kept enough faith to remain in the Christian mainstream, worshipping God.

Despite what is alleged by Don Cupitt in *The Sea of Faith* (p. 271), the God of thoughtful Christianity is not a 'cosmic Father Christmas' now producing only attitudes of 'nostalgia' and 'superstition'. Any crude theology, manipulation in the interests of power and denial of human dignity and creativity which have disfigured the record of Christianity are not the heart of the matter. They are in no way essential to the Christian belief in the reality of God – any more than the idea that the earth stays put at the centre of the universe was essential to Dante's belief in 'the love that moves the sun and the other stars'.

Don Cupitt's response is on pp. 283–6.

4

MAURICE WILES AND THE ACTIVITY OF GOD:

Does God intervene after creation?

Maurice Wiles has rightly been honoured by appointments to leading positions in English theology. He succeeded John Robinson as Dean of Clare College, Cambridge, in 1959, became Professor of Christian Doctrine at King's College, London, in 1967, and Regius Professor of Divinity at Oxford in 1970. In the Church of England he was for a time Chairman of the Doctrine Commission. And ever since I reviewed a couple of books by him rather rudely in the middle of the 1970s I have been troubled in conscience. I am going to reprint those reviews after deleting a few ephemeral references, but I have added a review of a book which I praised without reservations. I have felt troubled because I think the emphasis ought to fall on the virtues of this very learned, honest and brave theologian and on the importance of the task he has set himself – and because I do not think that in the space of a review I have ever managed to make clear what more I ask from him. So I have added some reflections based on his teaching in the 1980s. I do not yet discuss in any detail his teaching about the Incarnation, because that belongs to the next chapter.

Review of *The Remaking of Christian Doctrine* by Maurice Wiles (1974)

All who are seriously interested in the English debate about the restatement or revision of Christian belief should notice a new book. It consists of the Hulsean Lectures delivered at Cambridge a few months ago. Here is one of the most prominent theologians at work in England today getting to the heart of the matter, and doing so with an explosive frankness. But many readers are likely to be disappointed. The conclusions reached are mostly negative or, when positive, tentative. All this is deliberate. 'It is characteristic of all positions,' writes Wiles, 'that the more extreme their presentation, the more interesting they appear' – but 'if the middle position seems to us to be most true, we do not blame it for its less exciting and more attenuated appearance'. For example, it is exciting to regard revelation as 'a direct and utterly reliable communication of God to men in the dictated words of Scripture'; but it happens to be untrue, and our consolation is that it is 'religiously more profound' to have an 'account of God's dealings with mankind' in which 'the freedom of a fully human response is taken with full seriousness' (pp. 115–16).

Wiles also makes no apology for the fact that 'I have seldom quoted explicit texts of Scripture or specific conciliar decisions', one reason being that frequent quotations of that sort 'can very easily be taken to imply a falsely authoritarian view of their role' (p. 104). But this largely non-technical book is distinguished by its author's intellectual power (manifest in the rigour and brevity of every page) and by his courageous seriousness in tackling the greatest themes open to a theologian – God, the person and work of Christ, the Holy Spirit, the eternal hope, the nature of doctrine itself. He is relentlessly honest in relying on his own experience, study and thought. Before our eyes he is driven to faith and to agnosticism – and back again. Characteristically, when he has asked himself at one point whether he ought to dispense with the concept of God, he says: 'I resist. To do so would be to leave a whole dimension of human experience even more opaque and inexplicable than it already is' (p. 108).

He really does face, or imply, every conceivable difficulty. In most men's theology there is one blessed plot sheltered from scepticism. Not so here! Wiles observes that

> many of those Christian philosophers who are most acutely aware of the intellectual difficulties inherent in the basic affirmations of theism are almost naively credulous in their handling of the historical traditions about Jesus, while many of those who are most scrupulously critical in their assessment of those historical traditions seem unwarrantably easy-going in the confidence with which they continue to affirm their basic theistic convictions (p. 111).

He is determined to stay exposed to the icy winds. 'It is questionable how far we can know what was explicitly taught by Jesus; in so far as we can, it was taught within a first-century setting and needs translation before it can be incorporated into contemporary doctrine' (pp. 11–12). Again: 'I would want to argue that there is need for a far greater caution, a far more profound awareness of the indirectness of the language than has been customary' when talking about God (pp. 29–30).

Wiles denies himself the escape of appealing to the 'development' of Christian doctrine or to the guidance of the Holy Spirit. 'The concept of development does not provide any criteria for distinguishing between true and false developments' – while 'the concept of the Spirit's guidance *by itself* can be used to legitimate anything, which means that it can be used to legitimate nothing' (p. 13). It was said that the neo-orthodox Karl Barth put a bomb in the playground of the liberal theologians, but Wiles belongs to the bomb-removal squad. He summons us to a 'continually changing and essentially temporary . . . task' (p. 2) in remaking Christian doctrine for our generation, and offers us no alternative to hard thought. He remarks: 'To many a man not only in the pew but in the pulpit, the picture that I have been drawing will, I fear, seem a disturbing one. But theologians are made of sterner stuff' (pp. 48–9).

Plainly, if the reader's only difficulty is a reluctance to accept the stern task of honest thought, the reader is to blame – unless he can produce a valid certificate of exemption from all intellectual labour (which one would have thought unlikely in any reader able to climb into a pulpit). But there is something needlessly provocative about the tone which Professor Wiles adopts.

It may be that he reckons that the chief religious problem today is a pig-headed obstinacy in clinging to the past – for example to the old accounts, understood with a wooden literalism, of the atonement as a victory over demons or as a substitutionary sacrifice or as a reversal of the sin of Adam. If so, he may be wrong. Blind conservatism is a problem in some quarters. In many more, the problem is that nothing seems available to take the place of doctrine that has been disapproved, discredited or outgrown. And until a powerful new utterance of the everlasting gospel is proclaimed and popularised, it is psychologically unlikely that the conservatives will be prepared to abandon the old positions. If a vulgar analogy may be permitted, theological strip-tease is not interesting if the spotlight stays on the discarded clothes.

The emphasis which Wiles gives to his denials is not necessary if he is to state the truth as he sees it, for running through his book there are golden affirmations. 'There is a reality other than the human experiencing,' he writes, thus preserving the divine transcendence – 'but we are only able to speak of it indirectly by speaking of those experiences within which we are aware of its effective presence,' thus preserving the divine revelation (p. 27). 'We know Jesus, as we experience God, only in his effect upon the world, upon the church and upon ourselves' (p. 49). But God has some effect! 'Talk of God's activity is', as Wiles says, 'to be understood as a way of speaking about those events within the natural order or within human history in which God's purpose finds clear expression or special opportunity' (p. 38). And he implies a high doctrine about the 'expression' and 'opportunity' in the event of Jesus Christ.

'Talk of [Jesus'] pre-existence ought probably in most, perhaps in all, cases to be understood, on the analogy of the pre-existence of the Torah [the Law in the Old Testament], to indicate the eternal divine purpose being achieved through him, rather than pre-existence of a fully personal kind' (p. 53). So Wiles writes. It seems negative; but look closer and you will see that (as he says) 'Christ's passion is in some way a demonstration of what is true of God's eternal nature' (p. 79) and 'it is supremely through Jesus that the character of these purposes of God and the possibility of the experience of grace has been grasped and made effective in the world' (p. 122).

'Our talk of the Holy Spirit', Wiles adds in similar vein,

should perhaps be understood not as suggesting any specific or direct working of God upon the human personality, but rather as a reminder that the love of God is the source of all potentiality for good in the world and that to recognize that fact has a transforming effect upon our apprehension and our realization of that good (pp. 97–8).

Wiles virtually confines prayer to meditation, but he writes that 'the records of the Christ event and occasions of worship which focus on that event are particularly powerful agents in giving rise to . . . [the] awareness of God and of an ultimate divine purpose for the world' (p. 101). About our eternal hope, he is largely negative. The creed's talk of the 'resurrection of the body' is misleading, and alternative talk of 'personal survival' is little better. But he does say that it is possible for us to enter during this life into a fuller life of relationship with the bodiless and more-than-personal God, a relationship which will not be ended by death but rather consummated in a way beyond our imagination.

Asking what are the fundamental Christian beliefs, Wiles argues that the doctrine of the unique incarnation of God in Jesus Christ is not required for the whole pattern of belief to be true. But why he persists in taking such a negative view of the doctrine of the 'unique incarnation' is a bit of a puzzle. He rightly observes that the ways in which the New Testament, or the undivided Church's councils, or individual Fathers expressed this doctrine are not completely authoritative, or even meaningful, for most Christians today. He also makes some good points against some twentieth-century restatements of the doctrine – which is not surprising, since two of his main arguments are that all religious language is unsatisfactory and that Jesus is unique. But he himself seems to be engaged in an enterprise which is nothing less than the remaking of the statement that 'God was in Christ' in terms intelligible and credible in our time. As he puts it:

> The pattern of belief that I have been trying to develop is belief in God upon whom the world depends for its very existence, a God who cares about human suffering, who has a purpose for the world which men can come in part at least to know, and who elicits from men a mature response of faith and love in which sin can begin to be overcome and the goals of human life begin to be realized. Moreover, the central figure within history who focuses for us the recognition and the realization of these things is Jesus Christ (pp. 117–18).

It may be impertinent for this reviewer to describe Professor Wiles as an orthodox believer. But the pattern of belief which he allows us to glimpse seems to be potentially trinitarian. It is more or less what the New Testament was saying about Christian experience (in the Spirit) of the creativity, love and triumph of the Father as made known in his Servant, Messiah, Word, Image or Son. And, since he is a man of great integrity, we can take it that the reason why Wiles functions as a priest and teacher of the Church of England is that he, too, worships Jesus as the purpose of the Father, now in flesh appearing. It is therefore something of a puzzle why he is neither clear nor exciting about this basic orthodoxy, this essential Christianity. The answer seems to lie in one of the many deafening silences to be found in his book. Nowhere does he contrast the gospel with its alternatives; everywhere his concern is with the theological world, its tasks and its freedoms. His book is yet another reminder that the gospel comes alive when it is being tested against needs and against rivals. Christianity grows strong in the open air.

Review of *Working Papers in Doctrine* by Maurice Wiles (1976)

It is a collection of fourteen essays. They are not revised, and the brief new Preface is little more than a bikini to cover the skeletal creed which they offer for our critical attention.

The main problem which troubles Dr Wiles is not one which keeps most of us awake at night. It is the problem of the authority of the Fathers who taught the Church from the second to the fifth centuries. Ten years ago he published an excellent introduction to *The Christian Fathers*, and there can be no question that his patristic learning is deep. In his 1966 book he commended the study of the Fathers because they established 'a scheme of Christian theology which in its main features has remained normative for the Church ever since' (p. 7). The story of his mind over a decade seems to be a process of more and more radical questioning of this tradition. Already in his 1966 book he in effect urged us to be careful to purchase a return ticket when we visited the land of the Fathers. Now it often sounds as if he would not disagree wholeheartedly were we to decide to stay at home.

He reprints his 1969 paper entitled 'Does Christology rest on a mistake?' There he suggests that the belief in a 'distinct divine presence in Jesus', although a 'very natural feeling', in fact 'rests on a mistake'. It is important to see what he means by this provocative suggestion, which on the face of it implies that the Chairman of the Doctrine Commission of the Church of England is a Unitarian. But all that he means (it seems) is that the way in which the Fathers of the Church defined the 'distinct divine presence' rests not on a mistake but on an ancient metaphysical system involving a now largely forgotten use of philosophical concepts such as 'nature', 'substance' and 'person'. In other words, he is using the customary teaching device of stimulating by exaggerating when he holds an audience by using the exciting word 'mistake'.

In his very first essay Wiles takes issue with a previous Regius Professor of Divinity at Oxford, Leonard Hodgson. He quotes Dr Hodgson as saying that

> The doctrine of the Trinity is the product of rational reflection on those particular manifestations of the divine activity which centre in the birth, ministry, crucifixion, resurrection and ascension of Jesus Christ and the gift of the Holy Spirit to the Church . . . It could not have been discovered without the occurrence of those events, which drove human reason to see that they required a trinitarian God for their cause (p. 1).

The criticisms made by Wiles boil down to two. First, we cannot experience the eternal essence of the three divine Persons – only what they do to us. Second, we cannot experience precisely how the jobs are divided between the Trinity. (In creation, the Word or the Son and the Spirit have been said to be active as well as the Father . . .). But so what? We may agree with both these criticisms, but still be convinced with Hodgson that there is an experience which leads Christians to believe in the Trinity. Of course, experience cannot endorse all the refinements of the theology of the Cappadocian Fathers. Nor can 'the doctrine of the Trinity' ever be stated with a final authority by any teacher whatsoever. Hodgson repeatedly said so. But he was right to say more strongly still that 'the grace of our Lord Jesus Christ and the love of God and the fellowship of the Holy Spirit' are real enough and instructive enough. It is not at all necessary to claim, as Wiles does, that 'it is logically impossible for the doctrine to be known in any other way than by authoritative revelation' (p. 16) meaning by that last phrase a literal acceptance of the Bible and the creeds, a fundamentalist kind of 'revelation' which he emphatically rejects.

He gives us masterly expositions of the Fathers. When Origen taught that the Son was 'begotten of the Father' before all worlds, he taught that many other realities were eternal and that there never was a time when they were not; he was a Platonist. When Athanasius taught the full divinity of the Son, he taught (as did his enemy Arius) that the incarnate Second Person of the Trinity had no human soul; they both conceived of 'human nature' in a more abstract way than we can. We are not Arians – or Athanasians. When Apollinarius seemed to deny the full humanity of the incarnate Son, and Gregory Nazianzen replied that if human nature had not been 'assumed' it had not been 'healed', they too were citizens of an intellectual world which we cannot inhabit; for we do not think that human nature can be 'assumed' or 'healed' in that way, which seems to us remotely metaphysical. And so forth.

One by one the Fathers are lined up, closely inspected – and politely dismissed.

Essentially what Wiles objects to is what another Oxford patristic scholar, John Henry Newman, also rejected more than a century ago: Anglicanism as a 'paper religion' formally accepting the Bible, the Fathers and the Anglican formularies but not wrestling with truth and life. But it has been said that the tragedy of Newman was that he could not read German. For, while he was in agony about the insufficiency of the Fathers and the Thirty-nine Articles, a theological tradition (both Protestant and Catholic) was developing in Germany and was tackling the real nineteenth-century questions about God, Christ and the world. And the debate has continued. It is certainly surprising, and one hopes it is not merely impertinent, to suspect that Wiles does not know twentieth-century theology well enough. Of course he must have heard, read and pondered a great deal of it, but somehow – perhaps because it has been absorbed in the study of the very Fathers he now seems to think ultimately irrelevant – his published writing does not show much awareness that the questions he raises as if they were daringly novel have been answered, or at least debated at great length, with great integrity, and with some positive conclusions, by his own living colleagues.

Clearly he is capable of joining that discussion, and may well do so in future books. Here, for example, he writes that 'to speak of a God who acts in history' is a language

> very largely rooted in the fact that so much of the most profound personal experience has about it a quality of response; men have found a meaning and a sense of purpose, bigger than their own comparatively narrow concerns, being elicited, as it were by the events of history (p. 137).

That is an insight which could be followed up. But instead of developing it he leaves us now with the suggestion that, provided there is a 'genuinely open' search for truth and a 'serious attention to the Christian tradition', Christianity could in the future change very drastically from what it has been in the past since 'we cannot now foresee or foreclose where such shifts may take us' (p. 193). Well, perhaps. Such words are in one sense true, even platitudinous. But listen! 'I have not found myself able to propose any set of beliefs, or other distinguishing characteristics, which any Christian theology must include or exclude. This does not seem to me to be a matter of very great importance' (p. 192). After words so weary on the last pages of this book, who would preach a gospel, or deny it? Who would enthusiastically commit years of his life to the study of the Christian tradition, and who would live and work now in order to contribute to the dynamic restatement of the everlasting gospel for our time?

Review of *What is Theology?* by Maurice Wiles (1976)

The Regius Professor of Divinity in Oxford, who was Chairman of the last Doctrine Commission in the Church of England, has had a bad press recently. The Commission's final report, *Christian Believing*, seemed excessively disunited or vague about the central contents of the gospel; and his own book *The Remaking of Christian Doctrine* has been greeted with less than enthusiasm (with 'horror, dismay, protest and abuse' said its publisher, John Bowden, in a recent essay). Such a chorus of boos may well have distressed Dr Wiles, who previously enjoyed many years of calm as a lecturer in the theology of the Fathers, and who is personally a gentle and popular man and a transparently sincere clergyman.

His new book is excellent and not controversial. It is simply an introduction to the study of theology as it is currently taught, and it originated in lectures to first-year students in London and Oxford. It is true that a captious critic could complain that the tone is still very puzzled – in sharp contrast with (for example) the affirmative pride and joy trumpeted in Karl Barth's *Evangelical Theology*. Nevertheless, Wiles does introduce innocent students or general readers to the current scene (if one excludes conservative Evangelical or Catholic circles). The situation which students or readers will meet in the English-speaking world in the 1970s is certainly not one where the Barthian trumpets would seem in place, so that this professor's low profile and still, small voice will generally arouse sympathy, not execration. Moreover, all the many problems which Wiles mentions are real ones, and are likely to cause upsets unless approached, as the Prayer Book says about marriage, 'reverently, discreetly, soberly and in the fear of God'.

These are some of the problems. Is theology out of place in a university or on an intelligent reader's shelves because before it begins it blindly accepts the doctrines of the Protestant Bible or the Catholic Church, or because it depends on wallowing in emotion? If not – if it really is an enquiry learning from facts and worthy of rational people – exactly what is the status of those biblical and ecclesiastical statements, and those records of intense religious experience, which it does study? 'Theology', says Wiles, 'can very properly ask of its critics a readiness to put themselves in the way of the kind of experiences with which it purports to deal. But it must take seriously the reaction of those who do so and still find themselves unconvinced thereby of any reality of God' (p. 4). And that is typical of the balanced wisdom of the whole book.

Showing what Christian theology feels like 'from the inside', Wiles is entirely candid about the difficulties which a modern reader will encounter as he attempts to enter the thought-worlds of the prophets, the apostles, the Fathers and the Reformers; and he proves that his own mind is wide open to the correction and illumination that can come from other disciplines. He indicates here that theology can learn from literary criticism and historical research, from the natural and social sciences, from philosophy and psychology. Yet this book contains very few examples of the kind of coldly negative approach that has disappointed or angered many readers of his other books. The accounts both of traditionalism and of radicalism are, although of necessity not long, completely fair; and, although Wiles rightly presents his own point of view, his main concern is to initiate students into the craft, recognising that in due course they may reach conclusions different from his own.

The hesitant novices who read this book carefully will find many reasons to be grateful for a passport into a large and strange new world. How I wish I could have read such an introduction when I began my own study of theology a quarter of a century ago! And how I wish that the tact and love which Wiles lavishes on the students privileged to sit at his feet could be shown more plainly to adults who, in the miserable 1970s, long for a positive statement of Christian belief!

From the Fathers to Today

To make a positive statement of Christian belief in the spiritual climate of a country such as England towards the end of the twentieth century is no easy task except for a person who is not aware of the problems. Wiles is acutely aware of them. An expert in the history of Christian doctrine, he knows how confident many previous generations of Christian teachers were and how successful they were, or seemed, in their work at the time. He has more than once in his own books recalled a paradox: theologians of the fourth century acknowledged to the full the difficulty of saying anything significant about the eternal and infinite God who is 'ineffable' and 'incomprehensible' – yet they had the confidence to say a great deal with great effect on the Church. But in England a Christian teacher now has to work in an atmosphere which is much more sceptical about the value of his task, and being human he is likely to feel the scepticism inside him unless he can deaden it by an assertion of conservatism and orthodoxy so defiant that it may include a touch of hysteria. In particular he is in an exposed position if he is both an ordained priest, responsible to the Church, and a university teacher, responsible to an academic community which insists on intellectual fearlessness and rigour and which largely assumes that theology is a partisan defence of the indefensible.

'Such people live as it were in two worlds,' Wiles has written, 'however sure they may be that they are ultimately one.' Having been since 1970 both a canon of Christ Church, the beautiful and richly historic Anglican cathedral in Oxford, and a professor in that university, he writes about theologians:

> They are liable to be treated by their colleagues of the university as figures of faith, people whose faith is suspected of holding them back from making the most searching inroads into their subject and which may be thought to call into question the propriety of their position and of their subject's position in an open university. But at the same time and on the basis of the same activity they are liable to be treated by their colleagues in the Church as figures of doubt, people whose questioning approach is felt to be incompatible with their membership of the Church and their commission to preach the gospel (*Explorations in Theology*, 1979, p. 3).

In this spiritually uncomfortable situation theologians such as Wiles are challenged to do for our time what the Fathers of the Church did for theirs. It is a part of the endless task of translating a gospel originally expressed in answer to Jewish beliefs and hopes of the first century into 'something believable' (the phrase is T. S. Eliot's) in very different societies. The task began, according to the Acts of the Apostles, during Stephen's brief period as spokesman of the Greek-speaking section of the church in Jerusalem, and was carried on with more success by Paul as the apostle to the Greek-speaking Gentiles. In the twentieth century the task has been undertaken by Christians who have made the gospel relevant not only in the disillusioned thought-world which has its centre in Western Europe but also in settings where faiths of one sort or another flourish more easily – in the Americas (North and Latin), in Africa, in India, in China, in south-east Asia, in the islands of the Pacific, in Australasia, in the Caribbean, in the Islamic world and in the Russian empire. I have tried to write with this theme myself in *The Futures of Christianity* (1987), but can only marvel at the learning used so graciously by two professors, Ninian Smart in *The Phenomenon of Christianity* (1979) and Jaroslav Pelikan in *Jesus through the Centuries* (1985).

It is instructive to compare the world of the Fathers with other new worlds to which the universal Christian mission has been addressed. An amateur such as myself has the advantages of the presentations by Wiles himself of *The Christian Fathers* (1966) and *The Making of Christian Doctrine* (1967). It soon becomes obvious that the Fathers had to work in a situation not of their making, which meant that they were both specially privileged and specially handicapped.

They had the advantage of belonging to a Church which took the Bible seriously, so that they were saved from the temptation to pretend that the Christian theologian's responsibility is discharged if he sprinkles a little hot water on currently fashionable non-Christian ideas. But they had the disadvantage of belonging to a Church which generally venerated the Bible as a collection of perfect records and of propositions dictated by God. The exact nature of the inspiration of the Bible, as Wiles has pointed out, 'was not a subject with which the Fathers were very much concerned' (*The Making of Christian Doctrine*, p. 46). But anything like modern criticism, historical or literary, was out of the question. Either Scripture had to be treated as meaning literally what it said, with binding authority, or hidden meanings had to be found in the sacred text, often by an interpretation which delighted in discovering allegories which a Christian preacher could use but which strikes modern students as being fanciful. Thus the whole of the fourth gospel (including Jesus' 'I and the Father are one' at John 10:30) had to be taken as the very words of the historical Jesus; the practice of baptism 'in the name of the Father and of the Son and of the Holy Spirit' had to be traced back to Jesus himself (Matt. 28:19); references in the Old Testament to the appearance and activity of God, his angel or his wisdom, had to be taken as references to the Second Person of the Trinity who was to become

incarnate in Jesus; and down-to-earth items in the Old Testament
laws, or in the parables of Jesus, had to be taken as coded
instructions by God to the Christian Church in its daily life. The job
of the theologian was not to question any of this but was to arrange
the material according to its importance and expound it philosophically. Wiles has well stated the difference between this and
any modern approach. The concept of 'revelation' by God is
possible in our time as before, he grants. But he adds:

> The specific understanding which is excluded is one which
> isolates a particular area of the world and claims that that limited
> area contains religious truth in a form which may require human
> interpretation but which ought to be regarded as immune from
> the kind of critical assessment which is free to question or
> challenge its truth. We are surely bound today to say that there is
> no area of human experience, however special its importance,
> however justly entitled to be called divine revelation, which can
> be allowed that kind of immunity (*Working Papers in Doctrine*,
> p. 92).

The Fathers had the advantage, from a Christian point of view,
of living in a world where it was widely believed that humanity
needed to be 'saved'. An awareness of sin had grown among the
Jews, partly as a result of the destruction of their kingdoms by the
Assyrians and Babylonians and of their temple and holy city by the
Romans. As exiles or as subjects of an alien power, they felt that
God had punished them for their sins and their surviving religion
became more of an individual's quest for forgiveness and purity.
This element in the Jewish religious consciousness corresponded
with deep emotions in the Hellenistic culture and the Roman
empire, as is shown by the appeal of Paul's message of salvation.
The official religion of Rome and of the other cities around the
Mediterranean was strongly established. But it was too obviously a
tissue of legends, and in practice a celebration of worldly power, to
satisfy the individual's religious longings – longings which were
intensified by the psychological stress and damage caused by the
Roman empire's conquest and mixture of many peoples. In a world
made secure by Roman power, the insecurity of the soul could not
be answered by Rome's official religion. So, to fill a gap, the
'mystery' religions including the Gnostic movements arose – and
Christianity could be understood as one of them. The Bible, or
some less official gospel, could be said to provide the knowledge
(*gnosis*) which could rescue humanity from its plight. Initiation

through baptism could be presented as the illumination needed, and communion in the Eucharist as the 'medicine of immortality'. The work of the Church's Lord could be interpreted as the conquest of sin and death. But the Fathers who were able to find a receptive audience for such themes had the disadvantage of needing to state the gospel in mythological terms if it was to be hailed as a better alternative to the pagan tales about the gods. A 'myth' (such as the charming Indian tale of Krishna sporting by the river among the girls) is a story which on the face of it is like stories about everyday or historical events. But it does not recount actual events (little or nothing is known about the historical Krishna). In this story what are believed to be the spiritual processes of 'salvation' are dramatised, as a work of fiction can dramatise other spiritual processes which lie beneath its surface. (Thus the naked girl who blushes when she sees Krishna is held to symbolise the soul in humble penitence before God.) And so the Christian gospel was communicated as a myth. It was a story about the descent of the Redeemer, a divine or semi-divine being, into the world of sin, ignorance, death and darkness, in order to bring those who accepted him back with him into the world of light and divinity. And that story was so effective as an offer of salvation to that world that the Fathers were not inclined to probe it in order to separate myth from fact. It seems that only a highly educated minority in that ancient world ever raised any objection to Christianity because it was mythological. But in later ages, more anxious to separate fact from fiction, the question of how factual this mythology was became a harsh challenge to all the Fathers' orthodoxy. And in ages more anxious to separate divinity from humanity, the talk of the orthodox Fathers about God becoming man in order to make us divine has been suspect because it suggests a distinctly unorthodox repudiation of monotheism. Even when it is added, as it certainly ought to be, that the 'divinisation' (*theosis*) of man is achieved by God's grace the idea is very close to the denial of the transcendent unity of the one true God.

Spiritually and intellectually, however, the Fathers were on a level different from the tellers of tales about the pagan gods. Despite their use of mythology when offering salvation they had the advantage of taking God seriously. Socrates, Plato, Aristotle and their successors in Greek philosophy left a legacy of criticism of pagan mythology combined with an emphasis on the pure divinity of God and on the 'universals' in human experience. Such philosophy can be called 'metaphysics', as it was by Aristotle, because it goes beyond the physical. Christianity took over from the Neoplatonic tradition the insistence that God was 'without body, parts or passions', that God was spirit, simply and changelessly perfect, and that God's creation was real as a whole and not so real in its changing details. Thus the new religion lifted the idea of God above the pagan fables. Did it also lift the idea above the mythology to be found within Christianity's own Bible? The Fathers, with their very high doctrine of Scripture, did not think a demythologising programme an option for Christians. On the contrary, they believed that precisely because the one true God was not someone that mortals could understand or imagine, it was necessary for him to reach human minds by an authoritative revelation including what later generations would call mythology. But they accepted the challenge to integrate the biblical material with the philosophical tradition so as to reach a fully rational understanding of the divine reality. As early as around 175 Athenagoras was confident about the scope of Christian theology: 'what the union of the Son with the Father is, what communion the Father has with the Son, what the Spirit is, what the union of these three is and what the distinction between the united'. It was a programme not lacking ambition.

Moreover, the Fathers thought that Neoplatonic metaphysics had provided them with terms which could enable them to be sufficiently clear both about the eternal substance (*ousia*) of God and about the manner of God's activity (*energeia*) in the created world. They appeared to have inherited an intellectual fortune. But they had the disadvantage of being forced to use terms which had been designed to describe an eternal reality which was static because divine and a world which was viewed as a whole without much interest in its transient particulars. Their problem was something like the problem of explaining the development of an organism in biology in the terms of physics or chemistry. They could, and did, change the meaning of Neoplatonic terms when they baptised them for Christian use. But they could never fully overcome the problem of how to relate the motionless metaphysics of Greece to the Semitic world of the Bible, which is everywhere a world in which things and people are real one by one, in which divine and human passions are in conflict, in which God acts and is affected by other actions, and in which events and characters change. In the end the problem defeated them. That is not much to their discredit. Many other reputable thinkers have been defeated. Lessing's complaint has become famous. 'Accidental truths of history can never become the proof of necessary truths of reason', he wrote. 'That is the ugly, broad ditch which I cannot get across, however often and however earnestly I have tried to make the leap.' The question of how to relate the pure Being referred to in the Buddhist tradition as the 'Unbecome, Unborn, Unmade, Unformed' to the 'names and forms' of the world of phenomena has always in the end defeated mankind's ablest religious thinkers, including the greatest men in the Indian debate and those intellectual giants of Christianity, Judaism and Islam in the Middle Ages, Thomas Aquinas, Maimonides and Al Ghazzali (as Keith Ward expounded in his *Images of Eternity*, 1987).

Finally, the Fathers had the advantage of living under the Roman empire (or empires, western and eastern). The imperial peace meant that Christianity could spread quite rapidly around the Mediterranean and into the Roman provinces. It also meant that in order to retain its identity amid many competing religions, and in order to survive pressure and persecution from an empire which suspected that the refusal to worship gods including the emperor involved treason, the Church had to be as well organised as the empire itself. The Christian Scriptures were organised in a 'canon'; the Christian congregations were organised under bishops; the bishops were organised as the guardians of traditions said to derive from the founders (the apostles) and mostly enshrined in the Scriptures. All this gave Christianity a toughness which enabled it to appeal to the emperor Constantine, and to many who were glad to obey his edicts, giving it first toleration and then privilege. It seemed the one religion that would unify the empire, sanctify its government and uplift its morale and morals. Those who regret that the conversion of Constantine made Christianity the faith of millions have not thought about how impoverished the history of Europe and the world would have been without it. But with astonishing rapidity the Church which had been persecuted became a persecutor enforcing orthodoxy. The emperor, alarmed that the Church itself was not sufficiently united to perform this role, summoned a council of bishops to settle their theological disputes. It was the council of Nicaea in 325 and it acquired permanent authority. In 1964 the eminent Roman Catholic theologian, Bernard Lonergan, was still expounding the Christology of the New Testament and of the first three Christian centuries as *The Way to Nicaea* (translated into English in 1976). 'Those early Christian writers,' he taught, 'sometimes directly, sometimes indirectly, paved the way for the definition of dogma, without really knowing what they were doing' (p. 13). Wiles has analysed Nicaea's enormous prestige and influence in the fourth century:

> Even in the days of persecution the church had regarded the imperial powers that were as ordained of God; and then, almost overnight, God's viceregent was to be found no longer persecuting but presiding over the largest and most representative gathering of bishops in the church's history. Surely such a body in such a situation would be guided not merely to see the next step forward but to provide a firm and lasting answer on the fundamental issue of the church's faith (*Working Papers in Doctrine*, p. 43).

But the bishops who now proceeded to quarrel over rival interpretations of 'the faith of Nicaea' had incurred a major disadvantage. Theology was now entangled with imperial politics. Orthodoxy, although couched in the terms of metaphysics, became the law of the State. Heresy was often to be motivated by a dislike of the State. During its struggle to survive under the empire the Church had become more organised than Jesus and his apostles had ever intended. Now it was at least in danger of becoming an organisation spiritually different from the fellowship of the disciples gathered by the Lord who had been crucified under Pontius Pilate.

Wiles has paid to the theological achievement of the Fathers and the councils the greatest compliment which a man can pay: he has devoted many years of his life to studying it and to expounding it accurately and lucidly. He has protested that just because this is 'an approach which is not immediately congenial to us today, it is the more important that we resist the temptation to make a caricature of it' (*The Christian Fathers*, p. 108). He has finely written that

> the Fathers did not desert a living response to the person of Christ and turn instead to arid formulae about him. Rather, because their response to him was so dominating a concern, they did not shirk the obvious responsibility which that faith laid upon them of loving the Lord their God with all their mind and coming to grips with the intellectual implications of their faith (*Working Papers in Doctrine*, p. 38).

And yet over the years in the mind of this scholar the disadvantages of the Fathers have clearly outweighed the advantages. In the end he has seemed to cease to wrestle not only with Neoplatonic metaphysics but also with the tradition which they attempted to link with metaphysical descriptions of God: the tradition that God is powerfully active in the history of his creation.

In his Bampton Lectures on *God's Action in the World* (1986) he makes it plain that the change is due to the influence of a society which is in many ways unlike the world of the Fathers. Although he says that 'the view that I am outlining is fully compatible with a thoroughly positive attitude, which values the language of Christian tradition for the way it has served and continues to serve as the vehicle of genuine faith' (p. 10), actually the fear of fundamentalism is for Wiles so strong that it is thought necessary to construct a theology which appears to deny the Bible's central message about God's activity. There is such fear of mythology in religion that it is thought right to insist that in reality God never intervenes. And there is such fear of politics, including ecclesiastical politics, corrupting religion that it is thought right to reject the Christian Church's basic tradition that God *has* intervened somewhat like a monarch.

Wiles is anxious to welcome many achievements of modern thought which are (as I, too, am completely convinced) intellectually valid and spiritually beneficial. It was essential for us moderns to rid ourselves of the notion that every event that occurs has been caused by the predestinating determination of God – for that idea makes the problem of the existence of so much chance and evil in God's creation insoluble. It was also essential for us to abandon the belief that events are always being adjusted to suit the convenience of God's favourites – for that raises the unanswerable question why a good God does not favour the unfortunate. The right of a scientist to study nature, and of a historian to study the past, 'setting on one side any appeal to divine agency' (p. 6), is also essential, for in no other way could the regularities of nature and of history have been discovered as the foundations of all modern knowledge. The modern person who believes that God is 'the reason that entities occur at all' (p. 19) but who accepts the revelation by science of the regularities in nature has to acknowledge that the Creator has so arranged things that he is not needed like a technician who is often being called back to fix a faulty machine. Wiles quotes Austin Farrer: 'If God creates energies, he creates going activities. What he causes is their acting as they do' (p. 33). This action through regularities shows, as Wiles says (quoting Thomas Tracy), God's 'intentional self-restraint', his 'renunciation of certain uses of power' (p. 22). The Creator seems to have bound himself in that way. What usually gives rise to a belief that the universe *is* a creation, and not totally an accident in its origin, without any first cause, is marvelling at the thing as a whole. As Wiles puts it, the believer acknowledges 'the givenness of the world, with its remarkable physical balance which has made possible the emergence of human life and the conditions to sustain it' (p. 106).

But if modern religion does no more than marvel at the universe, it is likely to conclude that the 'God' of the theists is an old-fashioned name either for the universe (Spinoza's *Deus sive natura*), or for the 'life-energy' which arises on this planet, or for a spiritual or moral view of the life that has somehow emerged. Instead of referring back to Don Cupitt as an exponent of a 'non-realist' theism, I can refer to *Religion without Explanation* by D. Z. Phillips (1977) or quote Stewart Sutherland, a distinguished philosopher and now Vice-Chancellor of the University of London, who after rejecting 'the belief in a personal God who acts in history and in the world' concludes that 'what theism has preserved is the possibility of a view of human affairs which is not reducible to the view of an individual or group of individuals' (*God, Jesus and Belief*, 1984, pp. 200–1). I have to ask whether Wiles, who unlike Cupitt or Phillips or Sutherland does hold and teach that God is real, is really open to the possibility that God may act against evil because God is more than nature or life or spirituality or morality. I make (I am afraid, for the third time in this book) the obvious point that the problem of evil is crucial in any discussion about whether or not God is both transcendent and active.

God's Action against Evil

In *God's Action in the World* Wiles sums up the classic attempts which have been made to reduce the problem of evil to manageable proportions. We are told that what we call evil is necessary if the creation is to be distinguished from the perfect God; that much of evil is caused by the misuse of human free will, which on the whole brings many benefits; that the struggle with evil often strengthens and purifies human character; that it is reasonable both to believe that God somehow suffers in sympathy with us and to hope for the ultimate triumph of his purposes – a hope that entails the hope of heaven. And these are all valid points. But a reply has often been made by people suffering acutely, as well as by professional or amateur philosophers or by novelists of the calibre of Dostoyevsky or Camus. Wiles makes it himself. The reply is that such arguments are not enough consolation when one personally feels over-whelmed by evil or by sorrow for one of its victims. Is, then, the true view of the world tragic, with 'blind fate' ruling? It may be so. It must be so, in the last analysis, if the true view of the world is godless. But if so, we have to explain why so much of the world is experienced by us as good. And along with other religions Christianity says that God, who is different from his creation and to whom we ultimately owe the good in our normal experience, acts within his creation in order to deliver us from evil. For Christians, the supreme act is God's in Christ, the climax of many acts from man's primeval youth to our own century when evil has so often seemed to be reigning. And as Wiles once wrote:

> It is often claimed that the issues raised by the Fathers are issues of fundamental and perennial concern to Christian faith. The claim is just. For the fundamental question with which they were grappling was the question: what sort of God do we believe in in the light of the coming of Jesus Christ? (*Working Papers in Doctrine*, p. 95).

In the 1972 Cambridge symposium on *Christ, Faith and History* edited by Stephen Sykes and J. P. Clayton, Wiles responded to Peter Baelz's emphasis on the problem of evil by saying about the response of God: 'I fully agree that there must be room for the idea of special activity in some sense' (p. 36). But fifteen years later in *God's Action in the World*, although he apparently accepts John Hick's idea of 'God's continuous creation/salvation of the world' (p. 48), he advances a number of arguments against any belief in acts of God other than the creation. One is that this belief belonged to a culture which we cannot share. It was commonly believed in the pre-modern world that God, or the local god, acted frequently to bring a blessing or a curse, and the natural or historical expla-nation of events was often ignored or subordinated to this religious version. But my comment is that because the Bible and the world surrounding it were pre-scientific in tending to ascribe all events to the direct action of God, it is not necessary in logic to say that no events whatever are really in this category.

Another argument advanced by Wiles is that events regarded as acts of God can be analysed in terms of natural or historical causation, excluding God. Thus the exodus of Israel from Egypt over the Red Sea may not have involved any miracle. Even the

Easter faith of the Christians can be explained without any appeal to 'divine agency'. It may have arisen out of a natural recovery of faith in Jesus, possibly including 'appearances' which were 'psychical' experiences which in the present state of science are still classified as 'paranormal' but not as miraculous. (In *God's Action in the World*, pp. 90–3, Wiles modestly announces a suspension of judgement about the nature of the resurrection.) But my comment is that while the Old Testament includes some claims that miracles are knock-down proofs of the power of the Bible's God, generally in the New Testament miracles are seen as 'signs' which point those who are ready to 'believe' to the active God. Their miraculous nature cannot be proved so surely as to compel belief in an active God. (Thus even the resurrection of Jesus, the nearest that the New Testament gets to a knock-down proof, is not said to have been so certain and so public that it has knocked non-Christians down.) And the goodness of these miracles cannot be proved so surely as to prevent non-believers from saying that they are the work of an agent of Satan. As 'signs' they are mysterious and ambiguous, needing interpretation by faith if 'the finger of God' is to be discerned in them.

In a scientific age events which believers interpret as miracles can always be interpreted as merely natural events. For all that we actually know, that may be all they are: 'miracles' are what faith calls some events. However, it is not necessary in logic to say that believers are wrong to find 'the finger of God' in them, if first the legitimacy of belief in a creative and loving God who is capable of interventions has been granted. We may say that 'God did that' while from another angle it is equally right to say that 'nature did that'. Wiles has given us an analogy: we may say that 'Solomon built the temple' whereas from another angle it is true to say that stonemasons built it (p. 61). Elsewhere he has remarked that it is possible to speak of 'an active God whose action is to be seen "in" rather than "between" worldly occurrences' (*Working Papers in Doctrine*, p. 137). If this means that God acts in events which can also be interpreted in worldly terms, I think that this preserves what is essential – and, as I believe, true – in the Bible's message about the active God. But Wiles is, with characteristic frankness, more concerned to make explicit the differences between his teaching and the Bible's than to claim credit for similarities between them which may be no more than superficial. He writes:

There are exceptions, but I would judge that almost overwhelmingly the Bible's way of understanding those special events to which it bears witness is one in which the activity of God in relation to the worldly occurrences concerned is conceived to be of a different kind from that which is operative in the general run of worldly occurrences. Is it consistent then to regard the Bible as a religious authority, which as I have said seems to be an inescapable necessity for Christian theology, and at the same time to transform as drastically as my account would involve its own understanding of those events to which it bears witness? (*Working Papers in Doctrine*, p. 146).

Wiles is obviously irritated by being accused of merely reviving the Deism of the eighteenth century. While thinking 'revelation' unnecessary, Deism shared Christianity's belief in a perfectly good Creator of a sufficiently good world. The title of Matthew Tindal's volume of 1730 said it all: *Christianity as Old as the Creation or the Gospel a Republication of the Religion of Nature*. The Deists altogether denied that special activity of God which is associated with the concept of miracle. Wiles has written that

talk of God's activity is to be understood as a way of speaking about those events within the natural order or within the natural history in which God's purpose finds clear expression or special opportunity. Such a view is not Deistic in the most strongly pejorative sense, in that it allows for a continuing relationship of God to the world as source of existence and giver of purpose to the whole. It is Deistic in so far as it refrains from claiming any effective causation on the part of God in relation to particular occurrences (*The Remaking of Christian Doctrine*, p. 38).

More recently he has said that '"act of God" is a symbol which discloses an existing reality, namely that there are occurrences in the world which embody and express (in substantial if not in perfect measure) the will of God, either for mankind in general or for a particular person' (*Faith and the Mystery of God*, 1982, p. 27). On this basis, as he once told Professor Basil Mitchell, 'I want to keep open the possibility that the kind of account I should want to give of the central Christian events might perfectly properly be termed "revelation", and the word given a rather different definition' (*Theology*, 1980, pp. 109–10).

Whether or not Wiles deserves to escape the criticism levelled against eighteenth-century Deism, which was a semi-Christian religion, is a question of what weight is to be put on such words of agreement with the Christian tradition. What does it mean to talk about events in which God's purpose finds 'clear expression or special opportunity' or is 'embodied'? It is not enough for him to dissociate himself from Deism by saying that God is the 'source of existence and giver of purpose' to the whole world, because the Deists said that too. What he needs to do is to persuade his fellow Christians that the terminology which he prefers expresses the *newness* of the events which the New Testament celebrates – and their *God-givenness*. 'By symbolizing certain occurrences as God's acts, we create a new reality,' he has recently declared (*Faith and the Mystery of God*, p. 27). Well – all symbols do 'create' as well as 'disclose' reality, and Wiles says so. But it is the faith of the New Testament and of the Church that these events were created not by us but by God. Indeed, that was once the clear faith of Wiles. At the end of *The Making of Christian Doctrine*, in 1967, he looked forward to an approach to Christology 'in terms of the divine activity', noting that 'such an approach is fully in accord with the first basis of doctrinal work, faithfulness to the witness of Scripture' and that in the Christian tradition 'the fundamental language of salvation is of a work of God effected in Christ' (p. 179). But now I ask whether he has fully maintained that emphasis on the God-givenness of divine activity. He still speaks of 'the full instantiation of the divine offer and human response in the person of Jesus' or agrees with 'the conviction that in Christ we are truly directed and joined to the ultimate reality of the being and love of God' (*Theology*, 1988, pp. 305, 307). But is the life of Jesus God's new act against evil?

Of course the saving events which are together spoken of as 'the Christ-event' have not been seen in isolation from other events. Wiles quotes from Gordon Kaufman: 'it is *the whole course of history* from its initiation in God's creative activity to its consummation when God ultimately achieves his purposes, that should be conceived as God's act in the primary sense' (*God's Action in the World*, p. 29). Seeing the life of Christ as prophesied in the Old Testament was the New Testament's way of expressing that truth. Another way of expressing it was to develop the idea that Christ was 'pre-existent' before his conception. As a conservative theologian, Colin Gunton, has recently put it:

> Jesus of Nazareth is not simply an unprecedented irruption or intervention of God upon the stage of history. The love of God

which becomes actual in this truly human and historical life is continuous with the love that operates throughout it. As Athanasius says, 'the . . . Word of God comes to our realm, howbeit he was not far from us before' (*Yesterday and Today*, 1983, p. 133).

But the whole thrust of the parables of Jesus is that something new is taking place, new wine demanding new wineskins, a new banquet demanding a response to the invitation; and the whole thrust of the letters of Paul is that because of the newness of Christ life feels new for the Christians. And the New Testament would never agree with the idea that these events are entirely worldly or normal and that it is only their human interpretation that makes them seem new, since 'insight in any field of understanding may come at unexpected times and in unexpected ways' (*God's Action in the World*, p. 101). It is assumed throughout the Bible that when people interpret events rightly it is because God has directly inspired them, which is a form of new action. That has also been assumed in the history of the saints. Some of the saints have left behind them abundant evidence of their belief that God acted in events in their own lives and acted in their responses to those events. It is very difficult to take anything in their self-understanding seriously if that belief is totally rejected. Wiles comes nowhere near a sympathetic appreciation of them when he writes at the end of his discussion of God's providence of

the self-dedication of human lives such as those of a Paul or an Augustine. It is precisely in them that God's act finds part of its fulfilment, not because there are separate distinguishable divine initiatives in relation to them or to particular aspects of them but because the emergence of such lives is what God's one act deliberately seeks to make possible (*God's Action in the World*, p. 81).

The Fathers of the Church were among the hundreds of millions of Christians who have had to turn old languages to new uses in order to talk about a revolutionary new experience of grace and truth 'from the Father through the Son in the Holy Spirit'. Many images were used in attempts to describe the at-one-ment of God and man achieved by Jesus, but as Wiles observes,

there was a firm central core of faith to which those images were giving expression . . . It can fairly be conveyed as a belief that in the death and resurrection of Christ God had worked effectively in history to transform once for all man's status (or at the very least man's potential status) in relation to God (*The Remaking of Christian Doctrine*, pp. 62–3).

Of course the human response of Jesus to the Father, and the human response to Jesus of believers, are necessary parts of the at-one-ment, for it takes two to be at one. This is in keeping with the pattern by which, as Wiles finely says, 'God . . . makes himself known and available to man in love in the fullest way that is compatible with man's existence as a free being' (pp. 118–19). But that human response to the divine initiative is also fundamentally the new work of God. It is, to use the traditional term, the work of 'grace'. When the work of God in event and interpretation – the work which is called 'revelation' – touches the human heart, God's purpose is achieved. As Wiles has so well said, 'the vision to which it gives rise is of a love which combines urgency with patience, which takes no short cuts because it takes human freedom seriously, but which cannot be cut short because it cannot cease to love' (*Faith and the Mystery of God*, p. 61). And that is a vision of God to which the contemplation of nature as a whole or of history as a whole does *not* give rise.

There is a profound truth in David Hume's famous, if ironic, remark that the Christian religion cannot be believed by any reasonable person without a miracle. The point was made at length, and more expertly than I can manage, in J. L. Mackie's philosophical criticism of belief in God in *The Miracle of Theism* (1982), but I, too, have always thought that the philosophical arguments against the existence of a good God outweigh those for it, or at least suggest an inconclusive verdict – unless those arguments are answered 'miraculously' by some experience of God which atheists either do not have or do not acknowledge. Such experience gives rise to a sense of the presence of God or gods in many religious traditions, almost throughout the world and throughout history. That point was made with up-to-date learning in John Bowker's books *The Sense of God* (1973) and *The Religious Imagination and the Sense of God* (1978). But in particular the new experience recorded as revelation in the New Testament gives rise to the Christian belief in the loving God, in contrast with what nature may well suggest. As was well said in Gerd Theissen's *Biblical Faith: An Evolutionary Approach* (1984), nature often seems to reveal a merciless God who is on the side of the strong.

In the Christian tradition 'the God to whom I commit myself as a

Christian is a personal God, the living God, a God of love'. So Wiles has affirmed (*Faith and the Mystery of God*, p. 12). Therefore the essence of Bishop Joseph Butler's plea to the Deists of the eighteenth century is also the essence of a plea which I want to make with all due respect to this Christian scholar of the twentieth century who believes in 'a God of love'. He should also say that God's love is active. There are many difficulties in Christian faith, and many in atheism, but it is even more difficult to believe with the Deists in a God who is the good Creator, 'a God of love', but who leaves his creation, with all the evil in it, to its own devices after starting it off. That 'natural religion' was said by the Deists to be the conclusion of natural reason. But in response to the Deists Bishop Butler denied that their theology was reasonable as an account of a good God responsible for the creation we see around us. If God is at all like a good human parent in being personal, living and loving, it is extremely difficult to accept the Deists' belief that he is now inactive, doing nothing to save his children from evil. This insight is worked out by a scholar who is a philosophical theologian (as I am not) in John Macquarrie's Gifford Lectures which I review later (pp. 273–5).

The teaching which the Fathers gave in their own world, more than a thousand years before Bishop Butler, was their way of responding to the newness of God's saving acts. But if the witness of the Fathers is thought by Wiles (who knows much more about it than I do) to have been ruined irrecoverably by its fundamentalist, mythological, metaphysical and political elements, one can ask a Christian theologian to accept the witness of Jesus to the active love of the Father – the witness that is 'gospel' or 'good news'.

There are of course difficulties in recovering the exact words of Jesus, for the gospels were edited some time afterwards. And there are of course bits in the gospels which go well with Deism's picture of a non-interventionist Creator. Jesus is reported as having urged trust in the good Creator who clothes the grass of the fields (presumably through natural means) and who sends sunshine and rain for the benefit of just and unjust alike (presumably in the course of nature). Jesus is also reported as having urged the humble and patient acceptance of the Creator's method of working. The crop must be given time to grow and must be allowed to include weeds, as is natural. Because he does not intervene in our affairs as often, as publicly or as decisively as we should like, the Creator can sometimes be felt to be like an absentee landowner – and in the extremity God must be prayed to as the Holy One who appears to have deserted his suffering servant. But these are not the most prominent themes in what is reported to us as the Lord's teaching, and to concentrate on them, presenting them as the essential vision of Jesus, would mean rewriting the gospels. It would mean the construction of a Jesus who advised his hearers to relax because God was not more active then than at any other time. They would be sensible to pray but not to expect God to do anything more than he had already done. There was no bridegroom coming, no burglar breaking in, no master calling his servants to account. The nearest approximation to a crisis was that the hearers would miss much if they failed to welcome the wise insights of Jesus into the admirable way in which the world was operating; and they would one day die, when they would see for themselves how well things were working out. It would mean saying that God himself is like a judge who paid no attention to the unfortunate widow, like a neighbour who would not get out of bed to lend a loaf, like a housewife who lazily expected the lost coin to turn up, like a shepherd who was confident that the lost sheep would find its own way back, and like the father who, as he tucked into the fatted calf, vaguely wondered why the prodigal son was not yet home.

Maurice Wiles' response is on pp. 286–91.

5

GEOFFREY LAMPE AND THE INCARNATION OF GOD:

Was Jesus only a man filled by the Spirit of God?

As I tried to be fair about the teaching of the scholars I have been discussing, it became obvious that the subject which is called Christology is crucial in the debate stirred up by England's radical theologians. But the discussion of that subject has often been confusing. One reason for this is that most people are not familiar with this branch of Christian theology. John Robinson reported being asked in Cambridge whether Christology was 'something to do with crystals'. Yet Christology must matter to serious, thinking Christians. For it is something to do with Jesus Christ.

Even patient listeners have often found it difficult to decide what the radical theologians intend to say about him, however. If the incarnation is being called a 'myth', does that merely mean that the old ways of expressing the doctrine that 'God was in Christ' are being questioned, revised and where necessary replaced? Or is it intended to say that Jesus was among the prophets filled by the Spirit of God, denying that his human life was unique as God's new act? If the intention is to revise an orthodoxy which was phrased in words not our own, the debate about Christology has been, I reckon, a necessary part of the perpetually necessary updating of theology. But if the intention is to deny that God's active love was embodied in Jesus Christ, what is always essential to Christianity has been in some danger. And because their intentions have seemed unclear England's radical theologians have, I believe, so far failed to provide a positive and adequate Christology – one which will be appropriate to what Christians have wanted to say as a result of their experience of Jesus. Sometimes these theologians have struggled to provide that. But sometimes they have seemed to be reducing Christianity in order to fit into non-Christian categories without showing convincingly that the baby must go the way of the bathwater.

Before offering a few reflections I hope to convey something of the significance of the debate by reprinting reviews which appeared in the *Church Times* immediately five key books were published.

I wrote about a book of essays, *The Myth of God Incarnate*, edited by John Hick (1977). The other contributors were Don Cupitt, Michael Goulder, Leslie Houlden, Dennis Nineham, Maurice Wiles and Frances Young. With its attention-grabbing title, this deliberately controversial book which became a best-seller (by theological standards) was launched at a press conference in the Chapter House of St Paul's Cathedral. I appeared alongside the essayists (announced as *advocatus Dei*!) and saw that the most vocal journalists had come along in order to make fun of the theologians, who, they thought, had ceased to be Christians without realising it. They turned out to be right in one or two of the cases; Don Cupitt I have discussed, and Michael Goulder has bravely resigned as a priest, explaining that he has ceased to believe in God. But subsequent theology by Leslie Houlden and Frances Young (to mention only two names) was firmly in the Christian camp, and Professor Young's *From Nicaea to Chalcedon* (1983) was a history of ancient Christology so scholarly and objective that it was hard to tell her own opinions. At the time Professor Wiles took legitimate revenge on his critics by giving them a little lecture on historical Christology, which was not one of their subjects. But Professor Hick played into their hands by an instant reply. He said that Jesus was 'possibly the most wonderful man who has ever lived'. It was no mean compliment – but it was more reductionist than anything he had written and it was reported as a denial of Christianity.

A popular reply, *The Truth of God Incarnate*, edited by Michael Green, was rushed out, but two years later the results of a more leisurely and expert discussion were published as *Incarnation and Myth*, edited by Michael Goulder. The original essayists and some more traditionalist theologians had met in a conference for an exchange of reflections.

Three other books stood out in this controversy. One, *The Human Face of God*, was a product of John Robinson's many talents and was published nearly five years before *The Myth of God Incarnate*. My review of it may show why Robinson was critical of *The Myth*. In the last chapter of his own book he had made statements as unorthodox as anything there. But most of his book was an affirmation about Jesus Christ more positive than anything that emerged in *The Myth*, and, as I tried to show in my chapter on him, it was in the end this conservative side of Robinson that prevailed.

Another important book was *God as Spirit*, by G. W. H. Lampe, published in the same year as *The Myth*. The author was a professor in Cambridge from 1959 to 1980, after teaching in the universities of Oxford and Birmingham. Avoiding every trace of sensationalism, and basing himself on a close examination of the Scriptures and the Fathers, he was one of the most respected theological scholars of his generation and was to be specially admired for the calm courage with which he faced death by cancer. *G. W. H. Lampe: Christian, Scholar, Churchman. A Memoir by his Friends*, edited by C. F. D. Moule (1982), was the portrait of a saintly priest. It is a pity that his book, which was far more constructive than *The Myth of God Incarnate*, attracted less public interest and that the Oxford University Press allowed it to go out of print before it was reissued by the SCM Press.

In my review, however, I asked whether even this magisterial statement expressed the full truth. So in 1983 I was glad to welcome the publication of Professor James Mackey's *The Christian Experience of God as Trinity*. It was followed four years later by a very helpful book on *Modern Theology: A Sense of Direction*, but that is among the many relevant books which I must ignore here.

Review of *The Myth of God Incarnate* edited by John Hick (1977)

What do Christians nowadays mean if they recite the Nicene Creed and call Jesus 'God from God, Light from Light'? The divinity of Christ has often seemed the essence of Christianity; and unless Christians are fairly clear about what they think of Christ today, they are not going to get very far by being keen on evangelism or involved in politics or efficient in reorganising the Church. So it is important to meet the challenge of the latest explosion of English radical theology.

Why have seven Christian scholars chosen a title so likely to scandalise the faithful and embarrass parish priests as it gets talked about? Is it because they hope that the man in the street will thereby become the man in the bookshop? No, it cannot be. All the contributors hold academic posts and draw academic salaries; and they would presumably not choose a title merely because it is catchpenny or catchpound. The truth must be that they are worried. They seem convinced that most of their fellow Christians have not faced the facts, and that most of their fellow preachers have indulged in a conspiracy of silence.

Already there has been the suggestion (glad or angry, excited or weary according to taste): 'another *Honest to God*!' But the book is in fact a collection of essays by seven theologians. If there is to be a comparison, it ought to be with collective works such as *Essays and Reviews* (1860), which aroused a great Victorian controversy. The contributors to that volume were denounced as 'Seven against Christ.' But these scholars who join the fray in the 1970s do not intend to be against Christ. Professor Hick has a splendid passage on p. 172 beginning 'I see the Nazarene . . .' He speaks of 'the absolute claim of God confronting us, summoning us to give ourselves wholly to [God] and to be born again as his children . . .' He says that Jesus was 'so totally conscious of God that we could catch something of that consciousness by spiritual contagion'. Dr Nineham is probably the most radical of the contributors. Indeed he rebukes his own editor for speaking of Jesus as being 'totally conscious of God': such language is, he reckons, too high a mark in the examination. Yet even Nineham does speak of Christians as a group that views Jesus as 'the lens through which all the demands and promises of God to them are focused' (p. 200), and he includes himself in the group.

The essayists who now call the incarnation a 'myth' are sure that Jesus of Nazareth was a real man, with a mother and a father in the normal way. They are also sure that he had a human mind, which meant being limited in knowledge and outlook. He was a man who lived in a particular time and place – the only way in which a man can live. But the records about Jesus are limited, and the records that have survived all show that his teaching was full of images and arguments then familiar and now remote. They are not enough to prove beliefs that he was totally sinless, or completely devoted to God, or invariably loving, as Goulder observes (p. 53).

The Christians have also belonged to particular times and places. This has had at least three consequences. In the first place, the orthodoxy about Christ's 'person' uniting divine and human 'natures' was worked out within the thought-forms of a particular period in Greek philosophy. That world of Neoplatonic metaphysics was as remote from the first followers of Jesus as it now is from us. A. D. Nock is quoted: 'The Christian hope has its

roots in Palestine; Christian theology and above all Christology
have theirs in Alexandria' (p. 113).

Secondly, the most famous pictures of Christ in history (in paint
or mosaic or words or ritual) were set against a background which
now seems very dated. For example, Christ was depicted as an
emperor surrounded by the Byzantine court; Don Cupitt has an
iconoclastic essay on this. Within the New Testament there is talk
about Christ as the Divine Man descending from heaven to mediate between heaven and earth and to redeem a darkened mankind.
Such talk is strange to us, but was already familiar to the pagan
world to which it was first addressed.

Finally, in the nineteenth and twentieth centuries Christians
have evangelised the world as never before. Their gospel has been
that Christ is the world's only Saviour because the only incarnation
of God. They have presented Christianity as 'the true religion'
because the revelation in Christ was final. They have failed to
appreciate the spiritual wealth in traditions such as India's, venerable before Jesus was preached or born – whereas the fact is that
the demands and promises of God have been focused to non-
Christians through many non-Christian lenses.

So the essayists challenge their readers to be frank about what it
means to treat Jesus as a man of the first century AD; about what
ought to be said in his honour in modern thoughts, phrases and
pictures; and about his proper place in a world which has known
many saviours and revealers. They can use the word 'myth' because the word has a theological meaning altogether more polite
than its colloquial use. 'Myth' is, Wiles points out, a word less than
150 years old (p. 149). Hick uses it in the following sense: 'a myth is
a story which is told but which is not literally true, or an idea or
image which is applied to someone or something but which does
not literally apply, but which invites a particular attitude in its
hearers' (p. 178).

The book can proceed to speak of 'the myth of the incarnation'
because 'incarnation' is also a word with a technical theological
meaning. The word need not refer to the basic Christian claim that
God was present and active in the life of Jesus Christ. It can refer to
the much more developed Christology defined by the councils of
the Church in the age of the Fathers. To say that the incarnation is
'mythological' can be merely to say that these councils and the
Fathers behind them spoke in a way which cannot be ours unless
we simply repeat their orthodoxy parrot-fashion. But it was not the
biblical way either. Thus Maurice Wiles: 'Incarnation, in its full

and proper sense, is not something directly presented in scripture' (p. 3). So defined, the book's title and contents lose most of their offensiveness for those who are familiar and patient with theologians' habits.

By driving some sharp questions home, the book would disturb dogmatic slumbers. If there be anyone willing to study contemporary theology who is unaware, the book will make him or her aware. However, such a reader might be regarded as a mythological creature, for it would appear impossible that anyone capable of understanding this book has not already come face to face with the main problems of twentieth-century theology. Thus the book has much the same value as would be possessed by seven economists' essays written in 1977 to suggest that we really must do something about inflation. Books where these questions are openly discussed constitute a large section of the stock of any up-to-date theological bookseller. It is therefore disappointing that this book contains no essay where these recent attempts at restating Christology are treated with the scholarship they deserve. Instead, the essayists write sometimes as if they had just discovered the questions – like a passenger discovering the Pacific from the window of a jet.

Sometimes they write as if a few flip generalisations should be enough to persuade the reader not to bother with earlier attempts. Even Professor Hick, whose own previous writing has been very valuable, does not indicate how widespread and how deep has been the discussion about Jesus Christ in relation to non-Christian religions. Nor does the book explore the significance of recent attempts at popular reinterpretations of Jesus. There is no full treatment of 'liberation theology', which always involves a special Christology about Jesus the Liberator – although the literature on that mainly Latin American movement is already substantial. There is no study of the pop Christology so conspicuous in the Western world – although *Jesus Christ Superstar* has been one of the most successful shows of the 1970s. And many other silences speak more loudly about the essayists than about their great subject.

One appreciates that space was limited. But space has been found for historical essays by two of Professor Hick's colleagues at the University of Birmingham. Michael Goulder contributes a largely speculative study of the alleged Samaritan origins of Christological beliefs previously thought to have a Gentile Gnostic background. 'Paul', he tells us, 'appropriated the idea of Jesus'

incarnation in the course of dialectic with the Samaritan missionaries in Corinth and Ephesus between 50 and 55' (p. 79). Frances
Young's two essays are equally learned and much more reliably
historical, but for that very reason do not reach original
conclusions.

What is most needed at this stage of the discussion is not more
pleading that the questions need to be faced, but more careful
consideration of the work of those who have actually faced them,
both at the academic and at the popular levels. If this book had
included an adequate treatment of contemporary theology or
evangelism, it is unlikely that the editor would have written as he
now does in his Preface. There he sums up the main contrast as
being between 'a recognition that Jesus was . . . "a man approved
by God" for a special role within the divine purpose' (quoting Acts
2:22) and 'the later conception of him as God incarnate, the
Second Person of the Trinity living a human life' (p. ix).

No! The main contrast, surely, has been between two more
profoundly different groups. There are those who have taken the
quotation from Acts as meaning no more than that Jesus was a
prophet or leader not unlike Muhammad or Gandhi or Mao. And
there are those who have been compelled by their own experience
of his continuing power to say that his human life is the supreme
expression of God's own self, the embodiment of God's own love –
of course 'limited only by the receptive capacity of human nature'
(E. L. Mascall, quoted on p. 5). In the first group are the Unitarians, the Jews, the Muslims and many Hindus, not to mention
other theists who revere Jesus. In the second camp are the
Christians.

If this book had explored the meaning of the uniqueness of Jesus
in recent discussion, the essay by Frances Young would not have
been left unrevised. She claims that 'Jesus cannot be a *real* man and
also unique in a sense different from that in which each one of us is
a unique individual' (p. 32), and she adds for good measure (in a
note) that 'each man is potentially "God incarnate"' (p. 47). But
recent discussion has only served to show once again that, among
all the individuals in history, Jesus of Nazareth was and is solitary
in his claims, in his character and in his work – work which now
embraces nineteen centuries and all the continents. To list other
saviours and revealers is, in the end, to show that Jesus still stands
alone. Every man ever born, and every woman too, may be
potentially God incarnate. Or so Frances Young believes. It is
theoretically possible, and her experience of Birmingham is

enviable if it has suggested the theory to her. What we do know is that no one about whom we have any evidence has realised that potential in a way at all similar to the Man after whom Christianity is named.

While Christians have much to learn, they have no reason to forget that their Lord remains utterly unique. And they have no reason to cease to adore him as the Word, Image, Act or Son of the Father, now in flesh appearing.

Review of *Incarnation and Myth: The Debate Continued* edited by Michael Goulder (1979)

The British sales of *The Myth of God Incarnate* reached twenty-four thousand within eight months – a figure which shows that the British public is not quite so indifferent to basic questions about the truth of Christianity as is often supposed. And now most of the contributors have published a volume of reconsiderations, jointly with some of their most powerful critics – an action which shows that theologians are not quite so arrogant as is often believed. The volume is a carefully edited assembly of papers read at a private conference held in Birmingham last July. The chairman of that gathering, Professor Basil Mitchell of Oxford, although inclining towards the traditionalists, adds a fair assessment. 'If one thing emerged from our discussions', he observes, 'it is that the problems which confront contemporary Christian theologians are of enormous difficulty and complexity' (p. 240).

At times the confrontation of traditionalists versus radicals seems like a seven-a-side rugger match. Professor Wiles points to an either/or when he looks forward to the day when 'the view that Jesus is to be identified with God is replaced by one in which he symbolises and expresses God's action towards the world' (p. 7). But actually the whole drift of the argument is away from confrontation towards agreement to tackle the positive task of reconstructing Christology – a task which is, however, not tackled here.

The traditionalists either make, or are quoted as making, some very significant points about the difficulty and complexity lying just beneath the surface of the assertion that 'Jesus is to be identified with God.' When one thinks about it, one sees that it cannot be *literally* true that the man who walked in Galilee and died on Calvary simply equalled the infinite, eternal Creator of the universe. And of course the official theology of the Church has never taught that this was 'literally' true; hence the need of trinitarian doctrine. Professor Nicholas Lash rightly refuses to say 'yes' to the crude question, 'Is Jesus God?' – preferring instead (p. 41) a formula such as 'Jesus is the word of God incarnate.' Inevitably to talk about the presence of God in Christ is to talk about a mystery. At one stage Brian Hebblethwaite, the most definite Defender of the Faith among these essayists, claims that the incarnation is 'literally' true; but it turns out that 'literally' has a special meaning for him, since he recognises that talk about God in Christ must use analogies (pp. 27–8). He says that 'the popular Christmas carols will ensure that Chalcedonian orthodoxy will be remembered long after *The Myth* is forgotten' (p. 95) – whereas the whole point is that the carols are poetry, not philosophy. Bernard Lonergan is quoted as saying that even the use of a term such as (in translation) 'substance' in the classic definitions of the incarnation such as Chalcedon's is 'metaphorical' (p. 26). More than one contributor alludes to the insistence of Ian Ramsey that all talk of this kind legitimately includes an element of 'paradox' (pp. 52, 61). And surely the metaphors and paradoxes of poems are the best way of voicing the Christian response to this mystery.

There is also a strong insistence running through many of the essays that the incarnation is not to be isolated from the rest of God's activity, any more than the Christmas carols are isolated from the general festivities. Such isolation, says Moule, is 'nowhere to be found in the New Testament'. Nor is it the Catholic view, adds Wiles; God has spoken to us through mystical experience, ethical concern and human love. Hebblethwaite gladly grants Christianity does not, according to these essayists, teach that the incarnation or atonement changed the attitude of God towards mankind; here, too, Moule insists that such a doctrine is not to be found within the New Testament. And the unchanging God of Christianity is the universal God. John Taylor, Bishop of Winchester, is quoted as saying: 'We believe now that the Ultimate Reality upon which the faith of all believers is focussed in every religion is the same . . .' (p. 193).

There is, too, on many of these pages a frank admission that a developed trinitarianism is not to be found in the Bible. Instead various Christologies are experimented with, none systematically. As Professor Stanton demonstrates, in Paul's thought there is no speculation or emphasis on Christ's pre-existence. His concern is with the saving activity of God. So the Bible need not be

completely abandoned if we find the Greek philosophy of
Chalcedon hopelessly dated or the much earlier idea of Christ's
pre-existence before birth incredible. What matters for us, too, is
God's saving act.

However, the radicals are brought up against some sharp challenges, and in many places (not, alas, all) they seem to be taking
those challenges seriously. For it is not enough to say that Jesus
'symbolises and expresses God's action towards the world' – unless
one adds 'uniquely'. Jesus did not snatch at equality with God; yet
his name is above all other names.

Professor Stanton concludes that for Paul 'Jesus stood in the
closest possible relationship to God' (p. 157). Professor Moule says
plainly that, although Jesus did not go about saying 'I am God's
Son', we find in the synoptic gospels the quietly assumed and
exhibited presence of God's sovereignty where Jesus was. So 'the
impact made by Jesus on his own and the next generation is such as
precludes an estimate of him as no more than a man' (p. 149).
Many men have symbolised and expressed God's action, but there
has been only one Jesus.

In Greek *kurios* (Lord), used about God in the Old Testament,
is used about Jesus in the New. And Moule asks: 'Is it the function
of a merely human person to bestow life? Is creation a normal
human function? Or the bestowal of Spirit?' (p. 149). He shows
that for the early Christians life was life 'in Christ' although the
Christ spoken of was also a recent man in history; and prayer was
prayer 'through Christ', not merely following a dead man's example. The celebration of God's saving act in Christ necessarily
involves the adoration of Christ himself. Thus the radically reduced Christology of Don Cupitt is rejected as being unable to
cover the Christian experience of Christ. Bishop Lesslie Newbigin
moves into the attack out of his long experience in India. He asserts
that Cupitt's insistence that God cannot either intervene or suffer
(to use necessary analogies with human experience) arises out of a
definitely BC understanding of God. He adds for good measure that
the presentation of Jesus as 'an example of the god-filled life' is
Hindu.

The Christian experience of God through Christ was from the
beginning, and always has been, revolutionary. Since this is the
experience which Christian theologians have to interpret, Professor Lash's complaint is that 'the authors of *The Myth* are not
sufficiently puzzled' (p. 25)! He leads one to hope that the debate,
if pursued at this appropriate level in England as it is already being

pursued elsewhere, will persuade many radicals to be more humble before the experience of God in Christ which the Christian tradition has enshrined. Probably the now urgent reconstruction of Christology will move away from unnecessarily large claims that in the incarnation God's activity comes to a 'complete and perfect' expression when God is 'totally and absolutely' incarnate. (I quote Professor Moule.) Do we not need to be more cautious, more carefully trinitarian, more conscious that the full revelation is not yet? But an approach to a possible Christology for our times is indicated in Bishop Newbigin's creed: 'The life, death and resurrection of Jesus are, I believe, the decisive events in God's history with his creation' (p. 206). That approach avoids Greek metaphysics. But it does not cut the heart out of the Church's religion.

Review of *The Human Face of God* by John A. T. Robinson (1973)

It is now ten years since *Honest to God* was published, and Dr John Robinson has celebrated by putting into print, after much expansion, the Hulsean Lectures which he delivered at Cambridge in 1970. 'For ten years now', he writes in his Preface, 'I have promised myself that my next book would be on Christology, or the person of Christ' (p. vii). In the event, this latest book is his longest – which is not to say that it is a thoroughly great book.

Robinson recalls that 'in the same letter of April 30, 1944, Bonhoeffer bequeathed to us two searching questions: "How do we speak in a secular way about God?" and "Who is Christ for us today?"' If during the past thirty years, and particularly during the past ten, Christian theologians have gone a long way towards answering these questions (and such is the case), no small part of this achievement is due to the creative stimulus and to the serious suggestions to be found in Robinson's many writings. His new book presents Jesus as a real man in real history, yet also as the man whose life discloses ultimate reality. This is an achievement all the more important because there are still millions, including the young, fascinated by Jesus yet puzzled by who he is and what he means. Robinson calls it, in necessary paradoxes, the 'uniquely normal' humanity, the humanity that points 'Beyond'. And he quotes from Austin Farrer: 'the Man who lived God' (p. 185).

The picture of Jesus Christ which one gathers from a number of New Testament passages and from almost all the Fathers of the Church, and which one easily assumes to be the picture to which one must cling if one wishes to be a Christian, is the picture of a divine person descending temporarily from heaven to assume humanity like clothing, without being in the everyday sense a man. Robinson is almost everywhere wise enough not to pour contempt on that picture. For that picture remains a possible presentation or 'projection' of faith in Jesus. Although few would nowadays go so far as St Thomas Aquinas, who taught that 'when he ate and drank, it was a concession not to his necessities but to our habits' (p. 40), the traditional picture, or something like it, is still taken for granted in much of our worship and preaching.

Robinson, is, however, one of the numerous theologians who in our time declare frankly that for them, as well as for many Christians and almost all non-Christians, this picture is now largely unintelligible and has lost almost all its power. Moreover, these theologians demonstrate that another picture is possible, is intelligible, is powerful, and is Christian.

Certainly, the old picture is based on passages in the Bible. Yet Luther, as here quoted (p. 100), wrote: 'The scriptures begin very gently, and lead us on to Christ as to a man, and then to one who is Lord over all creatures, and after that to one who is God.' *In what sense 'a man'?* The historical Jesus was perfect man in two senses: first, he was completely human, and secondly he was perfected through sufferings (as it was put in the Epistle to the Hebrews). He was amazingly free of guilt, yet Mark's picture is of panic in Gethsemane and a sense of dereliction on Calvary. *And in what sense 'God'?* Robinson quotes a recent theologian, the American John Knox, as asking the key questions: 'How could Christ have saved us if he were not a human being like ourselves? How could a human being like ourselves have saved us?' – and as giving the two key answers: 'The divinity of Jesus was the deed of God. The uniqueness of Jesus was the absolute uniqueness of what God did in him' (pp. 89, 211).

Robinson himself thinks of Jesus thus:

that one who was totally and utterly a man – and had never been anything other than a man or more than a man – so completely embodied what was from the beginning the meaning and purpose of God's self-expression (whether conceived in terms of his Spirit, his Wisdom, his Word, or the ultimately personal relationship of Sonship) that it could be said . . . of that man, 'He was God's man', or 'God was in Christ', or even that he *was* 'God for us' (p. 179).

Jesus was the human face of God – but God has other faces. He has other 'modes of being' (which is Karl Barth's way of presenting the doctrine of God as Trinity). And there is a fuller revelation still to come; so the Bible says. Just as the coming of Jesus was no mere 'afterthought' in the mind of God (this may be held to be what lies behind the traditional, indeed biblical, teaching about the pre-existence of Jesus and about his virgin birth), so the glory of Jesus is not isolated but is the clue to the riddles of this bloodstained planet's life, of the inconceivably vast universe, and of God. Jesus, born as a man, is the key to the meaning of all things from the beginning to the end, the 'definite' revelation of God as *Abba*, Father, 'the embodiment of his nature and the enactment of his will' (p. 197).

But one remembers on reading this book why this learned and devout theologian, with a pastoral heart and a tirelessly industrious mind, has exercised for more than ten years the knack of making many of his fellow Christians hopping mad. For he has now written a book which is so scholarly as to make tough going for sensation-seeking non-theologians; yet instead of making an authoritative study of the New Testament, for example, or of the Fathers, he has sacrificed some of his space to matter more glittering than golden. This matter may all too easily distract attention from his deeply serious and deeply Christian teaching. To give only one example, he refers to a 'recently attested' disappearance of the body of a Buddhist holy man, 'so absorbed and transmuted that what is left behind after death is not the hulk of an old corpse but simply nails and hair' (p. 139). If the dematerialisation of a Buddhist can be 'attested', why – many readers will wonder – make such a fuss about passages in the New Testament which appear to contradict science?

Other passages throw out provocative suggestions that passages in the New Testament long supposed to mean one thing really mean another. These passages mostly concern the pre-existence and uniqueness of Jesus, Robinson's tendency being to assert that Jesus regarded himself, and was regarded by the evangelists, as '*a* son' rather than as '*the* Son' of God. Likewise much of his exposition of the origins of Christian doctrine depends on his belief – oddly enough, a 'conservative' belief! – that both the fourth gospel and the Epistle to the Hebrews are earlier in substance, and 'lower' in Christology, than is commonly agreed among the experts.

What is likely to matter far more to many readers of his new book is that some passages in it, particularly in the last chapter, appear to leave behind little but the nails and hair of the essential faith which inspired the New Testament, suggesting that

> . . . the realization is fitfully dawning that 'God' now means, for us, not an invisible being with whom we can have direct communication as it were on the end of a telephone, but *that by which he is represented*, his surrogate – the power of a love that lives and suffers for others . . .
> . . . If men are to believe in God, it can only be 'a-theistically', that is, as he is represented – above all in the irreplaceability of men (pp. 218–19).

What Easter Day showed is that

> the representative of God, the Christ, is not confined to the individual body of Jesus . . . The Christ lives on – in the lives of those who represent now the human face of God (p. 215).

So Robinson suggests. But to the early Christians God was in one vital sense supernatural. He was the Creator who held Abraham, Isaac and Jacob in eternal life, and who supremely had raised Jesus from the dead. Therefore he could be prayed to in love and joy. And Jesus was in one vital sense superhuman. Although the Church was his 'body', although the poor were his 'brothers', he was in his own glory, glimpsed in the Easter experiences; and, when the early Christians said that 'the Christ lives on', they were not thinking only, or mainly, about themselves or their neighbours. Some passages in Robinson's book if taken by themselves would suggest a religion of humanity connected with a dead teacher – a religion somewhat like Buddhism in its early days (with a new consciousness or godless bliss to be attained along a way pointed out by the Buddha). Coming from an interpreter of the New Testament, such passages show a failure of nerve.

Yet essentially this is a book by one thoughtful Christian for others. Its heart, which is a heart full of reasonable faith, deserves to be taken very seriously and very gratefully.

Review of *God as Spirit* by G. W. H. Lampe (1977)

On the face of it this new book, based on the Bampton Lectures delivered at Oxford in 1976 by the Regius Professor of Divinity in the University of Cambridge, may seem just one more negative onslaught against the Church's traditional teaching. But anyone who has the patience to take more than one look at it will see that it adds to the virtues of the radicals – seriousness about great matters, integrity in seeking and speaking the truth, the courage to innovate – the virtues of the conservatives. Here we find a humble sense of the power of Christian experience, a wish to help Christians to find a theology worthy of this power, an intimate knowledge and love of the Bible.

It may seem that the Cambridge professor has deserted the radicals with whom he has been identified. Lampe shows on his last page that he expects this reaction: 'Some will complain that . . . I have been more conservative than the present state of critical, historical, sociological, and religious studies warrants, particularly in my emphasis on the centrality and decisiveness of the action of God in Jesus' (p. 228). But he has not lost the teeth with which he has bitten Catholics and Evangelicals in various recent controversies in the Church of England. He does not think that the traditional trinitarian and Christological doctrines with their talk of persons, natures, wills and substance are satisfactory or, indeed, meaningful today. He does not think it probable that the tomb of Jesus was empty, and does not reckon that it matters decisively.

He attacks the notion, dear to Anglican Catholics (at least in the past), that episcopal confirmation 'gives' the Holy Spirit; he puts all the emphasis on baptism. He criticises many Catholics' understanding of the Eucharist when he writes: 'the reality which faith receives in the sacrament is the indwelling presence of God as Spirit' (p. 167). He also rejects the traditional Evangelical interpretation of the atonement as a sacrifice to appease the wrath of the angry Father, and the traditional Evangelical stress that only in Christ is God known. He has no patience with a fundamentalist view of the Scriptures, and more sympathy than respect for the spectacular manifestations of Pentecostalism. Beyond doubt he is a radical.

However, having demolished so many of the old ways of believing in God through Christ, he does not leave it at that, as has been the custom with all too many of his fellow radicals. 'The foundation of Christology', he writes, 'is the conviction that in Jesus God himself has acted. He has not addressed men from the far side of the gulf which divides Creator from creatures and urged them to repent. Through Jesus he has done for men that which they could not do for themselves' (p. 14). That is Lampe's foundation, too. Like Professor Peter Baelz, whom he quotes, he sees in Christ 'the ground for trusting and hoping in God, the example of trusting and hoping in God, and the source of inspiration and power to trust and hope in God' (p. 14).

The problem he faces is that he does not find the early Fathers' and councils' expositions of this foundation-fact helpful. It is not that he is ignorant of the Fathers; among his earlier publications was the massively learned *Patristic Greek Lexicon*. Nor does he wish to deny the incarnation; he writes of the 'real presence' of God in Christ. But he wants to put things another way. To him the incarnation is 'union between God and man at the personal level. This implies a union of will and a union of mind, a union in which the characteristic qualities of divine activity, above all self-sacrificing, compassionate, love, find expression in a human personality without derogating from its human freedom' (p. 12).

This exposition of the incarnation gets away from the ancient controversies, which Lampe (an expert in them) thinks led to dead ends. The theological model of God the Son 'almost inevitably tends to suggest either that deity revealed in human terms in Jesus is somehow other than God whom we conceive of as Father, or that God whom we acknowledge in Jesus was united in him with something less than a fully human personality' (p. 13). Instead of this 'model' of God the Son, Lampe prefers to interpret the incarnation in terms of the presence and activity in a human spirit of God as Spirit. By a 'human spirit' he means not a mere ghost but 'man as a rational, feeling, willing, personality endowed with insight, wisdom and moral sensitivity, capable of responding to God' – and by 'God as Spirit' he points not to a vague Something but to the living God of the Bible.

So he deliberately escapes from the Neoplatonic metaphysics used in the Athanasian Creed and other formulae of the faith, back into the world of the Bible where men and women were not Greek philosophers but Hebrews overwhelmed by God's actions for, among and in living people. But he also escapes from the Unitarian reduction of Jesus to the level of other great servants and prophets of God. To him, Jesus is 'God's self-revelation, no longer dimmed and distorted, as in other men, by the opaqueness of sin in the mirror which reflects and communicates it' (p. 24).

Obviously Lampe has not said the last word. My own view is that the account given of Jesus by the gospels can be fitted into this framework, but I do not think he does justice to Christian experience of Jesus after Easter – the experience which has seemed to demand the trinitarian way of talking about God's self-revelation.

He speaks of Christians experiencing 'God, the Spirit who was in Jesus'. But, like many another attempt to cut the knots in Christology, this is not fully true to life. It is true that the New Testament refuses to distinguish sharply between 'Spirit' and 'Christ' when referring to the eternal reality in which the Church even now lives; and it is true that the 'Christ' known by the saints is more than the rabbi from Nazareth. But still the Christian insists that 'Jesus is alive today' – personally, in eternal glory, but also still as the Lord with power to teach, heal and save. If the Christian is entitled to think this about Jesus, the Christian is entitled to say 'Jesus is Lord' with a passionately personal devotion. It is not enough to say with Lampe, who quotes the musical *Godspell*: 'Long live God!' (p. 155).

Review of *The Christian Experience of God as Trinity* by James P. Mackey (1983)

What sort of a life would best equip a man to write basic theology in the 1980s? I suggest that pretty well the ideal background would be as follows: a Roman Catholic priest decides that the intellectual obligations of that particular ministry are incompatible with his immense and growing stock of knowledge and independent thought, and therefore becomes a layman while remaining very much a Catholic Christian; a professor migrates from a famous campus in America to teach in the University of Edinburgh; a scholar deeply versed in biblical criticism becomes willing to tackle doctrinal questions with a profundity which involves some technical discussion, but insists on writing in a style which is readable, humane, even sometimes humorous; a man thoroughly aware of radical Christian and non-Christian attacks on the old orthodox statements of the faith is nevertheless determined to offer a reconstruction of doctrine which does justice to the intentions of the Fathers of the Church.

Ah, you say, that is a pipe-dream. Such a man exists, however – and he has written this splendidly positive book as a sequel to his *Jesus the Man and the Myth* (1979), which was rightly acclaimed as a judicious summary for Roman Catholics and others of the whole modern scholarly debate about the man from Nazareth.

Dr Mackey knows that the doctrine of the Trinity has often embarrassed those who would commend the gospel to the twentieth century. The adherents of other religions think that it worships three gods, one being a man (an operation which the Christian Church performs happily while largely ignoring that man's moral teaching). The atheists or agnostics who abound in the countries which once were Christendom regard this doctrine as the most notorious example of talkative Christianity's habit of trivialising the mystery which surrounds human existence; there is an atheism for God's sake. Even devout Christians have an attitude described by our author in a sentence to be relished:

> To the reflective Christian mind . . . it can be at best a mystery too soon, an intellectual obstacle on the obstacle course to heaven to be taken in stride with as little thought as possible; at worst, an intellectual conundrum comprising some strange celestial mathematics, some very abstruse philosophical concepts, and some theological reasoning that is, for most people, too clever by half (p. 3).

He goes back to the experience reflected in the New Testament in order to show that the early Christians did not lightly take a God-fearing Jew and make him into a new religion. No, if the Christian Scriptures are read without the trinitarian spectacles provided by a different century, we see that Emil Brunner was substantially right to put it like this: 'If the Name "Father" designates the origin and content of the revelation, the Name of the "Son" designates the historic Mediator, and the "Holy Spirit" the present reality of this revelation' (p. 41). This three-foldness in the Christian experience of God was what gave rise to the later doctrine when the Church had the leisure to indulge in metaphysics.

Basically Mackey wants Christian doctrine to be 'as it was in the beginning' – very firmly rejecting any tendency to add 'one or two more pre-existent divine beings to the one God who is worshipped in all three great monotheistic religions of the West' (p. 251). He is one of many contemporary theologians to regret the phrase 'three persons', if 'person' is understood in its modern meaning. 'Certainly,' he writes, 'it must be conceded that the answer to the questions, "Is Jesus divine?", and "Is the body of Christ, the eucharist[ic] community, divine?", is yes and no. But this is the absolutely orthodox answer' (p. 244). Always in the old orthodoxy the humanity of Jesus was affirmed along with the enfleshment of the Word, while the humanity of the Church has seldom required any emphasis. But the divine power at work in these known realities can be experienced. In demonstrating that the models used in the New Testament's Christologies were taken from non-Christian sources Mackey covers much of the ground of the essays in *The Myth of God Incarnate*, but he does so more deeply and satisfyingly, with a far more constructive conclusion. The incarnation of the pre-existent Son is, he thinks, a myth, once a very effective one; but the incarnation of God in Jesus the man is *not* a 'myth' in any denigratory sense.

Mackey's conclusion is, indeed, much the same as that of G. W. H. Lampe's masterpiece, *God as Spirit* – but his presentation does more justice to the Christian experience of the living Lord and the living community. Like Lampe, he knows well the philosophical background to the creeds called Nicene and Athanasian – and he agrees that, within the terms of that now-vanished background, the Church was right to reject the Arian idea of a semi-divine, pre-existent but created Son. True divinity is encountered in the man Jesus, and it is glimpsed in the Eucharist. Supremely it is seen in the love which took Jesus to his death.

Why Orthodoxy Needs Revision

Leonard Hodgson, an Oxford theologian, wrote in 1950: 'Religious creeds are concerned with the most profound, indeed the ultimate, mysteries, with problems concerning which only a fool or a knave could claim to have knowledge . . .' Archbishop William Temple, who died in 1944, wrote: 'To admit acrimony in theological discussion is in itself more fundamentally heretical than any erroneous opinions upheld or condemned in the course of the discussion.' In his posthumously published *Explorations in Theology* (1981), Geoffrey Lampe quoted both sayings with emphatic approval (pp. 5, 13), and I remind myself of them as I offer some reflections after a debate marked by courage in confessing ignorance.

We must start with the man Jesus. 'It may safely be said that practically all schools of theological thought to-day take the full humanity of our Lord more seriously than has ever been done before by Christian theologians.' So Donald Baillie recorded in a book which has become a modern classic (*God Was in Christ*, 1956, p. 11). This development in the tradition has (at least in my view) satisfactorily answered many objections to its ancient formulations. The belief that Jesus was born of a virgin and had no human father has been widely seen as separate from the belief that he was God the Son incarnate, so that it is possible to affirm the second, far more important, belief while being agnostic or sceptical about the history of the virgin birth – as many thoughtful Christians now are. The belief that the fourth gospel consists largely of the very words of Jesus, revealing his own understanding of himself, has been abandoned by most people who have really studied the differences between it and the other three gospels, and most people who have carefully read the other three while trying to exclude memories of the rest of the New Testament have seen how enigmatic Jesus is reported to have been about status. He seems to have called himself not 'God' or even 'Messiah' but 'Son of Man', which in different contexts may refer to the man who according to Jewish belief is to be vindicated by God as the representative of 'the saints of the Most High' (Dan. 7:13–14, 18) or may mean merely 'a man'. So it is much harder now to use the old argument that 'Jesus claimed to be God, therefore he was God or bad or mad.'

Nowadays it is seldom maintained by thoughtful Christians that Jesus was infallible about matters such as the authorship of Old Testament books or the diagnosis of diseases. Nor is it believed that there was a divine bit of him that did miracles and was exempt from suffering. He was not omniscient (all-knowing) or omnipotent (all-powerful). He was a man in every sense. He did not pretend to be, or seem to be ('docetism'); he was. This means that it is no solution to the Christological problem to say that the person of the Father lived in the life of Jesus, excluding any human personality ('monarchian modalism'). Nor is it a solution to adopt the fourth-century orthodoxy that the humanity assumed by the Son was 'impersonal', modernised by E. L. Mascall (*Theology and the Gospel of Christ*, 1977) to say that 'in Jesus there is no human ego'. Both solutions are incompatible with the completely certain truth that Jesus was completely human. If we ask why anyone ever thought that Jesus could be human without being a person, we have to remember with Maurice Wiles 'the Platonic approach, according to which humanity as such is a more fundamental and more real concept than individual man' (*Working Papers in Doctrine*, p. 45). I think that when he came to express his own opinion Wiles was perfectly right to say that Jesus, 'like every other human person, was a product of the evolutionary process, one whose particular characteristics were substantially affected by his heredity and environment with all the attendant limitations of psychology and knowledge'. Wiles also reminds us that the recognition of the full humanity of Jesus

> implies also ascribing to him that same genuine freedom which is constitutive of our existence as human persons. Affirmations of that kind are to be found in the writings of many who seek to maintain a highly traditional understanding of the incarnation as well as of people who advocate some substantial revision of it (*God's Action in the World*, p. 87).

Christians feel driven to try to relate the man from Nazareth to nature's Creator, as well as to human nature, because in what he does or is divinity seems to be displayed or implied. Günther Bornkamm summed many things up when he wrote in his *Jesus of Nazareth* (1960) that 'to make the reality of God present: that is the essential mystery of Jesus' (p. 62). Another German scholar, Ernst Fuchs, provided another summary: 'his conduct is neither that of a prophet nor of a teacher of wisdom, but of a man who dares to act in God's stead' (*Studies of the Historical Jesus*, 1964, p. 22). And a third, Wolfhart Pannenberg, has worked out what is called a 'Christology from below', with its basis in history and experience, particularly experience of the risen Lord. Such a Christology does not begin with the question 'How has the Second Person of the Trinity assumed a human nature?' It is faith which, 'rising from the historical man Jesus to the recognition of his divinity, is concerned first of all with Jesus' message and fate and arrives only at the end of the concept of the incarnation' – at the faith that 'Jesus was what he is before he knew about it' (*Jesus – God and Man*, 1968, pp. 33, 141). In *The Myth of God Incarnate* Frances Young echoed the general scholarly agreement that 'some pretty far-reaching claims' are implicit when the gospels 'correctly report' the message of Jesus: 'his healings display the forgiveness of God, his teaching is the word of God, the judgement of God can be seen in the way people reject or respond to him' (p. 17). And her own conviction was that 'Jesus "stands for" God and is the focus through which God is revealed to those who respond' (p. 22).

However, it does not necessarily follow that the language used about Jesus by the Fathers of the Church, or by its councils in the fourth, fifth and sixth centuries, is authoritative, or even meaningful, for us today. Although I would hesitate to say with John Hick that the Chalcedonian Definition of Christ agreed in 451 is 'a form of words without assignable meaning' (p. 178), I am deeply impressed by the fact that scholars such as Wiles and Lampe, who are experts on the work of the Fathers and the councils, and have given much of their lives to acquiring that expertise, find so little that is permanently significant or intelligible in the Chalcedonian Definition. Nor are these scholars being perversely English in believing that orthodoxy needs revision – as may be seen from, for example, Alister McGrath's *The Making of Modern German Christology* (1986), a book by a scholar who is certainly not a radical. It will not do for defenders of the Definition simply to be shocked that, as E. L. Mascall complained, 'in 1976 the Regius Professors of Divinity in the two ancient English universities, both being priests of the Church of England, declared explicitly their inability to believe in the Trinity . . . [All] that our leading Anglican unitarians have to offer us . . . is one third of the Church's God and one half of the Church's Christ' (*Whatever Happened to the Human Mind?*, 1980, pp. 98, 127). The Church's God and the Church's Christ need not be presented in the language of an antiquated mythology or philosophy. When this tragedy occurs, the reaction of Immanuel Kant is inevitable: 'The doctrine of the Trinity provides nothing, absolutely nothing, of practical value, even if one claims to understand it.'

Traditional language about God the Son coming down to earth from heaven as Redeemer needs to be recognised as 'mythological' in the sense of being a poetic attempt to express the belief that 'God was in Christ'. God cannot have needed to come 'down' in order to reach earth like an astronaut at the end of a voyage in space; logically, although not imaginatively, one might equally well speak of him coming 'up' from the depths. An expedition of that sort cannot have been necessary in order to put right a fall understood literally as Adam's fall from immortality and perfection through disobedience, for we know that the story of Adam, Eve and the snake was a Hebrew myth. And the Father cannot have refused to forgive the sins of humanity unless a price ('redemption') was paid to him in the shape of the sacrifice of the perfect Son, for such a theory is contrary to the teaching of Jesus about the Father's ever-ready forgiveness and also contrary to our own conviction that God, if he exists, cannot be morally inferior to human parents. And another point stressed by Wiles in criticism of the Church's Fathers is obviously correct, I think. He makes the point that (despite the claims of Athanasius and other Fathers) human nature need not be 'assumed' by a divine person if humanity is to be 'healed' or 'saved'. Many other possible ways for

God to heal or save effectively may be experienced or imagined. Some are set forth in the gospels.

Radically critical scholars such as Wiles and Lampe are among the Christians who are glad that the Catholic Church rejected the Arian view of Christ at the Council of Nicaea. By a coincidence 1988 saw the publication of two major works of English scholarship which did justice to Arius yet reached the same conclusion (*Arius: Heresy and Tradition* by Rowan Williams and *The Search for the Christian Doctrine of God* by R. P. C. Hanson). Arius took the references in the Old Testament to the Wisdom of God being created, and the references in the New Testament to the Son being subordinate to the Father, to mean that the Word of God, a being who was also Wisdom and Son, was a subordinate creature. It had not been necessary for him to exist; 'there was when he was not'. For the debate about Christology in the time of Arius, that denial meant that Christians could not fully encounter God in Christ: all that they could meet was a creature. But the pity was that the development of an orthodox Christology after this correct rejection of Arianism led the Catholic Church to enforce the use of what cannot be more than the paradoxes of poetry, saying that the Son was 'begotten' by the Father before time was, whereas the Spirit only 'proceeded' from the Father. And the anti-Arian development after Nicaea led the Fathers and the councils into dogmatic propositions which to many other thoughtful Christians in our own time seem meaningless or dangerous. It became the tendency of the theologians in the tradition of Antioch (most famously Nestorius) to deny the full divinity of God in Christ – and it became the tendency of the theologians in the tradition of Alexandria (most famously Apollinarius) to deny Christ's full humanity. When divine and human 'natures' and 'wills' were said to be united in one 'person' – 'without confusion, change, division or separation', it was said by the Council of Chalcedon in 451 – new meanings had to be given to all the Greek or Latin words behind these English terms, and still it was extremely difficult, if not impossible, to specify how the unity of the person of Christ was secured. Our modern understanding of personality has made it even more difficult to see how a man not believed to have suffered from the mental illness of schizophrenia could have had two 'wills' or a further 'nature' apparently parallel to his human nature. Traditionally it was said that the miracles of Jesus showed his divine nature, but such a distinction between humanity and divinity when reflecting on his life seems unnecessary. Many of the miracles were deeds other men could do: he is reported to have said so himself. And in the most human and most public sign of his life, his dying, he most clearly showed God's love in action. Indeed, a traditionalist such as Brian Hebblethwaite, who defends the doctrine of 'two consciousnesses' coexisting in 'God incarnate', also defends the traditional doctrine of the *communicatio idiomatum*, 'whereby the predicates appropriate to divinity and humanity may be properly applied to each nature in the hypostatic union which constitutes the Incarnation' (*The Incarnation*, 1987, p. 164). This makes it difficult to say what is the difference for practical purposes between the two wills, natures or consciousnesses said to be united in Jesus.

It is yet more difficult for those who affirm the unity of God (monotheists) to say how God the Son was a 'person' before the human life of Jesus began or how the Spirit is eternally a 'person'. When this language was developed in the fourth century by the three friends later called the Cappadocian Fathers, they passionately insisted that they were not talking about three gods. And it is certainly fair to emphasise that when they used the Greek word *hypostasis* they were not responsible for the misleading suggestions which followed its translation into Latin as *persona*. A *hypostasis* was not a separate, self-sufficient 'person'. It was an expression of *ousia* or 'substance' or 'being'; as Wiles has said, 'within a fully Platonist framework any individual concretion of *ousia* must necessarily have a lesser degree of reality than the *ousia* itself' (*The Making of Christian Doctrine*, p. 133). This was the background even when it was insisted that Father, Son and Spirit were equally of the divine *ousia*. The insistence on the unity of God could also be expressed by saying that only the Father was the 'source' or 'fount' of divinity, the Son and the Spirit being somewhat like the Father's two hands. But if the word 'person' is understood in anything like the famous definition of Boethius ('an individual substance of a rational nature') or in a modern way (such as 'a centre of consciousness'), the development of the Cappadocian Fathers' concept of God becomes tritheistic; for then 'three persons' means three gods. So Lampe concluded after long reflection (*God as Spirit*, pp. 136, 227) – I think, unanswerably, for it is not a good enough answer to say that tritheism was never intended. Lampe rightly regretted that the warning given by some theologians while orthodoxy was in the making against the dangers in the use of the term 'Son' was 'so lightly rejected' (p. 139). Although the communion (*perichoresis*) of the divine 'persons' is meant by orthodoxy to be much more, it proved very tempting for advocates of what is called 'the social Trinity' to think of the Father and the Son as holding an eternal conversation like two people – often with the Spirit as a third partner, or as the conversation itself, having to be called a 'person' because the Father and the Son were so called. I am not sure that this danger is altogether avoided in the two most able recent expositions of the doctrine of the 'social' Trinity, *The Trinity and the Kingdom of God* by Jürgen Moltmann (1981) and *Trinity and Society* by Leonardo Boff (1988).

It is also very difficult to see why the uniqueness of Jesus Christ, or of Christian experience of the Holy Spirit, means that the *eternal* being of the divinity experienced in the work of Christ or of the Spirit must be distinguished from the *eternal* being of God the Father. The gospels tell us about Jesus as a man who prayed to the Father amid real temptations, and it is generally agreed by scholars that, despite some passages in the fourth gospel, it is inconceivable that the historical Jesus believed that he was himself divine. The rest of the New Testament tells us about men and women who prayed to the Father in the power of the Spirit. Paul interprets the experience to the Romans (in his chapter 8, the peak of his theology) as the activity of the Spirit at prayer in them; 'through our inarticulate groans the Spirit himself is pleading for us' (Rom. 8:26). But it remains obvious that prayer, however completely inspired by God, has always been a human activity. It is dangerous to move far beyond the prayer of Jesus and the prayer of the early Christians into speculation about an eternal conversation between Father, Son and Spirit. The Spirit enables us to cry 'Father!' in prayer, but it does not follow that we can know what the Spirit as another 'person' says to the Father in heaven. And it is particularly dangerous to argue that unless we can know that there are these eternal relationships of love between the three eternal persons God cannot be called 'love' – for to say that is to say something that no Christian would wish to say. It is to say that the New Testament writers, and Jesus himself, who were not trinitarians in the sense now traditional, had no adequate reason to call God loving.

Recognising these dangers in talk about three persons, distinguished modern theologians have preferred to think of the Trinity as three 'modes of being' or 'of coming to be' (Karl Barth) or 'distinct manners of subsistence' (Karl Rahner). But even such phrases have their own dangers. In so far as they refer to mysteries beyond the reach of human experience, and therefore beyond the reach of human understanding, they may suggest that we know more than we do. As James Mackey points out, 'unless we can truly differentiate three distinct "modes of being" from each other and from one "something" which is not a mode of being, we shall have no warrant for using the formula at all' (*The Christian Experience of God as Trinity*, p. 143). Although there are obvious differences between human experiences of the creation, of Jesus and of the Spirit, we are taking a further step when we speculate about eternal differences within God. And we ought not to exaggerate the differences between the human experiences. It was the traditional, orthodox doctrine that the operations of the three persons of the Holy Trinity were 'undivided' when experienced from outside (*ad extra*) – for the Son and the Spirit were both at work in creation, the Father and the Spirit in sustaining the incarnate life of the Son, the Father and the Son in sending the Spirit, and so forth. And if this warning needs to be remembered when thinking about the Holy Trinity's work on earth, how much more do we need caution when trying to see differences within God's 'essence' or eternal being!

Is it essential to use traditional language about the incarnation because it is essential to Christian faith to say that in Jesus God is personally exposed to evil and suffering, and involved in the human agonies of life and death? Most Christians would agree with all their hearts and minds that God is indeed so exposed and so involved; it is thirty years since I wrote a devotional book called *God's Cross in Our World*. The title 'crucified God', made familiar to recent students of theology as the title of Jürgen Moltmann's great book (translated into English in 1974), was used by Tertullian in the second Christian century. In *The Myth of God Incarnate* Frances Young wrote:

> For me, experience of suffering, sin, decay and 'abnormality' as a constituent part of the world, would make belief in God impossible without a Calvary-centred religious myth. It is only because I can see God entering the darkness of human suffering and evil in his creation, recognizing it for what it really is, meeting it and conquering it, that I can accept a religious view of the world (p. 34).

And multitudes have felt the same, although naturally many Christians who see things in the same way would regret the use of the word 'myth' to refer to the entry of the real God into sufferings such as a crucifixion. But it does not necessarily follow that the activity of God which we have experienced in our experience of Jesus Christ involves the incarnation as traditionally conceived.

Such activity certainly involves God's presence in Christ, but it is equally certain that his presence is spiritual, not physical. God's presence is strongly real, but it is equally certain that when embodied in a man it is limited to a sphere narrower than the totality of his presence in his creation. For example, when we say that God's active presence was real in the dying Jesus – so that the ancient Christian poetic expression about 'the passion of our God' refers to a reality – we cannot mean that the Creator 'literally' or 'completely' died on a cross. What the cross shows is that when trying to think about the Creator in the light of the cross it is not wrong to think that his character includes love which suffers.

Once one absorbs these truths, one sees that a lot of rhetoric about traditional orthodoxy needs to be examined. 'I have no hesitation whatsoever in standing by what I wrote', said Brian Hebblethwaite in *Incarnation and Myth* (p. 28). What he wrote was that 'the human life lived and the death died have been held quite literally to be the human life and death of God himself in one of the modes of his own eternal being . . .' He repeated this position in his collected essays on *The Incarnation* (p. 49). But I submit that this stalwart traditionalist ought to have hesitated before this commitment to the statement that God 'quite literally' lived and died. I suspect that he has still not taken the measure of those who want to confine themselves (so far as is possible in the realm of religion) to facts which living people have experienced. It is disconcerting to find him speculating in his essays whether Christ would have come had there been no fall (yes) or whether he could have been born on another planet (no). The question is insistent: how on earth could you know? Is there, as Hebblethwaite claims, 'all the difference in the world' between what orthodox Christians want to affirm about Christ and what Professor Keith Ward, for example, says when he calls Jesus 'a man in whom the glory of God was manifested fully, and through whom God will bring to himself all who will respond' (p. 157)? Is it 'illogical' to say that 'God is love' unless one is also confident that long before there was a creation to love, God was himself differentiated into a loving 'society of two' (Farrer, quoted on p. 16)? Is it necessary to be sure about God the Son as a mode of God's eternal being before the incarnation?

It seems wiser to be content with the truth that all language, but particularly religious language, is the human use of a series of models, more or less inadequate, in order to talk about what can never be fully described, on the basis of experience which is also incomplete. At the end of his *The Shape of Christology* (1966) Professor John McIntyre wisely wrote that

> if models are the deliverances of imagination, we shall be a little reluctant to claim for them immediately the sanctions of faith. They do not come to us with the authority of Christ himself. They do not impose themselves on us with the dazzling light of truth. They represent our partial insights, our slow advance from a vantage-point. If we assign to them the sanctions of faith, very soon we find ourselves seeking to impose them on our fellows; or we set up the machinery of the Inquisition or its Protestant forms of anathema, which are not without their painful consequences (p. 175).

Who Do We Say He Is?

The language of the Fathers and the councils was not the language of the New Testament. Books by major scholars such as *The Christology of the New Testament* by Oscar Cullmann (1963), *The Foundations of New Testament Christology* by R. H. Fuller (1965), *The Humanity and Divinity of Christ* by John Knox (1967), *The Origin of Christology* by C. F. D. Moule (1977) and *Christology in the Making* by James D. G. Dunn (revised in 1989) are incontrovertible expositions of the fact that the titles given to Jesus in Scripture were taken from the surrounding culture because no other available titles could express the Christians' experience of God in Christ. That fact gives no support to any theory which seeks to look behind the curtain surrounding what human beings can experience. Cullmann wrote robustly:

> Because the first Christians see God's redemptive revelation in Jesus Christ, for them it is his very nature that he can be known only in his work – fundamentally in the central work accomplished in the flesh. Therefore, in the light of the New Testament writers, all mere speculation about his natures is an absurdity. Functional Christology is the only kind which exists (p. 326).

Wiles has agreed that 'Christ is a functional title. It indicates one who stands in a special relationship to God and who performs a work of ultimate significance for the life of man' (*Working Papers in Doctrine*, p. 39). An always honest theologian such as David Brown who wishes to defend the orthodox tradition which developed, and which said more than the New Testament does, finds that the best he can produce from Scripture is that Paul or John or the writer of the Epistle to the Hebrews 'may have attributed pre-existence to Christ without realising all its implications' (*The Divine Trinity*, 1985, p. 157). He argues accordingly that 'neither scriptural diversity nor scriptural language should be our final court of appeal' (p. 306).

Non-Christians such as Jews or Muslims are not the only people who regret any impression that 'God became man' in a way that obscures the differences between God and man. There is danger in the talk (not in the Bible or the Fathers) of Jesus as 'the God-man'. To many seriously thinking people talk about God becoming man seems as meaningless as talk about a man becoming a frog or (as Spinoza put it) about a circle becoming a square. Of course the capacity to 'become man' may be a part of the nature of God, a part which we cannot understand; the traditionalists are right to make this reply. But it is not, I submit, necessary to insist on language which we cannot understand in order to talk about what God has shown to us and done for us and among us. It may be possible to understand the apparently simple statement 'Christ is God' somewhat as most Christians probably understand the statement about the Eucharist, 'This is my body.' The bread does not become the body of Christ by a physical transformation; there is a spiritual presence of Christ in the Eucharist which makes the bread signify his life or 'body' to the believer. So it may be said that Jesus Christ is himself the supreme sacrament, signifying God. This seems to be an approach worth exploring as we seek a modern Christology with a biblical foundation.

In company with many other scholars Geoffrey Lampe treated most of the New Testament titles of Jesus as examples of Hebrew religious language. Thus he studied 'Christ' or *Messiah* (the agent or viceroy of God) or 'Son of God' (a title given to kings and other outstanding men). He knew very well how this biblical phase developed into the theology of the Fathers, as may be seen from (for example) his magisterial treatment of 'Christian Theology in the Patristic Period' in *A History of Christian Doctrine* edited for the use of students by Hubert Cunliffe-Jones and Benjamin Drewery (1978). But in *God as Spirit* he went back to the biblical origins. He wrote:

In Hebrew religious language 'Spirit' is one of those 'bridge' words which express the idea of God's outreach towards, and

contact with, the created world . . . They convey the idea of the
Creator addressing his rational creatures, inspiring, teaching,
commanding, warning, punishing, forgiving, rewarding, intervening to help and rescue, loving, and even standing in a
relationship to his people like that of a husband to his bride or a
father to a child. Among the many images which express this
idea of God in relationship are those of the 'word' which God
addresses, the 'angel' which he sends or which is his own
self-manifestation, the 'arm' or 'hand' or 'finger' which signify
his intervention in power, 'power' itself, which is God in action,
his 'face' which may be turned towards men or averted from
them, the 'wisdom' which is God's creative counsel and purpose
and which he also gives to human beings to enable them to fulfil
his purposes and respond to his demands (p. 35).

Most people have always thought not in abstractions but in
pictures and stories, and (although even scientists use models in
order to imagine realities sufficiently well for their work) this was
specially true in pre-scientific ages. Most people have also thought
that what is personal is what is most real. Even Plato, a philosopher
not incapable of abstract thought, pictured the Demiurge as the
agent of the supreme God in the creation (in the *Timaeus*). Philo,
the Jewish philosopher who was Paul's contemporary, wrote about
God's Word (*Logos*) doing that cosmic job. It was therefore
inevitable that in the Bible these ideas about God's relationship
with the world should be pictured and personified in a story. Not
only was the idea of the coming kingdom of God personified in the
picture of the coming of the Messiah. The idea of God's message
was personified in the picture of a messenger (in Greek *angelos*).
The idea of God's wisdom was also personified; there are several
poems in the Old Testament where Wisdom speaks. John opened
his gospel with the idea of the Word (*Logos*), perhaps quoting
from a hymn. Scholars disagree about the extent to which these
personifications were meant literally or were known to be nothing
more than images used to think about God. The question seems
unanswerable, because presumably some of the Hebrews were
sophisticated and reflective and most were not. In our own time
even highly intelligent writers or artists can get so 'carried away'
that they treat their creations as if they were real people. It is also
unclear whether these personifications were, or were not, thought
of as fully divine. In the Old Testament, for example, Wisdom
speaks sometimes as the sovereign God and sometimes as a

creature, created 'before all else that he made', at the one Lord's side during his creation of the earth; in chapter 8 of Proverbs both voices are heard. There was a basic ambiguity in the very idea of the *Logos* as the agent of creation. But what is clear is that the story of God sending his only son became the most powerful of all these images, because it spoke of a relationship which could be imagined by anyone with a tolerable father. It is also clear that no great problem was felt when Christians began to think of Jesus as the Son of God who had been sent from his heavenly home where he had existed in glory before he accepted his humiliation as a man. Paul, John and the writer to the Hebrews did so think, although their thought cannot be reduced to one simple story. It is highly significant that they felt no need to justify this development. It seemed a natural way of speaking about God's initiative – for, as John Knox wrote, 'it would have been quite impossible for any primitive Jewish Christian to entertain even for a little while the notion that God had merely happened to find a man worthy of becoming the Messiah' (*The Humanity and Divinity of Christ*, pp. 9–10). As Lampe wrote, to the early Christians

> Jesus was not just another prophet (though they did call him a prophet) to whom the word of God had been spoken; he was a personal embodiment of God's address to us; he was God's word or wisdom or spirit (in Hebrew wisdom writings those three terms are synonymous) incarnate (*Explorations in Theology*, p. 33).

Language about a 'pre-existent' person in eternity, God the Son, thus rose naturally out of the wish to say that Jesus was God's Son incarnate. So, much later, did much more sophisticated language claiming that God the Son 'assumed impersonal humanity'. But this was dangerous language, as the continuing history of Christian theology was to show. Lampe, after long and expert reflection, believed that 'they could have claimed for Jesus what their faith demanded without their doctrine running out into meaninglessness' (*Explorations in Theology*, p. 35). Therefore he (like John Robinson and many others) proposed a revision which surely need not shock any Christian. He proposed that we should think of Jesus as a person and of the God who dwelt and acted in Jesus as Spirit, not as 'a person' in the human sense. And at the end of his book *God as Spirit*, towards the end of his life, Lampe said what he thought was demanded by Christian faith:

I believe in the Divinity of our Lord and Saviour Jesus Christ, in
the sense that the one God, the Creator and Saviour Spirit,
revealed himself and acted decisively for us in Jesus. I believe in
the Divinity of the Holy Ghost, in the sense that the same one
God . . . is here and now not far from every one of us; for in him
we live and move, in him we have our being. In us, if we consent
to know and trust him, he will create the Christlike harvest; love,
joy, peace, patience, kindness, goodness, fidelity, gentleness,
and self-control (p. 228).

Lampe's version of the Christian faith was enough to inspire a
life full of that lovely harvest, just as Robinson's faith could be
known by its fruits; and what was true of these well-known
theologians now recently dead is true of others. So with deep
respect I welcome their positive affirmations about Jesus, the man
in whom God's active love is newly and uniquely embodied. But I
have to add that this new Christology, no less than the old, has its
dangers. So I proceed to some criticisms.

The Preface to *The Myth of God Incarnate* declared the conviction of all its contributors 'that Jesus was (as he is presented in Acts
2:22) "a man approved by God" for a special role within the divine
purpose' (p. ix). But that primitive Christology which is remarkably well-preserved by Luke in the Acts of the Apostles does not
express anything like the full Christian experience of Christ.
Paradoxically that full experience is better expressed at the beginning of Luke's gospel, where some of the phrases are also primitive
(such as the reference to 'the throne of his father David') but where
the poetry celebrates Christianity's conviction that the life of Jesus,
the Son of God who is 'king for ever', began in the heart of God, for
'the power of the Most High' overshadowed that life before Jesus
spoke a word. To say that such a man is only 'approved by God' or
only has 'a special role' seems an understatement.

Of course Jesus Christ is not now to be seen or touched or heard
in the same way as the rabbi from Nazareth was to be seen or
touched or heard. And of course the reality which Christians
encounter is bigger than the historical Jesus. The very word
'Christ' refers to the interpretation of Jesus by Christians. It is the
English version of the Greek translation of the Jewish title 'Messiah'. It became, as it did for Paul, more or less another proper
name for Jesus (which is the Greek form of Yeshua), implying far
more than 'Messiah' had ever done. Jesus was the risen Lord, the
Son of God. This is a reminder that all the events which are held to

be in a special sense 'acts of God' are *interpreted* events. What makes the impact is the interpretation of an event which could be interpreted otherwise. That rule applies to the 'Christ-event'. What Christians think of as 'Christ' includes the wonderfully inspired interpretations of the historical Jesus presented in the gospels, including the fourth, and in the gospel according to Paul. And there are other substantial reasons why the 'Christ-event' is for Christians bigger than the life of Jesus between his birth and death.

The influence of Jesus demands interpretation because it was so much greater after his death than before it – as well as for reasons even more unusual. While he was alive in the normal human and historical way he was misunderstood and deserted by his closest followers; they later reported that. After his death he was obeyed heroically and worshipped joyfully in a new phase to which the New Testament refers in its various ways of talking about the life and power of 'the Spirit'. So 'Christ' was experienced in the Spirit and the two were largely – although not completely – identified. As Lampe wrote:

> For them, as for all subsequent believers, it was the conscious-
> ness of finding inspiration and power for a life of sonship and
> brotherhood in the community that had its origin in the mission
> of Jesus which was the decisive factor in their identification of
> the 'Spirit of God' with the 'Spirit of Christ' (*God as Spirit*,
> p. 99).

This leads on into the second reason for thinking that what is interpreted as the 'Christ-event' is bigger than the life of the historical Jesus. The new community of Christians is itself involved in the new reality of 'Christ'. Paul wrote about life in the Church as life 'in Christ', and about the Church as the visible 'body' of the invisible Christ, because of his experience that to persecute Christians was to persecute Christ and to understand, love and serve them was to understand, love and serve him. But Paul was far from being the only Christian to connect the saints very intimately with Christ. And as the history of Christianity has lengthened and spread, it has been a fact of history that much of what is understood as 'Christ' has been contributed by Christianity interpreting Jesus and not based solely on the records surviving about the historical Jesus. The recorded teaching of Jesus has been seen in new perspectives, with a new emphasis and thrust. What is perceived as the essential message of Jesus has been applied to subjects which he cannot have covered such as the feudal system, African religion, modern capitalism or nuclear war. The activity which began in Jesus has been taken into countless new situations, to the ends of the earth – although always, as Christians always insist, in dependence on the Saviour and the Spirit. Notoriously this has quite often resulted in an image of 'Christ' contrary to the perceptions of Jesus by other Christians or by historians (such as the emperor-Christ or Christ the socialist). But on the whole this richness of development, sometimes referred to by talk about 'many Christs', has helped to make Christianity relevant and lively. The Church has often claimed too much for itself, and the compliment that it is 'an extension of the incarnation' is undeserved. But interpretation by the Church, in words and in lives, is part of what is meant by 'Christ'. There is a sense in which 'Jesus is risen in the *kerygma*' or gospel (a phrase which Rudolf Bultmann accepted as a fair summary of his theology).

However, the development has always needed to be checked by reference to the gospels and to definitely Christian experience. These controls are neither infallible nor complete, for the gospels and the experience must always be evidence both fragmentary and edited. But enough can be known about Jesus and about his impact to put him in control. And without this reference back to Jesus and the Christian community, 'Christ' easily becomes a term so vacuous as to be meaningless. The convictions that God's action in Jesus Christ is not his only action, and that the truth revealed in Jesus Christ is not the only truth, are meaningful, important and (I believe) correct. But there are great dangers in extending the word 'Christ' to cover all that is good or true, so that insights characteristic of existentialist philosophy or Hindu religion are said to be 'Christ', or the world's poor are said to be 'Christ', or evolution or sheer 'life-energy' is said to be 'Christ'. That kind of talk is often resented by Christians, with justice. It reduces their Saviour to a cipher – perhaps to a ventriloquist's dummy. But it is also resented by non-Christians, who find it intolerably patronising. And it is often rightly condemned by people who are concerned for the meaningfulness of language. For it misuses a title which only makes sense when applied to an individual, as if one were to call the world's poor or evolution or life-energy 'President'. (Did Bultmann mean existentialist philosophy when he said 'Jesus'? He was not always clear, but his teaching as a whole, including his sermons, shows that his intention was Christian. Robert C.

Roberts sympathetically criticised *Rudolf Bultmann's Theology* in 1977.)

If the use of the title 'Christ' is firmly anchored to the historical Jesus, as it ought to be, we have to attempt to answer the question what it means to call Jesus 'Christ'. It seems extremely important that our answer should affirm – as Jesus himself affirmed – that in this life God was active in a way that was unique. To say with Wiles that Jesus 'symbolises and expresses God's action towards the world' is not enough. In his *Explorations in Theology* (p. 24) Wiles expanded that estimate of Jesus to say this:

> He was not just one who had taught about God; he was not just one who had lived a life of perfect human response to God. He had lived a life which embodied and expressed God's character and action in the world. As prophets in the past had expressed the word of God that had come to them not only in speech but also in symbolic action, so in a far more comprehensive way did Jesus. The impact not merely of his teaching but of his whole person communicated the presence and the power of God with an unprecedented sense of directness and finality.

However, even this expanded verdict seems to me inadequate in relation to the evidence. In *God's Action in the World* Wiles rejects 'particular divine acts ensuring the birth of the particular person, Jesus'. To him, stories about such acts are merely 'a retrospective way of expressing the totality of his commitment to and fulfilment of the will of God for the world' (p. 89). But the logical conclusion of this line seems to be that Jesus was a very good man who had made himself that good. Every piece of evidence we have about him suggests that Jesus would have been horrified by such an idea. In keeping with the tradition of Jewish piety, Jesus plainly thought of himself as utterly dependent on the Father for anything that was good in his life or true in his teaching. Looking back on the work of Jesus, Christians were right to say that it had originated in God's love for the world – whether or not Matthew and Luke were right to say that it had not originated in Joseph's sexual love for Mary. In his *The God of Jesus Christ* (1984) Walter Kasper, the distinguished Roman Catholic theologian and bishop, showed how the doctrines of the pre-existence of the Son and the two natures in the incarnation – which he defended (as I cannot) – arose in the ancient world out of a simple insight which surely deserves defence by all Christians. 'In his being as Son Jesus has his radical origin in God and radically belongs to God. The turning of Jesus to the Father implies the prior turning of the Father to Jesus' (p. 171). Thirty years before, Donald Baillie had put the insight more simply: 'Whatever Jesus was or did, in His life, in His teaching, in His cross and passion, in His resurrection and ascension and exaltation, it is really God that did it in Jesus; that is how the New Testament speaks' (*God Was in Christ*, p. 67). Every piece of evidence we have about Jesus also suggests that like the early Christians he believed with his whole being that the Father was doing something new in his life. He co-operated not merely with 'the will of God for the world' but with the will of the Father *for him*, so that this new act of God might be consummated and God's kingdom might come on earth as in heaven. Believing that Jesus was right, I cannot say that Wiles has improved on his original perception that 'the heart of Christian faith is the person of Christ and what God has done in him' (*The Christian Fathers*, p. 24).

I also cannot say that Robinson's last chapter in *The Human Face of God*, called 'Man for All', is more persuasive now than when I first read it and thought it too vague. Finding the ideas of 'God' and 'Christ' everywhere, this over-generous Anglican bishop in the end located them nowhere. He wrote:

> God has emptied himself into Christ, and Christ into his fellow men . . . The Christ lives on – in the lives of those who represent now the human face of God . . . The 'implicit Christ', the 'greater Christ', to use Sölle's terms, is much, much wider than the church . . . Jesus is but the clue, the parable, the sign by whom it is possible to recognize the Christ in others (pp. 215–16, 239).

To say that is, I fear, to empty the terms 'God' and 'Christ' of Philip Toynbee, who was by no means a conventional Christian, picked on that last chapter as suggesting a religion that was not Christianity or even theism, despite the theological jargon. I think he was right. 'What happened at the Incarnation, if we can so put it,' wrote Robinson,

> is that God, the power of nature and history, the Logos or principle of the evolutionary process, began to be represented in a new way. The appearance of Jesus marked the emergence of a world 'come of age', whose ordering could no longer be understood on the model of a parent running the universe by direct rule, like 'the Lord' of the Old Testament. That had meant treating man as a minor . . . Jesus thereby represents a new

mutation in the development of spirit, as evolution begins, not merely – as Sir Julian Huxley has expressed it – to become conscious of itself, but through personal responsibility to incarnate God. Put the other way round, henceforth 'God' is to be represented no longer simply as a personified being over man's head, but in and by man and his responsibility (pp. 217–18).

That is a long way from what the gospels say about the historical Jesus, who prayed to the Father, all through the night if need be, in Gethsemane if need be, in order that he might know and do the Father's will.

Lampe did not allow himself to be led into such highly debatable territory. (Although his personal relations with Robinson were good, he did not mention *The Human Face of God* in his own *God as Spirit*.) But as I see it he contributed his own error to this debate, for he was wrong to deny the reality of what he called the 'post-existent Christ'. This denial seemed to him to follow logically from his rejection of traditional orthodoxy about the eternal Son's existence before the human conception.

In order . . . to interpret God's saving work in Jesus we do not need the model of a descent of a pre-existent divine person into the world. Nor do we need the concept of a 'post-existent' continuing personal presence of Jesus, himself alive today, in order to interpret our own continuing experience of God's saving and creative work (p. 33).

This was the part of Lampe's argument that seemed weakest to a number of critics, and it continues to puzzle me why he exposed himself to this criticism. As an expert in the history of Christian doctrine he knew perfectly well how central to the life of the Christian community has been the conviction that Jesus is the living mediator between the Father and humanity. 'The central conviction of all Christians', he wrote, 'is that Christ is the focal point of the continuing encounter between God and man which takes place throughout human history' (p. 13). He went on to say that 'in fact we need no mediator' because 'it is God himself, disclosed to us and experienced by us as inspiring and indwelling Spirit (or Wisdom or Word), who meets us through Jesus and can make us Christlike' (p. 144). But here Lampe went against what most devout Christians would say was their experience. As a New Testament scholar he knew perfectly well that the early Christians combined a belief that Jesus was 'in heaven' with a belief that spiritually he was 'with' them and 'in' them on earth, 'to the end of time'. Normally their prayer was to God 'through' Christ, but even in the Acts of the Apostles, where the emphasis is on the 'ascension' of Jesus into heaven and on the gift of the Holy Spirit at Pentecost, Christians are directly addressed by Jesus and address him. Their Easter stories need not be taken as completely accurate history, but even if they 'take the form of historical narratives in order to convey truth about Christian life as it is experienced by believers at all times', as Lampe held (p. 8; cf. p. 152), these stories do show how strong was the faith that after his death Jesus could meet Christians and transform them, so that their first creed was 'Jesus is Lord' (1 Cor. 12:3). And although their meeting with Jesus in the Eucharist was more mystical than physical, it combined 'remembrance' of the man in history with a 'communion' that made it much more than a memorial service.

These characteristics of early Christianity can be recognised as marking the whole story of this religion. The continuing personal presence of Jesus has of course seldom been experienced in a way that would make it right to compare the encounter to a conversation with an invisible man. Nor have experiences reported as 'visions' or the 'direct intuition' of Jesus been frequent or valid beyond questioning and testing. Nor has it been easy to separate the raw experience from the interpretation by images already in the Christian's mind through tradition. Nor has it been possible to demonstrate the validity and importance of this experience to people who find reports of it totally alien and puzzling. The Christian's experience of the risen Lord has been in all these respects like religious experience in general. But the experience has felt real – and felt stronger than the impression left by hearing or reading about a dead man. It has been more like a Jesus-shaped spiritual pressure on one's life, validated not by emotional ecstasies but by daily behaviour. That, as I interpret it, has been my own experience.

This experience is partly, but (it seems to me) not adequately, described in the more recent writing of Wiles. He says that 'there can be little doubt that Moses, Isaiah, Jesus and Paul all made substantial contributions to the development of our moral awareness' and that 'for one whose faith in God finds its shape through the records of Jesus, the direct address to Christ in the poetic form of hymnody or in the context of more informal occasions of prayer will not seem inappropriate' (*Faith and the Mystery of God*, pp. 107, 97). But Christian experience has been from very early days that in private prayer and public worship 'the grace of our Lord Jesus Christ', the graciousness of a living Lord, communicates the love of God and the fellowship of the Holy Spirit. This is much more than 'poetic' or 'informal' response to written records. It is – or at any rate, for most Christians it feels like – a response to a Lord who was dead and is alive for evermore.

As a Christian Lampe believed in life after death. He expressed this faith in a university sermon preached when he knew that he was dying (*Explorations in Theology*, pp. 130–7). He said that he had himself had 'an extremely happy life', but that 'for the many whose lives are oppressed, unfree, handicapped, sad death must be either feared as the end of any possible hope, or welcomed in sheer total despair, if this life is the whole story'. Moreover, even happier people must be aware of 'the constant incompleteness and rudimentary state of the outreach towards God'. The necessary 'transformation cannot be completed in these few years of life; and if those years are all there is for us, such glimpses of God as we now have are like a springtime without a summer to follow'. So he believed that 'the renewal of the inward man into Christlikeness . . . must be an infinite progress into the infinity of God' and he admired believers for whom 'those who died just happen to be no longer visible'. His last words were a reaffirmation of the faith that nothing 'shall be able to separate us from the love of God, which is in Christ Jesus our Lord'.

But if this Christian faith in life after death is true, it seems unnecessary and illogical to say, in the most extreme contradiction of the Easter faith, that of all the human race Jesus is the only one who is dead indeed. Lampe did not say that, but his dislike of the simple faith that 'Jesus is alive today' led him into many passages which suggest that the life of Jesus after death is so heavenly that it should not be reckoned as existence in any sense that mortals can recognise. Here, it seems to me, the nerve of the Easter faith of most Christians has been cut more severely than when the stories at the end of the gospels are not treated as historical; and I do not see why the operation is necessary for the sake of truth. It seems true to Christian experience to say that God, who was in the man Jesus between conception and death, has also been in his personality after death, still using that personality to communicate with those who will accept him.

For many Christians, this experience is still best interpreted by continuing talk about God the Son who existed in eternity before assuming a human nature, and when that orthodoxy has been revised so as to admit fully the fact that Jesus was a man there seems to be nothing in it that is obviously 'wrong' (i.e. demonstrably inconsistent or otherwise probably false) – *if* it is regarded as meaningful. David Brown, for example, does find meaning in such traditional language. He has offered a defence of *The Divine Trinity* complete with 'the uniting of a human nature into an already existing Person' and 'three consciousnesses' in the Godhead (pp. 123, 287). I respect his integrity and reckon that James Mackey (whose theology I prefer) went too far when he said in a review: 'One does get the impression at times that Brown could find reasons for believing just about anything' (*Religious Studies*, 1986, p. 159). Attacks of that kind inevitably evoke the rejoinder that radicals have not troubled to understand what the traditionalists are trying to affirm. Thus a reviewer of Mackey's own book wrote: 'Why study the Fathers at all?, one begins to wonder. For Mackey it seems to be a melancholy duty laid on those who recognize and wish to remedy the damage done to the Christian tradition in its formative phase'(Andrew Louth in *Theology*, 1983, pp. 449–50). But the discussion can be serious and constructive. And for those Christians who do not find much meaning in traditional orthodoxy, there is an alternative.

Ours need not be the alternative of a very weak Christology. By saying 'God was embodied in Jesus Christ' we can mean more than is meant by a compliment such as 'the Senior Tutor is the veritable incarnation of good sense', as Brian Hebblethwaite puts it (*The Incarnation*, p. 49). We can mean not a compliment to Jesus but the worship of God in Christ. We can satisfy what John Macquarrie, at the end of *The Truth of God Incarnate* (1977, p. 143), rightly said were the three minimum requirements in any interpretation of this doctrine: '(a) the initiative is from God, not men; (b) God is deeply involved in his creation; (c) the centre of this initiative and involvement is Jesus Christ'. We can do justice to what C. F. D. Moule, in *Incarnation and Myth* (p. 140), rightly says is demanded by 'the evidence from the beginnings of Christianity' – that Christ is on both sides of the distinction between the Creator and the created. And thus a reinterpretation of the doctrine can be in tune with the New Testament. As Colin Gunton has written:

The historical man Jesus is never construed apart from his meaning as the presence of the eternal God in time. The New Testament, if we take it seriously, will not allow us to choose between time and eternity, immanence and transcendence, in our talk about Jesus. The two are always given together (*Yesterday and Today*, p. 207).

If 'God was in Christ' is taken to mean that God was here met as light in a suffering and ignorant world, and as saving and healing activity which lifts us sinners from the dominion of death to abundant and eternal life, and as the love which is the first cause and the ultimate reality of the universe, then it is true to say that the person who has really 'seen' Jesus, in spiritual encounter and understanding, has spiritually 'seen' God the Father at work. The fourth gospel, expounding this, tells us that in Jesus we encounter a reality which is 'one' with the Father, which therefore is 'before Abraham was' and 'before the world began'. 'What God was . . . became flesh, he came to dwell among us' and is rightly prayed to as 'my Lord and my God'. But this gospel also preserves the distinction which is general in the New Testament between 'Jesus' and 'God'. It was written in order that we might believe that 'Jesus is the Son of God', the Son of the Father who is 'greater'. 'The only true God' has 'sent' Jesus. Elsewhere the mystery is expressed like this: Jesus the man is a part of the creation, to Christians the 'first' of all creatures, but also 'the image of the invisible God' (Col. 1:15). This suggests that the life of Jesus has an effect on us which is like the effect of another man but also like the effect of God. It is a mystery, but it may be compared with another mystery which is not a nonsense: our own thinking has both spiritual and physical aspects or levels, for it is both 'mind' and 'brain' and can be analysed as either. What the mystery of Jesus Christ means for practical religion, which is what matters most, has been well summarised by two eminent Roman Catholic theologians, Walter Kasper and Edward Schillebeeckx. The former constructed his *Jesus the Christ* (1976) around the faith that 'in Jesus Christ God himself has entered into a human history and meets us there in a fully and completely human way'. The latter, in his massive *Jesus: An Experiment in Christology* (1979), developed the idea of 'salvation in Jesus from God'. Such phrases may not go far enough to satisfy all Christians, but they go as far as the New Testament. And I suggest that what was good enough for the New Testament ought to be enough to point to what is essential in Christianity.

Am I ending this necessarily complicated discussion with a mere diplomatic formula, aimed at a shallow 'comprehensiveness', as Anglicans are often accused of doing to the detriment of theological integrity and clarity? I do not think so. I realise that many great

Christians – and multitudes of faithful, humble ones – would agree with Newman: they have thought with a passionate sincerity that every phrase in traditional orthodoxy is necessary in order to safeguard faith in 'God's presence and his very self' in Christ as 'a higher gift than grace'. But to my mind the practical consequences of a number of theological positions – the results for worship and life – may be equally Christian if they find room for the saving impact of God's grace through Christ. In *God Was in Christ* Donald Baillie (a great teacher of the Church of Scotland) success- fully built a bridge between the two positions by pointing out that what matters in the practical Christian life is 'the paradox of grace'; I live but Christ lives in me, Jesus lives but God lives in him, Jesus acts but it is the work of God. That seems enough. If one tries to go beyond that, probing the mystery, one gets involved in a difference of opinion about whether the Holy Spirit inspired orthodoxy as defined by councils of bishops in the period 325–452 in such a detailed way that its formulae (or most of them) are permanently authoritative for all loyal members of the Church – and the complex difference between what may be called traditionalism and what may be called modernism cannot be resolved by any simple argument. Yet both sides can unite in Christian worship and Christian life, acknowledging a saving mystery which cannot be put into words.

Reviewing *Incarnation and Myth* in *Theology* (1979, p. 451), Keith Ward complained about

> the greatest failure of the debate: the refusal to say just what Incarnation is. The verbal battle sounds intense, with cries of 'puerility' or 'bad scholarship' ominously sounded; 'God was personally present in Jesus', says one; no, 'Jesus was a man used by God, though admittedly in a unique way', says another. But is the battle more than verbal? To find that out, we need to know the difference between a man fully expressing God's love, and God being identical with a man; between qualitative and quantitative identity between man and God.

These are things which in my view we cannot know. I take Ward's point that further light could be thrown by studying 'the great amount of logical work done in philosophy on such concepts as "individuation", "identity" and "uniqueness"', and I have pon- dered *The Logic of God Incarnate* by Thomas V. Morris (1986), which was written as a response to the challenge which Ward voiced. But I still think it is too much to expect philosophy to throw any final light on the mysteries of the being and activity of God. It is, for example, too much to hope that 'a solid dose of logical care' will demonstrate that Jesus had two discrete minds, one unable to sin, the other being tempted (pp. 9, 142, 161). I believe that we have to be on our guard against supposing that modern logic could settle these controversies, where the Fathers' Greek philosophy failed. We cannot say just what the incarnation was, for we cannot find out. As Professor H. D. Lewis has wisely said after criticising radical theologians such as Lampe and Wiles: 'on the "how" the veil falls totally on us' (*Jesus in the Faith of Christians*, 1981, p. 73). What we can know is how the action, the embodiment of God in Christ, has an impact on us. In the words of Rudolf Bultmann, 'not what God is in himself, but how he acts with men, is the mystery in which faith is interested' (*Jesus Christ and Mythology*, 1960, p. 43).

Does this faith entitle me to recite in the course of worship – as I often do – the creed that is associated with the Councils of Nicaea and Constantinople and that is precious because inherited as a badge of unity by Christians of East and West? I think so, because I think that the language of that creed can be understood as the expression in the language of the fourth century of the faith which I share that Jesus Christ is absolutely unique among men. In this life, which began at conception but did not end at death, God has taken a unique initiative and exercised a unique continuing control; God has acted, making possible the uniquely full response and work of Jesus. So in Jesus God is present and God is active, with unique power 'for our salvation'. Uniquely, Jesus is the bearer of God's grace and the revealer of God's truth. In and through him, in the power of the Spirit, the one true God is to be worshipped and obeyed. For our living and dying he is God with us, God's life expressed in a human life and God's love embodied in a human death.

And I believe that the ordinary Christian thinking about Christ will always prefer the image of embodiment to the image of inspiration – in technical terms, will prefer incarnation to inspiration or indwelling. This is because the idea that 'God became spirit' suffers from two defects. One is that it can suggest that God is knowable equally everywhere, like the air – which denies the experienced uniqueness of the particular man, Jesus Christ. (Of course if 'spirit' suggests a powerful cleansing fluid or a powerful intoxicant this objection loses its force.) Another defect is that 'spirit' can suggest that God has remained aloof from our bodily experience. For human life is so largely *not* elevated above the physical. Although God's presence and power in a human life must be spiritual not physical, ordinary humanity does not often feel grandly inspired or able to identify fully with the inspired. One bleeds. One weeps. If one enters this world howling, if one is born into a family without economic or political security or social status, if one is an infant at the mercy of parents and diseases, if one grows up through the emotional storms of adolescence and early adulthood, if one earns one's living by doing a job which is obscure and not very interesting, if one has insoluble problems with the family and is misunderstood or abandoned by friends, if one is depressed and exhausted, if one is surrounded by physical or mental sickness, if one is categorised, marginalised and condemned by the authorities, if one dies painfully amid the defeat of one's dreams, one feels trapped, *embodied*. And then it can mean a very great deal if one believes that God, acting in Christ, wore our vulnerable flesh like a royal robe.

So I make no apology for being largely agnostic with regard to metaphysics such as the orthodoxy about the eternal relationships within the Trinity which was propounded by the Fathers and the councils. Nor do I apologise for being unable to say exactly how 'God acts' or how 'God was in Christ' in history. Those are matters beyond human understanding, or at least beyond my reach. But I still want to say that in order to be full Christians (not in order to speculate theologically) we need to believe in the new activity of God in Christ and to live in its light and power. For it can change our existence: that much we can experience and understand. I also want to argue now that we need not be so agnostic as some radical theologians think necessary about the history to which the New Testament witnesses – or about life-transforming relevance today.

The response by Maurice Wiles (pp. 286–91) alludes to this chapter.

6

JOHN BOWDEN AND THE FACTS ABOUT JESUS:

What do we know about the man behind the gospels?

Many people in our time suspect that modern theories about Jesus such as those of Robinson, Lampe and Wiles, and more traditional or 'orthodox' theories, all rest on a very flimsy basis of facts. Even my own suggestions may be criticised! So I now turn to a notable discussion about what can be known about Jesus historically. It was written by John Bowden, my successor as Editor and Managing Director of the SCM Press. But I do not find it easy to assess him. If I praise him I shall be accused, by critics and my own conscience, of too much loyalty to a friend and to a publishing house which I served for eight years with devotion and enjoyment. If I question him I shall be accused – again by my critics and my conscience – of jealousy of a man who as a highly successful publisher since 1966 has shown far greater ability than I possess. That has been confirmed by the respect and gratitude of all who study British theology, by the large sales and influence of many SCM Press books and by the award of an honorary doctorate of divinity by Edinburgh University, having particularly in mind his arduous labours as a translator. If I question him as to whether he has paid sufficient attention to *Christ in Christian Tradition: From the Apostolic Age to Chalcedon* or to *Christ: The Christian Experience in the Modern World*, I must not forget that those are the titles of learned masterpieces of Roman Catholic scholarship, by Aloys Grillmeier and Edward Schillebeeckx respectively, which together are more than 1,500 pages long – and which he translated.

However, John Bowden's own comparatively simple and short book *Jesus: the Unanswered Questions* (1988) bravely summed up in a vigorous, well-informed and readable way difficulties which have been set out at greater length in other books, and which are felt by many non-experts, but which have too often been ignored in the churches. The subject of Jesus is too important for it to be right to allow personal considerations to prevail. I therefore agreed to review the book for the *Church Times* and I am reprinting the review here. It has been shortened by two paragraphs in which I glanced at some of the scholarly arguments about the New Testament. My discussion in that tiny space was so brief as to be worthless, but I hope that my discussion here may show that I think that historical questions are important and must be answered by historical methods. After this reprint of my review I therefore offer some further reflections on these questions.

Review of *Jesus: the Unanswered Questions* by John Bowden (1988)

He has been haunted for many years by the question formulated by Dietrich Bonhoeffer: 'what Christianity really is, or indeed who Christ really is, for us today'. This has been to the great advantage of innumerable students of theology, professional or amateur; for, while Editor of the SCM Press, Dr Bowden has published books without number on one or other aspect of that question. Many of these he has himself translated from a variety of languages.

He has also felt driven to write some books of his own; and the fact that he has found time to do so demonstrates that the age of miracles is not over – whatever the theologians may say. One of these books, *By Heart* (1984), implicitly tells us why he remains an Anglican priest. Another, *Voices in the Wilderness* (1977), proclaims his belief that most of his fellow churchmen are shirking the question. Now he has published his own longest book, evidently intended to make the challenge inescapable. It is a valuable volume, partly as a summary of the problems which ought to goad the lazy-minded or the otherwise preoccupied, partly as a collection of footnotes that ought to stimulate anyone ready to be advised about further reading. I am glad that Bowden decided to make this expansion of a lecture which he gave to junior clergy and ordinands in Southwark Cathedral. They found him exciting. So did I, because I profoundly agree with him that vitally important questions about religious truths have been brushed under sanctuary carpets too often.

He is not one of those radical theologians who, as he puts it, leave the reader 'under a dark and leaden sky'. Almost a sixth of his book is a prologue in which he reminds us that being open to truth is, however painful, essential to true religion – and in his last chapter he returns with eloquence to the theme that a believer in God can find 'living with questions' not only endurable but actually a way of purifying and deepening faith in the Ultimate Reality. Those of us who are not ashamed to be called 'liberal' must be grateful for so powerful a statement of what is our own concern and our own experience. However, I am probably not the only liberal who would want to add that not all the problems here assembled are quite as 'unanswered' as is suggested. We can say this without departing at all from the insistence on honest truthfulness, and on the acceptance of all scientific, scholarly and social truths, which Bowden so correctly urges.

He rightly says that the life of the very varied churches can always be seen 'revolving round two focal points, not one: "Jesus" and "the Christ"' (p. 9). There is first the man of Nazareth for whose existence in history the New Testament is virtually the only evidence. But there is also Jesus in Christian experience; Jesus called by the Greek translation of the Jewish term for the great Liberator; Jesus called by many other names as endlessly he has been preached as Saviour, received as Lord, prayed to as Friend. For Bowden the problems concern both what we can honestly say about Jesus of Nazareth and what we can say with integrity about our Christ. His frequent answer to historical questions is that 'in the end we cannot really know' – and his frequent criticism of formal or informal Christologies is that they are in reality ideologies, reflecting the self-interest or perhaps the sentimentality of a particular group, often with little or no connection with the historical Jesus.

But I reckon that he often exaggerates the difficulties. Of course I do not deny the diversity of the Christians, in New Testament days, in history or in our own time. There are excellent summaries here of recent books where the evidence is set out incontrovertibly. But why must one say, as Bowden says, that the pro-Nazi German Christianity 'turned Christianity into a caricature of itself' (p. 122)? Surely, because it had given up any genuine attempt to relate the Bible to the contemporary situation. At that stage diversity had become heresy.

The Bible does not contain a biography of Jesus or a legislative code to control ethics. But it does witness to a historical Jesus of more substance than is allowed by Bowden or by the scholars whom he cites. And this is the Lord with whom all Christians must, so to speak, wrestle. Difficulties abound for people of the 1980s in some of the traditional interpretations of the fragmentary evidence provided by the New Testament. Bowden boldly and effectively forces the reader to consider these. But what a pity it is that he has muddled them up with unreal difficulties as if any stigma were good enough to beat a dogma!

The Quest of the Historical Jesus

Questions about the historical Jesus are certainly not confined nowadays to academic circles. From time to time the media mention them. In the *Sunday Times Magazine* published on Christmas Eve in 1988 the discussion was presented to a non-specialist public by the reproduction of attempts to portray Christ by a diversity of modern artists and film directors. 'Every screen portrayal has been vigorously denounced by one faction or another,' it was noted editorially, 'and only a handful of the 147 actors who have portrayed him have kept their careers intact.' Eight scholars gave their opinions. Two who are priests of the Church of England expressed contradictory views. For Don Cupitt, Jesus was a man for whom 'God is scattered and disappears into common humanity'; for Edward Norman, 'occasionally, in their enthusiasm for humanity and its needs, Christians see a Christ who is a bit too human'. For the Jewish scholar Geza Vermes, Jesus was 'an outstanding *hasid* or Jewish holy man', while Morton Smith sees only 'Jesus the magician'. For the Jewish scholar Hyam Maccoby, Jesus was 'a rebel against Rome'; for Bishop David Jenkins, 'his directness to God led to his being killed'. Father Jerome Murphy-O'Connor, a professor in the Ecole Biblique in Jerusalem, thinks of him 'in very concrete, human terms', but G. A. Wells, a professor of German in Birkbeck College, London, thinks 'Did Jesus exist?' a question which needs asking.

Some serious questions are raised here, and in my review I did not sufficiently stress the pain with which John Bowden sees them being brushed aside. In his book *Jesus: the Unanswered Questions* he writes that 'looking back at what I consider to be the best of the theology and biblical and historical research over the last twenty years I can see many signs of progress and positive development' (p. xiv). But in the churches the level of theological and historical knowledge and insight has – to judge from public debates – fallen appallingly and attempts to ask questions are largely frowned on. Instead, we are told that there is a 'turning of the tide', and that there is nothing wrong with traditional beliefs (seldom defined in any detail), which need only to be restated with renewed conviction and faith . . .

. . . Christian doctrine is still largely treated as the Bible used to be two centuries ago, presented as having such unique authority that it must have been made in heaven, rather than being the work of thinkers and negotiators at particular periods during church history, and therefore open to historical criticism and the problems of cultural relativism (pp. xiv, xvi).

I agree with much of this alarm about the intellectual quality of the neo-conservatism that has attracted too many Christians recently. I may boast that I fought a little of the necessary battle when on the basis of a pamphlet published by the Modern Churchmen's Union I tried to persuade the Convocation of Canterbury (a meeting of representatives of Church of England clergy) to welcome liberty of interpretation of the doctrines commonly called the 'virgin birth' and the 'resurrection'. Such liberty had been affirmed afresh by the cautiously balanced report of the House of Bishops on *The Nature of Christian Belief* (1986). Although I was supported, the majority of my brethren preferred to insist, more simply, that the events behind these doctrines had been physical and that this was 'the faith of the Church'. The debate did not reveal much awareness in the majority that most theologians would not say that Christians need insist on the physicality. Nor did the conclusion of the debate show much understanding of why the bishops had agreed to no more than the carefully phrased declaration that the Christmas and Easter narratives in the gospels 'express' the faith of the Church in its incarnate and risen Lord. Some bishops thought the story of the virginal conception 'imagery symbolic of divine truth' rather than 'historical fact', and their report recorded that the divergent views about the historicity of the empty tomb 'to be found among scholars of standing are reflected in the views of individual bishops'.

Bowden also voices a protest against the manipulation of other people by those who claim the authority to impose traditional doctrines. He gives as an example the imposition of 'distinctive views about biblical inspiration, about the person of Jesus, about moral behaviour, the marks of a Christian, and so on' as 'the watchwords of the group, the passwords of membership' in a close-knit group of fundamentalists (pp. 19–20). Later examples include the use of Christology to impose the doctrine of male supremacy: since God is Father and Jesus is Lord, maleness is superior and the man must be the head (pp. 94–5). Bowden has written short books introducing two leading theologians of our century, Karl Barth and Edward Schillebeeckx. While he pays tribute to Barth's greatness as a systematic theologian, he prefers the Roman Catholic scholar's openness to the questions being asked about Jesus and other Christian topics. He rightly sees that theology, despite its apparently academic and timeless character, can be used as a weapon of domination through brainwashing once it is no longer grasped by a passion for truth. I am reminded of Coleridge's warning: 'He who begins by loving Christianity better than Truth will proceed by loving his own Sect or Church better than Christianity, and end by loving himself best of all' (*Aids to Reflection*, p. 101).

No student of church history can deny that images of Jesus – the 'Christ of faith' – have been used in attempts to protect the Christianity of a particular time and place from the impact of truth and reality, and have also been used in attempts to control minds and spirits in the interests of the leadership of a particular Christian group. Sometimes such misuse of images of Jesus has been defended by claiming that it is justified by Christian experience, specially worship. But Bowden rightly points out that emotional experience, even the sacred experience of worship, ought not to be held to justify what is factually untrue or morally wrong. He draws a lesson from the development of the 'utterly fantastic' (p. 97) cult of the Virgin Mary. 'What can be said of the role of worship in connection with the development of the major Christian doctrines can also be said in connection with the development of Roman Catholic Mariology leading up to the doctrines of the Immaculate Conception and the Bodily Assumption' (p. 84).

However, these much-needed warnings are accompanied by some recognition that the 'Christ of faith' has not been merely a series of images belonging to the history of mysticism or to the story of ecclesiastical politics, groups with little connection with Jesus of Nazareth and justified by the irrational excitement of the worshippers' emotions. There have been checks in the Christian tradition on developments which were judged by the wisest heads in the Christian community to be illegitimate. Newman, who in 1845 first popularised the idea that there must be development in doctrines, wrestled with the need to distinguish sound development from unsound. Many theologians and church leaders have followed in his steps. In my review I referred to the rejection of 'German' (i.e. pro-Nazi and anti-Semitic) Christianity as an example of healthy controls on 'development', and there have been innumerable other examples in church history, although often the controls have taken a considerable time to be effective. And frequently the controls over strange interpretations of Christianity have been exercised by reminders about what we can know about the man behind the gospels, just as criticisms of the extravagances of developing Mariology have often been based on sobering appeals to the small amount of historical evidence about her. For example, where in the tradition of the Church we come across contempt for women, we turn to the attitude of Jesus as a higher authority; and where in the gospels we read examples of what Bertrand Russell called 'a vindictive fury against those people who would not listen to his preaching' (quoted by Bowden on p. 106), the Christian reaction is often to say that the compiler of the gospel has here coloured the actual words of Jesus by emotions deriving from the persecution of Christians by Jews after Jesus' death. The reason for this is that male chauvinism or 'vindictive fury' seems out of character with the reported life and teaching of Jesus taken as a whole. For the same reason sensational suggestions that Jesus enjoyed a sexual relationship with Mary of Magdala, or with 'the beloved disciple', are usually rejected, as are the theory that he advocated armed revolution and Albert Schweitzer's belief that he pinned everything on the kingdom of God coming within the next few months (or at least before his death) and tried to force its coming by taking on himself the necessary suffering, so that he died in despair at the kingdom's non-arrival. Pictures of Jesus as the friend and colleague of emperors can be faulted by looking at the historical evidence. So can the portrait of Jesus as a forerunner of socialism, the colleague of Karl Marx. The New Testament certainly shows the beginnings of a wide variety of devotional and theological interpretations of Jesus Christ, but in his great volume on *Christ* Schillebeeckx showed that the liberty to interpret had a limit. 'Is Jesus here the symbolic point of reference of a kind of *mysticism of being*? Or is a *historical* event really the specific Christian access to God? The New Testament defends the latter point of view, sometimes with great stubbornness' (p. 465).

In particular the historical fact of Jesus sets a limit to the use of Christianity in the service of political or ecclesiastical power.

Frankly I am surprised that Bowden, who translated Schillebeeckx's lengthy exposition of 'the grace of our Lord Jesus Christ' as the key idea in the New Testament, should apparently fail to see that Paul's converts (for example) were captivated by Jesus, as Paul had been, rather than captured by the sinister influences which Graham Shaw finds demonstrated in Paul's 'blatantly manipulative' prayers. 'The eschatological fantasies of the early believers are consistently exploited to inculcate an anxiety which only membership of the apostles' privileged community can allay'. So Shaw tells us (quoted approvingly by Bowden on pp. 126–7). This reduction of Paul to the stature of a salesman with sinister motives and techniques seems to me absurd. Shaw does not think that God is real or that Jesus Christ is alive; he showed that in his book on *God in Our Hands* (1987). But Paul did.

But what can be known by methods acceptable to 'ordinary' historians about Jesus of Nazareth?

This question has produced a vast discussion over the last century and a half, and elsewhere I have contributed what little I could to the debate, in addition to sponsoring some more expert ventures in 'the quest of the historical Jesus' while I was a professional publisher. I can, however, now save space by quoting eight points which Professor E. P. Sanders, who is in general highly suspicious of the treatment of history by Christian theologians, reckoned in his *Jesus and Judaism* (1985) to be facts 'beyond doubt' or 'almost indisputable' (p. 11). I quote them because Bowden does (p. 43). After quoting them I shall offer what seem to me to be reasonable deductions from these facts, or supplementary facts which are also almost indisputable, and then I shall explain why I think it necessary to repeat points usually thought to need emphasis no more than they need contradiction.

Sanders' eight points are as follows:

1. Jesus was baptised by John the Baptist.
2. Jesus was a Galilean who preached and healed.
3. Jesus called disciples and spoke of there being twelve.
4. Jesus confined his activity to Israel.
5. Jesus engaged in controversy about the temple.
6. Jesus was crucified outside Jerusalem by the Roman authorities.
7. After his death Jesus' followers continued as an identifiable movement.
8. At least some Jews persecuted at least parts of the new

movement (Gal. 1:13, 22; Phil. 3:6), and it appears that this persecution endured at least to a time near the end of Paul's career (II Cor. 11:24; Gal. 5:11; 6:12; cf. Matt. 23:34; 10:17).

1. Jesus was baptised by John the Baptist.

At least to some extent he identified himself with a movement of great religious excitement. It was one of a number of groups which expected a rapid transformation of the world by God and which prepared for that day by exceptional holiness of life. John baptised in the river Jordan, and the Essene monks who buried the Dead Sea Scrolls at Qumran lived not far away, with beliefs which were in some ways similar. But near the end of the AD 20s John challenged all who would listen, summoning those who were Jews to undergo the same ceremony of baptism that admitted pro-selytes, or converts, to Judaism. A new kind of Judaism was being inaugurated. However, it was an example of the humility of Jesus that he chose to be baptised among 'sinners'.

2. Jesus was a Galilean who preached and healed.

He was not a sophisticated city man. Brought up in the obscurity of Nazareth, he came from a background where religion was devout but often charismatic rather than formal. He expressed his religion by preaching about God, by comparing God's love with a good father's, and by so sharing his spiritual power that some were healed of mental or physical diseases understood (as was normal in that society) as demon-possession. The God whom he preached was a loving God who desired people's health. So – happy the poor, happy the mourners, happy the hungry! The impact of this message through such healings was strengthened by the character of the preaching. It was memorable because Jesus used short stories usually based on life as the common people knew it and sharply epigrammatic sayings sometimes based on the Hebrew Scriptures but not consisting of abstract or systematic theology or philosophy. He wrote no book.

3. Jesus called disciples and spoke of there being twelve.

He called all who heard him to a decision in response to God. As Schillebeeckx put it in *Christ*, the book which Bowden translated, 'Jesus announces the time of the disclosure of the kingdom of God.

That means that we must respond to it in the same way that we respond to the announcement, "Lunch is ready!"' (p. 543). Jesus wanted some to enter more deeply into his life and teachings, and to share his work more actively, than was possible for people who met him occasionally. He therefore gathered a fellowship, although it was informal, and he regarded it as very significant, linking it with the twelve tribes of Israel. He hoped for the acceptance of his message by all these tribes, and failing that stood in the tradition of other Jews who put their trust in Israel's faithful 'remnant'. To follow him was not only an individual matter. But he planned no institution.

4. Jesus confined his activity to Israel.

It was not very long before his life and teaching were regarded as the Saviour's by many Gentiles. But in his lifetime he belonged to his Jewish background and mainly conformed to it. Any contacts with Gentiles were incidental. He believed that the Jewish people had a unique place in God's purposes. Much of his teaching had parallels in the teaching of the Jewish rabbis who had been professionally trained for their work, as he had not been.

5. Jesus engaged in controversy about the temple.

He did not put the temple's sacrificial system at the top of the priorities of true religion, and he denounced some of the practices of the priests and their employees. He also denounced the pedantic rigorism with which some Pharisees applied the law of Moses to life outside the temple. For example, he healed on the Sabbath although the strict interpretation of the religious law was that this was justified only if there was a danger of death. And he had table-fellowship with people classified by the religious law as sinners. (Sanders plays down the evidence about the tension between Jesus and the official teachers of the law, but it remains strong evidence.) His parables are part of the evidence (although also played down by Sanders) that Jesus was a layman, sympathetic with the problems of the common people.

6. Jesus was crucified outside Jerusalem by the Roman authorities.

He was executed because Pontius Pilate thought that he was an actual or potential rebel. This was because he had spoken about the kingdom of God. Actually his message had been non-violent. That was why in Jerusalem he was not accompanied by anything like an army. He had concerned himself with the reign of God, and his followers went unpunished. But to the Roman authorities he was too similar to the Zealot rebels for it to be safe to discharge him as innocent once he had been accused as a trouble-maker. It was safer to torture him to death.

7. *After his death Jesus' followers continued as an identifiable movement.*

They were shattered by the ignominious execution of their leader, despite his and their hopes that the kingdom of God would be established in the near future. But about twenty years after the death of Jesus Paul was preaching in Corinth the message that he had 'received', presumably within a few years of that death and his own conversion: Jesus had been buried but was 'raised on the third day according to the Scriptures' and had appeared to named individuals and to groups. He reminded the Corinthians of this in a letter written about five years later. This was the main explanation that the Christians gave of the change from despair to a dynamic faith. Certainly it is remarkable that after some kind of 'Easter experience' their movement was spreading in Greece. 'What is unquestionably unique about Jesus', Sanders says, 'is the result of his life and work' (p. 320).

8. *At least some Jews persecuted at least parts of the new movement, and it appears that this persecution endured at least to a time near the end of Paul's career.*

Since Judaism at that time tolerated a variety of groups (Pharisees, Sadducees, charismatics, etc.), the reason for this persecution seems to be that the Christians were making claims about Jesus which some Jews thought blasphemous because incompatible with the fundamental Jewish belief in one God. Paul's surviving correspondence shows that Jesus was indeed given a highly exalted status in early Christianity, for example as 'Christ' or Messiah. The Proclaimer had become the Proclaimed, and his grace could be praised before mentioning God's love – because it was believed to convey God's love, particularly through the cross and resurrection.

The list of certain or 'almost indisputable' facts about Jesus given by Professor Sanders is indeed limited. It does not mention the preaching of the kingdom of God, although Sanders reckoned it 'unquestionable' that 'Jesus taught about the kingdom' (p. 307) and made this the theme of Part Two of his book, where he wrote: 'It is my own view that we can know the meaning of "kingdom" in the teaching of Jesus . . . in general . . . although we can be sure neither of every nuance nor of the full range of meaning' (p. 126). Even when Sanders' list is extended by himself (p. 326), or by me through the deductions or supplementary facts which I have only repeated from the work of many New Testament scholars, it may seem to miss out facts equally probable and important. It is almost certain that the Lord's Prayer was originally Jesus' own summary of his teaching. One clause in it voiced his simple trust in the heavenly Father for 'bread' day by day. Another reflected his insistence that the heavenly Father forgives us freely, so that we must forgive those who have sinned against us. (There appears to be a divergence at this second point from the standard Jewish teaching that God forgives only the penitent and that we should give to our enemies no less and no more than justice.) Another clause reflects Jesus' expectation of a time of testing out the climax of the struggle against evil – a time which would tear people apart unless God delivered them.

The list also omits any reference to the last supper (another 'almost certain' fact to Sanders, p. 307) and to the willingness of Jesus to put himself into the hands of his enemies in Jerusalem. It seems reasonable to conclude that he became convinced that his death was inescapable if the will of his Father was to be done. Other gaps in Sanders' list could be mentioned which are filled in by other scholars, although I do not pretend that anyone has got everything right in the scholars' debate about the historical Jesus. (A summary was provided by Professor James Dunn's *The Evidence for Jesus*, 1985, an invaluable popularisation of his more scholarly work which seems to me notably balanced.) Professor Sanders, introducing his *Jesus and Judaism*, was referring to that world of New Testament scholarship, not to ecclesiastical obscurantism, when he wrote: 'The dominant view today seems to be that we can know pretty well what Jesus was out to accomplish, that we can know a lot about what he said, and that those two things make sense within the world of first-century Judaism' (p. 2). And he himself concluded that 'these facts yield *certain* knowledge about Jesus of a *general character*. They allow us to understand him as a figure in religious history' (p. 321).

I therefore find it very hard to see why Bowden is so pessimistic about the possibility of knowledge of the historical Jesus. He quotes Anthony Harvey as saying that 'it can still be argued that we can have no reliable historical knowledge about Jesus with regard to anything that really matters' (p. 32) and the Bishop of Salisbury, John Austin Baker, as having once written that 'the Gospels cannot be said to give united support to any view of Jesus, orthodox or heterodox' (p. 33). He quotes Wayne Meeks as thinking that 'we probably do not have enough firm information to write anything like a rounded account of either Jesus' moral behaviour or his moral teaching' (p. 111) and H. J. Cadbury as being of the opinion that 'we are doubtless correct in supposing that Jesus called God "Father", but that the word was for him pregnant with meaning such as we give it, is not so probable' (p. 140). However, such quotations do not give the whole of the picture as most scholars see it.

Indeed, Harvey's book on *Jesus and the Constraints of History* (1982) began by pointing out that

> what we have to ask is not whether a given statement is true with a kind of supernatural certainty but whether the fact which it reports may be regarded as at least as well established as any other fact which comes down to us from antiquity. On this test we shall find that the evidence for at least the main facts of the life and death of Jesus is as abundant, circumstantial and consistent as is the case with any other figure of ancient history.
>
> There are of course many points of detail in the gospels which are by no means reliably established as historical facts . . . But there are also certain facts about Jesus which, by any normal criterion of historical evidence, it would be altogether unreasonable to doubt (pp. 5–6).

The evidence about 'his so-called messianic consciousness, his moral perfection or his relationship with his heavenly Father' is, Harvey grants, 'both insufficient and controversial', but all the rest of that book was an attempt to give 'a new turn to the argument' by demonstrating by 'accurate historical enquiry' that Jesus so acted under various constraints 'that he could be regarded as an actual agent of the divine, and become thereby an object, not only of our endless and fascinated study, but of our love and worship' (pp. 6, 10).

Bishop Baker's attitude has been roughly similar. In *The Foolishness of God* (1970) he emphasised the diversity in the pictures of Jesus given by the gospels (most notably the difference between the fourth gospel and the others) and in the images of Jesus in later Christian devotion. 'All presentations of Jesus edit or gloss the record.' But Baker did not stop at that point. 'It is this which makes the "quest of the historical Jesus", the attempt to arrive at some firm conclusions about what he really was, absolutely imperative' (p. 152). It was Baker's argument, expounded at length, that this quest is both possible for an honest student and favourable to an essentially orthodox theological conclusion. I understand that he suggested most of the wording of the doctrinal Declaration of Assent to which the clergy of the Church of England are now required to subscribe. It is printed in the Alternative Service Book of 1980.

The point made by Meeks about Jesus' moral behaviour and teaching seems valid if it refers to a 'rounded account' of details. We do not know how Jesus conducted his business as a carpenter, for example, or advised his friends about marriage problems. We do not know what political or economic policy he would have advocated if invited to address the Roman Senate on such a subject. In first-century Palestine he said nothing about abortion or nuclear disarmament. But the parables and sayings reported in the gospels tell us about the main themes of his moral teaching and give no hint that he was attacked for hypocrisy (except that he was charged with being too fond of food, drink and the company of bad characters to make a respectable rabbi). These parables and sayings have been edited in transmission, but they leave a general impression that is firm enough for us to know what kind of moral teacher Jesus was. As the cautious Sanders says in his *Jesus and Judaism*: 'It is not the case that I am decisively convinced that Jesus did not say the bulk of the things attributed to him in the synoptic Gospels, but rather that I regard the material as having been subject to change in ways that cannot be precisely assessed' (pp. 15–16). That leaves a lot of evidence still standing. And the point made by Cadbury about Jesus' comparison between God and a father seems valid if it reminds us that in those days good fathers were not expected to act quite as they are expected to in our society. But the parables which illustrate the divine fatherhood still convey a strong religious message to modern parents or their children, because the relationships with which they deal are still sufficiently familiar.

The Quest of the Relevant Christ

In every age Christians – not all of them, but the most truly Christian of them when they have had access to the gospels – have acknowledged a duty to relate their ideas and images to the challenging reality of the historical Jesus as set forth in the gospels. They have not needed to be scholars in order to do this. St Francis of Assisi did it when he became poor. Mother Teresa did it when she went to Calcutta. It is sometimes said that the compilers of the four gospels were interested only in reporting the traditions about Jesus current in their own communities and were not at all concerned to get back to the original. And certainly all the material in all of the gospels has been edited in order to make a theological or devotional or moral point. These are books by preachers. But it is equally certain that the gospels include some very Jewish things which Christian communities far from Galilee and Jerusalem in the second half of the first Christian century must have found strange, some things which they must have found impossibly idealistic because the glow of excitement about the imminent kingdom of God was fading, and some things which they must have found offensive (such as the taunt that Jesus was a glutton, drunkard and the friend of tax-collectors and harlots). And the whole style of Jesus' teaching through parables or epigrams was one which, it seems from the letters preserved in the New Testament, few Christians were imaginative and clever enough to copy. Frequently commentators on the gospels, radical or conservative in their own bias, indicate the presence in those documents of Palestinian earth. Real history is there in the patterns which the evangelists have made. 'Redaction criticism' (the study of the editing) is a well-developed discipline. And it is striking that the Acts of the Apostles, which tells the story of the foundation of the Pauline churches with heavy editorial touches, has not edited out all the awkwardness of real history. For example, it is a repository of fragments of early Christian beliefs about Jesus as 'a man approved by God' which the Pauline churches had rejected as inadequate. Conflict and development are quite often smoothed over, but they are not totally concealed. The author was, in a sense which we can recognise, a historian.

It is sometimes said that Paul held himself aloof from these historical questions. Bowden tells us that apart from the references to the last supper and the resurrection appearances in 1 Corinthians 11 and 15 'Paul says nothing that we can identify with confidence as deriving from Jesus' earthly life and ministry, and certainly gives us no clue as to how that was understood in the communities in which he worked' (p. 41). But this is an exaggeration. Paul did not use the gospels, which were not yet written, or write with a purpose like theirs. But he often urged Christians to a new life 'in Christ', and although this was an idea larger than any direct imitation of the historical Jesus, or any repetition of his exact words, a reference back to Jesus was often implied and sometimes stated. Thus the first letter to the Corinthians does not contain only the two exceptions to Bowden's rule which he mentions and which are profoundly significant exceptions. It proclaims Christ 'nailed on a cross' (1:23) and 'raised to life' (15:20). It gives a ruling 'which is not mine but the Lord's' (7:10). It bases Paul's apostleship on seeing 'Jesus our Lord' (9:1). The Christians who are now 'Christ's body' must be characterised by practical love, and it would be unreasonable to think that the hymn to love in chapter 13 praises virtues thought to have been absent in Jesus. And Paul repeats the prayer *Marana tha* ('Come, O Lord!') in Aramaic, the language of Jesus (16:22). To Bowden, the famous hymn in Philippians 2:5–11 is

> mythological, in that it is about a divine figure who sheds his divinity, is obedient even to death, and as a result of that obedience is given by God an even higher place than he had before. Though we may be deeply moved by its poetry, if we apply our minds to it we have to reflect that we are not divine beings who have shed our divinity, and that the question 'obedient to what?' is not answered (p. 92).

But Paul knew perfectly well that the Christians in Philippi were not divine and never had been. He wanted them to be like their Lord by contending for the gospel, by love for one another and by humility (1:27–2:4). He referred to something as down-to-earth as death on the cross as God's will, to which Jesus was obedient (2:8). There is a mythological background to this hymn, and it is one which the Catholic Church was to refuse to take literally when it rejected the Arian picture of Christ as neither fully divine nor fully human – but Paul's main purpose in his quotation is plain and simple, for it is the encouragement of behaviour in conformity with the life and death of Jesus Christ. 'Christian faith', wrote Schillebeeckx, 'is a remembrance of the life and death of the risen Jesus through the practice of becoming his disciples – not through imitating what he has done but, like Jesus, by responding to one's own new situations from out of an intense experience of God' (p. 641).

Bowden is rightly troubled by 'the chaos of Christian moral teaching' (p. 110). But he does not greatly assist the solution of this problem. As I and many others think, the solution is a strenuous, reasoned and active attempt to relate the moral challenge contained in the New Testament to our own ethical questions which arise from our own new situations. Bowden, in contrast, very strangely seems to think it right to accept – or at least to quote without refutation – criticisms of the moral teaching of Jesus which are either mutually contradictory or else manifestly unfair. An eminent Jewish scholar, C. G. Montefiore, is quoted *both* as saying that 'Jesus was not good enough to be God' (p. 106) *and* as complaining that his moral teaching was 'strung too high' (p. 108). New Testament scholars are said to have established that 'the expectation of the imminent end to the present age conditions the whole of Jesus' ethical teaching' (p. 115), but H. J. Cadbury's *The Peril of Modernizing Jesus* (1937) is quoted as asking: 'Did Jesus consciously plan his life at all? Might he not have led a basically unreflective vagabond life, with much of the purpose in it being projected on to it later from the Gospels onwards?' (p. 141). Cadbury is also quoted as pointing out that nowhere in the synoptic gospels 'is there a clear appeal to the rights or needs of another party or to the interests of society in general' (p. 109).

Bowden gives a long reference to Richard Robinson's *An Atheist's Values* (1964). 'It is difficult', Robinson remarked, 'to see what Jesus' law of love can amount to in view of his overwhelming insistence on the priority of the law of piety. We cannot give material help to our neighbours because the law of piety demands improvidence and poverty. We cannot take family love very seriously because it may interfere with our devotions.' Robinson went on to point to human ideals 'wholly absent from Jesus' teaching, later indeed adopted into Christianity but in fact illegitimately labelled Christian'. 'The ideal of truth and knowledge is wholly absent. On the contrary, Jesus poured contempt on the professors of knowledge and declared that the kingdom of heaven is hidden from the wise and prudent. There is no place for beauty or justice.' 'Above all', Robinson concluded, 'Jesus says nothing on any social question except divorce' (p. 107).

In Bowden's book these questions or objections are simply thrown at the reader and left unanswered. But there are answers, at least in my view. By what Harvey called 'any normal criterion of historical evidence' some facts seem to be, in the ultra-cautious phrase of Sanders, 'almost indisputable'. Jesus did not claim 'to be God' just like that. He was a monotheist who prayed. His sayings and actions, however, clearly implied a special sense of God's holy love and a claim to be God's special agent in bringing about God's reign; this was the 'piety' of Jesus. If God were to be allowed to govern on earth as in heaven, people's behaviour would have to be perfect, chiefly in reflecting God's forgiving and healing love. The challenge was urgent. It was more important than economic aims or family ties. Jesus hoped that the kingdom of God would 'come' fully and soon, and he lived and died to speed its complete arrival. He sacrificed himself and said that his followers must be prepared for their own crosses. But his conviction about this good news and this moral ideal – the supreme truth about God and man, the only truth of ultimate significance – did not mean that he was willing to legislate comprehensively in the style of the law of Moses and the rabbis' oral tradition. On the contrary, he announced his message and illustrated its demands and promises by parables, often drawing lessons from the beauty of the earth and from the prudence of the worldly. And he met some of the human needs which he encountered, as a sign that the kingdom of God was bringing forgiveness, healing and joy. He told others to do likewise, like the Samaritan who met the needs of the Jew. He is reported as promising the Father's kingdom to those who feed the hungry, give drink to the thirsty, welcome strangers, clothe the naked, help the sick and visit prisoners.

What can a life which seems to have been understood by Jesus himself in those terms mean to people who live in a society and culture he never envisaged? It is important to ask this question without despair, for it is not a question that is unanswerable, however great the difficulties may be. There are some encouraging words by G. W. H. Lampe in *God as Spirit*:

> Jesus the Jew, the apocalyptic enthusiast, the wandering exorcist and miracle-worker, and many other aspects of the figure portrayed in the gospels, is certainly strange to our world. Yet the idea of the Kingdom of God at least lends itself to reinterpretation, as the New Testament itself demonstrates, on lines which make it of the greatest possible significance to every generation; the parables in which its character is disclosed, the 'fruit of the Spirit' which is love, joy, peace, and the other great Jesus-like

qualities, and the tragedy and victory of the Cross, are in no way strange to our world; they belong to the essential nature of mankind at all times (pp. 103–4).

The interpretation of the idea of the kingdom of God has accordingly been one of the great challenges to all Christian theologians, from Paul and John onwards. It is a task that has been extensively and profoundly discussed by the great modern theologians including Bultmann and Tillich. Both men are rightly criticised as being too individualist and emotional, in the existentialist style, ignoring rather than interpreting the social and physical dimensions of the hope that the government of God would be established on earth as in heaven. In reaction against that style of theology, the eschatology of the New Testament (of the Revelation of John, for example) has been linked with the political theology of Christians who await a new social order in (for example) Latin America or South Africa. These Christians of our own time are ready to pay the price of martyrdom on the way and are strengthened by the dreams of a future society which sociologists call millenarian. Eschatology has also been linked with ecology, and so with the hope that the earth itself, now too often abused and polluted by human greed and carelessness, will be made glorious in beauty as a new spirit takes control of politics and economics. These hopes which may be called messianic have arisen with a force and an eloquence reminiscent of the New Testament – and they have come from Christian communities whose poverty is also reminiscent of the Church's origins. Here I need do no more than refer to the connection between the New Testament and the liberation theology of Latin America which Christopher Rowland explored in his *Radical Christianity* (1988) after writing magisterial surveys of first-century apocalyptic hopes in *The Open Heaven* (1982) and of the evidence about Jesus in his *Christian Origins* (1985).

However, there is abiding interest in the attempts of theologians such as Bultmann and Tillich to translate the personal element in the New Testament's eschatology, and many thoughtful Christians have taken them very seriously, finding them helpful and life-changing. These were attempts to describe the situation of man confronted amid his finitude, anxiety and evil by God and God's offer of new and eternal life. It is a travesty of the teaching of Rudolf Bultmann, for example, to reduce it as Bowden does. '"God"', he now interprets Bultmann as saying, is the word which people have used in the past as a focus for their ultimate concerns of life, death, guilt, hope. Now they must learn to discard the word and the outmoded cosmology that goes with it . . . Jesus lived with such freedom and openness that not even his death could destroy his impact, and the community inspired by him still finds itself moved to hope that the love he communicated is stronger than death . . . To say that 'Jesus is God' is not to affirm a supernatural incarnation but to accept that the man Jesus clarifies ultimate human concern and gives the clue to the meaning of human existence (pp. 65–6).

Such a summary does scant justice to a great Christian theologian. In the age of Hitler Bultmann passionately wanted to preach good news about God, and did so in (for example) sermons in wartime Marburg. He was sceptical about the historicity of much of the material in the gospels, partly because he did his critical work at a time before it was known that elements which seem to be (and may really have been) Hellenistic ('the Gnostic redeemer myth') also belonged to the Jewish thought-world in New Testament times. His *Jesus* (1926), although described by its translators as a 'strictly historical study,' included an early statement of the need of Christianity to come to terms with the difficulties as he saw them (and exaggerated them, as most New Testament scholars have come to think). Significantly, the book was translated as *Jesus and the Word* (1935). His later work shows that he continued to believe that the message of Jesus was the 'presupposition' of the New Testament theology which could be known in far more detail than that message – but the message was not totally unknowable, as may be seen from (for example) the first chapter of his *Theology of the New Testament*, translated into English in 1952. It is not surprising that his pupils, Günther Bornkamm and others, undertook the 'new quest of the historical Jesus' which was exciting while I was at the SCM Press. As his American lectures on *Jesus Christ and Mythology* (1960) showed very strongly, Bultmann wanted to strip away the 'mythology' in order that what was still intelligible and powerful in the message of Jesus about God, a message given by life as well as words, might guide the twentieth century through great spiritual problems.

This was not because he adhered to a tradition that Jesus provides the only source of truth about God. Bowden parodies the Christian tradition when he asks whether 'it is worth while any longer trying to trace our understanding of the nature of our relationship with God, redemption and forgiveness, exclusively back to some identifiable element in the life, character and activity of Jesus of Nazareth' (p. 145). Even the most Christocentric theologians, such as Karl Barth, have always found their authority in a 'Christ' wider than what is recorded about Jesus of Nazareth – the 'Christ' who is the Lord of the Church, the *Logos* or Word of God in all creation, etc. But countless Christians, both theologians and simple disciples, have found that what can be known about Jesus of Nazareth at the historical start of the wider 'Christ' provides the supreme evidence that God is real, loving and reliable, so that the hopes and fears of human existence lived outside this influence are eclipsed. And Bultmann was among them, being criticised for it by atheist existentialists. John Macquarrie ended his study of *The Scope of Demythologizing: Bultmann and His Critics* (1960) by noting that Bultmann had 'known where to set a limit . . . The limit to demythologizing is nothing other than the recognition of the difference between a philosophy of human existence and a religion of divine grace' (p. 244).

In 1963 I included in *The Honest to God Debate* a review by Bultmann (then approaching his eightieth birthday) of John Robinson's bestseller. He sympathetically outlined Robinson's attempt to express an idea of God, the 'depth and ground of all being', whose relation to the world 'belongs to his essential being' but who is also 'the transcendent, the unlimited'. I also included Bultmann's own popular account of the gospel (in Greek, *kerygma*) in a letter of that year to the Sheffield Industrial Mission. I believe this should not be forgotten as an example of the kind of answer which ought to be given nowadays to questions about Jesus.

By nature men live by their own will and want to achieve their security by their own power. That is what the New Testament calls sin. For the basic sin is not the breaking of moral commandments (this follows from the basic sin), but man's self-will and his intention of trying to live by his own wisdom and power. Need for acceptance also belongs to the life of man, and by nature man tries to satisfy this need for acceptance through his own power.

The grace of God is grace for the sinner. The *kerygma* tells the natural man (which we all are) that he can only find his security if he lets go his self-security and that he can only find acceptance if he lets it be given by God in the knowledge that without God he is nothing. The grace of God releases him from all feverish searching for security and from all resentments and from the complexes which grow out of an unsatisfied need for acceptance.

Since the *kerygma* demands the surrender of all human self-will and of all self-security, the *kerygma* of the grace of God seems to the natural man to be primarily a stern demand, an 'offence', a stumbling block. For to abandon himself to the grace of God means in fact that man must be ready to trust in the grace of God amid all the blows of fate, in all suffering. That is why the *kerygma* of the grace of God is at the same time the *kerygma* of the cross.

While the *kerygma* demands the surrender of self-will it also demands at the same time *love* of the other, of the 'neighbour'. For love means to live for the other, at the same time surrendering one's self-will and being ready to sacrifice one's self-security for the other. The surrender of self-will to God occurs in actual life through loving one's neighbour.

To such surrender to the grace of God and to the neighbour, the *kerygma* promises freedom, power and life. If a man gives himself up to the grace of God he is released from all anxiety for himself and his security, and in such freedom he gains a quite new power; for he gains along with it a new hope.

Together with the cross the resurrection is proclaimed. This means that the man who trusts in the grace of God, and who lets go all anxiety about security, is also freed from all fear of death. He knows that he is not the one who has to worry about his future. God takes care of it; God gives him his future and therefore God's grace encounters him even in death. We cannot of course form any clear picture of a life after death. Yet it belongs to the radical surrender to God's grace that we renounce all pictures of a future after death and hand over everything to the grace of God, who gives us what is to come. God is always the God who comes.

John Bowden's response is on pp. 291–6. The response by Dennis Nineham (pp. 296–306) also alludes to this chapter.

7

DENNIS NINEHAM AND THE RELEVANCE OF JESUS:

If revelation is culture-bound, is it authoritative?

Of all the essays in *The Myth of God Incarnate*, the Epilogue by Dennis Nineham was the most disturbing because in it an Anglican priest widely respected for his personal qualities and his eminence as a New Testament scholar seemed to be saying that the Bible has little to teach modern people. Dr Nineham is no ignoramus or amateur who might be motivated to advocate the exclusion of the Bible from serious attention because he has never given the Bible such attention himself. After teaching theology at Oxford for ten years (from 1944) he became Professor of Biblical and Historical Theology at King's College, London, Professor of Divinity in London University in 1958 and Regius Professor of Divinity at Cambridge in 1964, before returning to Oxford for another period of ten years, as Warden of Keble College, and a final spell as Professor of Theology in Bristol 1980–86. Yet in this essay of 1977 he appeared to have found as little of permanent significance in the study of the New Testament as Maurice Wiles and Geoffrey Lampe had found in the study of the Christian Fathers.

Am I being too negative about this essay in *The Myth of God Incarnate*? A fair verdict would certainly have to recognise that it deals with real issues in the historical study of the gospels – the issues with which I have attempted to deal in my chapter about John Bowden's book. A just judge would also notice that Nineham spoke on behalf of 'the Christians' when he declared that when

> this Christ is truly preached and they truly listen to, and hear, the preaching, he does something to them, he faces them with an inescapable choice. He shows them just what their previous way of living has been worth and puts before them an alternative possibility, the possibility of living entirely out of God's power

and grace. In other words, he is the lens through which all the demands and promises of God to them are focused (p. 200).

But Nineham, who in those sentences sounds very like Bultmann as quoted at the end of my last chapter, describes as 'very doubtful' the belief in 'an unchangeable fundamental structure of the human spirit as such' and therefore avoids Bultmann's insistence on the permanent and supreme importance of the New Testament. Nineham asks:

> Is it necessary to 'believe in Jesus' in any sense beyond that which sees him as the main figure through whom God launched men into a relationship with himself so full and rich that, under various understandings and formulations of it, it has been, and continues to be, the salvation of a large proportion of the human race? (pp. 202–3).

A just judge would notice the consistent reticence about the actual life and teaching of the historical Jesus. Indeed, Nineham thinks that Christ can only function *if* he is an ever-changing figure. 'Just as he changed greatly between apostolic and Nicene times, so he has changed down the generations and must continue to change if, as cultural change accelerates, he is to continue to mediate the nature, grace and demands of God to succeeding generations' (p. 200). And Nineham says that his aim is to stop attempts to claim 'uniqueness of some sort for Jesus on historical grounds' (p. 201). It seems, therefore, that in this essay in *The Myth of God Incarnate* all the emphasis is on the career of Jesus since his death. 'Perhaps we may put it like this,' he says: 'the career of the historical Jesus occurred at such a time and in such circumstances that it was like a lighted match applied to a powder-keg. The powder represents the religious expectations and aspirations of the period, which were many and varied . . .' (p. 199). And it seems a fair summary of Nineham's understanding of the influence of 'Christ', as expressed in this 1977 essay, that the influence is exerted without the gospels being in any important sense normative or authoritative. The match (the figure of Jesus of Nazareth) ignites the religious expectations and aspirations of a society that comes to be called Christian in the first Christian century or later – but it quickly burns out, and that, it seems to be claimed, is no great loss.

H. J. Cadbury is praised ('as usual, judicious', p. 189) and quoted as saying that the religion which became the Christianity of the Roman empire 'may have had but slight relation to the historical actuality of its founder' (p. 191). In his Preface to his book on *The Use and Abuse of the Bible* (1976), Nineham stated 'baldly' that

> within the community which has preserved the scriptures, and had its life and beliefs to a considerable extent moulded by them, my experience has been such that, unless I deny what I am deeply convinced on many grounds is real, I am bound to affirm the existence and initiative of God and the possibility and reality of personal encounter with him (p. x).

But that statement, however impressive, leaves open the possibility that the 'considerable' influence of the Bible on the Christian community may rightly be much less than the importance of the community itself, or of direct personal experience of God within it. In a lecture of 1969 included in his *Explorations in Theology* (1977, pp. 110–11), Nineham had answered the question whether the Christian community should regard the 'Christian atheism' then being propounded by some theologians as being a legitimate development. His reply showed the absence of any effective idea of biblical authority, which to him must mean the 'attempted reference to alleged objective norms from which logically irrefragable positions can be derived'. He put his trust in the hope that 'as I live and worship with them and with my other fellow Christians, in the community, under the power of the Spirit . . . we shall all come to recognize dimensions of our common life and worship to which the views they hold – or think they hold – fail to do justice'.

In contrast, I am interested in the question of historical truth because I think that it would be a great loss to Christianity and to the spiritual life of mankind if the evidence about Jesus contained in the gospels were ever to be moved from the centre of the prayers and moral efforts of the Church as a body or the individual Christian. Christianity, whatever else it may be, is always and everywhere discipleship. So it must rely on the gospels more than on any other source of guidance. They need to be interpreted by the reason and experience of those who read or hear them, but they are decisive in the sense that a response to the Jesus they tell us about is what makes a community or an individual Christian. In 1958 Nineham was saying at the end of a discussion of biblical authority that 'obviously the clue must be found in the figure and work of Jesus, on which all else converges' (*Explorations in Theology*, p. 74), and thirty years later I see no reason to disagree with that judgement made early in a distinguished career. I suspect that in recent years Nineham, who has given so much of his life and ability to the close study of the gospels, has grown so familiar with the subject as to be somewhat bored by it and somewhat insensitive to the immense contrast between it and other sources of inspiration for spiritual and moral growth.

In *The Myth of God Incarnate* Nineham stated that 'modern historical methods have rendered obsolete any talk of "assured results" in relation to the figure of Jesus' (p. 192) and also stressed the brevity of the gospels. 'B. H. Streeter once calculated that, apart from the forty days and nights in the wilderness (of which we are told virtually nothing) everything reported to have been said and done by Jesus in all four gospels would have occupied only some three weeks' (pp. 188–9). About the evidence which *is* in the gospels, Nineham made points intended to question the conventional Christian tributes to Jesus as the 'perfect' man, 'the man for God' and 'the man for others'. He quoted C. G. Montefiore's complaint that we have no single story 'about his doing good to and praying for a single Rabbi or Pharisee' (p. 189) – apparently ignoring the story in Luke's gospel that when being nailed to his cross Jesus prayed for the forgiveness of his enemies (a story surely in keeping with the rest of the evidence about the character of Jesus). Nineham asserted that Jesus' 'understanding of man's relationship to God might strike us as in some respects rather servile and juridical' because 'to describe God as "father" meant something very different in his situation from what it does in ours' (p. 193) – apparently ignoring the glimpse of home life (surely not untypical) in the parable in Luke's gospel about the father, the prodigal son and their final relationship of love, a parable surely not untypical of the teaching of Jesus, although the wording we have is Luke's. He complained about Jesus' lack of concern 'with altruism . . . or with the rights or needs of the other party' (p. 193) – apparently ignoring the parable of the good Samaritan given by Luke and the story of the judgement of the nations according to their response to human needs in Matthew 25:31–46. Nineham also recorded the complaint that Jesus 'condemned severely those who would not share his vision' (p. 189) but noted two points (p. 190) – that such a stricture on Jesus is 'not necessarily justified' (because reports of the anger of Jesus may have been edited by angry Christians) and that if Jesus had faults 'his faults were the price he paid for that passionate faith which enabled him to move the world' (a quotation from W. Durant).

I agree that history does not tell us enough about the psychology or actions of Jesus to justify any claim on purely historical grounds that Jesus was completely 'perfect' in relation to God or his fellow men. Indeed, I find it impossible to see how there could be such evidence about any historical figure that would convince all his fellow men. But I must add that the impact of Jesus on Christians has been such that the tradition in their faith that he was 'perfect' or 'sinless' (the New Testament prefers the second expression) is entirely understandable. For the impact of Jesus has been the centre of the impact of the Bible.

Let me quote Nineham's account of this impact, which he gave in a lecture that was the last in a series on *The Church's Use of the Bible* which he edited in 1963. He then wrote:

> Interpret the universe and live in it as if the biblical writers' accounts of an encounter with a living, loving, demanding, promising God were true, and see if their experiencc is validated in your own subsequent experience; some such appeal to personal experience is surely unavoidable. But it may be backed up, not only by appeal to the experience of others, but also by the claim that the life lived in accordance with the biblical interpretation of life seems to fit best into the scheme of things and make sense in the light of conditions as we know them (p. 160).

In *The Use and Abuse of the Bible* Nineham made it 'unmistakably clear' that he was *not* doubting that 'contemporary Christians have limitless truth to glean from the gospels' (p. 168) and gave us a slightly fuller and more approving account of the biblical view of life:

> The New Testament is pervaded throughout by a mood of joyful triumph and release, release from the various forces which have been making men's lives a misery and separating them from God and one another. There is a feeling that the great distance which had seemed to separate God and men had been annihilated and, despite the writers' full recognition of their sinfulness, they betray a sense of an intimacy with God at least as close as any that Abraham, Moses or the old Hebrew prophets enjoyed. God is no longer primarily king or judge, but father. There is everywhere a consciousness of a spiritual presence, a presence which puts an end to fear and loneliness and gives full confidence in the face of all enemies, both natural and supernatural, including death (p. 140).

In a lecture of 1966 included in his *Explorations in Theology* he maintained that

> it is as nearly certain as any historical fact can be, that the events in which the church originated were the life and activity of Jesus; so the Christian can be quite sure that in Jesus God was at work producing the community in and through which salvation should be available (p. 88).

He also maintained that although the details are more dubious 'the *general* trustworthiness of the gospel records has withstood criticism in the sense that no serious scholar now doubts either that Jesus existed and was crucified by the Romans or that his previous activity as exorcist, teacher and controversialist was broadly as outlined in the gospels' (p. 76).

Yet in a lecture of 1975 he claimed that

> no scholar today supposes that New Testament Christianity as it stands is a possible religion for modern Western man, or that the character, conduct and beliefs of Jesus, even if we knew far more about them than we do, could constitute as they stand the content of a modern faith (p. 156).

The explanation given was that what the New Testament says about Jesus must be interpreted afresh by succeeding generations, expressing the significance of the material not in terms of the 'totality' of the 'culture' which shaped the New Testament but in terms of the totality of some later culture. As he said in another lecture:

> You can only extract revelation from the Bible when you have decided on the terms in which you are going to 'translate', or 'demythologize', or understand, the biblical terms and images; and that means allowing your contemporary statement of the faith to be determined by facts and considerations not directly derived from the Bible at all (p. 101).

I hope it is clear from what I have written elsewhere – in my history of many varieties of faith in *Christian England* from the Romans to 1914, for example, or in my book on *The Futures of Christianity* – that I am among those who emphatically agree with Nineham that (as he said in another lecture) 'what the Bible means for us must be expressed in our own way' (p. 139). In the years to come, as in the past, 'New Testament Christianity' or the message of Jesus must be understood and interpreted in terms of one's own culture. In the Bible itself there is great diversity. And nowadays there would be almost as much agreement with Nineham among thoughtful Christians about other propositions. He maintains that the Bible is not 'a collection of inerrant propositions and irreformable demands and propositions, guaranteed by their direct divine origin as timelessly valid and universally binding' (*The Church's Use of the Bible*, p. 147) – for even when the Old and New Testaments are described as 'infallible' or 'inerrant', no conservative aware of the problems would go so far as to put their entire contents on that level. Many thoughtful Christians would, however, hesitate to go as far as Nineham in another direction, when he calls the Bible

> a kaleidoscope of writings, traditions and fragments which are often rather artificially stitched together, the products of prophets, poets, visionaries, wise men, historians, liturgists, theologians and many others, and reflecting, at first or second hand, some vivid experience of life, usually, though not always, life touched by the hand of God (*The Use and Abuse of the Bible*, p. 193).

The hesitation which I share about that description of the Bible would not be due to a desire to deny the human element in these diverse books. It would be due to a wish to acknowledge the element of divine inspiration, and to say with the Second Vatican Council (1965) that 'we must acknowledge that the books of Scripture, firmly, faithfully and without error, teach that truth which God, *for the sake of our salvation*, wished to see confided to the sacred Scriptures'. The words which I have just italicised can be understood as allowing poetry (for example) to be interpreted as poetry and as limiting the inerrancy of the Bible to 'saving' (not scientific, historical or legislative) truth. Such words have been so understood by many Catholic or Evangelical teachers of a conservative disposition. For a fuller discussion I refer to my dialogue with the Evangelical leader John Stott, in chapter 2 of *Essentials* (1988). A Christian need not be a naive fundamentalist, totally ignoring or rejecting modern scholarship, if he holds that the question about 'what the Bible means for us' must be answered by a genuine attempt to let the Bible speak to us about God and our salvation, avoiding a mere echo of opinions derived from other sources. 'The content of a modern faith' should be the Bible as we understand it, with other sources of inspiration added. The meaning of the Bible for us should determine what we believe as Christians.

In *The Use and Abuse of the Bible* Nineham repeatedly stated his position that many attempts to extract *the* meaning of biblical passages turn out to be something radically different from the meaning intended by the writers, where we can recover that original meaning – a qualification which is necessary not only because the biblical writings are often fragmentary or concise but also because the world of the biblical writers is distant from our own. 'Anyone who claims that a document "really" means something different from what it appears to say must be careful to ask himself how he knows and also what he means by the word "really"' (p. 65). And where *the* meaning is extracted in a form that can be understood by modern people, it often turns out to be what the modern Christian was going to say anyway. Thus Bultmann made the New Testament 'repeat endlessly the – admittedly vital – challenge to give up all the pretended securities derived from this world by which we try to bolster up the natural man, and to live entirely out of the future, out of God's resources' (*Explorations in Theology*, p. 4). Such modernising interpretations, Nineham asserts in *The Use and Abuse of the Bible*, end up with a less distinctive message than 'the various New Testament descriptions of what the divine intervention consisted in' (p. 177). But the descriptions of the divine intervention which the New Testament does supply cannot be accepted as they stand, for they produce 'the embarrassment of the modern scholar' as he asks:

> Whatever its exact form, what was the point and result of it? The conquest of demonic forces opposed to God? Victory over Sin and Death conceived as quasi-personal powers? The provision of an effective sacrifice for sin or of a new Adam who could undo the work of the old and be raised to be a universal figure in whom all could be incorporated?
>
> It is only by a very drastic and unhistorical treatment that modern, as distinct from ancient, theologians can harmonize all these. Moreover, even so summary a list makes clear that none of these images, as it stands, is going to prove acceptable in our totality (*The Use and Abuse of the Bible*, p. 177).

In reply to Nineham some theologians have said that he exaggerates the difficulty of moving from the world of the Bible to the world of today. This is because he exaggerates the 'totality' of a culture and therefore needlessly despairs about the possibility of the responsible translation of ideas from one culture to another. It has been pointed out that even within a culture dissentients do deny the truth of some beliefs held by the majority. Thus we read that the Sadducees denied that there is any resurrection, or angels, or spirits (Acts 23:8), and Nineham believes that Luke deliberately deleted from his sources any references to the death of Jesus as an atoning sacrifice (*The Use and Abuse of the Bible*, pp. 152–3). And it is also pointed out that much in human nature remains constant, so that questions and answers about truth formulated in one culture can be understood in another. Nineham's position was criticised along those two lines by C. F. D. Moule and John Barton in *Theology* (1977, pp. 33–4, 122–3; 1979, pp. 103–9, 191–9). Neither Moule nor Barton occupies a position anywhere near fundamentalism, but both were dissatisfied with Nineham's exaggeration (as it seemed to them) of the pastness of the past and the otherness of other cultures. In reply Nineham reiterated his stress on 'cultural relativism'. Each culture, he repeated, has its own 'totality'. And when pressed to acknowledge the constants in human nature across time and space, he quoted Ernst Troeltsch, a scholar whom we shall meet again in the next chapter: 'What was really common to mankind, and universally valid for it, seemed, in spite of a general kinship and a capacity for mutual understanding, exceedingly little, and to belong more to the province of material goods than to the ideal values of civilisation.'

A full debate about the truth of Troeltsch's assertion would obviously involve a full exploration of some very debatable territory studied by the rival experts in many academic disciplines. Evidence about the dissimilarity of cultures can be piled up. So can evidence about their 'general kinship and a capacity for mutual understanding'. When studying languages, an expert can stress either that they are often hard to learn or that they often display a common linguistic structure. When studying social systems, an expert can treat them either as oddities or as a species. When studying mythologies, an expert can declare either that they are even harder for a stranger to understand than the languages in which they are preserved in verbal expression, or that they contain many fascinating parallels because the 'archetypes' in human feelings and dreams correspond with similarities in human experience. And most experts, so far as I know, would draw back from any facile generalisation. It would be convenient to say that in the many years that have passed since Troeltsch's death the debate had been settled by advances in social anthropology, psychology,

linguistics, the study of world-views and religions and other disciplines. But alas, when conducted at a general level the debate
somewhat resembles a dispute about whether a bottle is half empty
or half full. In the last analysis one's general approach to complex
and ambiguous phenomena seems to depend on whether one is
temperamentally inclined to see the constants or the variables. The
general debate therefore continues and seems unlikely to end. And
it spills over into the debate about the intelligibility of ancient
literature. When we have deciphered the inscriptions of Egypt or
Babylon, are we much the wiser about the early centuries of
civilisation? How easy is it for a modern reader to understand an
ancient Greek tragedy, or the world of Shakespeare? How far can
we learn about God from the Hindu Upanishads, or about the
spiritual life from the Buddhist scriptures, or about our duties from
the Analects of Confucius?

What Must the Truth Be Now?

It may be more profitable if we concentrate on the most solid work
of scholarship that Nineham has so far published, his widely used
Pelican Commentary on *The Gospel of St Mark* (1963), and if we
ask the question which has often been quoted from Leonard
Hodgson: 'What must the truth be now if people who thought as
the biblical writers did put it like that?' (quoted in *The Use and
Abuse of the Bible*, p. 222). Hodgson himself commented that 'the
real object of our study is not what the men whose works we are
reading were *consciously aware* of thinking and saying; it is the
truth which was struggling to make itself known through minds
conditioned by their presuppositions' (quoted in *The Church's Use
of the Bible*, pp. 164–5). And Nineham understands Hodgson's
question to mean: 'what light can we get on our present situation
from the stories told about God and man by people of the biblical
era?' (*The Use and Abuse of the Bible*, p. 222).

This particular gospel seems a good test case. Of the four in the
New Testament it is probably the one that seems strangest to
modern readers, and particularly to modern middle-class readers
enjoying many privileges, partly because it contains comparatively
little of the teaching of Jesus and partly because it seems to
have been written for a Christian community in exceptionally
uncomfortable circumstances. So what can Mark mean to us?

Nineham convincingly demonstrates that the gospel in our hands is the product of a community's faith, interpreting what evidence it had about Jesus. For example, the two stories about the feeding of thousands seem to have been originally one story, now retold in two ways for purposes which cannot be known. That is not to say that the gospel is all fiction. On the contrary, 'we can often be virtually sure that what the tradition is offering us are the authentic deeds, and especially the authentic words, of the historic Jesus' (*The Gospel of St Mark*, p. 51). But there are limits to the extent to which the Marcan material which later gospels used can be relied on as eye-witness evidence for details (as Nineham showed in his *Explorations in Theology*, pp. 32–40). Sometimes words which probably represent what the eternally living Lord was believed to be saying to that community are put into the mouth of the historical Jesus. Examples may well be the declaration that all foods are clean (7:19) and the acceptance of exorcism in the name of Jesus even when not done by a Christian (9:39), for the rest of the New Testament contains evidence that no such instructions by Jesus were known in time to answer anxious questions on these matters. And chapter 13 of Mark's gospel seems to be coloured by memories of the fall of Jerusalem long after Jesus' death.

The commentary also shows that material in the gospel with a stronger claim to authenticity has been shaped to accord with editorial interests. Nineham attributes this to the religion of the community to which this gospel belonged and notes features which are difficult or impossible for modern people to understand or to accept. The Old Testament was regarded as a book containing accurate predictions of God's future acts of salvation, so that it was believed that it could actually supply information about the life of Jesus. Most of the Christians shared the general Jewish expectation of a final intervention by God in the affairs of this world in the fairly near future. For them,

> the Jesus of whose earthly life the tradition spoke was the same person whom they now knew as Lord and Son of God, and whom they believed to be sitting at God's right hand in glory, governing the universe on his behalf, and soon to come to earth again to judge and wind up the universe, and usher in a wholly new world-order (p. 18).

The earthly life of Jesus had included such powerful exercises of divine power that the Christians asked themselves why he had not been recognised as the Son of God or Messiah. This gospel provided an answer:

> According to St Mark, although the public ministry of Jesus was quite unmistakably the inbreaking of the kingdom of God, Jesus did not seek public recognition as the messianic bringer of the kingdom; on the contrary he silenced such recognition when it was forthcoming and took careful steps to hide his identity (p. 68).

In this gospel the parables are told in order to conceal the truth from the people (4:10–12). The first unrebuked acclaim of Jesus as Messiah or Son of David comes from a blind beggar during the last journey to Jerusalem (10:47); the first clear sign that Jesus accepts a messianic role comes during the palm-strewn entry to Jerusalem (11:10); and there is an explicit claim only under solemn questioning by the High Priest (14:62). Jesus, however, cannot escape publicity, because he shares the general belief in 'the existence of innumerable supernatural beings other than God' (p. 45), and aided by angels he battles with demons in public. His miracles are achieved by the supernatural power that also enables him to multiply food, walk on water, still a storm or blast a fig tree; and most of them end in the expulsion of demons who cause diseases. In short:

> Jesus, in Mark, comes before us not primarily as a teacher, but as the mysterious Son of God – a numinous and rather aweful figure whose work is to bring home to his generation the conviction that the end of this dispensation is imminent, and by his ministry and death to hasten the coming of the kingdom (p. 48).

All these ideas are, as Nineham frequently stresses, strange to modern people and scarcely (if at all) intelligible. But we must still ask: what must the truth be now, if people who thought as Mark and (presumably) Jesus himself did put it like that? Nineham has never answered that question at any length, understandably pleading in his commentary that it falls outside the scope of such a book. In his *Explorations in Theology* he says that 'in a life which has brought many extra-curricular chores and concerns, I have gone as fast as I can', asking for 'new imaginative categories and symbols' but not being the prophet who could supply them (p. 5). I also have too little prophetic inspiration to answer with any authority. But it does not seem to me that the question is completely unanswerable.

I can only repeat from previous chapters that it can be affirmed on purely historical grounds that Jesus is utterly unique among mankind's religious teachers. He did not claim to be God the Son, but he did claim that his teaching and work had a unique place in God's purposes. What he said and did needs to be related to problems with which (so far as we know) he did not deal, such as the question whether Gentile Christians could eat food considered unclean by orthodox Jews. By his spiritual presence Jesus has continued to guide Christians, but Christians always need to check what they think is his guidance by comparison with the gospels. To read the gospels with modern eyes is to see how profoundly Jesus and the first Christians were influenced by the Old Testament yet constituted a new phenomenon puzzling and shocking to the Jewish religious authorities of the time, so that both the Jewish background and that new age must be considered as the background to later Christianity. Jesus was naturally reluctant to accept the title of Messiah since in the popular mind it implied that he was a rebel against Rome. He exercised power which may be called divine or supernatural, but it was always as a humble man, the servant of God, the friend of sinners, the subject of Caesar and Pilate. We have no need to think that the reports of his miracles are entirely accurate or that the diseases which he cured (perhaps by eliciting faith and confidence) were caused by demons. We can also be agnostic about angels. What is essential, if we are to be full Christians, is to believe that God was then at work 'for our salvation'. We cannot share any hopes that the kingdom of God would arrive in the first Christian century but we can understand how the enthusiasm of people more closely acquainted with grief than with worldly power gave rise to such millenarian hopes.

So from Mark's gospel arises a question not about the general meaning of human life, or about the general relationship of God and man, but about Jesus and his significance for us. For this purpose this gospel, together with the rest of the New Testament, gives us adequate – I do not say 'complete' – evidence about the historical Jesus. I recognise that there are many debates between scholars about the extent and meaning of the evidence, but there is a widespread agreement which I outlined in the previous chapter, and I conclude that Nineham is being too pessimistic when he writes that 'the plain fact is that no picture of the historical Jesus has yet emerged – or ever seems likely to – which comes anywhere near commanding universal, or even general, agreement' (*The Use and Abuse of the Bible*, p. 165).

However, the New Testament does not merely provide information. The Jesus presented to us by Mark asks: 'But what about you? Who do you say I am?' (8:29). As Nineham says in his commentary, Mark's story including that question 'is not so much intended to describe faithfully what happened on the *first* occasion when Jesus was recognized as Messiah as to show what is essentially involved and demanded whenever such a recognition takes place' (p. 227). The answer to this question is not a story which 'co-stars Jesus and God' (if Nineham 'may put it so without irreverence' in *The Myth of God Incarnate*, p. 202). The Jesus who protested that 'no one is good except God alone' (10:18) would surely have agreed that 'any serious religious quest must be based on the recognition that the one God is the sole norm and source of all goodness, even of the goodness of Jesus in the days of his flesh' (*The Gospel of St Mark*, p. 274). And the right answer to our question does not assert that Jesus rescued men 'from otherwise unavoidable damnation': that answer, as Nineham rightly says, 'presupposes a later, sophisticated atonement theology' not in the gospels (p. 281). But the answer is 'yes' to the following questions which are, I think, asked by the gospel as Nineham expounds it section by section in his commentary. Did Jesus bring government by God into the affairs of this world? Did he conquer when he was tested by evil situations? Has he the right to call us to be his pupils ('disciples'), teaching us as one who has the authority to do so? Can his influence cure many of our diseases, assure us of God's forgiveness of all our sins, and bring a new joy into the world, replacing all legalism? Does it bring peace amid the storms of life and unity and calm to our divided and restless personalities? Does it feed our spiritual natures, open our spiritual eyes and cure our spiritual paralysis? Does his victory mean that we need not fear physical death, because he has revealed a Father who loves us for all eternity; that we are not chained by the habits or the guilt of our sinfulness, because he has made possible a new life?

It is surely very striking that Mark's gospel, written within and for a community whose beliefs are largely foreign to us, has been able, and still is able, to put these life-searching questions and to inspire Christian responses. I conclude that the gospel's authority as revelation, like the authority of the rest of the Bible, derives not from complete infallibility or inerrancy but from its power, in and through its human element, to communicate that truth which God wanted put into it for the sake of our salvation. If I may put it so without impertinence, commentators who concentrate on the differences between the first century and ours may obscure that authority, so that God's word does not speak to us, changing our lives. Nineham begins his commentary by saying that visitors to an ancient building 'can get a great deal out of going round by themselves without any guide or guide book, but if they have a guide who knows his job they are sure to get much more profit and pleasure from their visit' (p. 15). I am not so sure about this, although I have been explaining great churches to visitors for many years. If a visitor is constantly told that the beliefs of the medieval world are unintelligible or plainly untrue, and not much else is added, he may be deterred from seeing that a cathedral (for example St Mark's cathedral in Venice) is a beautiful building which was made by people not wholly unlike him and which can speak to his heart.

After this criticism of an expert by an amateur, it would be a fair challenge to ask me how I would guide a modern visitor round Mark's gospel. So I propose to reprint an introduction to Mark which I wrote after learning much from Nincham's commentary among others and which formed part of my paperback on *Jesus for Modern Man* (1975). It was based on the translation in the Good News Bible, and like that version (which has subsequently been revised) was intended for people as unsophisticated as the first readers of Mark's rough Greek. It began with a discussion of the gospel's authorship which I have deleted, for the discussion can never be conclusive. Although I am attracted by the tradition that Mark wrote for the church of Rome after the martyrdoms of Peter and Paul, as Nineham points out 'Mark (Marcus) was the commonest Latin name in the Roman empire'. And I agree with him that the question who wrote the gospel is '*comparatively* unimportant' (p. 39). To reprint my discussion of the authorship would be to distract attention from what I do want to say. What matters is the gospel's message – which I believe conveys if not always the very words of Jesus (how could any non-fundamentalist be certain of that?) at least a clear impression of the spiritual impact made by Jesus on his first followers and on at least some of those whom they recruited within approximately the first forty years of the Church's history.

I maintain, along with most of those who would call themselves both Christian and radical, that the force of this impact can be felt more than nineteen hundred years later, despite all the problems which mean that we cannot completely feel what people now long dead felt; and I maintain that the impact has been renewed as Jesus Christ has, as it were, stepped out of the past, and out of eternity, to be the living Lord for people of many generations and many societies. By referring to his 'impact' I refer to an impression akin to that made by a great hero of the past, but much more intense and therefore more deeply life-transforming. By calling him Jesus 'Christ' I repeat the acknowledgement, made earlier in this book, that he is Jesus as interpreted by a long line of Christians including Mark and the other evangelists. But I also repeat that the whole idea of this 'Christ' is given shape and force by the personality of the historical Jesus, a personality for which there is sufficient historical evidence in the New Testament.

In *God's Truth*, the book of essays that looked back on John Robinson's *Honest to God* over a quarter of a century, Nineham reiterated his belief that 'what people need is some approach to envisaging realities such as God, creation and providence imaginatively in a way which does no violence to the rest of what they know to be true' (p. 154). I believe that too. I also agree with Nineham that 'to be fully convincing' the image of God as the Ground of Being with which Robinson and others have experimented must be supplemented by 'a plausible account of how the personal and gracious character of innermost reality manifests itself in practice and makes a difference to the quality and outcome of life at the historical level' – for otherwise Christianity can offer only the nightmare vision described by T. W. Manson, in which there is, as it were, a thick plate-glass window between God and the world. 'The eye of faith can see through the window and observe that there is a God and that he appears to be benevolently disposed towards men; but nothing more substantial than signals of paternal affection and filial trust and obedience can get through' (p. 155). And like Nineham I am dissatisfied by the theology of Maurice Wiles, who seems to combine a belief that 'the unique phenomenon of Christ was not just a contingent event, but was directly due to the divine will' with a denial that there have been any 'divine interventions in history of the sort proclaimed in the tradition' (p. 156). But I cannot leave the problem at that point, unsolved while we await the light to be shed by some prophet or group in the future.

Nineham quotes Leonard Hodgson's lament that

> for too long study of the biblical writers (and for the matter of that, of patristics, scholastics, reformers and the rest) has been based on the assumption that someone, somewhere, at some time in the past, really knew the truth, and what we have to do is to find out what he thought and get back to it (p. 157).

That rejection of a purely historical theology seems valid to me (as to almost everyone else), not least in the field of ethics, where conditions have changed profoundly, and I am glad to have been taught by Hodgson and to have been involved in the publication of his book on *Sex and Christian Freedom* (1967), from which the quotation comes. But Hodgson would, I feel sure, have been dismayed by any association of his name with any suggestion that in relation to the central and permanent religious questions what is essential for our living and dying has *not* been revealed by God through 'someone' in the past, namely Jesus Christ. Even that revelation had to be made in terms of how people thought and hoped some two thousand years ago, so that we need not accept a belief in demon-possession causing diseases, or a hope for the imminent end of this age of the world, or a picture of heaven or hell, as authoritative for us without interpretation. But along with Hodgson and a great multitude of other Christians I believe that in Jesus Christ God has, as it were, broken through the thick plate-glass window. All Christian teachers including Mark are essentially witnesses who say how they see that act: Christianity is not their invention. And while Christian theology in any generation should not be merely historical, it should be at its best a commentary on what has already been revealed: otherwise it is not Christian theology. In his Preface to the 1968 edition of his Gifford Lectures called *For Faith and Freedom* Hodgson wrote, I think wisely:

To answer the question 'What is the Christian view of anything?' we have to take into account how the understanding of it by the New Testament Christians has been deepened and enriched in the experience of their successors, and is still being deepened and enriched by our experience of life in the world of today. It needs patience, the patience required first to get to know the minds of our predecessors in the context of their own age and then to consider what the thought of our own age will allow us to endorse and what it will bid us revise.

These Gifford Lectures by Hodgson were, among other things, a history of the very substantial efforts of theologians writing in English to do just that during the first half of the twentieth century. If we ask what made their efforts Christian, we find that Hodgson answered:

The only claim we can rightly make – and, if we are to be true to our faith, it is the claim we must make – is that once for all in history, in Palestine some two thousand years ago, God did something which is of significance not only for all mankind but for his whole creation . . . The character of Jesus Christ is to be determinative for our thought of God . . . I have tried to show that Christian faith, while it forbids us to claim knowledge we have not got, gives us light enough to walk in the way that leads to knowing more. By this faith I have tried to live, and in this faith I hope to die (pp. 70, 221, 224).

An Introduction to Mark's Gospel

When Mark wrote an hour of testing was upon his readers. He put down the agonised prayer of Jesus in Gethsemane: 'Father! My Father! All things are possible for you. Take this cup away from me. But not what I want, but what you want' (14:36). The gospel is a call to be ready to share the cruel death which had destroyed all that was mortal of Jesus. It is a gospel for martyrs. A climax comes when Peter has rebuked Jesus for speaking about being put to death. Jesus rebukes Peter: 'Get away from me, Satan. Your thoughts are men's thoughts, not God's!' Then Jesus calls the crowd with his disciples, and tells them: 'If anyone wants to come with me, he must forget himself, carry his cross, and follow me' (8:33, 34).

The whole gospel is a call to personal devotion. The first words spoken by Jesus in it are: 'Come with me' (1:17). The gospel is a call to humility. 'Whoever wants to be first must place himself last of all and be the servant of all' (9:35), and the message must be received with a childlike humility (10:15). The gospel is a call to a single-minded purity. 'If your hand makes you turn away, cut it off! It is better for you to enter life without a hand than to keep both hands and go off to hell, to the fire that never goes out' (9:43). The gospel is a call to poverty. 'It is much harder for a rich man to enter the kingdom of God than for a camel to go through the eye of a needle' – although those who have left everything in order to follow Jesus are promised compensations including eternal life 'and persecutions as well' (10:25–30). And the gospel is a call to a courageous faith. 'If you do not doubt in your heart, but believe that what you say will happen, it will be done for you' (11:23).

Those who want to be with Jesus in his kingdom must drink his cup and be baptised in his way – which means that they must suffer (10:35–45). 'You will be arrested and taken to court. You will be beaten in the synagogues; you will stand before rulers and kings for my sake, to tell them the Good News . . . Men will hand over their brothers to be put to death, and fathers will do the same to their children; children will turn against their parents and have them put to death. Everyone will hate you because of me' (13:9–13). The Lord who makes such promises arouses bewilderment and fear. 'Jesus was going ahead of the disciples, who were filled with alarm; the people who followed behind were afraid' (10:32). Modern scholars who believe (as many do) that the gospel originally ended at 16:8 can point to the fact that the last words are typical of the atmosphere: 'they were afraid'.

But 'this is the Good News about Jesus Christ, the Son of God' (1:1)! The suffering prophesied by Jesus for himself and his followers has a glorious ending, for 'whoever loses his life for me and the gospel will save it' (8:35) and 'whoever holds out to the end will be saved' (13:13). On the other hand, hell will be the punishment of those who falter: 'there "their worms never die, and the fire is never put out"' (9:46, 48). And on earth the Jews who reject Jesus will experience 'trouble . . . far worse than any the world has ever known' (13:19). The fatal Jewish revolt against the Roman empire began in 66. Mark wrote at a time when his readers had to be warned against 'false Messiahs and false prophets' (13:22). One reason why this is Good News is that the other news is so bad.

Mark gives the Good News simply by announcing the victory of Jesus Christ over *evil* (in the shape of the demons who caused diseases), *sin* (in many shapes, beginning at 2:5), and finally *death* in the shape of hideous torture and execution, the worst punishment that the Romans could inflict.

He conceals nothing as he depicts the weakness of the human emotions of Jesus. 'Jesus was filled with pity' – but the Greek word may mean 'anger' (1:41). 'Jesus spoke harshly' (1:43). 'Jesus was angry' (3:5). Jesus was thought by people – it seems, including his own family – to have gone mad (3:21). Jesus was sleeping, and was woken up with the demand: 'Teacher, don't you care that we are about to die?' (4:38). Jesus was 'greatly surprised' at his rejection by his home town, where 'he was not able to perform any miracles', but the fact was that the people who had watched him as a boy and as a young man could say only, 'Isn't he the carpenter?' (6:1–6). Mark does not pretend that Jesus had all the answers. With a perfectly normal human ignorance Jesus had to ask a man his name (5:9), ask who had touched him (5:30), ask how much bread they had (8:5), and ask what they were arguing about (9:16). He did not know when the end of history would come (13:32). Jesus asked: 'Why do you call me good? No one is good except God alone' (10:18). In distress before his death, he told his friends: 'The sorrow in my heart is so great that it almost crushes me' – and he begged them to stay awake and give him companionship (14:34). The dying words of Jesus were: 'My God, my God, why did you abandon me?' (15:34). But the victory over evil, sin, and death tells its own story – that Jesus is the Son of God. Writing in the style natural to him and his readers, Mark dramatises this story by giving the cries and screams of the demons: 'You are God's holy messenger!' (1:24), 'You are the Son of God!' (3:11).

Mark's gospel does not explain the mystery of why the Son of God had to undergo such suffering, or the mystery of why he was not acknowledged. As to the first mystery, there are only hints of an explanation when it is said that the death of Jesus will 'redeem many people' or be a ransom liberating them from slavery (10:45) and when at 14:24 there is a reference to 'my blood which is poured out for many, my blood which seals God's covenant' (or completes the new agreement between God and his people). As to the second mystery, the explanation is offered that Jesus frequently ordered silence about his own status – silence from the demons and even silence from the disciples (8:30). According to Mark, it was only when Jesus was solemnly and repeatedly questioned by the High Priest that he made his claim publicly (14:61, 62). But Mark gives no reason why Jesus had wanted such silence.

Ever since William Wrede published a book on this 'Messianic secret' in Mark, in 1901, many scholars have supplied the answer that in fact the historical Jesus never claimed to be the Messiah, but that Mark shared the faith of the Church in AD 65 that Jesus had been the Messiah all along; therefore Mark had to do his best to explain why the claim was not more public. All that we need observe here is that mystery surrounds the Jesus of Mark. There seems to be no time for intellectual reflection; the pace is breathless. The mystery remains – but its practical consequences are not left at all obscure.

Mark's aim was to make the love and the demand of Jesus Christ so vivid that the persecuted Christians would feel themselves in the shoes of the rich man kneeling before Jesus on the road. 'Jesus looked straight at him with love and said, "You need only one thing. Go and sell all you have . . . then come and follow me"' (10:21). For this purpose Mark became (so far as we know) the first man to write a gospel – because it seemed necessary to give more than a few sayings of Jesus, and when telling the story of Jesus it was necessary to tell of more than his last hours. He wanted to show how the teaching had expressed the life, and how the life had led up to the death. In his gospel, facing death gives the unity. The enemies of Jesus plan to kill him as early as 3:6. At the centre of the gospel lie three solemn prophecies of the Passion (8:31; 9:30, 31; 10:32–34).

Mark's use of the phrase 'the Good News' or 'the gospel' in his first sentence was the reason why the new kind of book that he invented came to be called by a new name: *a* gospel. Scholars suggest that there were three thoughts in the mind of Mark when he used the old phrase about *the* gospel. He would remember the Good News in chapters 40–55 of the prophetic Book of Isaiah. He would remember that 'the Good News' had been one of Paul's favourite expressions. And he would remember how often 'good news' was announced in the propaganda of the cult of the divine Emperor. So he told the story of Jesus – the Messiah promised to Israel, the Son of God who had redeemed many people outside Israel, the King whose victory had come through endurance.

In his gospel a 'young man wearing a white robe' tells the women in the empty tomb of Jesus: 'Now go and give this message to his disciples, including Peter: "He is going to Galilee ahead of you; there you will see him, just as he told you"' (16:7). Did Mark end by relating an appearance of the victorious Jesus to Peter in Galilee? If so, the ending has been lost. What we can be sure of is that Mark believed that Jesus Christ would show his victory to all who let him lead them into life and death.

Dennis Nineham's response is on pp. 296–306.

8

JOHN HICK AND THE
UNIQUENESS OF JESUS:

Is Jesus of Nazareth the world's only Saviour?

In this chapter it is appropriate to leave the confines of England. In 1986 a meeting of distinguished Christian theologians was convened at the Claremont Graduate School in California by John Hick, an Englishman teaching there as a professor. He had edited *The Myth of God Incarnate* in 1977, and when the conference's main papers were published (in the USA in 1987 and in Britain in 1988) the title chosen recalled that earlier controversy. It was *The Myth of Christian Uniqueness*. Hick's co-editor was Paul Knitter, an American scholar and Roman Catholic priest, already noted for his book *No Other Name?* (1985). He explained in his Preface to the new book that the contributors, all Christians, were explorers. They were moving

> away from insistence on the superiority or finality of Christ and Christianity toward a recognition of the independent validity of other ways. Such a move came to be described by participants in our project as the crossing of a theological Rubicon. In the words of Langdon Gilkey, it represents 'a monstrous shift indeed . . . a position quite new to the churches, even to the liberal churches'.

The book conveniently pulled together a growing discussion about the position of Christianity among the world's religions. The literature on this subject is very large. Some 'selected readings' were edited by John Hick and Brian Hebblethwaite as *Christianity and Other Religions* (1980), and in 1987 I offered my own contribution in *The Futures of Christianity*. But this project led by Hick had a special importance. It gathered scholars from the First and Third Worlds, Catholic and Protestant, female and male, who had given the issues sustained attention. It challenged them to express themselves maturely, clearly and concisely. It exposed them to each other and to more conservative theologians, and it gave them a chance to revise their positions.

In his Preface Knitter confessed that the group's proposals were still 'inchoate and controversial'. As I see it, the book's title was partly to blame for this. For Christianity's uniqueness is no myth. In the book Aloysius Pieris rightly remarks:

> That Jesus is unique is obvious even to Buddhists, just as Christians would hardly question the uniqueness of Gautama. Is not each one of us unique? The issue is whether Jesus' uniqueness consists of his absoluteness as conveyed by certain christological titles, and whether the uniqueness of Gautama should be understood in terms of the absoluteness that the word *dharma* or, as in certain schools, *Buddha* seems to convey (p. 171).

Knitter defends the book's title on the ground that talk about the uniqueness of Christianity, 'like all mythic language, must be understood carefully; it must be interpreted; its "truth" lies not on its literal surface but within its ever-changing historical and personal meaning. This book, then, rather than intending to deny Christian uniqueness, wants to interpret it anew' (p. vii). But I have to repeat that the word 'myth' usually suggests a story that is simply untrue – as when John Hick once described the story of Adam, Eve and the snake as 'a mythic conception which does not describe an actual event in man's history or prehistory' and went on to demolish it as an explanation of the problem of evil (*Evil and the God of Love*, 1966, p. 181). If we come across a newspaper article headed 'The Myth of British Superiority' we do not expect its conclusion to be that Britain *is* best. I also repeat that the word 'myth' can be used in a more positive sense, as when Hick wrote: 'By Christian mythology I mean the great persisting imaginative pictures by means of which the corporate mind of the Church has expressed to itself the significance of the historical events upon which its faith is based' (p. 281). So it may be appropriate to describe talk about the 'pre-existent' Second Person of the Trinity becoming incarnate with a virgin mother as 'mythological' because there a story is being told somewhat like stories commonly called 'myths'. But the proposition that Christianity is unique is not a picture or a story, and to say that it is a 'myth' in a book's title is, I think, an error if the intention is, as Knitter claims in his Preface, 'to proceed as cautiously as possible'.

The reader who has not been put off by its title finds that the book demands a sympathetic patience. No clear answer to the question about the 'absoluteness' of Christianity emerges. The dictionaries tell us that 'absolute' originated in the idea of something being detached from something else, so that it came to mean perfect or complete in comparison with something imperfect or incomplete; and the history of European philosophy tells us that it was Hegel who made the Absolute the climax of his intellectual system. But no thoughtful Christian can hold that Christianity, whether understood as a collection of doctrines or as a collection of people, is utterly detached from the general history of religion or perfect or complete in every sense – and certainly Hegel did not think that Christianity as known to history was the Absolute. The question about the 'absoluteness' of Christianity therefore boils down to the question: is there any sense in which Christianity offers us absolute, perfect or complete truth?

The End of Christian Exclusivism

It is a question which in the history of modern theology was particularly stimulated by Ernst Troeltsch, the German scholar whom we have already met in connection with Dennis Nineham. Before his death in 1923 he pressed home the challenge to apply a modern historical approach (*Historismus*) to Christianity's dogmatic claims. Historical knowledge, he argued, could never yield a complete certainty either that reported events had actually occurred or that they had the religious significance claimed for some of them. All religious claims about past events must therefore be understood in their historical setting, as expressions of faith within humanity's various cultures living or dead. This version of *Relativismus* well deserves a scholarly study such as Sarah Coakley's *Christ without Absolutes* (1988). For Troeltsch, 'relativism' meant a move away from the claim made in the first edition of his *Die Absolutheit des Christentums* that Christianity was the culmination and convergence of all religion. Dr Coakley traces how he came to think instead that while Christianity was for the West 'God's countenance as revealed to us' (p. 37), in other cultures God may be experienced in different ways and there can be no perfect revelation of 'the Absolute' until the end of time.

The contributors to *The Myth of Christian Uniqueness* were theologians who had travelled the same path as Troeltsch and had gone further – partly because in our time all the great religions have made converts outside their homelands. It may be thought offensive to describe them, as Troeltsch did, as the religions of 'racial groups' outside the West. It certainly would be offensive to suggest that no 'racial group' sees any alternative to the absolute validity of its own inherited religion. However, it is clear that, developing Troeltsch's insights which were in their period astonishingly prophetic, these theologians of the 1980s rejected the understanding of Christianity's absoluteness which can be called 'exclusivism', defined by Knitter as the belief that there is 'salvation only in Christ and little, if any, value elsewhere' (p. viii).

Many Protestants have expressed exclusivist attitudes. Speaking for Catholics, the Fourth Lateran Council endorsed the much earlier claim (formulated by Cyprian in the third and Augustine in the fourth Christian century) that 'outside the Church there is no salvation at all'. And texts from the New Testament can be cited to support a stern position. In the Acts of the Apostles (4:11–12) Peter is said to have proclaimed to a Jewish religious court after a miracle of healing: 'This Jesus is the stone rejected by the builders which has become the keystone – and you are the builders. There is no salvation in anyone else at all, for there is no other name under heaven granted to men, by which we may receive salvation.' In John's gospel (14:6) the farewell discourses of Jesus include the statement: 'I am the way; I am the truth and I am the life; no one comes to the Father except by me.' But actually these passages, whatever may be their authenticity as the words of Peter or his Master, were not written with any thought of the existence of religions such as Islam, Hinduism and Buddhism. They affirm the Christian experience of salvation, meaning primarily healing, through the power of Jesus and of access to God as Father through Jesus the mediator, but it seems unreasonable to use them as definitive answers to questions which had not been felt in anything like their modern shape. Equally relevant, or irrelevant, are texts which take a more positive attitude to non-Christians, such as Paul's declaration that what can be known about God is plain to non-Christians because God has shown it to them (Rom. 1:19) and the speeches attributed to Paul about the nations groping after God (Acts 14:16–17, 17:27).

It is, however, as certain as anything can be in this field that the historical Jesus did not say that only his disciples could be 'saved'. He taught that God would forgive those who forgave each other and those who were merciful. Matthew's gospel warns us that 'when the Son of Man comes in his glory and all the angels with him, he will sit in state on his throne, with all the nations gathered before him' (25:31–2) – and the great blessing, 'come enter and possess the kingdom that has been ready for you since the world was made' (25:34), will not be given on the basis of whether or not people have already said 'Lord, Lord' to him (7:21). At least it is agreed by all Christians (except those who hold the monstrous doctrine that in his wrath God has predestined some or many or most of his children to everlasting punishment) that the New Testament is correct to say in several places that it is God's will that all should be saved. Some 'universalists' are confident or 'practically certain' that this will be the case; others, including myself, hope so and trust so, but have to leave room for human free will to choose evil to the uttermost and therefore final annihilation. I agree with John Hick's *Evil and the God of Love* that

> a universe in which a loving response to God is guaranteed could be only a poor second best to one in which created beings . . . came freely to love, trust and worship him. And if we attribute the later and higher aim to God, we must declare to be self-contradictory the idea of God so creating men that they will inevitably respond positively to him (pp. 310–11).

If 'salvation only in Christ' is taken to mean that the possibility of ending up in heaven is confined strictly to those who before their deaths have explicitly accepted Jesus Christ as Lord and Saviour, or who have been faithful members of the Church (however defined), most Christians now cannot believe it. Such exclusivism was hard to reconcile with what many Christians knew or felt in the centuries when the status of the non-Christian religions was not considered with any great care. Passages can be quoted from the Fathers and many other respected teachers, extending the idea of 'the Church' outside which there is 'no salvation' to include the saints of the Old Testament and all good pagans. In our time, when the size and antiquity of the human race have been realised as never before and when Christians have more knowledge and understanding of other religions than ever before, exclusivism is incompatible with a conscience instructed by some awareness of the fatherlike love of God and of the goodness and truth to be found in the vast history of the non-Christian majority of humanity. Accordingly it has been Roman Catholic doctrine for many years that God may be trusted to be merciful to non-Catholics who 'desire' to be baptised although that desire may not be 'explicit' – and also to non-Catholics who are 'invincibly ignorant' of the Catholic faith because living beyond the reach of missionaries or having access to inadequate missionaries only. Going further, the Second Vatican Council declared in 1965 that 'the Catholic Church rejects nothing of what is true and holy' in non-Christian religions, believing rather that among 'those who through no fault of their own do not know the gospel of Christ', or 'have not yet arrived at an explicit knowledge of God', 'whatever goodness or truth is found' is 'a preparation for the gospel'.

In *The Myth of Christian Uniqueness* that generosity is cited, along with teaching by leading Roman Catholic theologians such as Karl Rahner and Hans Küng. This explicitly states the hope and belief that God will welcome non-Christians into heaven, so that non-Christian societies are not the cesspits of evil which some Christian missionaries thought they saw, and the non-Christian religions which are so important in those societies are themselves ways which end in salvation. Such ways of salvation can be called 'extraordinary' (Rahner) if the emphasis is on Christianity as in some sense normative – or 'ordinary ways of salvation' (Küng) if the emphasis is on the numerical preponderance of non-Christians in history and in the contemporary world. As Hick put it in *The Myth of God Incarnate*: 'if . . . we call God-acting-towards-mankind the Logos, then we must say that *all* salvation, within all religions, is the work of the Logos and that under their various images and symbols men in different cultures and faiths may encounter the Logos and find salvation' (p. 181).

Many passages in *The Myth of Christian Uniqueness* suggest profound reasons for the modern Christian rejection of exclusivism. The many warnings in the gospels against spiritual pride may be applied to the claim that Christianity is simply 'the true religion' if that claim is intended to suggest that Christians can speak the truth, the whole truth and nothing but the truth about God. There would be much sympathy among Christians in our time with the reminder offered by two Indian contributors (Raimundo Panikkar and Stanley J. Samartha) of the Hindu insistence on mystery. About all religious words or pictures or stories it must finally be said *neti, neti* ('not this, not this'). When approaching God we are all like blind men grasping different parts of the elephant, as in the famous Indian story, and the Ultimate Reality cannot be pinned down in 'names and forms'. However, the sense of mystery is compatible with a non-fundamentalist belief in revelation. Gordon

Kaufman raises, I suggest, an unnecessary objection when he says that

> A contemporary theology, informed . . . by a thoroughgoing historical consciousness, would not be in a position to claim – as Christian theology has so often in the past – that its assertions were directly and uniquely authorized or warranted by divine revelation . . . Christian theology would understand itself in essentially the same terms that it understands other religious activity and reflection – namely, as human imaginative response to the necessity to find orientation for life in a particular historical situation (p. 12).

To claim that theological assertions are 'directly and uniquely authorised or warranted by divine revelation' sounds like extreme fundamentalism if, as seems to be the case, the claim excludes any human or cultural element in the Scriptures or in the religious tradition. In common with most contemporary Christians I think that such an understanding of 'revelation' is false. But the alternative stated by Kaufman, stressing exclusively the 'human imaginative response', is not the only alternative. One may also believe that God has revealed himself, necessarily using symbols belonging to the human world. (In the original Indian story a godlike prince is able to see the elephant as a whole – but has to explain the elephant to men who remain blind.) I also reject any suggestion that the Christian must exclude divine inspiration and revelation from non-Christian activity and reflection. As Kaufman himself says, religious assertions can be 'in some significant sense grounded in God, as "ultimate point of reference"' – a grounding which we can 'articulate' in 'the concept of revelation' (p. 12). Revelation, I conclude, is everywhere – but everywhere it is a mixture of what is of God and what is of man.

Another reason for rejecting exclusivism is the recognition of the fact that most adherents of a religion adhere to it because they were born into it – whether that birth is regarded as 'accidental' (as generally in the West) or as the working out of justice as a reward or punishment for good or evil done in previous lives (as is the Indian tradition). In particular it seems deeply wrong for Christians to argue that God will give no one except them a chance of heaven. Christians have belonged – usually by birth – to societies which have foully ill-treated 'heretics' and 'unbelievers', often claiming a justification in Christianity for their sins. So far from being entitled to claim a monopoly of God's mercy, they have often needed that mercy more than the non-Christians who were their victims. In his mercy God may be asked to forgive past Christian sins which may be excusable because they arose out of sheer stupidity in thinking that loyalty to Christ meant complacent pride in being a Christian, or which arose out of sheer insensitivity to the difficulties of religious thought and language, or which arose out of sheer ignorance of the goodness and truth in non-Christian traditions. But there is far less excuse now than in the old days for the arrogance or ignorance of exclusivism, and *The Myth of Christian Uniqueness* is to be congratulated on the energy with which it drives another nail into the coffin of that outdated tradition. Hick is in my view happily correct when he observes that 'the Christian mind has now for the most part made the move from an intolerant exclusivism to a benevolent inclusivism' (p. 22).

Including Non-Christians

'Inclusivism' is described in the Preface to *The Myth of Christian Uniqueness* as a position 'which recognizes the salvific richness of other faiths but then views this richness as a result of Christ's redemptive work and as having to be fulfilled in Christ' (p. viii). This position is rejected because it does not seem to take non-Christian religions seriously except as dim reflections of a redemption which Christianity alone knows fully and as preparations for a gospel which Christianity alone possesses. As Tom Driver complains, in this position

> there is no need to listen to the non-Christian at any fundamental level. To be sure, inclusivists might see that other religions contained some practices and insights that might 'enrich' their understanding of Christ, but there would be no reason to listen at the level at which their own form of faith, their commitment to Christ, might be called radically into question (p. 208).

Stanley Samartha speaks of 'exclusiveness and its patronizing cousin inclusiveness' (p. 79). Strong, and I think justified, exception is taken to Karl Rahner's proposal that 'non-Christians seeking the good and the true' should be regarded as 'anonymous Christians'. This proposal was generous in intention and was a major improvement on the exclusivism which had dominated Roman Catholicism. But it seems to deny the right of non-Christians to be themselves and to affirm their own understandings of the good and the true. Christians have been offended when they have been patronised by other religions – by the attitude of some liberally minded Jews that the New Testament is a popularisation of Judaism for Gentiles, by the Quran's attitude that biblical personages including Jesus were anonymous Muslims, by the attitude of Hindu advaitists that worshippers of the personal God (*Ishvara*) are really worshipping the *Brahman* better described as impersonal, or by the attitude of some Buddhists that all human enlightenment is a reflection of the Buddha's. People have been more inclined to engage in inter-religious dialogue when Christians, Jews, Muslims, Hindus, etc., have agreed to start accepting the differences between the religions, with each religion defining itself and being respected for what it is. Hick convincingly criticised Rahner in chapter 4 of his *Problems of Religious Pluralism* (1985), as did Knitter in chapter 7 of his *No Other Name?* A similar objection could be raised to talk about the 'latent church' outside the 'manifest church' of Christianity, as suggested by the Protestant theologian Paul Tillich.

Hick also objects to the idea that non-Christians are included in God's mercy solely because of 'the divine pardon bought by Christ's atoning death' (*The Myth of Christian Uniqueness*, p. 23). This idea was implied in Rahner's two axioms: 'God desires the salvation of everyone. And this salvation willed by God is the salvation won by Christ.' In the journal *Faith and Philosophy* (1988, p. 376) Hick expressed this objection concisely and in my view persuasively. Having drawn attention to the similarity of the moral and spiritual transformations advocated and achieved by all the world's great religions, he wrote:

> It has to be acknowledged that the immediate ground of their transformation is the particular spiritual path along which they move. It is by living in accordance with the Torah or with the Quaranic revelation that Jews and Muslims find a transforming peace with God; it is by one or other of their great *margas* that Hindus attain to *moksha*; it is by the Eightfold Path that Therevada Buddhists come to *nirvana*; it is by *zazen* that Zen Buddhists attain to *satori*; and so on. The Christian inclusivist is then, by implication, declaring that these various spiritual paths are efficacious, and constitute authentic contexts of salvation, because Jesus died on the cross; and, by further implication, that if he had not died on the cross, they would not be efficacious. This is a novel and somewhat astonishing doctrine. How are we

to make sense of the idea that the salvific power of the *dharma* taught five hundred years earlier by the Buddha is a consequence of the death of Jesus?

My own conviction is, however, that at-one-ment with God should be understood in one or other of the ways which avoid the error of supposing that God the Father's pardon needed to be 'bought' or 'won'. God's mercy was *displayed* on the cross of Jesus, who was a 'sacrifice' (a means of approach to God) provided for our benefit by God's love. And a Christian who worships the God of love will be wise not to pretend to be able to define the grounds on which God will have mercy on those who have not identified themselves with the sacrifice provided. In the gospels Jesus is not said to have taught that humanity's forgiveness would depend on his death. (I attempted to summarise what the New Testament does say in chapter 3 of my dialogue with John Stott in *Essentials*, applying it to non-Christians in chapter 6.)

It is surely understandable that so many Christians, mindful of what they themselves owe to the saving 'grace' of Jesus Christ, have believed that the salvation of non-Christians is always and everywhere accomplished by Christ's grace. It seems to me right to say that any salvation is accomplished by God's love which is revealed to Christians in Christ's grace, supremely in the death on the cross. But the acute psychological problem felt by non-Christians arises because Christian claims have so often been made in ways which are far from gracious. The cross was painted on the shields of anti-Muslim crusaders. I noticed in Sarah Coakley's study of Troeltsch that (although he afterwards changed his tune) in 1910 he produced a revealing image of Christians steaming across the oceans to patronise other cultures. He was saying that 'Jesus is the embodiment of superior religious power, embellished in ever new ways in the course of thousands of years, whose heartbeat is felt throughout the whole of Christendom, even as the vibration of a ship's engine is felt in every nook of the whole ship' (p. 170). Among non-Christians the word 'Christ' is almost inevitably heard as a reference to 'Jesus Christ' as preached by the Christian Church – and the word 'Church' is almost inevitably heard as a reference to the institution which has been identified with the evils of Europe and the Americas and of their colonial and neo-colonial expansion. For people who feel like that – as millions do – the idea of universal salvation by the grace of Christ is heard as the claim that the religion of Europe and the Americas

monopolises salvation – much as their business used to mono-
polise international trade. Christians ought to be sensitive to this
reaction where Christianity is heard as colonialism, for they would
react in a similar way to suggestions that the enlightenment of
humanity is made possible by the enlightenment of Gautama the
Buddha or by the delivery of the Quran to the Prophet.

For these reasons I cannot entirely agree with the defence of the
tradition of inclusivism offered by Gavin D'Costa in his careful
study of *John Hick's Theology of Religions* (1987). In his concern
to vindicate other Roman Catholic theologians, he seems not to
appreciate fully the scandal of an arrogance which has sounded
patronising even while it was being generous. But I need to face the
question: what is the alternative to that objectionable kind of
Christian inclusivism? And so I need to consider the alternatives
put forward in *The Myth of Christian Uniqueness*.

Hick has often compared 'God' or 'the Eternal One' or 'the
Real' with the sun around which circle the religions, which are
compared with the planets. So Christianity is 'one of a number of
worlds of faith which circle round and reflect that Reality'. He
made that image famous in a lecture of 1972 reprinted in *God and
the Universe of Faiths* (1973, pp. 120–32). Christianity, he says, is
'*one* of the great world faiths, *one* of the streams of religious life
through which human beings are savingly related to that ultimate
Reality Christians know as the heavenly Father'. But he asks:

> Can it be more than a hangover from the old religious imperial-
> ism of the past to insist upon attaching a Christian label to
> salvation within these other households of faith? This would be
> like the anomaly of accepting the Copernican revolution in
> astronomy, in which the earth ceased to be regarded as the
> center of the universe and was seen instead as one of the planets
> circling the sun, but still insisting that the sun's life-giving rays
> can reach the other planets only by first being reflected from the
> earth! (*The Myth of Christian Uniqueness*, pp. 22–3).

Panikkar, however, does not wish to compare the religions with
planets circling round a sun which represents 'that Ultimate Reality Christians know as the heavenly Father'. He writes: 'the center
is neither the earth (our particular religion), nor the sun (God,
transcendence, the Absolute . . .). Rather, each solar system has
its own center, and every galaxy turns reciprocally around the
other'. He calls this 'the theanthropocosmic insight' in which 'all is
implied in all' and 'each person represents the community and each

tradition reflects, corrects, complements, and challenges the other' (p. 109). And Paul Knitter now accepts Panikkar's displacement of 'God, transcendence, the Absolute' from the centre. He pleads guilty to the charge of

> implicitly, unconsciously, but still imperialistically imposing our notions of Deity or the Ultimate on other believers who, like many Buddhists, may not even wish to speak about God or who experience the Ultimate as *Sunyata*, which has nothing or little to do with what Christians experience and call God (p. 184).

As I see things, the picture of each religion as a whole galaxy circling round other galaxies, not around any one centre, is helpful in one way. It rejects the tendency to exaggerate the unity which exists between the faiths as they are. Hick has written that

> apprehensions of the Eternal having arisen with the force of revelation in the minds of certain supremely enlightened spirits, have become mixed with different streams of human culture, conceptualized in terms of different philosophical traditions, and subject to different historical influences, to constitute the vast religio-cultural complexes which we know today as the great world faiths (*Death and Eternal Life*, 1976, p. 32).

The Myth of Christian Uniqueness rightly stresses that for many practical purposes there is, or could be, a unity in the shared ideas of justice and peace, and a shared commitment to struggles for better societies, and Paul Knitter finely expounds the potential in all the religions as inspiring resources for human liberation. But in the specifically religious sphere – for example, in the deepest questions about what 'liberation' is – there are many differences between these faiths. They do not agree about what constitutes human nature, enslaved or free. As Gordon Kaufman says,

> there really is no . . . universally human position available to us; every religious (or secular) understanding and way of life we might uncover is a *particular* one, that has grown up in a particular history, makes particular claims, is accompanied by particular practices and injunctions, and hence is to be distinguished from all other particular religious and secular orientations (p. 5).

Still less is there agreement between the faiths about the Reality that transcends humanity. As Langdon Gilkey says, 'no one doctrine in any . . . system of symbols . . . can be abstracted out and be established as universal in all religions . . . God is as similar – *and* as different – from the ultimate principals of Hinduism and Buddhism as are the Christ and Krishna or the Christ and a Bodhisattva' (p. 41). So Knitter concisely and correctly (I think) maintains that 'philosophical maturity demands that we accept that all knowledge is "theory-laden"; different societies have different plausibility structures; each religion is speaking within its own "language game"' (p. 183). And Panikkar points out that if religions are compared with rivers, the most that can be said truthfully is that they meet in an ultimate reality without names or forms, as all the water in the rivers meets in the clouds in the sky, from which eventually it will 'pour down again into the valleys of mortals to feed the rivers of the earth' (p. 92).

Another merit in the comparison between a religion and a separate galaxy or distinct river is that it rejects the tendency to pretend that one can be a profound religious believer without being committed, or at least inclined, to a particular and unique way of being religious. As Hick notes:

> The importance of religious beliefs to the believer lies ultimately in the assumption that they are substantially true references to the nature of reality; and the importance of religious practices to the practitioner lies in the assumption that through them one is renewing or deepening one's relationship to the transcendent divine Reality (*Problems of Religious Pluralism*, p. 16).

Living in a particular galaxy cuts one off from the possibility of living as a being who had evolved in another galaxy might live, and swimming in one river means that one is not swimming in another. In a somewhat similar way, taking a religious stance in one tradition means belonging somewhere. Some element of absoluteness remains. As Langdon Gilkey says, the alternative is a relativism where

> God, Christ, grace and salvation, higher consciousness, *dharma*, nirvana and *mukti* alike begin to recede in authority, to take on the aspect of mere projections relative to the cultural and individual subjectivity of the projectors, and so in the end they vanish like bloodless ghosts. We have no grounds for speaking of salvation at all, a situation of relativity far beyond asking about the salvation of *all* (*The Myth of Christian Uniqueness*, pp. 43–4).

The practical way of coping with this problem is indicated by Gilkey in his chapter. He concludes that 'the infinite mystery is . . . understood as redemptive power and promise, and truly so understood – and yet the grace there known far transcends the bounds of its own manifestation to us and is creatively present in symbols derived from other manifestations' (p. 50). That seems to me a wise conclusion. It shows how all can be included in God's salvation of humanity without letting go of the definitely Christian experience of God's redemptive power and promise.

Christianity's True Uniqueness

I am typical of many Christians in our time when I reject Christian exclusivism. I agree that the Ultimate Reality is truly worshipped whatever names and forms of divinity are used, because I agree that the Ultimate Reality does not insist on the correct names and forms being used if the worship is sincere in the intention to worship what is really ultimate. In other words, God hears. However, it does not follow that all names and forms are equally true as accounts of the Ultimate Reality. I reckon that some correspond with the Reality better than the others. And so, I hope, does Hick. Criticising Wilfred Cantwell Smith in *Truth and Dialogue*, which he edited in 1974, Hick wrote that 'to say that whatever is sincerely believed and practised is, by definition, true, would be the end of all critical discrimination, both intellectual and moral' (p. 148). Nor does it follow, I think, that a religion is properly honoured when it is said to be so unique as a 'form of life' with its own 'language game' that it cannot be understood at all except by its adherents. A dialogue between believers in different religions, or between them and non-believers, is full of problems and dangers, but there can be a common search for a truth which is understood as more than the internal coherence of that religion's claims. It would be an insult to all religions to forbid the discussion of their truth understood as their correspondence with the Ultimate Reality. In *No Other Name?* Paul Knitter voiced the objection which almost all religious believers would have to any idea that 'anything goes; any creed, code, or cult can express the mystery of the Ultimate as long as it is personally appropriated, as long as it fits the needs of many' (p. 52). In his *Problems of Religious Pluralism* Hick said that 'we have . . . two tools with which we can try to measure and grade aspects of [the world's religions]. One is reason applied to their beliefs; and the other is conscience, or moral judgement, applied to the historical out-working of those beliefs' (p. 79).

After using these tools to the best of my limited ability I have to say that the self-revelation of God proclaimed by Christianity – I do not speak of the totality of the belief and behaviour of Christians – is in my view superior to all the other religious visions. In that sense I call it 'final' and shall continue to call it that unless I become aware of a better vision.

The Christian message that the will of God is our peace, and that God blesses the peacemakers, is, I think, better than visions of a warrior-god, including the pseudo-Christian idea of the crusade. I am conscious and deeply ashamed of the record of violence which is the disgrace of nominal Christians. It is an example of the terrible penalty that is paid when religion becomes the badge worn by tribalism, nationalism or imperialism and when orthodoxy becomes the test of loyalty to a social unit. In the case of Christianity the record is particularly atrocious because of developments far distant from the New Testament. The Catholic Church triumphed so completely in Western Europe that heresy could be regarded as thoroughly anti-social and even the Inquisition, which was terribly similar to the Gestapo, the KGB, the Red Guards or the Pol Pot thugs, seemed holy. Protestant or Catholic Christianity became part of the ideology of nations which were able to conquer and exploit much of the world through the use of naval skills and gunpowder before quarrelling between themselves and using even more lethal technology for their own destruction in the two world wars. But before all this is blamed on the Christian religion we ought to recall how completely the founder of that religion renounced and denounced violence. We ought also to remember that other religions, when given opportunities similar to those of the nominal Christians of Europe, have often also been corrupted by association with violent men.

I cannot agree with Rosemary Radford Ruether, who writes in *The Myth of Christian Uniqueness* (as elsewhere) that

> there is no historical basis for assuming that the religiosity of Pueblo Amerindians or ancient Canaanites, who saw the divine power in natural processes of fecundity, as well as in the establishment of human order and harmony, was less moral than Christianity. It is interesting that Judaism and Christianity have traditionally seen ancient Near Eastern religions as the epitome

of 'immoral religion' because of their possible use of sanctified sexuality, but have not seen their own sanctified warfare as comparatively more problematic (p. 141).

I am amazed that Dr Ruether, a distinguished champion of Christian feminism, here seems insensitive to the degradation of women in fertility rites such as those of Canaan. She is also unjust to the extent and influence of Jewish and Christian protests against the barbarity of war. She can be defended, of course. Her motive when she attacks Christianity is Christian. This and many other passages in *The Myth of Christian Uniqueness* are inspired by a healthy Christian self-criticism thoroughly in keeping with the spirit of the gospels where (for example) the apostles are repeatedly presented as cowardly fools. Indeed, the whole book is an example of the willingness of most contemporary Christians to admit that in the history of Christianity there is much that is tragically wrong when Christians have departed from the original message of love. But *that* message is morally supreme.

Jesus is believed by Christians such as me to be the utterly unique embodiment of God's own love. No doubt many tributes paid to him in devotion have been poetic rather than coldly scientific, but when I call him 'Lord and Saviour' I am not merely praising him with the kind of licence that is allowed to young men who sing songs in praise of the unique excellence of a beloved girl. I am making a serious comparison between him and humanity's other teachers. All humanity ought to venerate Gautama the Buddha and Muhammad the Prophet: to have any other attitude would be to condemn oneself. But those men, who in the history of religion came nearest to Jesus in religious influence, disclaimed the unique role in the fulfilment of God's saving purposes which Jesus claimed. They did not say that they were acting in God's place: to Gautama all talk about God or gods was unimportant and to Muhammad any claim to be more than a prophet was blasphemy encouraging idolatry. They did not say that they were removing the barrier, or bridging the distance, that prevented his children from knowing, trusting and obeying God as Father. On their own showing it would be inappropriate to call either man 'Lord and Saviour'. This is not surprising, for the whole idea of 'the Saviour', although it seems to have been taken over from the propaganda praising rulers of the Roman empire, has become Christian in its religious meaning. To call Jesus the world's only Saviour ought to be no more offensive to non-Christians than calling Gautama the

Buddha ('Enlightened') is to Christians. Christians can gladly accept that Gautama was indeed supreme in the achievement of 'enlightenment' as understood by Buddhists.

This conviction has been shared by John Hick, at least in his earlier writings. In an essay of 1983 reprinted in *Problems of Religious Pluralism* he observed that 'a demythologised Christianity has . . . the disadvantage that it does not really require or therefore sustain the magic and mystery, the bright colours and warm feelings and deep mythic resonances of Christmas and Easter', but he hoped that

> we can dismantle the myth, and speak instead of Jesus as a man who was startlingly open to God, and who saved people by making real to them the divine presence and the transforming divine claim upon their lives, thus setting up a new way of salvation within human history – the way of discipleship to Jesus as he is mediated to us through the Bible and the Church (p. 14).

Hick then held that the grace, 'which occurs whenever a human being freely responds to God, was more fully exemplified in the life of Christ than in any other life' (p. 63), although he was attracted by the idea that 'whenever and wherever the grace of God is effective in men and women, evoking self-giving love for God and neighbour, to that extent God has become incarnate within human history' (p. 57). And as recorded in his *God and the Universe of Faiths*, he taught in 1966 that 'the idea which has sustained Christianity is that this *agape* [love] which we see reflected in the mirror of the gospel records at work in human time, in particular finite situations, is none other than the eternal and universal *Agape* of God' (p. 153). So 'Christ is the Christian's image of God' (p. 178). To say 'Jesus Christ is God' without any explanation is to say something too simple and therefore either meaningless or misleading. But Jesus

> had only one nature, and this nature was wholly and unqualifiedly human, but the *agape* which directed it was God's. There was only one will, that of the man Jesus of Nazareth, but again the *agape* that was the ruling motive of his life was God's *agape* for mankind (p. 163).

In *The Myth of Christian Uniqueness* the matter is not put perfectly by Stanley Samartha when he tells us that

> The distinctiveness of Jesus Christ does not lie in claiming that 'Jesus Christ is God'. This amounts to saying that Jesus Christ is

the tribal god of Christians over against the gods of other peoples. Elevating Jesus to the status of God or limiting Christ to Jesus of Nazareth are both temptations to be avoided (p. 79).

These are surprisingly slipshod statements to come from a scholar who has rendered long and distinguished service to the World Council of Churches, organising dialogues between representatives of the world's faiths. Without repeating my earlier discussion of the incarnation of God in Christ, I may simply say that Christians do not merely elevate a man to the status of God in a tribal spirit. They worship Jesus as the human embodiment of the One. Thus St John's gospel, which has Thomas cry 'My Lord and my God!' (20:28), also has Jesus say 'my Father and your Father . . . my God and your God' (20:17); and later doctrinal developments have all retained monotheism, at least in intention. But I may also simply say that no one and nothing else should be called 'Christ' by Christians because for them there is no parallel to the embodiment and disclosure of the loving activity of the one real God in Jesus of Nazareth.

Not even the Prophet of Islam is for Christians another 'Christ'. Wilfred Cantwell Smith tells us that 'God has played in human history a role in and through the Quran, in the Muslim case, comparable to the role in the Christian case in and through Christ' (p. 64). The truth of that statement depends, I suggest, on what one means by 'comparable'. Certainly such a comparison is in order. It is undeniable that Muhammad has brought many millions to monotheism and to a high morality. I do not see how any sensitive reader of the Quran who believes in God could deny that God inspired many parts of it, but a detailed comparison between the Quran and the New Testament's witness to Jesus shows many differences, and I do not see how anyone claiming to be a Christian could prefer the Quran or put it on the same level as teaching about the character of God. Hick once said that for him the 'appropriate' response to Jesus is to call him Saviour, whatever may be the right understanding of the mythology about Jesus. 'For it is through Jesus that we have encountered God as our heavenly Father and have entered into a new life which has its ultimate centre in God. The absoluteness of the experience is the basis for the absoluteness of the language' (*God and the Universe of Faiths*, p. 172). In comparison, he said that the 'myth' that the Quran was 'divinely inspired down to the last syllable' is 'true' in so far as 'an attitude of reverent obedience to the holy book' is 'appropriate' (p. 175).

There spoke a Christian. I should expect a Muslim to speak differently.

The Christian claim which I have restated so briefly can, I think, be justified because the public and recorded influence of Jesus on the history of the world has been utterly unique in at least two ways. No other teacher has so powerfully expounded the idea of God as both eternal and loving ('Our Father in heaven'). He expounded it by how he lived and died as well as by his words. And no other teacher has produced Christian saints – the sinners who have been dominated, transformed and made holy by this idea of the eternal, loving God, and always in dependence on Jesus.

In *The Myth of Christian Uniqueness* Hick tells us that 'we have no good grounds for maintaining that Christianity has produced or is producing more saints, in proportion to population, or a higher quality of saintliness, than any other of the great streams of religious life' (p. 23). The truth of that statement depends on how 'saints' are defined. It seems obviously true that multitudes of people in non-Christian traditions (including Islam of course) have been and are much further advanced than most Christians in 'the transformation from self-centredness to Reality-centredness', as Hick expresses it. But interpretations of Reality can be very different. As Hick has noted elsewhere, 'the world may be experienced as God's handiwork, or as the battlefield of good and evil, or as the cosmic dance of Shiva, or as the beginningless and endless interdependent process . . . within which we may experience *nirvana*; and so on' (*Problems of Religious Pluralism*, p. 27). 'Reality-centredness' could be a word implying any one of these views of life. It could also commend itself to a Freudian or a Marxist. Hick adds – of course, correctly – that there is an overlap between the Christian faith in God as Creator and Father and 'the Muslim awareness of the Real as Allah the Merciful, the Compassionate', as there is an overlap with some beliefs held in other religions. He also correctly points out that Buddhists are agnostics about the Creator, not necessarily atheists. In dialogue other points may be discovered at which the religions come fairly close (p. 93). But dialogue also shows how deep the differences are, so that truth-claims do conflict. There is a conflict about whether it is useful to compare the Ultimate Reality with a person (despite Hick's claim in *Problems of Religious Pluralism*, p. 98, that the answers yes and no would be *equally* 'authentic'). And there is a conflict about whether or not it is best to compare God with a consistently loving and forgiving parent. So without denying that every great religion is 'built upon an authentic human perception of the Real' (p. 107), we have to consider the possibility that the Ultimate Reality may be pictured better as 'the Ultimate Reality Christians know as the heavenly Father' (as Hick has put it) despite the many errors and omissions to be found in the history of Christian theology. In reality Being may be more ultimate than Emptiness (the Buddhist's *sunyata*), and Love than Chance or Death, so that the only Source and Ground of all that exists or is possible is the one whose most important characteristic, love, may be described and lived out better by Jesus than by anyone else. If the Christian picture for all its limitations is truer to Reality than the non-Christian pictures are, then the Christian saints are closer to Reality than the multitudes of non-Christian saints are. Since I hold that this is the case, I cannot accept Hick's recent argument for the parity of all the world's saints.

It also seems to me that remarks made by Hick in *The Myth of Christian Uniqueness* on the contributions of the diffused influence of Christianity to the rise of science and democracy in the modern world are surprisingly superficial. He stresses that 'Christianity can claim no proprietary interest in the modern scientific enterprise', since many prominent churchmen offered either no encouragement or else downright opposition to that enterprise and its utilisation by technology. For him, Christianity's special relationship with science 'consists simply in the fact that it was the first of the world faiths to be hit by the impact of the new empirical knowledge and outlook' (p. 26). As for the rise of democracy, he reckons that 'the belated and still often wavering conversion of the churches to the ideals of human equality and freedom is a very recent development, which is now also occurring within the other world traditions' (p. 28). But such verdicts do not do justice to the Christian contributions. Both modern science and democracy arose during centuries when the non-Christian world was held back by conservatism and fatalism. Nowadays that remark must sound like an insult to non-Christians, but the historical evidence supporting it is massive. The Asian belief that the present incarnations of people are due to their behaviour in previous lives did encourage the acceptance of two disastrous ideas – that the poor deserve to be poor and that escaping from life with its cycle of reincarnations is much more important than transforming life. Other religious traditions, in Islam or tribal Africa or America, also had a strongly conservative influence which often supported social and technical stagnation. In contrast, science and democracy arose within a

Europe (and its North American offshoot) saturated by the Christian tradition. It is very difficult to believe that this was a pure coincidence.

Of course that religious tradition did not by itself give birth to science or to democracy. The birth needed a marriage between the religion which was still immensely powerful in that society and the new economic, social and intellectual forces which we call the Renaissance and the Enlightenment. But the religious tradition brought to that marriage powerful and fertile convictions deriving in the last analysis from the closely observant love which Jesus had both for nature and for human nature, particularly the human nature of the poor. In the Christian tradition nature was regarded as largely orderly, largely beneficent, sacred because created 'good' but not so sacred as to be called 'god'. People marginalised by economic and political power were believed to have been made 'in the image of God' and to have been loved by Jesus to the point of healing them and dying for them; and Christianity held that somehow God had expressed himself in a human life, in the flesh of a poor man. These Christian convictions were held by many of the pioneers of modern science and democracy. To exclude them from the factors making for the birth of the modern world seems unrealistic as history.

The direct or diffused influence of Christ or Christianity, in the making of saints or in the making of the modern world, may have been ultimately pernicious if Jesus Christ was wrong about the character of the Ultimate Reality. If Jesus was wrong, Professor Tom Driver may be right when in the last chapter of *The Myth of Christian Uniqueness* he says: 'Christianity, Judaism and Islam have almost always taught that God is active in history, but they have tended to combine this teaching with an unfortunate concept of divine transcendence that suggests (and sometimes insists) that God's essence is outside time and space' (p. 211). Driver offers as a better alternative the theory that 'God surpasses human beings by becoming *more*, not less, involved in creation. God is God by virtue of being more, not less, historical than we' (p. 212). I have not found that Driver's books, to which he refers the reader, entirely clarify these mystifying meditations, but I am not sure that this matters much. What does matter is what Hick states eloquently in *Problems of Religious Pluralism*:

> Each of the great religious traditions affirms that in addition to the social and natural world of our ordinary human experience

there is a limitlessly greater and higher Reality beyond or within us, in relation to which or to whom is our highest good. The ultimately real and the ultimately valuable are one, and to give oneself freely and totally to this One is our final salvation/liberation/enlightenment/fulfilment (p. 39).

What also matters is the possibility that the picture of God given to us by the life and teaching of Jesus Christ corresponds with the Ultimate Reality sufficiently to mean that for practical purposes this account of God is superior to others, although not perfect or complete. In this connection I was struck by a reference to human sexual reproduction when reading Hick's *Death and Eternal Life*. It may serve as an unusual parable about the uniqueness of Jesus and of the Christian insights and the Christian saints:

Each of the four hundred million or so sperm cells carries, in its details, a different genetic code. But only one out of these four hundred million can win the race to the ovum. Nevertheless this vast number is apparently needed. A single sperm, unsupported by its millions of companions, would not be able to make its way across the mucus area at the entry of the uterus, up the Fallopian tube, and through the membrane protecting the egg (p. 36).

Of course to say all that about Christ should not mean denying that Christians have much to learn from non-Christians. On the contrary, it is urgently imperative that we should learn. Jews, whose religion is by far the closest to Christianity, can teach the Christians who have been their persecutors about the unity and holiness of God and about the community whose life is purified by that vision and upheld by it through many disasters. Tribal Africans, whose religion was often despised as 'barbaric paganism' by Christian missionaries and colonisers, can teach the Christians about communion with neighbours, with the dead, with nature and with the God who is in and over all. And the great religions of the East can teach great lessons. I entirely agree with Paul Knitter that the more that the Christian community 'realizes that its savior *really* does make God known, the more it realizes that this God is a mystery ever more than what has been made known – the *Deus semper major*, the God ever beyond' (*No Other Name?*, p. 202). And I return to the traditional Christian teaching that Jesus Christ is *totus Deus, non totum Dei*, 'wholly God but not the whole of God', once endorsed by Hick (*God and the Universe of Faiths*, p. 159).

And of course to say all that as a Christian should not mean denying that there are difficulties in the central Christian ideas about God. But to get help in that field, I shall now briefly refer to some of the books of John Hick, one of the most impressive and persuasive Christian theologians of our time. Rather than quote extensively from his own popular presentations of his developing thought, with significantly varying titles – *Christianity at the Centre* (1968), *The Centre of Christianity* (1977) and *The Second Christianity* (1987) – I shall concentrate on his big books.

John Hick as a Christian Theologian

Faith and Knowledge was first published in America (by Cornell University, where Hick was then teaching), in 1957. Ten years passed before it was first published in Britain, in a revised edition, but it was fortunate for British readers that Hick's growing reputation as a lecturer in Cambridge University resulted in this fine book being made available to them. It had been written while its author was serving as a Presbyterian minister in Northumberland. It included a few explicit references to that pastoral experience and was throughout suffused by a spirit combining Christian piety with a sharp philosophical acumen. It was a contribution to what was then the contemporary discussion about the nature of religious faith.

This early book defended 'faith' as a claim about how things really are. As Hick summed it up in his Preface to the reissue of 1974, 'the claim to be conscious of the divine presence is not merely the expression of an idiosyncratic "slant" upon the world, but involves an assertion which is factually true or false because it is, if true, subject to verification within future human experience' – after death (p. viii). A religious faith's truth or falsity can be discussed rationally. 'All sorts of accidental circumstances may predispose us towards a proposition; the mere fact that it is widely held in the society around us is often sufficient . . . But it would clearly be absurd to suppose that the truth varies geographically with the liveliness of the local options' (p. 13). Christian faith in God is defined as 'the conviction that all life is under the control of a single, sovereign, personal will and purpose whose scope includes and yet transcends this present world and whose fulfilment secures man's deepest happiness and well-being' (p. 215). This conviction is held to be reasonable although the events on which it is based may also be described scientifically without any reference to God. Raw experience often is ambiguous, and the raw experience of life as a whole must be interpreted if it is to make sense. Faith is the religious interpretation just as atheism is a secular interpretation. A catalyst is needed to produce the interpretation: 'In Christianity the catalyst of faith is the person of Jesus Christ. It is in the historical figure of Jesus the Christ that, according to the Christian claim, God has in a unique and final way disclosed himself to men' (p. 216). And 'there is, I think, no room for debate as to the content of the basic claim of Christian faith concerning Christ . . . Christ is in some sense both God and man' (p. 220). The 'threefold sense of a divine purpose and love and forgiveness embodied in Christ was later reflected in the thought of the Church as the dogma of Christ's deity' (p. 226).

In *Arguments for the Existence of God* (1970) and elsewhere Hick has shown his thorough appreciation of the fact that the most serious objection to Christian faith arises from the tragic reality that the world believed to be created and controlled by God contains so much evil. His discussion of this mystery has been as profound as any of the books to which I referred in my earlier chapters and in *Evil and the God of Love* (1966) presented the results of study and reflection over a period of five years. The book was a masterpiece. With learning but also with clarity it argued against many attempts to explain the problem of evil in the Christian tradition – the attempt to show that all that exists is somehow good at least from God's angle; the attempt to prove that what seems to us evil is necessary if there is to be a distinction between the imperfect creation and its Creator; the attempt to classify evil as mere 'non-being'; the attempt to blame the apparent strength of evil on the rebellion of Adam and Eve and on the transmission of their sin through the lust of sexual intercourse; and the attempt to praise God for his justice in consigning so many evil, or at least non-Christian, sinners to everlasting punishment in hell. Elsewhere Hick has summed up his fundamental criticism of all these theories: 'The idea of a perfect creation going wrong entirely on its own is self-contradictory. Man would never in fact choose wrongly unless there were some flaws either in himself or in his environment' (*The Centre of Christianity*, p. 84). In contrast with these doomed attempts at an explanation, in *Evil and the God of Love* he has frankly acknowledged that much of the terrible reality of evil in the creation remains a mystery, as much good does, so that the interpretation of raw experience by faith or unbelief is needed. But he has pointed out that much evil is the result of actions by sinners who have been given free will because their Creator wants their free response in love – and that much evil can be seen to be redeemed, even on this side of the grave, because through dealing with it sinners are made into saints. As John Keats wrote: 'Do you not see how necessary a World of Pains and troubles is to school an Intelligence and make it a Soul?' (p. 295).

Above all, Hick has affirmed a faith in the ultimate triumph of God beyond the grave, as the Creator brings final good out of evil. Although insisting that the story of the fall is a myth of limited value, he found a truth in the exclamation of the ancient Easter liturgy: 'O fortunate crime, which merited such and so great a redeemer!' (p. 280). Although usually critical of the theology of St Augustine, he has endorsed the great Augustinian saying that 'God judged it better to bring good out of evil than to allow no evil to exist' (p. 182). As Hick put it:

> It is claimed – reducing the argument to its bare bones – that the evils of this life are necessary to prepare us as moral personalities for the life of the future heavenly Kingdom, and that they are justified by the fact that in that Kingdom all evil will have been left behind and unimaginable good will fill our lives (p. 387).

The discussion of the problem of evil in the non-Christian religions was not considered in *Evil and the God of Love*, but in the light of Hick's later development one point deserves special emphasis. A spiritually adequate – not an intellectually complete – answer to this problem was found in the idea of God as personal and loving. Hick quoted the insight of Irenaeus, who in the second century was Christianity's first systematic theologian, to the effect that 'man has been created for fellowship with his Maker and is valued by the personal divine love as an end in himself. The world exists to be an environment for man's life, and its imperfections are integral to its fitness as a place of soul-making' (p. 263). This insight goes back to Jesus himself, for 'this characterization of God as the heavenly Father is not a merely random illustration but an analogy that lies at the heart of the Christian faith' (p. 294) and 'the supreme insight and faith of New Testament monotheism' is that 'God loves *all* His human children with an infinite and irrevocable love' (p. 131). Moreover, Hick repeatedly says that the victory of good over evil in the story of Christ's life and death has been decisive for his own faith. In other words, according to this masterly book, only if the essential Christian picture of God corresponds with the Ultimate Reality (not perfectly or completely, of course) can the existence of so much evil be reconciled with a rational belief that our world is created by that Reality.

Published ten years after *Evil and the God of Love*, *Death and Eternal Life* may seem to be a book by a different author. Hick has now been influenced profoundly by his move from Cambridge to be a professor in the university of a great industrial city with a multi-faith population, Birmingham – and also by studious visits to India and Sri Lanka. He wishes to offer his new book 'not primarily as a contribution to christian theology, but rather as a christian contribution to global or human theology' (p. 27). Accordingly in its pages we find that he respectfully considers both the scientific understanding of personality and Asian mystical traditions including the *Tibetan Book of the Dead*. He insists that if the West is going to ask the East to consider sympathetically the traditional idea of the resurrection of the body, the East is entitled to ask for a similar sympathy with its idea of the reincarnation of the soul. But I hope I am not being unfair to a richly meandering argument if I record my impression that at the end of it Hick does make a contribution which is persistently Christian.

To be sure, the Christian faith in life after death is purged of many of its expressions which in the past have been so popular as to be considered official. It is assumed that modern Christians do not share the hope that makes the New Testament both exciting and strange – the hope that the living and the dead will be united in the kingdom of God in the near future. We are told in chapter 15 that belief in 'the resurrection of the body' should not suggest that our corpses will be revived or that the pictures of the joys of heaven and the torments of hell are true literally. It means 'the resurrection of the person', preserving 'the inner character of the individual' (p. 371) in relation to other persons as well as to God, 'expressing the personality within its new environment as the physical body has expressed it in the earthly environment' (p. 186). Such a resurrection depends entirely on the eternal God's love for us as persons: it is 'a gift of divine grace' (p. 181). It does not depend on the resurrection of Jesus as 'the coming forth of a miraculously re-vivified body from the grave' – although 'so long as we do not insist upon any dogmatic definition of its precise nature, we can assert that beyond all reasonable doubt what has come to be called "the resurrection of Jesus" was a real occurrence' (p. 171). The 'real interaction after his death between Jesus and the disciples' (p. 173), producing a conviction which 'could . . . have had as its simplest and perhaps most likely basis a vision or visions, perhaps only momentary, of Jesus as a majestic figure shining in super-natural light' (p. 177), powerfully strengthened the existing Jewish belief in life after death. So the treatment of some popular Christian beliefs as mythological may seem to many Christians to be drastic. But it preserves the central teaching of Jesus on this subject, reported in three of the gospels to be that God *is* the God of Abraham, Isaac and Jacob, persons who are still loved by God after their deaths: 'God is not God of the dead, but of the living'.

Far more drastic is Hick's treatment of Hindu and Buddhist beliefs in the rebirth of souls in new lives on earth. Here, we are told, is 'a mystic truth' (p. 355). These beliefs have offered a solution to the problem of evil, for they 'relieve God of this responsibility and make our *karmas* responsible' (p. 302). But they turn out to be untrue, unless it is an adequate translation of reincarnation to say what Hick says. This is his demythologised version of the idea: 'we all exist within the common karmic history of humanity, inheriting a world which others have fashioned and fashioning a world in which others must live', so that although 'we do not return in person to bear in later earthly lives the conse-quences of our present actions . . . *someone* will have to bear those consequences' (pp. 357–8). And beyond the grave there is the possibility – no more – of 'a series of lives, each bounded by something analogous to birth and death, lived in other worlds in spaces other than that in which we now are' (p. 456), as we are purged before our entry into the Celestial City and 'the beatific vision in which the finite spirit knows God directly as the ultimate reality of all being' (p. 207).

There are, I understand, some Hindus and Buddhists who would accept these two ideas as an adequate translation of the traditional idea of the reincarnation of souls in new lives on earth, but they seem to be few in relation to the total community of Hindus or Buddhists. They are proportionately fewer than are the Christians who translate 'the resurrection of the body' as 'the resurrection of the person' (of Jesus or of anyone else), in relation to the total number of Christians. Damage seems to have been done to the heart of Hindu or Buddhist faith. For it does seem very damaging to their spiritual authority if one says that Gautama the Buddha and the Hindu sages were wrong to teach people to fear the possibility of another life on earth, and that what was true in their teaching was only the condemnation of selfishness. This seems far more damaging than it is to say that Jesus and the first Christians were wrong to hope that the kingdom of God would 'come' quickly, because the infinitely more important ideas of God and of God's reign can be rescued from the disappointment of that hope about a date.

A unity between the world's faiths is sought in the common emphasis that the selfishness of the ego must die, spiritually and physically, in order that the person may be united with other persons and with God without ceasing to be a person. Hick admits that at first sight 'in Buddhism as well as in Hinduism there is a radically negative attitude to that which in the Semitic faiths is said to endure for ever as the object of God's eternal love' (p. 427). *Nirvana* has been understood by many Buddhists, and it seems probable by the Buddha himself, as the extinction of personality as a candle is 'blown out' (which is what *nirvana* means) by the wind. Many Hindu sages have held that *Atman* is ultimately identical with *Brahman*, 'the One without a second' – 'the collective human self being ultimately identical with God', as a Christian would put it (p. 464). But Hick stresses that the ordinary devotee in popular (*bhakti*) Hinduism and northern (*Mahayana*) Buddhism 'has affirmed a continuing identity in which the soul is both somehow part of the life of God and yet somehow still exists in a personal relationship of love to God. And that is what Hick affirms in the end: 'the unity of mankind in a state in which the ego-aspect of individual consciousness has been left behind and the relational aspect has developed into a total community which is one-in-many and many-in-one, existing in a state which is probably not embodied and probably not in time' (p. 464). Clues to the understanding of this idea are said to lie in the Christian traditions about the unity of three 'persons' in the Godhead and about the unity of Christians as limbs of the Body of Christ.

In all his books Hick places great emphasis on religious experience and pays far less attention to the idea of God's self-revelation. This emphasis is certainly necessary if one is trying to vindicate faith in God, or talk about God, as meaningful: such faith or talk arises out of religious experience. But surely we also need to consider what is said to be experienced. If only ordinary life is under consideration, many people will deny that the Christian interpretation is sensible. If extraordinary events or states of mind are said to be the vital experiences – ecstasies, visions or miracles – many people will reply that they have not had such experiences and do not wish to have them, because they prefer being calmly reasonable to what sound like moments of hysteria. But if it is claimed that God is revealed in a holy book or a holy community –

for Christians, in the witness of the Bible or in the life and worship of the Church – then at least something definite and familiar is being pointed to, and the claim that God can be known through it can be thought about rationally. Christians should not be frightened of their dependence on what they regard as God's self-revelation by the fear of fundamentalism, which is by no means necessary. Despite his many references to the scriptures of the world, I have to ask whether Hick has not been too nervous of being thought a fundamentalist.

One advantage of more emphasis on 'revelation' is that it encourages a stress on the limits of human knowledge in the sphere of religion. If our experience is clearly limited and conditioned by many non-religious factors, and if the revelation available to us clearly uses symbolism, story-telling, poetry or mythology in the attempt to speak about what lies beyond our experience, then we are encouraged to be cautious in our theology. Despite his many references to the mysteriousness of religion, I have to ask whether Hick has been sufficiently cautious. In *Death and Eternal Life* he gives us a good many pages of speculation about possible lives after death – lives which seem to be half in space and time and half out of them. The simple truth, at least to my simple mind, is that any talk about eternal life which uses the dimensions of space and time is mythological. For the individual, space and time as we know them and can think about them end at death. If this truth is granted, talk about more than one life in eternity is seen to be a mythological way of expressing the hope of progress, growth or purgation, just as talk about the resurrection of the body is seen to be a mythological way of expressing the hope that eternal life will be at least as personal as the life we know.

So to my mind, everything ultimately turns on the question about the reality of the God who loves us enough to give us eternal life. I base my trust in that God on the life and death of Jesus Christ, and on what has followed them, much more than on anything else in the world. And that is also the heart of such an answer as I can give to the problem of evil. I find it surprising that in *Evil and the God of Love*, despite the many references to God's victory over evil in Christ, there is not a greater emphasis on the revelation of God's suffering on the cross. Like most Christians in our time Hick believes the cross shows that God suffers, but he does not seem to use this faith as the Christian key to the mystery of evil. He certainly believes that we see in the life of Jesus 'a supreme instance of that union of divine grace/inspiration with creaturely freedom that occurs in all authentic human response and obedience to God', and he quotes Baillie and Lampe as expressing that belief more fully. And he believes even more than that. 'Surely we must say that the historical Jesus possessed, exhibited, incarnated, as much of the infinite divine love as could be expressed in and through an individual human life.' (I take these recent formulations from his essay in *Encountering Jesus*, edited by Stephen T. Davis, 1987, pp. 18, 21.) But I ask whether he has given enough importance to the supremacy of the cross of Jesus in proclaiming the God of love. Does he not underestimate the difference that Christianity makes when (unlike most Muslims) it asserts that Jesus the Word and Son of God really did die on the cross?

If God is in any way responsible for the presence of evil in his creation, even if only by permitting it – and that is the thrust of Hick's argument, with which I respectfully agree – the problem of evil is intensified unless we can believe that in some way God himself suffers alongside his creatures, somewhat as a decent parent does and wants to do. Of course, I do not suggest that God suffers against his will as we do; or that God suffers because of his sin, as we do; or that God suffers without hope, as we can do when at or near the despair of suicide. His suffering must be more like the pangs of childbirth. But I hope that God suffers, because if he does it shows that he loves, and I am assured by revelation that he does because his love is embodied supremely in the dying Jesus. And that is the most profound reason for the orthodox Christian insistence, which I share, that the life of Jesus embodies the active love of God and is not merely an example of a very good and heroic man responding to the love of God. I do not suggest that the interpretation of his agonised death as the revelation of divinely suffering love is clearly prominent in the New Testament: it is not. But I know that it has been, and is, prominent in the Christian Church in our century, and I believe that here is an example of the developing guidance of the Church by God as Spirit.

Hick has developed his attitude to non-Christian religions in the course of study, dialogue and reflection. In his book *John Hick's Theology of Religions*, which I have already mentioned (p. 222), Gavin D'Costa concluded that 'over the years he has moved from Christocentrism to theocentrism to a Reality-centrism' (p. 162), but that sympathetic critic also held that Hick has remained a Christian, in a way that cannot be fitted into 'Reality-centrism'. I agree that 'Reality' is still Christlike for him. So I valued the opportunity to review his most recent and most comprehensive (though not novel) treatment of the subject, *An Interpretation of Religion* (1989). Other Christian theologians have also developed their thinking, and I have added reviews of books which three of the most interesting – John Robinson, Ninian Smart and Hans Küng – wrote after exposure to other faiths. The question running through all these books is whether a Christian theologian can take a neutral, or even detached, attitude to the religions of the world, however eager he may be to do them justice and learn from them. And these books suggest that the only possible answer is no. Christianity's uniqueness is no myth: it goes very deep. For Jesus is unique. Salvation is everywhere, but since I have tried to explain what I mean by 'Saviour' I can say that there is only one Saviour.

Review of *An Interpretation of Religion* by John Hick (1989)

In this expanded version of his Gifford Lectures delivered in the University of Edinburgh, Professor Hick sums up the teaching given in previous books including his contributions to those landmarks in recent theological controversy, *The Myth of God Incarnate* and *The Myth of Christian Uniqueness*. But here his teaching is not provocative or fragmentary. It is put in the context of nothing less than a short history of religion. Well-informed, well-matured, this plea for religion and its pluralism is consistently impressive and (to my mind) mostly convincing.

About half the book argues in defence of religion against modern sceptics. Religion, he insists, was in all the pre-modern ages found wherever humanity was found. 'The view that belief in the supernatural is universal has been completely confirmed by modern anthropology' – as Talcott Parsons is quoted (p. 21). In our time this vast phenomenon deserves an interpretation which is religious, not reductionist – and which acknowledges that religion has sought and worshipped the Real, so that 'non-realist' religion of Don Cupitt's kind 'cannot credibly claim to represent the message of the great spiritual traditions' (p. 208).

That does not mean that religion is a simple affair. It consists of religions which often make truth-claims incompatible with the claims of their rivals – and within each of the great religions there is a great variety. Conrad Hyers is quoted: 'if a religion is given enough time and space, whatever its initial and prevailing orientation, it will eventually take up almost all, if not all, possible positions on any of the fundamental religious questions' (p. 341). None of the important truth-claims of any religion is provable. The universe is ambiguous. The believer can point to many things about it. Reason can show both that God may exist and that this is an important question. Basing one's life on one's answer to this question is reasonable. But religious belief remains belief. There are always other facts which tell against it, and clever and honest people can always argue against its validity.

But since the 'axial' period of prophets and sages (800–200 BC) all the great religions have encouraged belief in the Real, either as the personal God or as the impersonal Absolute – and have also encouraged belief that the Real is the good destiny of humankind. Those beliefs have produced saints in all the religions, with hope for lesser mortals whether in the Jewish hope of the imminent arrival of the kingdom of God or in the Indian hope of the final bliss after hundreds or thousands of reincarnations. Religion, says Hick, teaches a 'cosmic optimism' despite the grimness of many religious descriptions of the present human situation.

Often people's 'different beliefs lead to their acting ethically in the same way' (p. 315). Almost everywhere in high religion one finds the Golden Rule: love your neighbour as yourself because of the Real. And almost everywhere one finds the rule about the condition of spiritual progress: transcend selfishness. A Sufi mystic is quoted: 'No one will find his way to the Court of Magnificence until he is annihilated' (p. 50). Almost everywhere, too, thoughtful teachers of religion say that the Real cannot be pinned down in human categories. St Thomas Aquinas taught: 'The thing known is in the knower according to the mode of the Knower . . . We cannot grasp what God is, but only what he is not and how other things are related to him' (pp. 153, 247).

Christians have been specially prone to forget this and to banish to hell all those who do not accept their particular understanding of the work of Christ. Hick is himself a Christian, and the influence of Jesus is so pervasive in this book that his name is not indexed. But with pleasure he makes the points that the teachings of Jesus were 'directly practical and existential' (p. 262) not theological, and that in them 'there is no suggestion that the heavenly Father's loving acceptance was conditional upon his own future death' (p. 245).

I think Hick is right to expect that 'during the next hundred years most educated Christians will have come to take for granted a pluralistic understanding of the religious life of the world, with

Christianity seen as part of that life' (p. 377). Why, then, am I not convinced by this book's minimising of the uniqueness of Christianity?

It is because the account of the Real emerging here does not support the Christian hope and the Christian ethics that are taught clearly by Hick himself (sometimes very rightly in condemnation of Christian practice). When the Real is described, the description accords with the wisdom of Hindu and Buddhist sages but not with the wisdom of the cross. 'The Real', we are told, 'is the ground of our values, in that it is the ground of our existence and nature; and it is good in the sense that it is to be rejoiced in as the basis of the limitlessly better possibility that is open to us' (p. 338). To the Christian that says something – but does it say enough? 'The Real', we are told,

> cannot be said to be one or many, person or thing, conscious or unconscious, purposive or non-purposive, substance or process, good or evil, loving or hating. None of the descriptive terms that apply within the realm of human experience can apply literally to the unexperienceable reality that underlies that realm (p. 350).

To the Christian that is a healthy warning against glibness – but in the light of the cross (and of what went before and after it) surely it can be said that the first term in all those couples is the better, because the more appropriate as a pointer.

Hick often argues that correct theology is not vital to the human transformation which can be called salvation or liberation. He admires the Buddha, who said that just as the ocean tastes only of salt so his teaching tastes only of salvation, not speculation. And he admires two Indian pictures of religion: the water in a jar is coloured by the jar, but break the jar and the water and air in it join the Whole. But if the Real 'cannot' – or need not – be compared with unity, personhood, consciousness, purpose, substantiality, goodness and love, is there much sense in the Christian teaching that the best ethics is the imitation of Christ and his Father? And if the Real is not that, is there much sense in the claim that when united with the Real after death humankind will be compensated for all the ills that flesh is heir to?

There is a contrast between the Christian vision of the Real exhibited on the cross and (for example) the 'general Indian conception', said to be 'a whirling cosmic process which does not come from anywhere and is not going anywhere' within which 'streams of conscious life, falsely positing their own autonomous existence, are subject to the self-centred craving in virtue of which life is to them suffering, anxiety, unsatisfactoriness' (p. 64). And despite all the unity between the religions, at this point people who can must choose.

For himself, Professor Hick chose long ago and has never abandoned his choice. Here he says it again: 'Jesus is the one through whom my own consciousness of God has been largely formed' (p. 216). Is it arrogant to say that this all-embracing book, while properly penitent about the arrogance of Christians, has a 'cosmic optimism' which shows that it could only have been written by a believer in the Christians' God?

Review of *Truth is Two-Eyed* by
John A. T. Robinson (1979)

It so happened that I read an advance copy of Bishop John Robinson's *Truth is Two-Eyed* some weeks ago in Jerusalem. Tertullian's question many centuries ago was: 'What has Athens to do with Jerusalem?' In other words: What has Greek philosophy to add to the biblical revelation? The question to which Dr Robinson addresses himself is: What has Jerusalem to do with Delhi?

In the new question 'Jerusalem' stands for the religion of the biblical prophets, for whom the living God acts in history and the holy God commands the love of neighbour. For Christians, 'Jerusalem' stands supremely for the redeeming action and instruction recorded in the gospels (a kind of book no other religion possesses). Dr Robinson wishes to be loyal to that tradition of prophets and apostles. Notice, for example, his insistence that the text 'the kingdom of God is within you' implies not a purely individual and internal mysticism but 'the total transformation of this world-order'. 'Right politics *is* religion', he writes (p. 70); 'it is what to know the God of history means'. And 'Delhi' stands for what seems to be the totally different tradition of the religious East. Here the divine is seen in the repeated, otherwise meaningless, cycles of nature; and the human problem is how to escape, to be united with the divine as salt is dissolved in water.

Robinson alludes to some of the many recent publications which have recommended meditation to the West and liberation to the East, but his focus is not on such practical concerns. He has been fascinated to discover fresh, serious, constructive thinking among Indian Christians about the fundamental faith in God through

Christ, and he wants to report it. So he invites us to enter the East-West dialogue at a deeper level of thought.

When viewing God, he suggests, West and East alike need two eyes – one which concentrates on love for the God who can be addressed personally, and one which concentrates on reverence for the God who is everywhere, in us all and in all matter, although also infinite. At present the West too easily domesticates and trivialises the personal God. But with an equal honesty Robinson points out that the East too easily submerges all the values of personal identity and purpose in a nameless, formless One, with the result that in this life people give up the struggle for the personal fulfilment of all. Many quotations are assembled to show how, from the Bible to the present day, the prophets of West and East have striven to correct the deficiencies in the single-eyed vision. The West has been told by its own sons that 'Your God is too small.' When *Honest to God* was published, some discerning critics lamented that Robinson seemed unaware of the protests by the Christian mystics against the little God – but, if that was a defect, then he has certainly made up for it since. And he has been encouraged to find many Hindu, even Buddhist, teachers urging a loving devotion not far from the Christian worship of God.

He delights to quote Eastern religious poetry comparing God with the fragrance of a rose. The analogy may imply: no rose (no world), no fragrance. But he also exhibits with pleasure an Indian Christian poem extolling God as 'the seedless Seed of the tree of becoming'. That second image beautifully preserves the Jewish-Christian-Muslim insistence that the one true God is the Creator. In the teaching of the fourteenth-century English priest who wrote *The Cloud of Unknowing*, God 'is thy being but thou art not his'. The encounter with Hindu images of God has helped Robinson to be more 'unknowing', freed from the 'Latin captivity' of theology; and he hopes that it will help us also to see how great and how near is our God. But he is not impressed by the Eastern feeling that history is a spiral, making no progress (although for the East's sake he is prepared to imagine history as a series of ascending spirals). He grants the recent great popularity in India of the *Gita*, where Krishna appears to instruct his devotee about the duties of life; but he cannot help noticing that the main point of the *Gita* is that the devotee ought not to hesitate to engage in a civil war, since in the long run we are all dead and reborn. For this Christian bishop the world's history has a meaning, seen most clearly when God shines through the life of Jesus as the Christ.

Those who felt that passages in his *The Human Face of God* (1973) were obscure or heretical in tendency will be interested to note that, in this latest book, Robinson firmly dissociates himself from radicals who have surfaced since he did. Contributors to *The Myth of God Incarnate* argued that the whole idea of the uniqueness of the incarnation was an import into Christianity and should now be exported into oblivion. Robinson disagrees. He is sure that it has been the glory, not the shame, of Christianity from the beginning that the Word became flesh, that God's 'self-expressive activity' spoke with the voice and died with the blood of a historical man. Without this, Christianity 'is nothing'. In our time it is therefore not enough to say, as many Hindus say, that Jesus is one *Avatara* among many – or to say, as many Buddhists say, that Jesus is one *Bodhissatva* among many. Robinson did not like the picture of Jesus among many equals that dominates the Remakrishna headquarters in Calcutta.

Jesus is 'the Christ'! This means that the Jew who died some 1,940 years ago, and who was first understood in terms of Palestinian messianism, has risen to become universal. The early Fathers of the Church, using the pagan terms of their day, loved to speak of the 'seeds of light' planted by God throughout the world around Jesus the Light. Robinson is similarly keen to acknowledge that God has never left himself without a witness; and to acknowledge that the supreme witness of Jesus the first-century Jew to his Father can be understood by non-Jews in terms of Greek, Hindu, Buddhist, African, scientific or other thought.

What most interests him here is the fertility of recent Indian Christology. Indian Christians have made experiments which have not used the old Greek or Latin categories such as *persona* or *hypostasis*. Some of these experiments have failed to preserve the religious values of the old orthodox Christology defined at Nicaea and Chalcedon; they have surrendered too much to Hinduism, just as *The Myth of God Incarnate* surrendered too much to Western secularism. But the surrender is not necessary. What is necessary, if the Christian gospel is to be intelligible in new worlds, is the experiment in communication, in earthing, in embodiment. As Robinson interprets some Indian experiments in Christology his pleasure is evident, for they confirm the words of the American theologian Schubert Ogden: to say 'only in Jesus Christ' means that 'the only God who redeems any history . . . is the God whose redemptive action is decisively represented in the word that Jesus speaks and is'. A wise Indian Christian leader, M. M. Thomas, has commented: 'Probably this is the only form of universalism which can ultimately be called Christian' (p. 124).

His passage to India did not leave Robinson starry-eyed about Hinduism as a whole – or about the Indian Church as a whole. But he saw enough to persuade him that he had seen a star in the East. And it helped him to worship Jesus as the Christ. This book is not an easy read for an idle hour. It abounds in difficult ideas, and the difficulty is increased by the richness of its quotations. And the conclusions are not very controversial; there will be no sensation, no big sales. But this Cambridge scholar's willingness to be exposed to the unfamiliar East has led to an intellectual and spiritual achievement of no mean order.

Review of *Beyond Ideology* by Ninian Smart (1982)

The name of Professor Ninian Smart as author is enough to recommend any study that he may make of the contemporary dialogues between the great religious faiths and secular worldviews. Dividing his time between the University of Lancaster and the University of California, he has been in a position (if that is not too static a word) to advise the BBC on its famous TV series about world religions, *The Long Search*, and to write a row of wellknown books. Himself an Anglican priest, he is clearly determined to be humbly fair to those noble and subtle non-Christian visions and values by which many millions of his fellow men live. In this book, based on Gifford Lectures delivered in Edinburgh in 1979–80, he moves beyond description to offer some judgements, although very gently.

He assumes that, towards the end of the twentieth century, man remains a basically religious animal. Marxism has been greeted by many as the key both to the understanding of the past and to the mastery of the present; but now there are many Marxisms, and almost all of them seem 'tired'. Of all the secular ideologies in the modern world, nationalism has been the most compelling. Marxism has most effectively kept its appeal in situations where that liberating key which enthusiasts had glimpsed turned out to be a useful tool in nation-building. Yet nationalism is no more able than is Marxism to answer the questions about individual destiny and meaning. These questions are asked persistently whenever humanity can raise its eyes from the material necessities, and Smart observes that the most influential answers have continued to be provided by two international religions: Christianity and Buddhism. (His remarks about the deliberately unclear Hinduism and the all-too-clear Islam, although illuminating, are brief.)

Christianity and Buddhism have kept their spiritual power over the centuries because, to a world experienced as tragic, they offer a 'critique from the sacred Beyond'. Their insights are still expressed in great stories or 'myths'; in monastic orders and consecrated buildings; in richly different religious developments bound up with the cultures of whole peoples (there is a division in Buddhism rather like the Catholic–Protestant split in Christianity); and, above all, in teachings which are able to pierce through materialism to the soul of the individual, winning countless converts to the stony way of self-denial for the sake of a spiritual reward beyond tragedy. All this gives to religion a gravity which the cheerful slogans of Marxism or nationalism, shouted to drown the rattle of the guns, cannot rival. And there is no immediate likelihood that either Christianity or Buddhism will fold up. Our world is pluralist. The hope for humanity (which badly needs hope) must be that each faith will provide its own grounds for strong support to 'the concept of the sanctity of the person and the notion that politics is in the end about happiness' (p. 12). Thus the idolatry of Marxism or nationalism, with its demands for human sacrifices, can be countered.

It is tempting for those who wish to encourage the Christian-Buddhist dialogue to claim that the Buddha was from the first regarded as a living Saviour, like Jesus; that the 'self' from which he claimed to liberate his disciples was merely the 'ego' or the 'lower self' or the 'flesh' against which Christians too have waged war, that the goal he set before them, *nirvana*, was very like the Christian's heaven. But Professor Smart firmly maintains that Buddhism, when true to itself, teaches that the Buddha is happy precisely because he is entirely dead, with a self wholly dissolved in a *nirvana* which is emptiness. Despite some attempts to work out a Christian, or at least a Western, Buddhism, it is immensely difficult for Christians or ex-Christians to enter sympathetically into the Buddhist diagnosis of the human condition. It seems to be escapist (more than once Smart notes how it could not regenerate China). And, when it is presented as the solution to the problem of how to avoid endless incarnations, it is easy for those who inherit the biblical view of life to say brusquely: 'the cycle of births is not our problem.'

Similarly, as many missionaries have found in Asia, it is immensely difficult for Buddhists to respect a religion which prays to a personal, passionate and active God and has as its central image a man in agony on an instrument of torture. Such a religion seems trapped in the world of suffering and 'impermanence' – when mankind cries out for liberation from misery through the extinction of all cravings in that ultimate bliss which is 'not-born, not-become, not-made, uncompounded'. Many Buddhists would despise Christianity even if they could forget the colonial uniform which it wore in the past.

Clearly there is scope for many authors with some knowledge of both to attempt to explain the two religions to each other. The simplest way in for the Christian is to welcome from Buddhism the gift of peace of mind through meditation, through the realisation of the truth that nothing matters so much as it seems to at the time. The best way in for the Buddhist is through the idea of compassion. But the conversation about transcendence needs to go deeper than that, and Smart draws his wisdom from the necessary level. He is deep not only in his knowledge but also in his sensitivity to the power of religion. When he mentions sacramental acts such as the Christian Eucharist, or archery, sword-play or the tea ceremony in the Japanese version of Buddhism, he never mocks. He always asks what these rituals mean as, clutching at symbols, man meets the mystery of the Beyond. His sympathy falters only when he meets some of his authoritarian fellow Christians, 'flourishing Bibles with fabulous confidence, frenetic in their assurances that Jesus loves us and all is well with the world' (p. 196).

Review of *Christianity and the World Religions* by Hans Küng (1987)

Since Professor Hans Küng was declared by the Vatican to be no longer qualified to teach as a Catholic theologian, he has gone from strength to strength. Not only has he attracted ever-larger audiences in Tübingen, where the university has remained his base; his admiring public is now world-wide, partly as a result of many lecture tours. He is specially honoured in England.

Christianity and the World Religions is the fourth big book to present his teaching at greater length, with deeper learning and with a more massive documentation of other studies than is possible in a lecture. He may or may not remain a Roman Catholic (he does in his own eyes). What is certain is that the Vatican's displeasure has helped him to become a universal theologian.

Since he followed up his *On Being a Christian* with volumes which directly address the secular mind of the modern West (*Does God Exist?* and *Eternal Life?*), it was thoroughly fitting that he should tackle *Christianity and the World Religions*. He has maintained his own standard. This new *magnum opus* constitutes a rich education in a field which must concern every seriously thinking Christian.

Of course Küng's approach does not coincide with the convictions of all Christians. He is a total believer in the merits and the urgency of very careful, very charitable, very scholarly and very spiritual dialogue between Christianity, Islam, Hinduism and Buddhism – the four religions surveyed historically and philosophically in this book. Many Christians are still suspicious of such studies and conversations, or passionately opposed to them, because it all seems a betrayal of the uniqueness of the gospel. In particular many Christians in Islamic or Buddhist lands, or in India, have little sympathy with a religion which they or their parents have rejected and which has rejected them. The comparison seems to be between light and darkness; and a good many New Testament passages make it. But personally I found this book immensely encouraging. In part because I live in a London where many faiths are at home, I have tried to read a good deal about these religions in their own environments and to see a little of them with my own eyes. I have relied on the considerable number of British scholars who are now experts. And I have reached certain conclusions.

How heartening it is when along comes Küng with almost superhuman sizes in brain and heart; with a large library of books in German which I haven't read; with a small army of research assistants; with thanks, too, to hosts in many countries; and, most important, with three other Tübingen professors (Josef von Ess, Heinrich von Stietencron and Heinz Becheret) who between them write about half the book on the basis of their specialist knowledge of the non-Christian faiths! It is heartening because the conclusions are essentially the same as the lessons I have learnt from British scholars. No attempt is made to pretend that the four religions all say the same thing. As Professor Küng offers his 'Christian response' to each expert presentation, he constantly guards against that mistake. He thinks it patronising and misleading, although well-intentioned, to say that good non-Christians are 'anonymous Christians' (as Karl Rahner did). But he is quite sure that all these religions can learn from each other.

He argues for a Christian position that Jesus of Nazareth is the supreme revelation of God, but does so having taken the trouble to learn and, where his habitual honesty suggests that it is necessary, to apologise. Maybe some non-Christians will, like the Vatican, criticise him: but the only factual mistake I spotted in my ignorance was in the first sentence (there are now over 5 billion people living on this earth, not 4.8). If his assessments of other faiths are rejected – and how hard it is even for the most sympathetic outsider to see what a believer sees! – there can be no legitimate complaint that he attacks others while sparing Christianity. The historical criticism that he applies to Muhammad, or Gautama the Buddha, or the evolution of Hinduism (properly, not an 'ism' but a 'collection of religions'), is applied to the evidence about Jesus. He rebukes Islam for its legalism, or Buddhism for its dependence on monasticism, but also condemns aspects of his own Catholic heritage. He probes the luxuriant mythology and the flourishing popular religion of India, but is realistic about similar elements in Catholicism, respecting them but not pretending that they are the pure knowledge of the One.

His criticisms may be resented because they come from a European in the post-colonial age. But on many pages he alludes to scholars born within the non-Christian traditions who have themselves dared to be critical – Muslims who have very tentatively begun to move from Quranic fundamentalism; Hindus who acknowledge that religion has strengthened stagnation and exploitation; Buddhists who are quietly sceptical about the reality of the problem to which the Buddha addressed himself (the prolongation of suffering through reincarnation). And the final effect is not critical but positive. We are entering, says Küng, the post-modern age, when around the world sensitive people want to see science, technology and industry subjected to human welfare – not materialistic individualism, but the relations of men and women to nature, to their fellows, to society and to ultimate reality.

Jesus is the best teacher of this new age. But Christianity needs the passion of the Muslim's adoration of the ultimate reality as One God, for Islam's challenge can undo some of the harm done by the Church's total separation from its roots in Jewish monotheism. And Christianity needs the insistence of the Eastern religions on experience – through nature (it is brilliantly explained how Hindu images respond to nature's varying moods), through the community (preserved in the East by domestic and public ritual as well as by the family), through solitary meditation (where the Christians are the amateurs). Only a Christianity able to learn or re-learn these things can rise to the challenge. And only such a Christianity will be in a spiritual condition where it can say convincingly: 'The Allah you already know is fatherly; the One you already seek has come among you as a man in history; the Nirvana you already desire is negatively No-thing, but much more interestingly Being-itself, the Source and Goal of a creation which is good because created out of joy'.

John Hick's response is on pp. 306–10.

9

WHAT, THEN, SHOULD WE BELIEVE?

Because of my clumsiness the previous chapters may have been misunderstood. They may have conveyed the impression that I have little sympathy with the 'turbulent priests' whom I have discussed. It may seem that I fail to appreciate what they have done to awaken the Church of England (in particular) from its dogmatic slumbers and to ask radical questions echoing around that part of the world which is interested in English-speaking Christian theology. But John Robinson, Don Cupitt, Maurice Wiles, Geoffrey Lampe, John Bowden, Dennis Nineham, John Hick and their collaborators have all laboured mightily, with sweat of mind and heart, in the spirit of Alec Vidler's introduction to *Soundings*. 'It is time for ploughing, not reaping,' Vidler wrote in 1962,

> for making soundings, not charts. If this be so, we do not have to apologize for our inability to do what we hope will be possible in a future generation. We can best serve the cause of truth and of the Church by candidly confessing where our perplexities lie, and not by making claims which, so far as we can see, theologians are not at present in a position to justify (p. ix).

As I look back on *Soundings* I gladly reflect that in England there have been many attempts by Christian communicators and pastors, as well as by lay people in conversation with friends and neighbours, to restate Christianity in language which makes sense towards the end of the twentieth century. The plea for 'Beginning All Over Again' which Howard Root made could not be taken literally by Christians, and it is perhaps a comment on the proposal that its author became the Director of the Anglican Centre in Rome and the Archbishop of Canterbury's Counsellor on Vatican Affairs. It is also noteworthy that the contributor to *Soundings* who handled the challenge of science to theology was to write as Archbishop of York: 'The truth is that doctrinally the Church of

England remains where it always has been' (*York Diocesan Leaflet*, February 1989). But there have been many new beginnings as the biblical and Christian tradition has been made more relevant to contemporary quests for meaning and morality in life and to new interests in spirituality. It has been made relevant to the questions being asked by the poor, the young and women, and to the concerns for peace and the environment. And I am glad that the intellectual difficulties outlined in *Soundings* – my subject in this book – have been expounded with unforgettable effect by the authors whose books I have summarised and criticised. Robinson made millions listen to his plea for realism and honesty in thinking and talking about God and about Jesus. Cupitt has voiced the very widespread conviction that the old forms of belief in God resulted in attitudes which degraded and damaged humanity. Wiles has reached beyond his own world of theological scholarship to ask what it means to say that 'God acts'. Lampe, another scholar of high eminence, compelled thought about the searching question: What does it mean to say that 'God was in Christ'? Bowden has sharpened modern questions about Jesus as a figure in history and Nineham has demonstrated the strangeness of much in the New Testament as modern eyes look at it. Hick, Smart and others have made inescapable questions about Christianity's position amid humanity's other religions. One does not have to agree with all the answers offered by these radicals in order to congratulate them on their questions.

What, though, have been the results of radical theology as taught by these and other scholars, and as spread by a little army of popularisers including publishers and authors, and TV and radio producers and performers, as well as preachers and teachers? One result has been that many people in England and elsewhere who identify themselves as 'Christians' in one sense or another have had to learn to 'live with questions' – with questions which were not faced so frankly before the 1960s. No longer is it obviously true that, as Alec Vidler said at the time of *Soundings*, 'there's been so much suppression of real deep thought and intellectual alertness and integrity'. Loyal Christians are no longer so frightened of questions. And many others who were already asking these questions silently have dared to ask them out loud, knowing that they will not be prosecuted or excommunicated or even thought eccentric. All this must be to the benefit of the Christian Church if, as Vidler claimed in 1962, 'the cause of truth and of the Church' is a single cause.

But there has also been a conservative backlash which has simply and vigorously reaffirmed one expression or another of what is called in the American song the 'old-time religion'. Various explanations of this phenomenon have been advanced. Stalwart conservatives naturally give the chief emphasis to the work of the Holy Spirit: God has 'owned' and 'blessed' evangelism proclaiming 'the full gospel' along traditional lines. If we seek any further explanation, we may observe that many people do not find it easy to live with questions and denials in the sphere of religion; they want religion to be a rock, not a crumbling sandcastle. And most Christians do not find it easy to accept a version of Christianity which seems to have no room for trust in God as Father or for the imitation of Christ – where apparently not only is the Father unknowable, but also the Son. All forms of Christian 'radicalism' or 'liberalism' may be rejected, or deeply suspected, as tending towards that destruction of faith in the Father through the Son, when people do not want to be walking question marks following in the steps of a crucified enigma.

In England the most vigorous expression of religious conservatism has been mainly Evangelical or Pentecostal, but sociologically and psychologically similar factors have strengthened a Catholic or Orthodox conservatism elsewhere (and in England to a certain extent). The strength of this neo-conservatism was seldom expected in the 1960s but has turned out to be a major phenomenon, pushing the spirit of the 1960s into nostalgia for those who were young and involved then, and for others into distant history. Those offering themselves for ordination have been mainly conservative in disposition and the inclination of many of the clergy and laity already supporting the local churches has been similar; and those church leaders who could be called 'radical' or 'liberal' have been heavily criticised.

This reaction is surely understandable. But an orthodoxy which is deaf will not retain for long the allegiance of thinking people. Basic questions of belief can be brushed under the carpet for a time. Attention can be concentrated on general sentiments in favour of stability in family, neighbourhood and nation; or on the aesthetic appeal of traditional beauty in morals, buildings, music or words; or on the warm fellowship of a congregation or smaller group; or on the attraction of an authoritarian figure outside the family during the emotional upheavals of adolescence. There can be much emphasis on the intellectual and personal faults of the innovators in theology. But however effectively the carpet may conceal the basic questions, most thinking people will see enough of what is, and what is not, on display in this house of traditional orthodoxy to know that it is not their home.

By now it will, I hope, be obvious that I am convinced that the best course in this very dangerous situation is the positive restatement of the Christian faith in terms which will preserve its essential substance but also seem realistic and true to as many in the surrounding society as are prepared to consider it sympathetically. But equally obvious is the difficulty of knowing what the 'essential substance' is. What is truth, as opposed to ephemeral or wrong-headed fashion in the thought of one day and one place? These problems confront all who around the world and across history have struggled to restate the Christian gospel in the language of a particular culture. But so far as I know the problems have never been greater than when the task concerns a society which is to a large extent 'post-Christian'. Such a society contains many conservative believers who resent modernisation; it thinks it knows what Christianity is, although it is often ignorant; it is likely to have a bias against the Church because of some memory of the past; it is also likely to have a soft spot for what it thinks is the simple truth about God which the Church has obscured; and in daily practice it often worships what Christianity has for long regarded as idols.

In the atmosphere of such a society it is, I have found, absolutely necessary for the Christian to be soaked in a very different atmosphere – the Bible's, whether the Bible is read privately or is communicated in the course of the Church's worship. As I hope I have shown in my references to the New Testament in this book and in my *A Key to the Old Testament* (1989), I am not defending fundamentalism or anything like it. I agree with the criticisms of that position set out in, for example, John Barton's *People of the Book?* (1988). I also agree with him about the current dangers of fundamentalism: 'Times have changed indeed, and irrationalism rather than rationalism now seems (to me at least) to be the enemy of true religion. The religious world today is full of credulity and a seeking of six impossible things to believe before breakfast' (p. 38). But experience has convinced me that (as John Barton needs no telling) it is not enough for Christians to be guided by the newspaper read at breakfast. We must become citizens of what Karl Barth called 'the strange new world within the Bible' (*The Word of God and the Word of Man*, 1928, pp. 28–50). There (whatever some scholars who have perhaps grown over-familiar with the Bible may say) 'the Lord hath more truth and light yet to break forth out of his holy Word'. (The name of the Puritan minister who thus assured the Pilgrim Fathers before they embarked on *The Mayflower* was John Robinson.)

I am going to end my part in this book by reprinting some more reviews. They describe attempts to relate a faith with a recognisable foundation in the Bible to contemporary questions. The first review welcomes teaching by the present Regius Professor of Divinity in Cambridge, Stephen Sykes, that the identity of Christianity consists not in theological agreement but in a shared spirituality. But other reviews record the emergence of some intellectual agreement. One welcomes a book by an American theologian, Sallie McFague, written among the English in Cambridge. Another pays tribute to a philosophical theologian, John Macquarrie, who has taught in Glasgow, New York and Oxford. Another applauds the religious wisdom of a scientist, John Polkinghorne, now President of Queens' College, Cambridge. The third presents a report in which a Doctrine Commission of the Church of England managed to express an agreed faith. And finally I review two books of theological essays published in 1989 and summing up a century's developments in the study of Christian doctrine. But I have to stress that Sykes is fully aware of the seriousness of the issues at stake in many theological disagreements (he would be the last man to advocate any kind of anti-intellectual pietism) and that the positive statements by the other theologians have been reached after a long wrestle with the hard questions. Like Jacob in the old story, the thoughtful modern believer emerges from his night-long wrestle and walks into the dawn 'limping'.

When John Polkinghorne, for example, asserts that there is still room in a world-view thoroughly influenced by modern science for a world-transcending God who 'intervenes in' or (better) interacts with his creation, he is no simpleton. He is a highly qualified scientist, and his voice is joined by a chorus of honest thinkers who hold together up-to-date science and Christian theology while recognising that they are very different disciplines. As a physicist he is encouraged in his religious faith by the thought that the universe is not seen by most contemporary scientists as a rigidly determined, entirely predictable machine. Matter-energy is seen to be a dance of particles, open to novelty because full of chance, with cause-and-effect like a network not a chain. Other scientists with other specialisms would stress what is known about matter-energy at its most complex, for example in the human brain. This brain is a product of evolution. It has emerged in a universe full of 'fine tuning' which has this marvellous outcome, but we do not find in its activity determinism by simple physical causes. Amid the mystery of the mind-body relationship we feel free to make our own decisions in response to many non-physical influences. The point for theology in this scientific situation (here described inadequately, of course) is that science itself has changed since it was thought to rule out the active God. As ever, science proves nothing religious – but on this showing God may act afresh in the dance of the particles; God may bring progress out of novelty made by chance; God may influence our minds by his new acts. God is, in Karl Barth's phrase, 'the One who is free to love'. In prayer we join our freedom to his.

In a series of broadcasts subsequently expanded into a book called *The Turn of the Tide* (1986), Professor Keith Ward explored the background to such thinking. He interviewed a considerable number of scientists, philosophers and theologians, and he concluded that the progress of knowledge in these spheres 'has actually made Christian belief seem much more acceptable now than it might have seemed forty or fifty years ago' (p. 8). Many intellectuals still think all religion self-evident nonsense; many believers depend on their emotions rather than their minds in 'a blind fundamentalist conservative reaction against the Enlightenment' (p. 25); 'there has been an almost complete failure of religious education in Britain' (p. 114); but reasoning people can reasonably believe. As Ward, himself an Anglican, noted: 'at the time I write this both the Professors of Philosophy at Cambridge are Catholics and two out of the four Professors of Philosophy at Oxford are Christians of a Catholic tradition' (p. 72). And he found Christian theology, studying the material of Christian belief, to be 'in a lively and confident mood' (p. 133), with 'a creative refashioning of ancient traditions in the light of new perceptions' (p. 127). His analysis of the situation in theology was much more confident than the kind of diagnosis offered by some of the scholars discussed in this book, who seem close to despair about the gap between the Church and the contemporary world of informed and honest thought. A part of this theological confidence was, as Ward reported, a new mood in biblical studies. Graham Stanton, Professor of New Testament Studies at King's College, London, said:

> Over the last twenty years or so there has been quite a significant change . . . On the whole, there is now more agreement than

there was that we have a fairly reliable portrait of Jesus of Nazareth in our Gospels. Roman Catholics, conservative evangelicals and scholars who would make no particular claims, do agree on the general reliability of the portrait of Jesus (p. 101).

The problem confronting Christian theology seemed to Ward, as he surveyed the scene, to be essentially one of communication with people not fully aware of the change in the intellectual climate.

John Macquarrie's work is an example of this mood of thoughtful confidence. Now an Anglican priest in retirement, he came into my life when he was a university lecturer in Glasgow and a Presbyterian minister, specialising in the challenging theology of Rudolf Bultmann and in the existentialist philosophy which lay behind it. From 1960 to 1966 I had the privilege of publishing his books *The Scope of Demythologizing, Twentieth Century Religious Thought, Studies in Christian Existentialism* and *Principles of Christian Theology*. He also achieved the feat of translating Martin Heidegger's *Being and Time* into what was more or less English (in collaboration with Edward Robinson). Long after he had become an Anglican and an Oxford professor (and I had ceased to be his publisher) he achieved another feat. His book *In Search of Deity* (1984) deserved, I thought, not a review but an ovation. Before he wrote that, his *In Search of Humanity* (1982) took account of the great contributions made by the sciences and by the philosophies to our understanding of ourselves. It avoided any static picture of 'human nature' or 'the human being'. Instead it stressed that the 'human becoming' develops from its physical basis by responses, relationships and choices – including the responses, relationships and choices of religion. Thus he combined a full acceptance of science with a clear statement of the central insights of the existentialist philosophers.

As another example of thoughtfulness behind confidence, I may briefly refer to his *Principles of Christian Theology* (in its revised edition of 1977). That book faced many modern problems. It quoted with sympathy the famous formula of St Vincent of Lérins, who died before 450, about Christian faith as 'that which has been believed everywhere, always and by all'. But it also recognised the necessity of development in doctrine by endorsing some less familiar words where St Vincent looked forward to 'a great increase and vigorous progress in the individual man as well as in the entire Church as the ages and centuries march on, in understanding, knowledge and wisdom' (p. 19). Philosophically the book was sophisticated. It welcomed the decline of naive ideas about God which picture him as a man standing apart from the world but occasionally intervening to put it right ('anthropomorphism' and 'interventionism'). God is Holy Being, the Being that lets all beings exist:

> The primordial Being of the Father, which would otherwise be entirely hidden, flows out through expressive Being to find its expression in the world of beings. Christians believe that the Father's Being finds expression above all in the finite being of Jesus, and in such a way that his being is caught up into Being itself (pp. 199–200).

Historical questions were also confronted. It was, for example, taught that no one should be deterred from the Christian faith through inability to accept the doctrine of the virgin birth of Jesus since 'there can be little doubt that the stories that have come down to us are legendary rather than historical' (p. 280). On the 'empty tomb' tradition he asserted:

> Not the discovery of an empty tomb but the 'appearances' of the risen Lord to his disciples seem to be the origin of belief in the resurrection of Jesus . . .
> There would be no profit in speculating about the nature of these appearances, any more than trying to establish that the tomb was empty (pp. 288–9).

The Doctrine Commission which reported to the Church of England in 1987 shared this sensitivity to modern problems combined with a positive faith. It had two recent predecessors. An earlier commission ended its work in 1976. Most of its report, *Christian Believing*, consisted of essays by individual members, including Geoffrey Lampe and Dennis Nineham. But in the joint report there was much emphasis on the problems which all recognised. The first sentence described Christian life as 'an adventure, a voyage of discovery, a journey, sustained by faith and hope, towards a final and complete communion with the Love at the heart of all things' but it was quickly added that there are problems about 'the pastness of the past' in the Bible and in the Church's tradition, and about the capacity of human beings to talk sense about God. 'God is far beyond the compass of any words we can use of him' (p. 16) and 'right from the very beginning of Christianity there is pluriformity in the faith, just as there had been in the faith of Israel before it' (p. 28). It was acknowledged that many members of the Church of England either 'have difficulties about individual clauses in the creeds' or feel that 'they can neither deny nor affirm the creeds' (pp. 36–7).

Another Doctrine Commission reported in 1981 on *Believing in the Church: The Corporate Nature of Faith*, but it did not submit any joint report at all. Instead individual members published essays of high quality and Anthony Harvey described the atmosphere in the final essay:

> Can it be that the Church does not know what it believes? Have the foundations been shaken beyond repair? Must every doctrine commission (like this one) disappoint the faithful by discussing only *how* we believe, and drawing back before the (as it seems) far more urgent question of *what* we believe? These questions, and the dismay and insecurity they cause, are inevitable so long as the model with which we work is that of the individual believer having his faith supplied and monitored by the institutional organs of the Church. But they lose much of their menace if, as we have argued, the faith of both the Church and the individual is more accurately described as a kind of 'corporate believing', in which the individual, directly or indirectly, contributes to the formation of church doctrine at the same time as the Church, through its worship, its ethos and its historic formularies, moulds the belief of the individual. The novel thinking of a radical theologian, or the explorations of small groups in the Church into new ways of formulating and expressing their Christian faith, can then be seen, not as a challenge to traditional doctrine which must at all costs be answered, but as a necessary stimulus to the kind of thinking which must go on at all levels if the Church is to maintain a vigorous life (p. 287).

This is how Harvey saw the way ahead:

> Continued attention to Scripture and tradition, making full use of the results of modern scholarship; critical and informed participation in worship; prayer which shows sensitivity to the real needs of the contemporary world; dialogue with men and women who hold a different world-view or profess a different religion – all this and more must be engaged in by church members according to their gifts and aptitudes, and constitutes that corporate believing which in turn acts as a principle of

verification and control over the individual's quest for truth. But
. . . no final and authoritative statement is possible; at most one
can describe the flavour of contemporary theological discussion,
or establish the broad lines within which inquiry may be
conducted (p. 289).

Many Christians have, however, wanted something more definite than that. In the year before *Believing in the Church*, an
Alternative Service Book had been authorised for use in the
Church of England that contained a large number of prayers which
implied strong, and strongly traditional, religious beliefs. The
language had been somewhat modernised and some old beliefs had
been quietly scrapped, but no one claimed – or complained – that
the book represented a theology that had been revised radically.
Its conservatism is a reminder that the development within professional theology of a style of thinking that is both rooted in the
tradition and open-mindedly up-to-date and truthful (the style
which is characteristic of all the books I am about to discuss) has
not yet been translated into language which non-experts can
understand and accept as the fire and the light in their lives. So my
conclusion is uncertain. It remains to be seen whether Christian
believing will remain so often, and so tragically, polarised between
radical explorers and conservative worshippers, but I am sure that
this is not necessary. What was finely called in *Soundings* 'the cause
of truth and of the Church' had been well served by much of the
work of radical theologians writing in English between 1962 and
1989. Such work deserves a sympathetic, although not an uncritical, welcome. Much of it is, or ought to be, in the cargo as new
waters in the ocean of truth are entered.

Review of *The Identity of Christianity*
by Stephen Sykes (1984)

What is essential in our religion? It is a question which must strike
many people in our age, when Christianity is immersed in so many
changes and involved in so many dialogues – with secularism, with
Communism, with Islam, with the Eastern faiths – that it often
seems that there is no firm identity. One can reckon that, even in
the Church of England alone, there are at least two Christianities
flourishing.

So the question is insistent for anyone contemplating the Christian movement in contemporary reality or in history. What is the

foundation to which all the rest is superstructure, the spirit to which all the rest is body, the centre to which all the rest is circumference? It may be hoped from the title of this book that the question is answered by a new formula. Not so! 'I propose', writes this distinguished theologian, '. . . not merely that it is inconceivable that Christians could agree with each other, but also that it is actually undesirable that they should do so – with the proviso that they should share enough in common to be capable of worshipping together' (p. 8).

Sykes has reached this conclusion as a result of his study of the books of fellow theologians. No doubt he is aware of less academic factors in the debate, but his own approach is very much that of a professor, as a rich appendix of footnotes and bibliography would demonstrate to anyone in doubt. His sub-title frankly limits the field: 'Theologians and the Essence of Christianity from Schleiermacher to Barth.' He stresses that the men he has studied did wrestle with the question – and did so with considerable integrity and sophistication. That gives his study a unity, although Schleiermacher's thought was scarcely known by another of the giants, Newman; while Harnack's ideas were publicly and indignantly repudiated by Loisy, as were Troeltsch's by Barth. The big six here presented were united by a common calibre rather than by any consensus, and their inability to agree does suggest that the notion of an 'essence' to be recovered, defined and perhaps enforced as a series of dogmas is a mirage.

However, certain trends do emerge out of the disagreement. One is a feeling that, if there is an 'essence', it must be one that can be shown to have been present from the beginning. Newman was accused of justifying the development of Christianity's essence into the dogmas of Trent and the Vatican, but he was prepared to reduce the foundational doctrine of the Church to the Petrine confession: 'Thou art the Christ, the Son of the Living God' – and he insisted that 'as the Church does not know more than the Apostles knew, there are many questions which the Church cannot answer' (p. 51).

Later, Harnack did offer simple doctrines as the 'essence' – the fatherhood of God, the brotherhood of man. But he warned himself: 'We must not be like the child who wanted to get at the kernel of a bulb, went on picking off the leaves until there was nothing left, and in the end could not help seeing that it was just the leaves that made the bulb' (pp. 135–6). In response to Harnack, Loisy argued that, for devotional purposes, the Catholicism of the early years of this century should be treated as, so to speak, the bulb. But Loisy was intellectually unhappy with dogmatic Catholicism and was totally rejected by the Vatican he thought he had been defending. He loved that beautiful bulb, but in the 1900s he could not quite bring himself to believe in it. And so the debate continued. Karl Barth made the essence 'the Word of God', but that idea, too, was open to criticism. Every attempt to define the essential content of the Christian faith will seem to some Christians too much and to others too little. Barth, for example, was criticised for accepting too many or too few traditional words.

Sykes therefore puts his whole emphasis on the willingness to worship together. Christ 'did not found Christianity' in the sense of bequeathing a doctrinal system. ('Rather,' he says on p. 20, 'Christianity was founded by Jesus' earliest followers on the foundation of his transformation of Judaism.') But, while the 'faith which is spread by appeal to the teaching and example of Jesus has certain inherent ambiguities which will give rise to different interpretations' (p. 23), what unites Christians is the awareness of a new possibility of access to the Father through the Son in the Spirit. There, and only there, is the essence. His argument is that

> internal doctrinal conflict may actually serve a constructive purpose in the Church so long as there is a tradition of communal worship, centrally authorized, in which the symbols and rituals of the Christian faith are openly spoken and performed, and the whole Christian community opened up to the interior dimension of the self-offering of Jesus (p. 285).

One merit of this emphasis on worship is that it limits the power of either church leader or theologian to say who is in and who is out of the essential faith. Sykes has an acute understanding that power is at stake in many apparently theological discussions – and that Professor Küng wields power no less than the Pope. He wants to get away from the obsession with jurisdiction or the 'teaching office' into the more ethical and spiritual atmosphere epitomised by the definition by Gregory of Nyssa: 'Christianity is the imitation of the divine nature' (p. 214).

Review of *Models of God* by Sallie McFague (1987)

This book is in a sense English. Largely written during a sabbatical year in Cambridge University, it is justly commended by Professor

Maurice Wiles of Oxford as an 'example of a rather rare species – a work of radical theology which is constructive and relevant in character, while remaining at the same time self-conscious and responsible about the theological method it follows'. But Sallie McFague is a professor at Vanderbilt Divinity School, Nashville, Tennessee, and before I praise her constructiveness I shall offer a few English observations about her distinctly North American background.

As a citizen of a democratic republic she insists that some of the models of God which are most prominent in traditional prayers do not work well in our time. The English, although they are accustomed to a monarchy, deserve to be reminded that any royalist or lordly theology seems nowadays a very odd interpretation of the gospels. At the other extreme it can be said in this book that 'if Jesus is not a king but a servant, then God should be spoken of in "servant" language in relation to the world' (p. 56). But for McFague the image of Jesus the Servant appeals no more than the image of God the King. It is out of a society which in its wealth is not typical of the millions in our world who are still enslaved economically that she says that 'the language of servitude is no longer current, respectable or significant for expressing the distinctive and unconventional kind of love epitomized on the cross' (p. 56). Out of a background of a power not typical of most human experience she writes that 'until a few generations ago, nature appeared more powerful than we are' (p. 13). Had this sensitive North American theologian been at work in Latin America, Africa or Asia, far more attention would have been paid (some *is* paid) to the model of God as Liberator. The cry of the bulk of humanity, in this as in every previous age, remains a cry for deliverance from very tangible forms of slavery by mighty acts of God – which, of course, do not exclude acts such as the divine inspiration of hard work and of technological and political change; and to this cry the image of Jesus who suffered like a slave under Pilate because he believed in the Kingdom of God remains powerfully relevant. And if the image of God as Liberator seems to lack power in a North America which is thought not to need liberation, perhaps the image of God as President or as manager is worth exploring, in order to express the simple sense that we need God.

As a theologian coming from one of the most democratic societies in the world, and from the world's most super superpower, McFague insists that it is not right in our time to leave matters such as the avoidance of nuclear war and the conservation of the environment to the professionals or to fate. We are responsible – and how urgent it is that we should 'learn to live politically in the world in which we already live scientifically' (p. 5)! I have to admit that many of the English share the common human tendency to regard religion as a private affair with little connection with such daunting problems, despite all the exhortations. McFague's emphasis on the people's political responsibility is a very healthy challenge to the privatisation of religion. But her book sometimes seems shallow in the appreciation of personal religion, where historically the quest has been for liberation from the sin that separates the soul from God. The ideal, surely, is that a strong personal religion should support a strong involvement in social problems.

McFague claims the support of the gospel of John for her belief that 'the basic relationship between God and all others cannot be one-to-one; or rather it is one-to-one only if it is inclusive of all. It is not individuals who are loved by God . . . but the world' (p. 86). Most readers of that gospel will think that this ignores its insistence on new birth into the believing minority, but the interpretation is fairly typical of a general failure to explore the depths of personal religion in Christian history. In defiance of the history of mysticism and devotion, we are told that 'the metaphors of God as King, ruler, lord, master and governor, and the concepts that accompany them of God as absolute, complete, transcendent and omnipotent, permit no sense of mutuality, shared responsibility, reciprocity and love (except in the sense of gratitude)' (p. 19). When informed by McFague that if God is imagined as a king 'the world is empty of God's presence, for it is too lowly to be the royal abode' (p. 65), one remembers that in Catholic and Orthodox spirituality things of the world – bread, wine, oil, water, pictures, churches – are very often vehicles of the real presence of God. Francis of Assisi, like his Master a lover of nature, lay on the floor all night saying *Deus meus et omnia*. And to speak of 'the traditional Christian, and especially Protestant, view of sin as corrupting, depraving and making worthless both human beings and the rest of creation' (p. 133) is to use a generalisation which is questioned by most of the history of Christian civilisation.

McFague dislikes the traditional penitent's talk about sin as a person-to-person affront to God. 'To sin is not to refuse loyalty to the liege Lord but to refuse to take responsibility for nurturing, loving and befriending the body and all its parts' (p. 77). She also dislikes talk about the Spirit making the communion of saints. For her such ideas are 'individualistic' and 'elitist', so that 'the Spirit is not a strong candidate for imaging God's sustaining activity' (p. 171). In her own theology the models of God as a judge condemning what is unworthy of humanity, and as an artist patiently creating what is lovely, are conspicuous by their absence. So is the image of Jesus as personal saviour; for her, 'it is not what one individual did two thousand years ago that is critical but what we, with God, do now' (p. 54). She makes these denials partly because the Bible seems to mean little to her. 'It is not so much an interpretation that one looks for in the Bible as a process, not so much a content as a form' (p. 43). The reduction of the Bible to a 'process' which provides some of the 'form' of contemporary Christianity, but without supplying decisively much of its content, has resulted in a blindness to most of the story of Christian spirituality.

But what gains there are from her confidently, even breezily, fresh approach! She takes seriously Dennis Nineham's point that many of our contemporaries 'find it hard to believe in God because they do not have available to them any lively imaginative picture of the way God and the world as they know it are related' (p. 31).

She rightly takes a pride in pointing to pictures of God which can communicate the Christian belief in the God who is 'on the side of life and its fulfilment' (p. xii) to the people around her. She stresses that these, too, are only pictures, like the traditional pictures which she discards as impotent in an 'ecological, nuclear age' (her sub-title). For her all theology is 'metaphorical', the eternal essence of God being unknowable. Although she has come to prefer the word 'model' to 'metaphor', since 'a model is a metaphor with staying power' (p. 34), she wisely insists that 'models of God are not definitions of God but likely accounts of experiences of relating to God with the help of relationships we know and understand' (p. 39). However, the ultimate scepticism of recent French deconstructionists such as Jacques Derrida ('there is nothing outside the text') is not for her. For all her rejection of metaphysics, she reckons that some texts, some models, are better than others as signs indicating the better approach to reality. She has no interest in 'a byegone world, one under the guidance of a benevolent but absolute deity, a world that is populated by independent individuals (mainly human beings) who relate to one another and to other forms of life in hierarchical patterns' (p. 3). There must be a new world in theology. But she wants models that teach responsibility for all forms of life inclusively, that destabilise 'conventional expectations and worldly standards' and reach out 'to the weak, to the outsider, to the stranger, to the outcast' (p. 47). And a reader outside the USA cannot help reflecting that the models she likes are specially appropriate to a nation dedicated to the proposition of equal rights for all, a proposition which has quite recently been extended to include blacks, women and nature herself.

She is positive but also thoughtful in recommending the image of the world as God's body. Although the image has a long history – explored together with some of the accompanying philosophical problems in Grace Jantzen's *God's World, God's Body* (1984) – it seems particularly full of significance in the USA. There most people believe in God. They also believe in taking care of their bodies by diet and exercise. But tragically often their sense of power over unlimited natural resources has led to the pollution or exhaustion of those resources – and may now lead to a nuclear winter in which this planet will be ruined. So McFague is hitting the ball like the best of baseball players when she communicates the sacredness of the creation by comparing it with a body as an expression and instrument of God's life and love, and when she calls on all her fellow Americans to treat the world with the care which most of them already lavish on their own bodies. She wants them to think of Mount Everest as being 'befriended', not 'conquered' (p. 9). But she is not a pantheist. She wants to preserve a difference – although not a gap – between God and the world, remarking that merely 'to believe in the trustworthiness of things or that the power in the universe is gracious' (an optimistic belief characteristic of one strain in American religion and sometimes articulated by professional theologians) is to say 'something important but very imprecise' (p. 44). She tells a fellow theologian, Gordon Kaufman, that it is not enough to think of God as the 'unifying symbol of those powers and dimensions of the ecological and historical feedback network which create and sustain and work to further enhance life' (p. 18). And 'I do not believe that the reduction of the personal God to hidden creativity or unpredictable grace is desirable or necessary' (p. 80). So she admits the limitations of this model of the world as God's body, for if thinking about God as personal has value it means that the logic of the model should not be pursued to the narcissistic extreme of saying that when God loves the world she merely is a body loving herself. God may be distinguished from the world because she is the Creator of the world – much as 'we may be said to be spirits that possess bodies' (p. 71).

McFague therefore accompanies that picture of the world as God's body by pictures of God as mother, as lover and as friend. The last picture is something of an anticlimax, although it has the merit of distinguishing between God and sex – a point which needs making in the USA, and not only there. In this book the emphasis is on the model of God as mother. In one of her infrequent references to history the author quotes Julian of Norwich: 'we owe our being to him and that is the essence of motherhood' (p. 115). But the contemporary appeal of this model, as compared with 'father', is that fathers have often been thought of as condemnatory. 'What the father-God gives is redemption from sins, what the mother-God gives is life itself' (p. 101). Mothers have usually been more successful than their partners in demonstrating that 'parental love wills life and, when it comes, exclaims: "It is good that you exist!"' (p. 103). And the divine acceptance and desire is driven home by the model of God as lover as well as Love.

There are dangers in these models as in all others. McFague is not interested in the danger of encouraging a religion which promises fertility through magic including temple prostitution and sacred orgies. In North America that may be said to belong to the past – where, however, it was prominent, as the Old Testament shows. The audience to which this book is addressed knows that productivity, agricultural as well as industrial, comes through technology not through the impregnation of Mother Earth with human seed. But some dangers in thinking of God as mother or lover are fully recognised – for very North American reasons. 'Reuther and Tillich note the difficulty with this imagery: it can tend towards infantilism; it can suffocate and "swallow"' (p. 116). And 'the problem with introducing a feminine dimension of God is that it invariably ends with identifying as female those qualities that society has called feminine. Thus, the feminine side of God is taken to comprise the tender, nurturing, passive, healing aspects of divine activity' (p. 99). That is objectionable because in the contemporary USA the old-fashioned idea of femininity is generally rejected in favour of an image of woman as fully equal with man in healthy toughness and determined efficiency. The image of God as a mother must not be allowed to suggest that God is a wimp.

The great merit of this book is that it is constructive. But it has a further merit: it never pretends that the models of God which it recommends out of the North American experience are perfect. On this basis its author may welcome some criticism by an Englishman. It is typical of the differences between our countries that the English state the problems and the Americans do the job.

Review of *Science and Providence* by John Polkinghorne (1989)

It is perfectly right to ask whether a suggested religious belief is in accordance with religious experiences, past or present, and in particular to enquire into its relationship with what Scripture affirms on the basis of experiences believed to be crucial. It is, after all, through experiences which lead back to Scripture that people come to believe anything in a religion such as Christianity. But in our time it is also right to ask whether a suggested religious belief is compatible with scientific knowledge.

That question is best discussed by scientists. Most scientists are very reluctant to venture into a field so big and so controversial, but fortunately in recent years in England a considerable body of expert science-and-religion literature has appeared. This new paperback by a Fellow of the Royal Society and former Professor of Mathematical Physics, now a priest, lists many other up-to-date books and (while having its own slant) is supremely useful as a summary of their wisdom.

In *One World* (1986) and *Science and Creation* (1988) Dr Polkinghorne presented his world-view. It is a vision of one world which can be described both in scientific and in religious ways – because science says that here is a marvel of indeterminancy ('chance') being brought into stable patterns ('order'), with matter, life and mind as one continuum, and because religion says that this whole chancy, ordered, beautiful thing is created and sustained by the Mystery to be named as God. In this book he goes over some of the same ground, pointing also to other books such as D. J. Bartholomew's *God of Chance* (1984), Hugh Montefiore's *The Probability of God* (1985) and Arthur Peacocke's *Creation and the World of Science* (1979) and *God and the New Biology* (1986). And he leaves a final and convincing impression that science does support (without proving) the belief that we and our environment are indeed 'the creation'. On any other showing, it is very, very difficult to explain why the universe should be so amazingly well-adjusted as our environment. In this world, we are at home!

But then Polkinghorne comes to questions about a specifically Christian theism. He asks whether 'a personal, interacting God is a credible concept in this scientific age'; whether miracles are possible because God acts, for example in response to prayers. And to such questions he answers yes, disagreeing not only with non-Christians but also with radical theologians such as Dr Maurice Wiles, whom he gently accuses of misunderstanding science.

He does not expect a lot of miracles, for he does not want what Austin Farrer called 'the God of kicks and halfpence'. His God is the God of majestic order, and he dislikes any talk about a divine 'interference' in nature. Equally he dislikes attempts to describe God's activity without a sense of mystery. He is acutely aware of the reality of the evil permitted in God's creation, attributing it to the free wills of human beings and to the 'free processes' of nature, with which God does *not* interfere as if he were a clockmaker adjusting the hands of a clock. The vast reality of evil is one of his reasons for rejecting pantheism or the idea that the universe is God's 'body'. But he holds with Augustine that 'God judged it better to bring good out of evil, than to allow no evil to exist'; 'if Augustine was mistaken, then this world is indeed one without meaning and hope' (p. 64).

His own hope is great because he also holds that God is free to perform miracles, understanding miracles as 'perceptions of a deeper rationality than that which we encounter in the everyday occasions which make visible a more profound level of human activity' (p. 51). And he finds intimations of this in recent scientific discoveries suggesting that we live in 'a universe endowed with becoming', with 'genuine novelty possible in cosmic process', so that 'genuine freedom for ourselves, and for God, is not ruled out' (p. 2).

In his view this justifies prayers for healing (and even 'perhaps' for rain). It also justifies the belief that God has interacted with the world to the extent that he 'has actually lived the life of a man'. And it justifies the belief that God will go on interacting with his creation. 'The only certainty is God himself. Our ultimate hope rests in that faithfulness which will not abandon anything of value once it has come to be' (p. 90).

Einstein declared his belief in God because he marvelled at the order in nature: 'God does not play dice'. But Polkinghorne has also been very deeply impressed by the emergence of novelty out of what looks like chance in the play of the elementary particles and in the rest of nature. For him, that kind of dice-playing is what has made progress in evolution possible. And that scientific world-view strengthens his faith in the divine Player who is free to end his game in triumph. If I may vulgarise his argument, God plays with loaded dice.

Review of *In Search of Deity* by John Macquarrie (1984)

One kind of belief in God is specially vulnerable to attacks by modern atheists. God has been pictured as a celestial Mrs Thatcher (except that the picture is of a man) – a God who frequently intervenes from on high in the sluggish habits of nature or history. That evokes the response, even among some theologians, that we must take leave of such an interfering, domineering God. If we like we can call nature or history 'God' (pantheism); but it is often claimed that the only logical stopping-place in the escape from the transcendent God as traditionally pictured is the rejection of religion altogether, as one vast illusion.

So the extremists suggest. But there may be a middle way between the discredited old picture and the new total atheism. If so, the English, and particularly the Anglican, love of comprehensive moderation and eirenic balance may mean that English theologians have a vocation to propound it. Since 1970 Professor John Macquarrie has taught in Oxford, where he is also a canon of Christ Church. By birth a Scot and by education a Presbyterian, he has defined and defended the English and Anglican middle way with the force of a convert. *In Search of Humanity*, published a couple of years ago, depicted *homo sapiens* against the background of modern science, psychology and philosophy but essentially as a religious animal. Now, in a book based on Gifford Lectures delivered in St Andrews, he argues for a balanced belief in the One – sometimes he feels that the word 'God' has been too disastrously trivialised – who is worthy of worship.

He reaffirms his conviction that anthropology almost necessitates theology, since human nature is such that faith arises naturally from it. He also repeats his conviction that the control of the technological revolution demands the recovery of the faith that man is responsible to God for the welfare of the world. 'Nowadays,' he writes, 'natural law seems to be just about as unpopular as natural theology. Actually, I think that they stand or fall together, and I am committed to both of them' (p. 217). But if natural law is to be 'founded in the divine nature and reflected in human nature,' it obviously depends on belief in the Law-giver – and it is equally obvious that this belief has been eroded or at least challenged by modernity. The question which needs to be asked of the modern atheist is whether the God he has rejected is the only God in whom it is reasonably possible to believe.

Macquarrie displays much sympathy with intellectually and morally serious atheism. He, too, rejects the idea of a God external to the universe but intervening in it from time to time. 'To hold such a belief, and at the same time to assent to the basic assumptions of the scientist, does not seem to me to be logically possible' (p. 39). Certainly the existence of such a God cannot be proved – and, when the attempt is made to prove it, the argument tends to reduce the Creator to being one thing among many or one cause among many.

Moreover, such a God is morally repulsive if he is presented as being aloof from the disorder and suffering of the creation. The questions arise inevitably. Why doesn't the Almighty Father intervene more often? Is he asleep up there? If, with that capacity to swoop down and sort things out, he is the paymaster of righteousness, why don't the good prosper more reliably?

There is, however, another road to faith in God. 'That to which your heart clings and entrusts itself is, I say, really your God' (Luther, quoted on p. 26). God is 'Something than which no greater can be thought' (Anselm, quoted on p. 27). God is so mysteriously transcendent over the world around us that the mystery of his reality may be called No-thing, but he is also rightly called Holy Being, the source, ground and goal of all that merely exists. He is not created by our dreams, fantasies, ideals or prayers. He is the One on whom the many depend.

This God is to be adored, not analysed. The true worshipper who senses God's greatness is 'lost in wonder, love and praise'. But this God also expresses himself in creation – he 'lets be', he 'gives'. And like a friend, he makes himself known by acting; Macquarrie, although he heartily dislikes the word 'intervene', is clearly not a Deist who believes that God's work is confined to creation. Like an artist, God puts something of himself into what he makes, so that the creation is both something distinct from the Creator and also an emanation from him, a flowing-forth or radiation. And in the end all things return to, and are fulfilled in, that One. The relation of the Creator to the creation is, on this showing, best understood through the comparison with human love. Love does not dictate; but, also, love does not sit aloof. Love acts gently because love cares so much. It is no more true to say that 'God minus the world equals God' than it is to say that a father does not care what happens to his children. Yet love has its own power, a faint echo of God's ever-creative power. That is the true miracle.

Such, put briefly, is Macquarrie's account of God. It acknowledges both that God is incomprehensible and that he is experienced; both that he is infinite and that his relationship to us is personal; both that he is felt to deserve worship as being supremely good and that it is impossible to fit his activity into any normal categories, intellectual or moral. And this account is here expounded with a passion which a mere summary cannot convey – partly in the author's own words and partly in a series of studies of philosophical theologians of the past.

Macquarrie has written a book which incorporates the best of faith in God as 'the One' and 'the Other' with the best of Spinoza's pantheistic faith in *Deus sive natura*, 'God or nature'. It is a noble book about the God who, in modern times as in ancient, may be believed in by the free, informed mind and worshipped by the mature soul. For such a masterpiece gratitude is too small a word.

Review of the Doctrine Commission's report
We Believe in God (1987)

The latest report of the Doctrine Commission of the Church of England outlines a coherent and convincing doctrine of God. That might seem an easy task for a church committee. But in a situation where more must be attempted than the simple repetition of old doctrines, the commission has summarised the best current theology. The report ought to be read, marked and inwardly digested by literally everyone who teaches or preaches in the Church of England. And it would help anyone else who thinks seriously about a faith under the kind of *intellectual* challenge that is offered by the climate of thought in England.

I stress the 'intellectual' because inevitably the report does not say much about the social pressures for or against religion. It is a report by theologians; when it glances at past theological controversies, it ignores the social factors. It is sympathetic with the liberation theology which gives the top priority to *praxis* and in particular to the fight for social justice, but its own emphasis is on the individual's prayer and reflection and it refers to poetry rather than to politics.

I also stress the 'English' in this theology because little space is found for dialogue with the great religions outside the tradition of the Europe which once was Christendom. Much of the experience of prayer is acknowledged to be common ground with non-Christians; but in the most original chapter (7) the trinitarian nature of Bible-based prayer (to the Father, through the Son, in the Spirit) is stressed without urgent attention to the questions about non-Christian spirituality.

There are only a few paragraphs about the challenge of feminist theology. Although they are thoroughly sensitive and sensible paragraphs, like the rest of the report, the proportions would have been different in the American Church. But I do not criticise these limitations. They make it possible for the report not to be too long – and to be agreed unanimously by a commission coming from many backgrounds.

The commission obviously wants to be loyal to the Church's faith based on the Scriptures, and in its own deviations from inherited dogma or old-world piety it is gently eirenic. Nevertheless it sometimes sticks its neck out in a way which may invite some traditionalists to look to their axes. Will all Evangelicals like this: 'The more carefully one studies the Bible, the more one becomes aware of ideas of God and responses to him which seem actually to conflict with one another' (p. 3)? Will all traditionalists like this quotation from Reinhold Niebuhr: 'There is no social evil, no form of injustice, whether of the feudal or the capitalist order, which has not been sanctified in some way or another by religious sentiment and thereby rendered more impervious to change' (p. 18)?

This report has a tone different from *Christian Believing* and *Believing in the Church*, which came from previous Doctrine Commissions: it agrees about what is believed! It is also different from the recent statement from the House of Bishops of the Church of England on *The Nature of Christian Belief*: it cannot leave the impression that good pastors are papering over deep cracks. If it does not break new ground, it authoritatively (with that *magisterium* which can be exercised by completely honest people who have calmly mastered a subject) maps the field where treasure is to be found.

It gets beyond the polarisation of liberal and conservative theologies to teach that while all images of God are only 'models', only fragmentary, helpful but corrigible, God is there – and can be known to be there even in the Dark Night of the Soul. He is boundless but 'at least personal' (William Temple, p. 43); he can seem powerless but 'God is willing to fail until He can have the only success love would value' (John Oman, p. 135). In reply to secularists (some of whom are ordained nowadays), it is finely said that 'God' is not a word which we use to describe the universe of the depth of our relations with each other. Rather, what God truly is, is what constrains and sets a limit on our approximate language about him' – just as what the universe truly is, is what constrains the approximate language of science. So religious language makes use of poetry and – yes – myths, but it is not merely 'mood-expressing, attitude-evoking' any more than poetry or mythology always is.

Brilliant chapters summarising current biblical scholarship have as their central statement: 'The most notable feature of Jesus' spirituality was that, without in any way denying the law, he did not relate to God through the Law but directly as "Father", and invited his hearers to share in the same relationship' (p. 81). Simone Weil, who fully shared in our own tormented century, wrote: 'In my arguments about the insolubility of the problem of God I had never foreseen the possibility of that, of a real contact person to person, here below, between a human being and God' (p. 125).

But what does God do when he has to accept that he must work towards his vision in imperfect material, the Creator being like an artist more than like a computer-programmer? What does he do when the very climate that is needed to sustain life on this planet brings disasters to his children? What does he do when his own children fail to respond to his love? What does he do when his incarnate love is crucified? The commission gives a clear answer: God is never totally defeated – as sometimes we can see, when we look back over a tragedy which seemed to be breaking us and find that it fits into a pattern of victorious love. But 'the idea that God loves his creatures as a Father loves his children and consequently suffers when his creatures fail to respond to that love is at the heart of the Christian understanding of God' (p. 157). And this answer is given despite 'the most venerable theological position' (p. 159) in the Christian thought of past ages – which is that God cannot change and therefore cannot suffer.

'Christians,' the report concludes, 'are those who enter into the long-suffering patience of God, sharing his victory over evil by absorbing it in inexhaustible forgiveness' (p. 161). Previously the commission has observed that 'we no longer believe' that God is 'correctly described as a being seated on a celestial throne who regularly consigns large numbers of human beings to a place of torment somewhere below the earth' (p. 29). At any rate this report offers a constructive, and now semi-official, alternative to an image of God which 'we' may not believe, but which millions of people probably still think is what the Church teaches.

The pity is that it has taken the present series of Doctrine Commissions twenty years to get to this point. Nothing could be more important or more urgent for the Church than this kind of positive teaching about basics. Only so can Christian faith be commended to people such as the doctor in a novel by Salman Rushdie, 'unable to worship a God in whose existence he could not wholly disbelieve' (p. 12).

Review of *Keeping the Faith* edited by Geoffrey Wainwright and *The Religion of the Incarnation* edited by Robert Morgan (1989)

In 1889 eleven Oxford theologians wrote a book of essays 'to put the Catholic faith into its right relation to modern intellectual and moral problems' and called it *Lux Mundi*. Now the centenary of that publication, which became a landmark in English theology, is commemorated by the appearance of two books of essays – one by present or recent members of the Faculty of Theology in Oxford, the other by a wider circle, the editor being a British Methodist scholar now teaching in the USA and the first contributor being Stephen Sykes, Regius Professor of Divinity in Cambridge. The two books, when taken together, provide a rare and very interesting opportunity to assess the present situation in English-writing theology, not only in contrast with *Lux Mundi* but also in an atmosphere somewhat different from the 'radicalism' which was inaugurated by the 1962 volume from Cambridge, *Soundings*.

In both books of the 1980s the atmosphere is one of a quiet, chastened confidence that an essentially but not exclusively traditional faith is able to stand up to modern intellectual and moral problems. The confidence is not so great as that of the Victorians – but in both books historical essays point out that Oxford in the 1880s was a scene very different from anything that exists anywhere a century later. In the 1880s Nietzsche was recording the 'death of God' in Germany or at least in his own tormented spirit. But church life in Britain was then flourishing and expanding; so was the British empire, among races that theologians did not hesitate to call 'uncivilised' and 'savage'; and Oxford was the nursery of a governing class, with science scarcely old and respectable enough to join the nursery and morals still usually what a

Sunday School teacher would approve. No one foresaw that a quarter of a century after *Lux Mundi* the lamps would go out all over Europe.

Today not only has the ascendancy of Europe been ended. So has the complacency of European (including English) Christianity. Many challenges have been heard in the churches – and have produced self-questioning and revision. Introducing the new book from Oxford, Robert Morgan notes a 'turn of the tide in Anglican theology against doctrinal reductionism'. But he dissociates this from more extreme forms of neo-conservatism and from 'the more cheerful neglect of theology in large sections of church life'. And he adds two wise sentences. 'Far from the best insights of liberal theology being repudiated in English Christianity, they are widely taken for granted. But there is a growing recognition that they do not suffice to nourish a minority church in an aggressively secular society' (p. xi).

On the one hand, liberalism or radicalism has made the point that, as John Barton puts it later, 'theology is not a game played among those already in a charmed circle, but a set of assertions about the way things really are; and if it fails to connect with what may be discerned through other modes of study, history, the natural sciences, and so on, then it is saying nothing worth saying' (p. 69). So Barton criticises the idea that Christian theology is 'narrative theology', repeating the story told in the Bible without connecting it with the rest of our knowledge and experience.

On the other hand, the Bible does tell a story which is good news for sinners. Both books quote Archbishop William Temple's reflection, as the Second World War was further wrecking European self-assurance, that what is needed now is a message of salvation. That is what makes theologians of the 1980s dissatisfied with the destructive radicalism of the 1960s and later. In *Keeping the Faith* (a title which speaks volumes) Professor Sykes dismisses 'the notorious theological happening of the 1960s, the so-called "death of God" or "secular theology" movement' (p. 14); from Minnesota Robert Jenson marvels that 'a few years ago it was possible to create a stir . . . on the odd supposition that the Christian God's being "incarnate" is a problem, whereas, of course, the real problem has always been how to identify the Christian God *apart* from incarnation' (p. 25); Principal Forrester of New College, Edinburgh, remarks that 'the panegyrics for secularization . . . forgot . . . that a secular society may be diabolic, idolatrous and exploitative' (p. 256); and Bishop Lesslie

Newbigin, so far from being overwhelmed by non-Christian religions, says that 'there is much in the Gospels to suggest that it is not in religion but in the ordinary human relationships of loyalty, trust and kindness that the light of God is to be discerned' (p. 325).

So in the new Oxford book Rowan Williams moves to switch off the gentle Christmas light which for the Victorians illuminated their whole world: 'It is not "the Incarnation" that is the basis of dogma, but judgement and conversion worked out through encounter with the telling of Jesus' story' (p. 87). And this author of a learned study of the Arian controversy sees 'the novel dogmatic expressions of Nicaea and Chalcedon' (p. 95) as elaborations of the simpler creed that 'We believe in one Lord, Jesus Christ' – a creed which is most alive when affirmed against Nazism, for example, or *apartheid*.

What, then, should theologians be saying when the background is not one of German or South African evil, but is a secular society where, as the chaplain of the Oxford college where Newman was an undergraduate puts it, 'sin is out of fashion, the Devil is a joke and God irrelevant' (p. 162)? How should theologians reason in a climate which, as Daniel Hardy observes, seems to be tending towards a 'post-modern' denial of factuality and rationality even within the sphere which was occupied – at first, at theology's expense – by science?

In *Lux Mundi* Scott Holland reinterpreted 'faith' not as assent to doctrines or to miracle stories or to proofs of God's existence from the excellence of nature, but as 'a living friendship with God'. In these books it is agreed that becoming a Christian does not mean merely making a private choice of a lifestyle because it seems to be one's 'thing' (which is a secular estimate of religion) but involves 'the intention and passion which move a believer's self-understanding into the narrative of the people of God and sustain it there' (Sykes, pp. 20–1). Professor Maurice Wiles of Oxford has often seemed very radical. But here he writes: 'The Christian, who finds the spiritual transformation to which the New Testament bears witness a continuing reality within the community which finds its faith in God through Christ, may still speak of Christ as the embodiment of the reality of God for him or her' (p. 84). Richard Norris of New York hears this as the scriptural way of talking: 'Human persons and communities are envisaged habitually in the setting of a relation – at once dependent and responsive – to a "Beyond" which invokes, sustains, enlivens and addresses them in and with their natural and historical world' (p. 80).

The distinctiveness of this meeting with God through the Christian community and its Scriptures becomes clearer because now the environment does *not* easily prepare for the gospel, as the Oxford Victorians tended to suppose. Andrew Louth quotes the spiritual isolation and agony of the Welsh priest-poet R. S. Thomas (pp. 35–6), and it is striking that the priests who contribute from amid the piety of America find that even in that church-going society, as Robert Jenson says, 'the hardest thing in the world is to look an acquaintance in the eye and tell him or her that he or she is wrong about religion' (p. 32). In his essay on Christian ethics Keith Ward stresses that in the Bible-based community ethics must be the imitation of Christ, not merely a Christian veneer on 'natural law' – for we must 'pattern our lives on the nature of God' (p. 237). And the same approach is taken by the Evangelical essayist in the Oxford book, Alister McGrath, although he also stresses that Christ is no mere example.

Of course these men (and how out-of-date it already is that no essayist in either book is a woman!) are not fundamentalists. Perhaps the best essay of all is by a Roman Catholic professor, David Power, on the senses in which Scripture and Tradition are authoritative. This is a much more sophisticated account than was Charles Gore's essay in *Lux Mundi* which, however, drew on his head the wrath of the conservatives of his day. But throughout both books it is seen that Christians need to gain from their Saviour through their Church and their Bible strength to fight against evil and to live in the dawn of the kingdom of God. Two of the brightest and best of Oxbridge, David Brown and Brian Hebblethwaite, devote serious essays to the problem of evil, both concluding that the problem becomes tolerable (never soluble) if it is believed that God is himself willing to suffer alongside his children and if in the end 'all the world's sufferers are raised, forgiven and transformed in order to share in the final consummation of all things' (Hebblethwaite, p. 75).

It is remarkable that in neither of these books – nor in *Lux Mundi* – is there any metaphysics about the Trinity or the incarnation. What is in focus is God's grace as it reaches struggling mortals. The old theories about the atonement are also boiled down into the celebration of God's saving grace in essays by Paul Avis and Trevor Williams. The cross is 'the outpouring of divine love to win us back to God' (Avis, p. 147). The sacraments of the Church are seen in biblical terms, partly as recollections of Jesus (a 'disturbing memory' as well as a comfort) – but mainly as anticipations of the final kingdom of God. This is of course the theme featured in the ecumenical document on *Baptism, Eucharist and Ministry* (1982) over whose making Geoffrey Wainwright presided. The Reformed scholar J.-J. von Allmen is quoted: 'Sacrament takes place when the age to come chooses, touches, exorcises (or pardons), occupies and consecrates an element in this age and thereby makes itself present' (p. 344). The future breaks in because God breaks in – that, in a world more evil than Oxford knew in 1889, is what is affirmed by a religion based on the Bible.

RESPONSES

Don Cupitt

The Vision of Christ that thou dost see
Is my Vision's Greatest Enemy . . .
                        William Blake

The non-realist interpretation of religious language which has become very widespread around the world in recent years is not a pure innovation. Among the precursors of it that I have elsewhere cited are fideism, biblical and Protestant voluntarism, and especially the long tradition of the Negative Way in theology. To keep the gods describable, the ancient Greeks had always kept them finite. When after Plotinus (third century AD) the God of mainline Christian Platonic theology finally transcended the categories altogether and became infinite, he thereby became officially ineffable and incomprehensible. So our religious language ceased to be able confidently to latch on to an Object external to it – and the seeds of modern non-realism were sown. Non-realism is not an aberration, but has grown directly out of the highest of high orthodoxy (which, as David Edwards will know, is what happened in my own well-documented case).

A further impetus to the emergence of theological non-realism was given by the two great founders of modern thought, Kant and Hegel. Both were Lutherans, but both knew that the age of supernatural belief had ended. For Kant, God was an Ideal of Reason and a moral postulate: hence my phrase, 'a guiding spiritual ideal'. For Hegel, God coincided with the universal human Spirit unfolding in history towards its consummation: hence the occasional use by me and other non-realists of the Feuerbach-Jung notion of God as the greater Self that we are to become, and our occasional talk of God as having in Christ and the Spirit 'died' into humanity.

All major subsequent theologians have been greatly influenced by Kant or Hegel or both, so that the greater part of post-Kantian theology *can* be read in a non-realistic sense. Of course, any text is capable of various readings, and there is no such thing as the one True reading. But a text like Kierkegaard's *Purity of Heart* certainly can – as I reported back in the 1970s – be read non-realistically. God is real as one prays to him. God is within religious language and practice. God, exacting, transcendent, just, holy and merciful, functions as an eternal standpoint within the religious consciousness, from which one's life is assessed, examined and judged. It is most important to understand that a writer such as D. Z. Phillips uses all the customary language about God to just the same effect as a realist, while yet in the philosophy of religion he is in fact a non-realist. So far as everyday religious practice and utterance are concerned the non-realist may well be indistinguishable from the realist, and one may have to search for very small tell-tale signs to spot the difference. There may not be any, in which case the writer can be understood either way. For example, T. S. Eliot was certainly exposed to the non-realistic interpretations of religious language that are to be found in his philosophical master F. H. Bradley and in Indian mysticism, but I cannot just now recall a text where Eliot is explicit about his own view.

However, during the 1980s I have obviously done more than offer a philosophical analysis of standard idioms. I have also wanted to destabilise standard idioms, putting forward a range of philosophical arguments about the endlessness of interpretation, the social and historical relativity of all meaning, and the provisional and humanly manufactured character of truth in the modern period. From these and other considerations it follows that in our time we must see realities of every sort as established only within our ever-changing human conversation. There is no faculty in a modern university that any longer transmits fixed, objective and given Truth. In every faculty, including that of theology, truth is now a running debate. You can only report the current state of the argument. That is all there is. So we have now got to see religion in a quite new way. It is not a supernatural datum. It is an ever-renewed imaginative and productive human activity. Thus my late-1980s 'post-modern' writings have come to look rather like radicalised versions of the Roman Catholic modernism of the early years of the present century.

How well David Edwards understands the history of philosophy and theology, the issue between realists and non-realists, and the present state of Christian thought, I leave it to the reader to decide. But the tone of what Edwards has written points to a third level of disagreement between us. He would presumably profess himself content with the faith and the Church as he first received them and as they still are, whereas I want root-and-branch reform as soon as possible. The values that David Edwards still seems to cherish are to me anti-Christian and even demonic. That we are in a frightful mess should have become apparent just these past few years, just in Britain. Or indeed, just these past few years, just in Rome.

The problem is partly one of the political context. Right-wing politics assigns a number of roles to the Church, as an arm of the heritage industry, as a concealer of the reality of social change, as a legitimator, and as an engine for the mass-production of authoritarian personalities – all of which ought to be making us Christians very rebellious indeed. But apart from all that, the Church is in any case still locked into a hopelessly inappropriate medieval world-view, a paranoid patriarchal rationality, and a psychologically repressive vocabulary, which are preposterously at variance with her claim to stand for human redemption. Until we put things right, the whole apparatus will increasingly do people more harm than good.

It is no use saying that there have been some humane and reasonable modern theologians. If there have been, they have made no difference. Look at the texts in our standard authorised prayer books and hymn books. How much has changed? Take a devotional companion such as Milner-White's *Daily Prayer* (one of the very *best*) and analyse in the manner of modern literary theory just what values are being recommended, what ethical and ontological scales are being constructed, and what world-view is being presupposed. The results, I promise, turn out to be quite horrifying to a present-day sensibility.

The chief reason for this extraordinary value-shift is that in recent years *feminism has spread to men*. I warned nearly twenty years ago that feminism was going to present a major challenge to the Church, but for a long time it seemed that the radical Christian feminist critique of the Church's language and institutions was going to be ghettoised or kept out on the periphery. Now, however, the revolt is spreading to men as well. A great deal of what has come down to us now feels like sexist ideology grown old and very sick. Even a fairly old-fashioned and unreconstructed heterosexual male like me finds it unendurable. We cannot defend it. We must clean it up, for what on earth can be the point of waxing indignant in defence of a form of Christianity that no longer makes people whole?

We must change, and the sooner the better. My recent writings may seem inadequate to me and highly excessive to others, but I have at least been attempting to open some pathways of intellectual, moral and religious renewal. And since the Church can only be changed from within, I shall stay and serve her as best I can. Fortunately, Anglican formularies nowhere say either that the Church is infallible and irreformable, or that priests have got to be metaphysical realists.

Maurice Wiles

David Edwards' reaction to what I have written about the activity of God is representative of what many intelligent and reflective Christians feel. Christian faith is reflected in Scripture and in many of its principal doctrines seems to imply a number of discrete 'acts of God' in the course of human history. Edwards is sufficiently a man of his time to acknowledge that he cannot accept as true every traditional account of such 'acts of God'. But he is also convinced that the basic concept of special divine actions is so integral to Christian faith that it has to stay.

Once it is acknowledged that there is a problem about such talk which needs to be worked at, we have a starting-point for constructive discussion. One of the first points that needs to be made is that the concept itself is not a straightforward one. In whatever sense God 'acts', he is not an agent in just the same way that we are. There is nothing particularly 'radical' about that insistence. It is a common feature of the main theological tradition. To deny it is to treat God as one more individual agent within the world, and no longer as the ground and source of all existence. And so it is surprising that, for all his acknowledgement of difficulty in identifying particular acts of God, Edwards does not seem to feel any difficulty about the concept itself. What he wants to see maintained is 'the Christian Church's basic tradition that God *has* intervened somewhat like a monarch' (p. 115).

The language of 'intervention' (let alone the human model he uses on that occasion) seems to me altogether inappropriate. Not only does it suggest the idea that God's agency is parallel with ours, but also the idea that there are times when God is not acting. Yet every Christian wants surely to speak of God as always at work. When I have spoken of God's one act as the act of creation, I have stressed that I am speaking of creation as a continuing and still unfinished process. So it does not carry with it the implication that he is a God 'who leaves his creation . . . to its own devices after starting it off' (p. 123). The whole process is God's action in the sense that it is a purposive happening, which is only possible because God wills it and makes it possible.

But 'intervention', if a clumsy and to me unacceptable word, is designed to indicate that we do differentiate between the various things that happen in the world and speak of some of them as God's actions in a special sense. Edwards thinks that my recent suggestion that we should speak of the whole creative process as God's one act represents a going back on an earlier recognition that 'there must be room for the idea of special activity in some sense' (p. 117). But that is because he has too simple, too univocal, an idea of divine activity. The language of God's action is used in Scripture in highly interventionist ways (parting the Red Sea, effecting a virginal conception, etc.), but it is also used of bringing about God's purpose in more indirect ways through the medium of human agency. That human agency may be a matter of evil human actions (Joseph's brothers selling him into slavery in Egypt, Judas' betrayal of Jesus, etc.). In those cases God's 'acting' has surely to be understood in a very Pickwickian sense: God somehow ensures that the evil acts of men and women, for which they are fully responsible, contribute to the fulfilment of the divine purpose. In other instances it may be a matter of the inspired action of a prophet or saint, consciously seeking to fulfil God's will. It is with reference to such cases that I would want to use the language of a special divine activity.

I do not think Edwards wants to deny any of that as far as it goes, but he wants to say more – quite a lot more. But before we go on to consider what more, it needs to be pointed out that the rhetorical peroration (p. 124) in which he suggests that on the basis of my views we could all relax and wait to discover after death how well everything has been working itself out is just that – a rhetorical peroration that bears no serious relation to the views I have expressed. Indeed, if one were to argue in that kind of way at all, one could just as well claim that the more place one allows to special divine action or providential ordering of events, the stronger the case for easy-going human relaxation.

But despite this lapse from serious discussion, there is an important issue at stake about which Christians ought to be concerned and where the right answer is not self-evident. Does God 'intervene' in the course of events to bring about such contra-natural occurrences as a virginal conception or to determine what happens in the future in answer to prayers for healing or for rain? The underlying regularity of the way the world works at the macroscopic level seems to me to be such that some kinds of purported 'miraculous' happening ought to be regarded as strictly inconceivable. But I do not believe the world to be a mechanistically closed system of such a kind that the possibility of all 'miraculous' or providential occurrences can be ruled out in advance as inconceivable on scientific grounds. Nor can we draw a precise line between what kinds of 'miracle' are and are not possible. There is murky ground between the absurdity of the sun standing still and the experienced reality of apparently spontaneous healings.

But are such unexpected occurrences, whether recorded in Scripture or experienced in apparent answer to prayer, to be understood as specifically initiated actions of God? Or are they to be seen as unusual but highly positive occurrences within the diverse pattern of events that make up this strange world, stable but amenable to novelty, which God is in process of creating? The general stability of the world is a positive God-given characteristic of it, without which personal human life as we know it would not be possible. The special divine acts which Edwards (along with very many other Christians) wants to insist on are therefore bound to be relatively few. Are they, limited though they may be in number and extent, crucial, as he and others suggest, for the maintenance of a genuinely Christian belief which can speak of God as a loving personal Father?

The problem is too big to deal with in all its complexity in a brief response of this kind. Let me therefore concentrate on one important aspect of it, which Edwards alludes to more than once. No problem is more difficult for the theist than the problem of evil. Evil cannot be 'explained', and most attempts to do so demonstrate a moral insensitivity that ill becomes the Christian apologist. But we have to take the fact of evil very seriously in determining how we should envisage and speak of God's relation to the world. There does not seem to be any possible way of understanding the presence of evil in God's world other than one that sees it as integrally related to human freedom. Moral evil or sin is a by-product of the exercise of that freedom which makes possible our personal life and our relationship with God. Natural evils are perhaps best understood as an inescapable by-product of that generally stable ordering of the world that, we have claimed, is the necessary backcloth for human freedom and personal life. That does not, it cannot be too strongly emphasised, 'explain' the existence of evil, but it seems to provide the only conceivable context within which the Christian believer can view it, the only one which does not leave it in absolute contradiction to his or her affirmation about the sovereignty and the love of God.

It is in the context of that conviction that I want to respond to Edwards' question as to whether I am 'really open to the possibility that God may act against evil' (p. 116), or whether for me God has to be seen as 'inactive, doing nothing to save his children from evil' (p. 123). On his account of God's relation to the world, which allows for some, admittedly limited, number of divine interventions in answer to prayer or for the better providential ordering of the world, such special actions are naturally seen as evidence of God acting against evil. But fearsome evils still remain. And we have to ask: Do not many of the often claimed acts of God, in response to prayer for example, seem trivial compared with those evils that appear to have been allowed to continue unchecked by divine action, frequently despite much believing prayer? On the account that I am suggesting, in which such special actions are ruled out as logically incompatible with the divine self-limitation implicit in the creation of the world as a setting for the emergence and growth of free human persons, no such problem arises. God is active against evil in the only way in which it makes sense to speak of special divine activity within our world – by the inspiration of men and women to work for the overcoming of evil and the creation of that good which is the goal of the whole creative purpose. Neither account (both inevitably oversimplified in so brief an exposition) is without its difficulties. But it seems to me that my account is not only truer to our experience of how things are in the world, but actually coheres better with belief in a God whose true face we see in Jesus Christ than does the more traditional account. Even, or as I am tempted to say especially, in relation to the intractable problem of evil, which Edwards is inclined to see as the Achilles heel of my approach, it can stake a claim to the greater religious depth.

But even if the account I have been giving of how God may be understood to act in the world were thought to carry conviction at the more general level of experience, Edwards still wants to ask whether it can do justice to Christian talk about the resurrection. He himself speaks of the resurrection as among those 'mysterious and ambiguous' '"signs"' which point those who are ready to believe to the active God' (p. 118). For me too the resurrection is a sign of hope that the way of Jesus is the way of God and that it will serve to bring God's purpose in creation to fulfilment, however uncertain in the light of the evidence I may have to remain about the nature of the historical events that followed on the death of Jesus. But precisely because of its 'mysterious and ambiguous' character the 'active God' to whom it points for the believer need not be the interventionist God whom Edwards insists is the only adequate God for Christian faith.

The same basic issue is at stake between us in relation to the wider question of the person of Christ, which Edwards deals with at more length in the ensuing chapter. He approves my insistence that Jesus 'like every other human person, was a product of the evolutionary process, one whose particular characteristics were substantially affected by his heredity and environment with all the attendant limitations of psychology and knowledge' (p. 144), and in the light of that and other allied insights acknowledges that 'a lot of rhetoric about orthodoxy needs to be examined' (p. 151). And this leads him to be critical, in my view appropriately critical, of attempts to spell out the implications of that orthodox rhetoric by people such as Eric Mascall (pp. 144–6), Brian Hebblethwaite (p. 151) and Thomas Morris (pp. 166–7). What he wants to hold on to is a midway position between their attempts to understand God's action in Christ and the very different kind of account that I have offered. But what is for me disappointing about his own contribution to the discussion is that he nowhere spells out his own views in a manner that might give some precision to that midway position. He speaks of 'poetry' which celebrates the birth of Jesus as something that 'began in the heart of God, for "the power of the Most High" overshadowed that life before Jesus spoke a word' (p. 156), and goes on at crucial moments to insist with Donald Baillie that 'whatever Jesus . . . did . . . , it is really God that did it in Jesus' (p. 160), or to affirm with Edward Schillebeeckx 'salvation in Jesus from God' (p. 165). But the issue that I have been struggling with is what sense or understanding to give to such statements. And that task he does not even seem to attempt. He may have examined the orthodox rhetoric, but having done so he ends up by simply repeating it. I do not claim that what I have written about God's action, about the resurrection or about the person of Christ is *the* correct spelling out of Christian truth. It is rather an attempt to offer an intellectually and religiously coherent account of some central affirmations of Christian faith. That, as I see it, is a crucial part of the theologian's role. And what is so offered needs to be assessed and criticised by others who see things differently. But the critic who is to be taken most seriously is one who is prepared to offer some alternative account that deals more satisfactorily with the problems that have been raised. It is because I do not find even the outline of any such alternative account implicit in what Edwards has written, that he does not persuade me to retract the interpretation of Christian faith that I have tried to set out in my writings.

John Bowden

Dear David,

Since we have known each other now for twenty-five years, and since what comes over most strongly from your comments on my book *Jesus: the Unanswered Questions* is the very profound way in which I and my writing affect you (more strongly than you yourself may perceive), it seems most appropriate to reply to you in the form of an open letter. I much prefer to address *you* with an audience listening in than to address an audience *about you*.

However, despite the personal form of this response, its personal content will be less than that of your comments, because what we are discussing is, in that lovely old hackneyed phrase, 'something bigger than both of us' – namely the truth, or as near as we can get to it. I am particularly grateful to you for the time and trouble you have taken to read and write about my book, because one of the great weaknesses of contemporary Christianity is that theological books are still being read and consumed in large quantities, but not really studied, discussed and argued about. And anything that furthers thought and discussion is a good thing. However, I do wish that you had not felt it necessary to be quite so personal (especially about yourself: at times you read like a kind of twentieth-century Paul on the defensive), because I think that your feelings have prevented you from reading with sufficient objectivity and attention to detail the books you discuss (including mine). That means that you do not do justice to the substance of some very important issues which are there to stay, even if not many people (though more than you might think) have the openness and patience to recognise them.

Above all, it would have helped if, either in your *Church Times* review which you reprint or in your comments, you had summarised the overall argument of my book rather than discussed bits of it apart from its main thesis. So I must begin by outlining the argument – though I hope that your readers will get hold of a copy of *Jesus: the Unanswered Questions* for themselves; otherwise there isn't much point in either your remarks or mine.

My book is partly a personal quest for God, who is greater than Jesus, but alongside that is in fact above all about power. Christianity is a religion of power and the use of power, whether in the Church of England to which we both belong; the Roman Catholic Church and its wealth, promises and demands; or the world-wide Evangelical movement. Now in all these Christian traditions, and in many others, that power, which is exercised in the name of Jesus, the Christ, can be liberating, refreshing and creative, rising up from our deepest spiritual well-springs; or it can be self-seeking, manipulative and tyrannical. The name of Jesus has been used in connection with both these kinds of power within the churches all down Christian history, and from time to time we need to analyse the present state of affairs to see how healthy it is. I feel that the present situation in our churches is very unhealthy, above all in that too many people who exercise power are pretending that there are no questions when there are all too many questions (look only at the sinister debates over the role of women in the Church), and that these questions must be raised if we are to have a worthwhile belief in God – who was even the focus of Jesus' own belief.

Most of my book is therefore questioning: questioning for the purpose of liberation. You call yourself a liberal; if I had to give myself any label I would call myself a post-liberal. Because it is quite clear to me that what we must do at this point in our Christian (and human) history is to attempt to change things on a very wide scale – and in the Church that is always particularly difficult. In our Western world most mainstream churches, at any rate, have been happiest when maintaining a *status quo*, preferably one which does not set them too far apart from the society within which they exist. But for many Christians who have left or are leaving the churches, or are just clinging on inside, the *status quo* now is virtually unbearable because the churches have, as corporate bodies, apparently stopped thinking, let alone acting, on those things which really matter. The questions I ask in my book are very relevant to this. To keep to the issue of the role of women in the churches and society, my approach to Jesus of Nazareth in the chapter you have chosen to discuss pays close attention to recent feminist scholarship and the considerable change it has made to many people's understanding of the New Testament. I looked hard for anything of any kind about women, whether in the first-century world or in ours, in your comments, and found them exclusively male. My questions are, of course, relevant to a much wider range of issues, from the relationship between world faiths to attitudes about the future of our planet, but that should have made the point.

I was quite surprised that you took as the focus for your comments just one chapter from my book, the third, because it was one which I felt to be perhaps the least controversial of all. It just describes, neutrally and I think fairly, the present state of New Testament scholarship relating to Jesus. Within that scholarship there is so much difference of opinion that, as I shall argue shortly, the only word for that is uncertainty – and that is the way things are, whether one likes it or not; even whether one accepts it or not (like the universe, it's there).

As I began my book by explaining, I started my theological studies under demanding teachers, having my nose rubbed in the gospels, and in so doing entered into a complex scholarly discussion which is still going on. I have tried to keep up with it as much as I can, and I have many New Testament scholars as friends, so if I have any theological speciality, it is here. By contrast – and I'm sorry, but I must make this point since we are concerned in a quest for the truth, the evidence, and how things are, not second-hand opinions – you did not have your nose rubbed in these particular texts and therefore cannot be expected to see them in quite the same way. You are a historian, not a New Testament scholar or a theologian; and therefore when it comes to questions of assessing New Testament evidence, you must inevitably be at a disadvantage. (It is significant, for example, that although you have some biblical references to Paul, you do not make a specific reference to any saying of Jesus in the synoptic gospels.)

And that in fact puts me at a disadvantage, too, because some of your comments are a mixture of so many presuppositions and ifs and buts that it is very difficult to get us both on to some ground where discussion can take us forward and be constructive. But let me try.

Among others, I make three points: 1. While we can certainly recognise a 'synoptic Jesus' (from the gospels of Matthew, Mark and Luke) which is different from the Jesus of the fourth gospel or Paul's Christ, there is such uncertainty about what he said and did when we get down to details that 'there is a good deal that we probably do know about Jesus; the trouble is that we can rarely, if ever, be sure precisely what it is' (p. 32). 2. Take widely praised books about Jesus and read them one after the other (Dodd, Bornkamm, Sanders, for example): after the first you will have a clear and attractive picture, but read the second and the picture will be very different; read the third and it will be different again. You cannot easily add together the 'findings' of New Testament scholars here: Dodd would certainly have disowned most of Sanders' work! *The only reasonable name for such disagreement is uncertainty*. 3. The character of the Christ of Paul and his Christians in Greek cities is demonstrably very different from that of Jesus and his followers in rural Palestine – and the difference increases as time goes on.

But let's begin with just Professor Sanders, as you clearly set much store by him and develop his 'eight points'. (In passing, though, I should comment that it is quite out of the question that Professor Sanders would accept the use you make of his book, which you clearly haven't checked out with him: the significance of the quotation from his p. 2 which appears on your p. 180 is very different in its proper context: there it is (a) describing the reaction to Bultmann's exaggerated position, to which we shall be returning because you seem to like it so much; (b) setting up a kind of Aunt Sally which he is going to batter.)

I want to look in a bit more detail at Sanders' point 8: 'At least some Jews persecuted at least part of the new movement and it appears that this persecution endured at least to a time near the end of Paul's career', on which you comment (p. 179): 'Since Judaism at that time tolerated a variety of groups (Pharisees, Sadducees, charismatics, etc.), the reason for this persecution seems to be that the Christians were making claims about Jesus which some Jews thought blasphemous because incompatible with the fundamental Jewish belief in One God.'

I don't think that you realise that here Sanders is making quite a subtle point which cannot be developed as you would want. Note 'at least some Jews . . . at least part of the new movement'. This indicates that we have to take into account that in the period in question both Judaism and Christianity were differentiated within themselves. In chapter 5 of my own book, which you have ignored, I write about the way in which Christians and Jews parted company in the first century and I reflect current thinking in the Christian–Jewish dialogue (of which you implicitly approve) that the parting of the ways was not over the person of Jesus (I quote Lawrence Shiffmann, 'There was no sin in making the error [as it was to the Tannaim] of believing someone to be the Messiah') but over the observance of the law, and in particular the regulations over 'clean' and 'unclean food'. Paul's letters (e.g. Gal. 2, the episode with Peter) and the episode of the Hellenists and Stephen in Acts 6 illustrate this tension, which virtually disappeared, largely because the fall of Jerusalem in AD 70 also resulted in the decline of Jewish Christianity. But it is now regarded as a misconception to think, as you do, that the reason for the persecution was because Christians were making claims about Jesus which Jews thought to be blasphemous (the gospel of John reflects a different, later stage).

You do tend to write as though creating a portrait of Jesus is a matter of getting a basic outline (perhaps provided by one scholar), the 'gaps' in which can be filled in from others. But the problem is that if you do pick and choose among modern New Testament scholars, because their presuppositions are so complex and so different, you land in real trouble. It's a bit like that old parlour game in which someone draws a head, passes the paper round, someone adds a body, someone adds legs and – shamelessly to borrow from another similar game – 'the consequence is' a monster. By monster I mean a picture of Jesus of our own making which never existed, a subtle idol created by human beings (see my p. 140). It is in that context that I ask the question that you call a parody, as to whether it is still worthwhile trying to trace our understanding of the nature of our relationship with God, redemption and forgiveness to the life, character and activity of Jesus of Nazareth (my p. 145, your p. 188). I clearly think that the creation of monsters is more of a danger than you do, which is why I have this particular concern. And because I have this concern I have to ask you: Is there not too much about your views of Jesus which reflects David Edwards and his experience and place in the Church of England (and elsewhere) for others to be completely happy with? To keep to Professor Sanders: you borrow from him, but I'm sure *you* wouldn't be happy with the Jesus as apocalyptic prophet who emerges from his *Jesus and Judaism*. That is why I think that in fact there is greater safety, and insight into the nature of God, in a more sceptical position.

Talking of scepticism, we must move on to Bultmann. I'm amazed, truly amazed, that you manage to use Bultmann at the end of your comments as a stick with which to beat me over the head. Not that I'm not delighted, because as you will know I have an enormous admiration for Bultmann, though he seems increasingly to have been of his time and place.

You say (p. 188) that Bultmann wanted to strip away the 'mythology' in order that what was still intelligible and powerful in the message of Jesus might guide the twentieth century. But it was a bit more complicated than that. Look at the long passage from Bultmann with which you end your article. Where is the word Jesus? Where is there anything about Jesus? As those familiar with Bultmann's work would expect, Bultmann talks about *kerygma*, grace, cross, resurrection and so on. Although very late in his life Bultmann slightly changed his views, he argued that for Christians it was not only impossible to know more about Jesus than that he was, but also illegitimate. 'Christ encounters us in the *kerygma* and nowhere else.' That statement encapsulates Bultmann's theology. And the first chapter of his *Theology of the New Testament* to which you refer (p. 188) was 'prolegomena' to New Testament theology, not that theology itself. (Many people disagree with this, as I do myself, but that is what Bultmann actually thought – see Walter Schmithals, *An Introduction to the Theology of Rudolf Bultmann*, 1968.) It was, of course, precisely because of Bultmann's scepticism that Günther Bornkamm tried to make a fresh start in the 'new quest of the historical Jesus' which you once found exciting (p. 188); I am, of course, rather more doubtful, for reasons which I explained in my book (p. 152).

I could go on a good deal longer, but there I must stop. My views, not yours, are in fact under discussion. I don't think you even begin to see the strength of my case.

Dennis Nineham

The burden of David Edwards' complaint seems to be that I exaggerate: (a) the historical untrustworthiness of the gospel records, or at any rate the difficulties involved in discovering the historical truth about Jesus; and (b) the extent of the differences between diverse cultures and the difficulty we have, as a result, in (i) understanding, and (ii) appropriating, the attitudes and beliefs of cultures very different from our own.

Broadly, and with certain reservations, I accept the quotations Edwards has assembled as giving a fair account of my position on both matters. Some of the reservations to which I refer are of a general kind, others are more particular. Of the general reservations two perhaps deserve a brief airing. First, Edwards does not really make clear that over the forty-odd years of my working life

my ideas have changed – and I hope I may say developed – a great
deal. I make no apology for that; it would be a poor scholar who
never allowed the evidence to alter his or her ideas. In fact in both
the areas which are of concern to Edwards my doubts have steadily
increased. Long before I became his pupil, my old tutor, R. H.
Lightfoot, a traditionalist by temperament, if ever there was one,
had been forced by years of gospel study to the conclusion that, as
he put it in his Bampton Lectures, 'the form of the earthly no less
than of the heavenly Christ is for the most part hidden from us. For
all the inestimable value of the gospels, they yield us little more
than a whisper of his voice, we trace in them but the outskirts of his
ways'. My own studies have convinced me that that is no more than
the truth; indeed I doubt if most of us have yet taken the full
measure of it. As I confessed in a book review for a recent number
of the *Journal of Theological Studies* (1986, pp. 440–1), reading I
have done over the past year or two has persuaded me 'that even
now enlightened biblical scholars tend to overestimate the amount
of historical fact behind the biblical texts and the possibility of
discovering it and basing interpretation on it'. By the same token,
the more I study cultures of much earlier times, the more impressed I become by the depth of the differences which divide our
culture from them. It is perhaps as well to say at once that a careful
reading of what Edwards has written in this and preceding chapters
has done nothing to change my mind on either issue.

The point about the development of my ideas seemed worth
mentioning because, if it is not taken into account, what were in
fact developments from one position to another could be mistaken
for inconsistencies within a single more or less static position.
There are, I think, hints of such a mistake, or misrepresentation, at
one or two points in Edwards' essay.

My second general reservation is this: it is no doubt unavoidable
in an essay such as Edwards' – though if so, it perhaps puts a
question mark against the worthwhileness of the whole exercise –
that only conclusions should be quoted, lack of space preventing
the inclusion of the facts and reasoning on which they were based.
In several books and almost innumerable articles over the years, I
have made great efforts to document and explain fully the grounds
for the conclusions at which I have arrived. In the – inevitable –
absence of all this from what Edwards has written, my position is
bound to appear as, to some extent, a matter of taste and temperament, or even whim. A considerable element of subjectivity
undeniably enters into the sort of differences of opinion being

canvassed here; no reader of Edwards' account of his own position, for example, can miss that element. Yet I venture to hope that anyone who reads in full what I have written, evidence and all, will come to feel that there is much more to it than that.

Then I have a number of detailed reservations about the fairness of Edwards' account; by way of example, three of these perhaps deserve mention. On p. 194 he accuses me of 'apparently ignoring' the account in Luke 23:34 of Jesus' last words on the cross. In fact any ignoring there may be is on his part, for the very next sentence to the one he quotes reads: 'Luke 23:34 is of doubtful range and of doubtful authenticity'. The words are a quotation from Montefiore and are fully justified. In presenting Luke 23:34 as authentic words of Jesus Edwards should have made clear the great weight of scholarly opinion against him. The best-known English commentator on Luke's gospel, J. M. Creed, brackets the words, on the basis of the manuscript evidence, as not being an original part of the text. In so doing he follows Westcott and Hort, and the same line is taken by the most up-to-date critical editions of the Greek New Testament. In that case, so far from being authentic words of Jesus, these are not even authentic words of Luke! Inattention on this scale both to what I have written and to the questions raised by modern scholarship is remarkable.

Secondly, Edwards accuses me of ignoring the parable of the prodigal son as evidence for the meaning of Jesus' teaching. In arguing that the connotations of the word 'father' were different in the time of Jesus from what they are now – a contention with which he seems to agree in his essay on John Bowden – I have, he says, ignored the evidence of the parable. He must know that a plausible case has recently been made out for questioning whether the parable goes back to Jesus. (See John Drury, *The Parables in the Gospels*, 1985, which also gives grounds for doubting whether the parable of the good Samaritan goes back to Jesus, a question relevant to p. 194. This book was reviewed by Edwards.) In any case this is of all parables one of the hardest to interpret; Professor C. F. Evans, for example, has listed a number of conflicting interpretations. Even if the one Edwards seems implicitly to choose is the right one, it by no means follows that the 'glimpse of home life' it affords is 'typical', or that the teaching of the parable, so interpreted, is 'not untypical' of the teaching of Jesus. These are simply *ipse dixits*.

Thirdly, Edwards takes me to task (p. 203) for claiming that 'no picture of the historical Jesus has yet emerged . . . which comes anywhere near commanding universal, or even general, agreement'. Yet such a claim is simply a statement of fact. From D. F. Strauss in the early nineteenth century, through writers such as Renan, Holtzmann, Seeley and Weiss to Schweitzer, and from such twentieth-century scholars as Kautsky, Loisy, Guignebert, Goguel, Glover, Klausner and Montefiore to Bultmann, Bornkamm, Conzelmann, Dodd, Vermes and Elliott, innumerable masters of the subject have attempted a reconstruction of the historical Jesus. If Edwards can show that these accounts, widely – in some cases wildly – differing from one another, are in fact harmonisable, or that any one of them commands universal, or even general, consent, then he knows something not revealed to other scholars. Perhaps what he has in mind is the so-called 'new quest of the historical Jesus', associated with the names of such scholars as Bornkamm and Käsemann; certainly for a time these writers were felt in certain circles to have cracked the problem at last. More recently, however, damaging criticisms have been levelled against their conclusions and their presuppositions; and their accounts must now be seen as no more than so many further items to be added to the list of variant reconstructions referred to above. Theologians must take on board the fact that *provisionality* is an inescapable characteristic of all conclusions arrived at by means of modern historical method.

With regard to the question of cultural differences, Edwards devotes several pages to it, claiming, fairly enough, that opinions about it vary widely, and attributing this variety in large measure to differences of temperament among those who hold them. A great deal of what he says here seems to me justified, though he may exaggerate somewhat; for example, despite his claim about the unwillingness of experts to generalise in the matter, Sir Isaiah Berlin, than whom there could hardly be a greater expert in the field, is prepared to dismiss outright, as 'fallacious', any 'belief in a fixed, ultimate, unchanging human nature'. In fact that seems to me on the extreme side, and I have frequently quoted with approval the words of the American literary critic Lionel Trilling, who wrote that 'to suppose that we can think like men of another time is as much of an illusion as to suppose that we can think in a wholly different way' (*The Liberal Imagination*, 1964, p. 187).

My difficulty with this part of Edwards' essay is that, having opened the question up in an interesting way, he then abruptly shies away from any attempt to discuss how it should be resolved, simply remarking that it will be more 'profitable' to turn to something else. Such a move is remarkable since it means that the whole question with which, according to the title, the essay was to be concerned is simply begged, and so is the historical question along with it. For the view we take of the historical accuracy of New Testament statements will depend quite largely on our assessment of one element in the culture of the New Testament period, namely the attitude taken towards the past and (giving) accounts of the past. In my submission, the attitude with regard to this matter then was so very different from our own that to approach their statements about the past with questions and presuppositions native to our culture is inevitably to mishandle and misrepresent them. To be more specific: for them edification was a value in writing about the past at least as important as accuracy, which was in any case impossible for them, at any rate to anything like the degree to which we demand it today. As they saw it, to have written an account of the past which did not conform with the religious beliefs of their time would have seemed irresponsible, whatever the evidence available might be. Indeed lack of conformity with current religious belief would have seemed to them a sure sign of falsity in any report, however strong its external attestation might be. To discuss the sort of questions Edwards raises without teasing out these issues is to risk superficiality.

It is quite clear where Edwards' sympathies in the matter lie, but he offers no grounds for them, apart from one brief argument and the statement that Drs Moule and Barton regard my position as involving exaggeration. The last is certainly true, but it hardly proves anything; it would be easy to produce the names of scholars who think I have got it about right, as Professor Trilling in fact did, or who feel that I seriously underestimate the differences, as Sir Edmund Leach did in his last book, and as Sir Isaiah Berlin presumably would. As for the argument referred to, it appears to be simply what used to be called an *ignoratio elenchi*, an attempt to disprove what has not been asserted. No one doubts that within a given culture some people may disagree with the beliefs of others. That is because they share a common set of primary presuppositions on the basis of which there can be a meeting of minds. Participants in a common culture can understand one another's positions and put forward arguments, for or against, intelligible to the other side. The whole question at issue, however, is whether differences in fundamental presuppositions between different cultures are so deep as to make such a process difficult or impossible on a cross-cultural basis.

Since Edwards puts forward his own position as a better alternative to mine, some comment on it from me is presumably expected. The first thing that strikes one is the high degree of subjectivity involved in it. Words such as 'sure' and 'surely' recur repeatedly (e.g. three times on p. 194). To preface a statement with the word 'surely' does nothing to advance any argument. It simply makes clear that, from the viewpoint adopted by the writer, what follows seems virtually self-evident; and perhaps also that the writer expects most of the readers he envisages to share his viewpoint. The matter of the correctness or otherwise of the viewpoint in question is left exactly where it was.

Edwards says roundly 'I believe . . .', 'I maintain . . .', 'I feel sure . . .', and no one will question his right to do so; as we have seen, a degree of subjectivity is unavoidable in connection with questions such as these. What is important, though, is that expressions of subjective opinion should be recognised for what they are, and not accorded any more authority than that deriving from the fact that they are the opinions of such an able and widely read scholar. It has always to be borne in mind that there are other scholars just as able and widely read who hold a very different opinion, in this case, for example, Professor Rudolf Bultmann, on any showing the doyen of modern New Testament scholarship. The point is important because it applies to many passages in Edwards' essay where he might seem at first sight to be stating established facts, for example the statement on p. 202 beginning 'I can only repeat . . .', or that on p. 206, 'a personality for which there is sufficient historical evidence . . .' It should especially be remembered when he says on p. 206 that he 'cannot leave [an important] problem unsolved'. Such a statement reveals him as one of those R. H. Lightfoot used to describe, after Meredith, as 'hot for certainties'. (*Ah what a dusty answer gets the soul/When hot for certainties in this our life!* Contrast Keats' commendation of 'negative capability'.) More seriously, it leaves him no alternative but to go on as if the problem *had* been solved, and solved in the way that he would like. If so, what follows in the essay must be read with a question mark against it in case he is wrong about the solution of the unsolved problem he has taken as his starting-point. The point is the more important because, as we have seen, he proceeds in the same sort of way over the unresolved problem of cultural differences on p. 200, and he does the same on p. 210 over the important question of Jesus' messianic consciousness.

A related point arises on p. 205 in connection with his rejection of my suggestion that a visitor to an ancient building needs a guide. Certainly, as he says, a building visited without a guide, or alternative means of access to the sort of information a guide might impart, may 'speak to the heart', indeed speak very powerfully; but that was not quite the point I had in mind. An unguided and uninformed visitor must be very careful to make no historical or other factual claims about the building or any part of it. I once took a recently arrived visitor from Australia, who had never before been in a country with a long history, to see a large Victorian building; he was, understandably, much impressed, but, until corrected by his 'guide', quite convinced that the building dated from the Middle Ages! Being impressed by a phenomenon confers no right to make historical judgements about it. Being impressed by the figure of Jesus portrayed in the gospels gives no one the right to pass judgement on its historical authenticity. Without accusing Edwards of making any such illegitimate transition, I draw attention to the amount of emotional capital he clearly has invested in the hope that one side of the present debate should prove to have the right of it, as witness his words on p. 193 that 'it would be a great loss to Christianity and to the spiritual life of mankind' if the gospels were to prove incapable of fulfilling certain functions. Where such strong emotional forces are at work, the utmost care must be taken to see that the evidence is weighed with scrupulous impartiality. That it would be edifying if it were true is not something that can be allowed any weight whatsoever in determining the truth or falsehood of a historical claim. I am not *quite* persuaded that Edwards has kept that cardinal historical principle in the forefront of his mind throughout his writings. Many theologians do not.

The tour of Mark's gospel Edwards himself undertakes (pp. 208–11) is difficult to assess. What exactly is he doing? Is he simply explaining how the gospel speaks to his heart, in the hope of facilitating its having a similar impact on others? That is certainly what p. 205 would suggest; but if so, he lets the gospel speak to him without as much regard as might have been exacted for what Mark himself sought to convey. For example, he says nothing about the important insights the evangelist wished to communicate through the way he told and juxtaposed the stories of the stilling of the storm and the Gerasene demoniac (4:35–5:20), the curing of the blind man at Bethsaida and the opening of the disciples' eyes at Caesarea Philippi (8:22–30), or the curing of Bartimaeus and the immediately ensuing passion narrative (10:46ff.). On the other hand it is very doubtful whether Mark will have seen – or would accept – a number of the inferences Edwards draws from some of his passing remarks. For example, it must be doubted whether he saw the question in 5:30 as proving that Jesus was capable of ignorance – even if he believed that to be the case, which I doubt. The question, like the one at 8:27, is a question only in form; Athanasius may profitably be consulted on that.

Is Edwards, then, seeking to uncover the historical substratum beneath Mark's gospel? If so, it is strange that he nowhere refers to the serious doubts which have been raised about the historicity of a number of the incidents to which he refers, for example those in 4:35ff., 14:32ff. and 15:34.

A similar ambiguity hangs over the section on p. 204 where he discusses the issues to which the gospel seems to him to give rise. For example, he asks, avowedly expecting the answer 'yes', whether Jesus 'teaches us as one with the authority to do so, and the right to call us to be his pupils'. If we reply in the affirmative, to what does that commit us? Edwards himself says (p. 203) that we cannot share Jesus' fundamental expectation, generally regarded as undergirding the whole of his teaching and ministry, namely that his appearance on the scene heralded the imminent end of the world; at a guess Edwards feels the same about Jesus' teaching on the eternal tortures of hell or his blanket prohibition of divorce. (Jesus replaced all legalism, he says, p. 186.) How then are the visitors he guides round the gospel to distinguish the teaching Jesus *has* the authority to impose? It can hardly be on historical grounds, for no one nowadays will reject the eschatological teaching of Jesus on that score. Is it then a matter of intuition, along the lines of Coleridge's claim that 'whatever *finds* me bears witness for itself that it has proceeded from a Holy Spirit'? Probably it is, and, if so, none the worse for that. It needs to be pointed out, however, that in that case what 'finds' Edwards, or, in his own words, 'speaks to his heart', is neither the historical Jesus nor the Jesus of St Mark. It is a Jesus who can speak to twentieth-century Western readers. Accordingly, I am not altogether clear how his position differs from the one he quoted from me on p. 192. ('Just as he has changed . . . so he must continue to change . . . if he is to mediate . . .')

Another puzzling section of Edwards' essay is the one on p. 197 in which he distinguishes between 'saving' and 'scientific, historical and legislative' truth in the Bible. On the face of it, this is a surprising distinction in relation to the New Testament, which is generally supposed to have intertwined historical claims and saving belief almost inextricably. St Paul declares roundly, for example, 'If Christ has not been raised . . . your faith is null and void' (1 Cor. 15:14). It would be difficult to go further than that in lining up faith with historical claims. However, for purposes of clarification, let us take as an example the more or less unqualified assertion in Hebrews 9:22 that 'without the shedding of blood there is no forgiveness'. That is a text which appears to have no scientific or historical element, and it is quite clearly a faith-statement, and a very important one; to a considerable extent the teaching of Hebrews, and indeed of the rest of the New Testament, is tied up with it. To many of the peoples around the Mediterranean basin in the first century it was what T. E. Hulme called 'a doctrine felt as a fact' – it seemed simply self-evident. Yet modern Western readers will find it hard to accept. They are likely to feel that, so far from blood-shedding being self-evidently necessary for forgiveness, it is not necessary at all. They will be unable to see an intelligible connection of any kind between forgiveness and blood-shedding. Does Edwards mean that because this statement is a biblical faith-claim, and as such inerrantly true, we have to accept it although it seems unintelligible in the context of our culture? That would indeed imply a tough doctrine of inspiration; and how many more such things should we be invited to believe? Perhaps that is not what he has in mind; but if not, what becomes of the 'inerrancy' of 'saving truth' in the Bible?

Of the many other points I wish I had space to raise I will conclude with one which concerns the central theme of Edwards' essay, the concept of the culturally conditioned. At various points he interprets the significance of Jesus in categories which might *seem*, at any rate, to be native to first-century culture. For example, on p. 209 and elsewhere he writes several times of the victory of Jesus over evil, sin, death and so on. He speaks, for instance, of Jesus' victory over 'death in the shape of hideous torture and execution, the worst punishment the Romans could inflict' (p. 209). In itself, undergoing the agony of crucifixion is not a victory. In the case of someone who faced death in that form – or any other – with dignity, courage and lack of bitterness, we might well use the word victory; but that would be in a metaphorical sense, and if we had to press the metaphor, we should have to say it was victory over the self and its baser urges, not over death itself. The New Testament uses the language of victory in an altogether more robust way, but that is because the New Testament writers envisaged death, sin and the like as themselves (quasi-)personal powers, or as the direct work of personal powers, over whom victory was possible in an almost literal sense. (See my remarks as quoted on pp. 198 and 201. In an age which can no longer interpret death in that personal way, as ultimately the result of the fall, but must see it as an inevitable concomitant of biological existence, what does Edwards mean us to understand when he talks of Jesus as having 'overcome' it? The question is important because it arises in connection with a number of the other categories in terms of which he invites us to interpret the 'work' of Jesus.

It is to be hoped that nothing in the above will appear ungracious. Edwards asked me for a frank response to his essay; I thought he meant what he said and I have tried in the space available to meet his request. Any impression of abruptness that may have been given either by his essay or by my response to it is no doubt due to the fact pointed out on p. 297 above. Limitation of space has meant that out of two structures of presupposition and argument, each a whole and more or less coherent, only the conclusions could be brought to view and attention, rather like the visible parts of two icebergs. As a result, positions have had to be stated and rejected somewhat summarily. G. L. Prestige once characterised the gulf between Cyril of Alexandria and the Nestorians as 'a chasm of mutually omitted contexts'. *Si parva licet componere magnis*, something of the same sort may be said about the present discussion. The point may be illustrated by means of two examples.

As is clear from p. 193 and elsewhere, Edwards feels that Christianity must 'always and everywhere' rest primarily on the gospels; and he holds that belief because, as he has written elsewhere, that is what Christians have always done in history. To me such a claim is by no means self-evidently true. For one thing, it has *not* always been like that. St Paul, for example, not only had no gospels on which to rely, but he paid scant attention, in framing his beliefs, to the traditions which the gospels would contain when they eventually appeared. More seriously, the cultural changes of the past two hundred years or so seem to me so profound and far-reaching as to rule out the use of the past as a compelling precedent in the way suggested. In articulating its beliefs, the Christianity of the future will have to rely on the insights and illumination granted to contemporary Christians – very much including the so-called laity – on a scale altogether greater than it has ever done in the past. The balance between authority and experience will, and should, alter.

As a second example we may take Edwards' implicit presumption that the truth is likely to be found in a middle position between two extremes. In the present essay, for instance, he seems to feel that any position which lies between the 'fundamentalist' extreme on the one hand and the 'radical' on the other is at least a candidate for serious consideration. This, once again, is an unargued assumption. There has certainly been a great deal of talk in the Church of England down the years about the virtues of the *via media*, but much of it has been loose and unreflective; so in the hope of stimulating reflection I will conclude with some characteristically trenchant words of Albert Schweitzer, who did not share the assumption at all. 'Progress', he wrote,

> always consists in taking one or other of two alternatives, in abandoning the attempt to combine them . . . The pioneers of progress have therefore always to reckon with . . . those who go on believing that it is possible to combine that which can no longer be combined, and in fact claim it as a special merit that they in contrast to 'one-sided' writers, can do justice to the other side of the question. One must just let them be, till their time is over.

John Hick

I appreciate, gratefully, David Edwards' generosity of spirit in being willing to read carefully a colleague's fairly extensive writings, and to find much to approve, as well as identifying important points of difference. I agree with him (as against another friend, Don Cupitt) in affirming the reality of the transcendent. I agree with Edwards also in affirming the salvific character of the Christian life, at its best, as an authentic and sufficient path of human transformation from self-centredness to a new orientation centred in the divine Reality or, in Christian terms, in God. But rather than elaborate on our agreements it will be more useful, in these few pages, to concentrate on the differences. Edwards remains on the other side of the theological Rubicon which separates an inclusivist from a pluralist understanding of the place of Christianity among the religions of the world. I would like to try to make clear what the difference is, and why I still prefer the pluralist option.

We should begin, I think, at the concrete historical end. Edwards says that 'the self-revelation of God proclaimed by

Christianity – I do not speak of the totality of the belief and behaviour of Christians – is in my view superior to all the other religious visions' (p. 226). Now it is entirely natural, and indeed predictable, that one who has been spiritually formed by the Christian vision should feel that it is normative, and indeed superior to all alien visions. I certainly began my own Christian life (at the age of eighteen) with this feeling, and continued to think in that way for many years. In the same way a Buddhist or a Hindu or a Jew or a Muslim is likely to feel that his or her inherited vision is superior to that of all other traditions, including Christianity. But how do we proceed beyond this very natural starting-point? I suggest: by looking at the fruits of these visions, in human life, both personal and communal. If the function of the religious traditions is to be enabling contexts for the transformation of human existence from self-centredness to Reality-centredness, to what extent do they succeed? The broad answer seems to me to be that the great world faiths are extremely different but, so far as we can tell, more or less equally effective paths of salvation/liberation. They seem to produce saints – persons in whom the salvific transformation is far advanced – to much the same extent. It is true, indeed a tautology, that 'no other teacher [than Jesus] has produced Christian saints – the sinners who have been dominated, transformed and made holy by this idea of the eternal, loving God and always in dependence on Jesus' (p. 230). Of course, only Christianity produces Christian saints! But if a Buddhist writer were to claim unique superiority for the founder of his own tradition on the ground that no other teacher than the Buddha has produced Buddhist saints, Edwards would at once recognise the logical circularity; and a like circularity is present in his own argument. The question is not whether other religions produce *Christian* saints, but whether they produce their own saints, and how these compare with the Christian variety. The question is not easy to answer; but my own interim conclusion, arising from both reading and observation, is that the saints of the other great world traditions have been and are comparable with their Christian counterparts in the degree to which they have been transformed from self-centredness to Reality-centredness. As in the Christian tradition, some have withdrawn from the world into monasteries, nunneries and solitary hermitages, while many of those whose names are known to us have been active teachers, organisers and leaders – for example, Shankara, Boddhidharma, Shinran, Kabir, Nanak, Ramakrishna, Gandhi . . . etc. These seem to be comparable in quality, so far as our human judgement can tell, with St Paul, St Thomas Aquinas, St Francis, St Catherine of Genoa, Martin Luther, Albert Schweitzer . . . etc.

Societies are much harder to transform than individuals, for lovelessness more easily becomes institutionalised than love – hence, in Reinhold Niebuhr's phrase, moral man and immoral society. The records of the great religious traditions in influencing societies, so as to create favourable conditions for human transformation, have been uneven and generally dismal. Each record shows relatively good and relatively bad aspects and moments. Edwards is acutely aware of the historical record of Christian societies in violence, intolerance, anti-Semitism and racial oppression. Societies presided over by the other world faiths have produced their own evils, sometimes similar and sometimes different. They all affirm, and can be judged by, the same basic principle of love, compassion, the unselfish seeking of the welfare of others. But the comparative assessment of these vast internally diverse phenomena, spanning many centuries, is an almost impossibly complex task. How are we to weigh the endemic poverty and lack of social justice afflicting many traditional Muslim, Hindu and Buddhist societies against the endemic violence, social injustice and institutionalised hatred, culminating in the twentieth-century Holocaust, of so many Christian societies? My own interim conclusion (for which I have presented the reasons in several writings) is that there is no good ground for a claim on the part of either Christianity or any of the other world religions to stand out as manifestly morally superior.

In general, my regretful perception is that Edwards has not transcended the sense of comfortable superiority endemic among Western Christians who see the religious life of the rest of the world through narrow, tinted church windows. This enables him to accept such out-moded stereotypes as that *nirvana* means for Buddhists extinction. It also enables him to say that 'no other teacher [than Jesus] has so powerfully expounded the idea of God as both eternal and loving' (p. 230). In many cases we do not really know with certainty what elements of the New Testament teachings about God come directly from Jesus. Recent scholarship (see, for example, Paula Fredriksen's *From Jesus to Christ*) has shown a considerable continuity between Jesus and other Jewish teachers of his day, particularly in Galilee. But beyond this, his teaching about the eternal and loving presence of God is paralleled in the Hindu *bhakti* tradition, in many of the Muslim Sufi teachers, in the teachings of Guru Nanak (the founder of Sikhism), in Amida Buddhism, in the teachings of many of the Jewish rabbis and, as a vision of the infinite out-going compassion at the heart of the universe, in much of Mahayana Buddhism. In all these cases the infinite love of the eternal is powerfully expressed, as also is the appropriate human response of mutual love. Even the striking paradoxes of Jesus' teaching are paralleled elsewhere: for example it was the Amida Buddhist teacher Shinran who said, 'Even a good man will be received into Buddha's land, how much more a bad man'!

We who have been formed by the Christian tradition can and should rejoice in Jesus' teaching concerning the love of God and the call to love our neighbours. But in doing so we do not need to denigrate the comparably powerful teachings of the same kind by which people in other traditions have been formed and by which they are – so far as we can tell, to much the same extent as in Christianity – being salvifically transformed.

This pluralistic view of the great world religions as independently authentic contexts of salvation/liberation leads one to favour a particular kind of Christology which has been developed, generally for other reasons, by a number of contemporary theologians. For from the traditional dogma that Jesus was literally and uniquely the Son of God it follows that Christianity, uniquely, was divinely founded and is accordingly superior to all other religions. Since Christianity does not in fact seem to be superior, however, perhaps it had a human founder. Perhaps the idea of Jesus as Son of God is a metaphorical rather than a literal truth. Certainly in the ancient world 'son of God' was a common metaphorical designation for anyone who was believed to be close to God, doing God's will. Kings (including the kings of Israel – see Ps 2:7; 2 Sam 7:14), emperors and holy men were often called 'son of God'. Jesus was clearly, in this familiar metaphorical sense, a son of God. It was when the gospel went out into the Gentile world that the Hebraic metaphor was eventually transposed into Greek metaphysics, and Jesus, son of God, became God the Son, Second Person of the Holy Trinity.

The original metaphor can be described, in a technical sense familiar in modern theology, as a mythological mode of speech. Thus to speak of 'the myth of God incarnate' is to suggest that the idea of divine incarnation is a metaphorical or mythological idea. As metaphor it is (we Christians believe) a true metaphor: Jesus really was so open to God that God as Spirit was working in and through him for the salvation of those who have been influenced by him. But the mythic character of this truth means that it does not preclude God having also acted in other ways, in and through other lives and other events, for human salvation within other streams of history.

But David Edwards has done so much to expand the Christian vision, and to make it plausible in the contemporary world, that I still hope one day to find him expounding a pluralistic understanding of the wider religious life of humanity.

BIBLIOGRAPHY

Thomas Altizer and William Hamilton, *Radical Theology and the Death of God* (Harmondsworth: Penguin Books, 1968)

D. M. Baillie, *God Was in Christ: An Essay on Incarnation and Atonement* (London: Faber & Faber, 1956)

J. A. Baker, *The Foolishness of God* (London: Darton, Longman & Todd, 1970)

Baptism, Eucharist and Ministry (Geneva: World Council of Churches, 1982)

James Barr, *The Semantics of Biblical Language* (Oxford: Clarendon Press, 1961)

Karl Barth, *Evangelical Theology: An Introduction* (London: Weidenfeld & Nicolson, 1968)

Karl Barth, *The Word of God and the Word of Man* (London: Hodder & Stoughton, 1928)

David J. Bartholomew, *God of Chance* (London: SCM Press, 1984)

John Barton, *People of the Book?: The Authority of the Bible in Christianity* (London: SPCK, 1988)

Leonardo Boff, *Trinity and Society* (London: Burns & Oates, 1988)

Günther Bornkamm, *Jesus of Nazareth* (London: Hodder & Stoughton, 1960)

John Bowden, *Edward Schillebeeckx: Portrait of a Theologian* (London: SCM Press, 1983)

John Bowden, *Jesus: The Unanswered Questions* (London: SCM Press, 1988)

John Bowden, *Karl Barth: Theologian* (London: SCM Press, 1983)

John Bowden, *Voices in the Wilderness* (London: SCM Press, 1977)

John Bowden (ed.), *By Heart: A Lifetime Companion* (London: SCM Press, 1984)

John Bowker, *Licensed Insanities* (London: Darton, Longman & Todd, 1987)

John Bowker, *The Religious Imagination and the Sense of God* (Oxford: Oxford University Press, 1978)

John Bowker, *The Sense of God* (Oxford: Oxford University Press, 1973)

David Brown, *The Divine Trinity* (London: Duckworth, 1985)

Emil Brunner, *Truth as Encounter* (London: SCM Press, 1964)

Rudolf Bultmann, *Jesus and the Word* (London: Nicholson & Watson, 1935; London: Collins Fontana, 1958)

Rudolf Bultmann, *Jesus Christ and Mythology* (London: SCM Press, 1960)

Rudolf Bultmann, *Theology of the New Testament*, vol. 1 (London: SCM Press, 1952)

H. J. Cadbury, *The Peril of Modernizing Jesus* (New York: Macmillan, 1937; London: SPCK, 1962)

Keith W. Clements, *Lovers of Discord: Twentieth-Century Theological Controversies in England* (London: SPCK, 1988)

Sarah Coakley, *Christ without Absolutes: A Study of the Christology of Ernst Troeltsch* (Oxford: Clarendon Press, 1988)

Scott Cowdell, *Atheist Priest?: Don Cupitt and Christianity* (London: SCM Press, 1988)

Oscar Cullmann, *The Christology of the New Testament* (London: SCM Press, [2]1963)

Hubert Cunliffe-Jones (ed.), assisted by Benjamin Drewery, *A History of Christian Doctrine* (Edinburgh: T. & T. Clark, 1978)

Don Cupitt, *Christ and the Hiddenness of God* (London: Lutterworth Press, 1971; London : SCM Press, 1985)

Don Cupitt, *Crisis of Moral Authority* (London: Lutterworth Press, 1972; London: SCM Press, 1985)

Don Cupitt, *The Debate about Christ* (London: SCM Press, 1979)

Don Cupitt, *Explorations in Theology* (London: SCM Press, 1979)

Don Cupitt, *Jesus and the Gospel of God* (London: Lutterworth Press, 1979)

Don Cupitt, *The Leap of Reason* (London: Sheldon Press, 1976; London: SCM Press, 1985)

Don Cupitt, *Life Lines* (London: SCM Press, 1986)

Don Cupitt, *The Long Legged Fly: The Theology of Longing and Desire* (London: SCM Press, 1987)

Don Cupitt, *The Nature of Man* (London: Sheldon Press, 1979)

Don Cupitt, *The New Christian Ethics* (London: SCM Press, 1988)

Don Cupitt, *Only Human* (London: SCM Press, 1985)

Don Cupitt, *Radicals and the Future of the Church* (London: SCM Press, 1989)

Don Cupitt, *The Sea of Faith: Christianity in Change* (London: BBC Publications, 1984)

Don Cupitt, *Taking Leave of God* (London: SCM Press, 1980)

Don Cupitt, *The World to Come* (London: SCM Press, 1982)

Don Cupitt, *The Worlds of Science and Religion* (London: Sheldon Press, 1976)

Don Cupitt and Peter Armstrong, *Who Was Jesus?* (London: BBC Publications, 1977)

Stephen T. Davis (ed.), *Encountering Jesus* (Atlanta: John Knox Press, 1987)

Gavin D'Costa, *John Hick's Theology of Religions: A Critical Evaluation* (Lanham: University Press of America, 1987)

The Doctrine Commission of the Church of England, *Believing in the Church: The Corporate Nature of Faith* (London: SPCK, 1981)

The Doctrine Commission of the Church of England, *Christian Believing* (London: SPCK, 1976)

The Doctrine Commission of the Church of England, *We Believe in God* (London: Church House Publishing, 1987)

C. H. Dodd, *The Founder of Christianity* (London: Collins, 1971)

John Drury, *The Parables in the Gospels: History and Allegory* (London: SPCK, 1985)

James D. G. Dunn, *Christology in the Making: A New Testament Inquiry into the Origins of the Doctrine of the Incarnation* (London: SCM Press, 1980,[2] 1989)

James D. G. Dunn, *The Evidence for Jesus: The Impact of Scholarship on Our Understanding of How Christianity Began* (London: SCM Press, 1985)

David L. Edwards, *Christian England* (London: Collins Fount, 1989)

David L. Edwards, *The Futures of Christianity* (London: Hodder & Stoughton, 1987)

David Edwards, *God's Cross in Our World* (London: SCM Press, 1959)

David L. Edwards, *Jesus for Modern Man* (London: Collins Fontana, 1975)

David L. Edwards, *A Key to the Old Testament* (London: Collins, 1976, [2]1989)

David L. Edwards with John R. W. Stott, *Essentials: A Liberal-Evangelical Dialogue* (London: Hodder & Stoughton, 1988)

David L. Edwards (ed.), *The Honest to God Debate* (London: SCM Press, 1963)

Paula Fredriksen, *From Jesus to Christ* (New Haven, Conn., and London: Yale University Press, 1988)

Ernst Fuchs, *Studies of the Historical Jesus* (London: SCM Press, 1964)

R. H. Fuller, *The Foundations of New Testament Christology* (London: Lutterworth Press, 1965; London: Collins Fount, 1969)

Charles Gore (ed.), *Lux Mundi: A Series of Studies in the Religion of the Incarnation* (London: John Murray, 1889)

Michael Goulder with John Hick, *Why Believe in God?* (London: SCM Press, 1983)

Michael Goulder (ed.), *Incarnation and Myth: The Debate Continued* (London: SCM Press, 1979)

Michael Green (ed.), *The Truth of God Incarnate* (London: Hodder & Stoughton, 1977)

Aloys Grillmeier, *Christ in Christian Tradition, Vol. 1: From the Apostolic Age to Chalcedon* (London and Oxford: Mowbray, 1965, [2]1975)

Colin E. Gunton, *Yesterday and Today: A Study of Continuities in Christology* (London: Darton, Longman & Todd, 1983)

R. P. C. Hanson, *The Search for the Christian Doctrine of God: The Arian Controversy 318–381* (Edinburgh: T. & T. Clark, 1988)

Anthony Harvey, *Jesus and the Constraints of History: The Bampton Lectures, 1980* (London: Duckworth, 1982)

Adrian Hastings, *A History of English Christianity 1920–1985* (London: Collins, 1986)

Brian Hebblethwaite, *The Incarnation: Collected Essays in Christology* (Cambridge: Cambridge University Press, 1987)

Brian Hebblethwaite, *The Ocean of Truth* (Cambridge: Cambridge University Press, 1988)

Martin Heidegger, *Being and Time*, trans. John Macquarrie and Edward Robinson (London: SCM Press, 1962)

John Hick, *Arguments for the Existence of God* (London: Macmillan, 1970)

John Hick, *The Centre of Christianity* (London: SCM Press, 1968, 1977)

John Hick, *Christianity at the Centre* (London: Macmillan, 1968)

John Hick, *Death and Eternal Life* (London: Collins, 1976; London: Macmillan, 1985)

John Hick, *Evil and the God of Love* (London: Macmillan, 1966; London: Collins, 1968, [2]1985)

John Hick, *Faith and Knowledge: A Modern Introduction to the Problem of Religious Knowledge* (Ithaca, NY: Cornell University Press, 1957; London: Collins, 1974)

John Hick, *God and the Universe of Faiths: Essays in the Philosophy of Religion* (London: Macmillan, 1973)

John Hick, *An Interpretation of Religion* (London: Macmillan, 1989)

John Hick, *Problems of Religious Pluralism* (London: Macmillan, 1985)

John Hick, *The Second Christianity* (London: SCM Press, 1987)

John Hick (ed.), *The Myth of God Incarnate* (London: SCM Press, 1977)

John Hick (ed.), *Truth and Dialogue* (London: Sheldon Press, 1974)

John Hick and Brian Hebblethwaite (eds), *Christianity and Other Religions: Selected Readings* (London: Collins Fount, 1980)

John Hick and Paul F. Knitter (eds), *The Myth of Christian Uniqueness* (London: SCM Press, 1988)

Leonard Hodgson, *For Faith and Freedom* (Oxford: Basil Blackwell, 2 vols 1956, 1957; London: SCM Press, 1968)

Leonard Hodgson, *Sex and Christian Freedom* (London: SCM Press, 1967)

The House of Bishops of the General Synod of the Church of England, *The Nature of Christian Belief* (London: Church House Publishing, 1986)

Eric James, *A Life of Bishop John A. T. Robinson: Scholar, Pastor, Prophet* (London: Collins, 1987)

Eric James (ed.), *God's Truth: Essays to Commemorate Honest to God* (London: SCM Press, 1988)

Grace Jantzen, *God's World, God's Body* (London: Darton, Longman & Todd, 1984)

Daniel Jenkins, *Beyond Religion: The Truth and Error in 'Religionless Christianity'* (London: SCM Press, 1962)

Walter Kasper, *The God of Jesus Christ* (London: SCM Press, 1984)

Walter Kasper, *Jesus the Christ* (London: Burns & Oates, 1976)

Alistair Kee, *The Roots of Christian Freedom: The Theology of John A. T. Robinson* (London: SPCK, 1988)

Alistair Kee, *The Way of Transcendence: Christian Faith without Belief in God* (Harmondsworth: Penguin Books, 1965; London: SCM Press, 1985)

Paul F. Knitter, *No Other Name?: A Critical Survey of Christian Attitudes toward the World Religions* (London: SCM Press, 1985)

John Knox, *The Humanity and Divinity of Christ: A Study of Pattern in Christology* (Cambridge: Cambridge University Press, 1967)

W. G. Kümmel, *Introduction to the New Testament* (London: SCM Press, 1977)

Hans Küng, *Christianity and the World Religions* (London: Collins, 1987)

Hans Küng, *Does God Exist?: An Answer for Today* (London: Collins, 1980)

Hans Küng, *Eternal Life?* (London: Collins, 1984)

Hans Küng, *On Being a Christian* (London: Collins, 1977)

G. W. H. Lampe, *Explorations in Theology* (London: SCM Press, 1981)

G. W. H. Lampe, *God as Spirit* (Oxford: Clarendon Press, 1977; London: SCM Press, 1983)

G. W. H. Lampe (ed.), *A Patristic Greek Lexicon* (Oxford: Oxford University Press, 1961)

H. D. Lewis, *Jesus in the Faith of Christians* (London: Macmillan, 1981)

Bernard Lonergan, *The Way to Nicea: The Dialectical Development of Trinitarian Theology* (London: Darton, Longman & Todd, 1976)

Thomas Luckmann, *The Invisible Religion: The Problem of Religion in Modern Society* (London: Collier-Macmillan, 1967)

James P. Mackey, *The Christian Experience of God as Trinity* (London: SCM Press, 1983)

James Mackey, *Jesus the Man and the Myth: A Contemporary Christology* (London: SCM Press, 1979)

James Mackey, *Modern Theology: A Sense of Direction* (Oxford: Oxford University Press, 1987)

J. L. Mackie, *The Miracle of Theism: Arguments For and Against the Existence of God* (Oxford: Clarendon Press, 1982)

John Macquarrie, *Principles of Christian Theology* (London: SCM Press, 1966, [2]1977)

John Macquarrie, *The Scope of Demythologizing: Bultmann and his Critics* (London: SCM Press, 1960)

John Macquarrie, *In Search of Deity: An Essay in Dialectical Theism* (London: SCM Press, 1984)

John Macquarrie, *In Search of Humanity: A Theological and Philosophical Approach* (London: SCM Press, 1982)

John Macquarrie, *Studies in Christian Existentialism* (London: SCM Press, 1960)

John Macquarrie, *Twentieth Century Religious Thought* (London: SCM Press, 1963, [2]1981)

E. L. Mascall, *Theology and the Gospel of Christ: An Essay in Reorientation* (London: SPCK, 1977)

E. L. Mascall, *Whatever Happened to the Human Mind?: Essays in Christian Orthodoxy* (London: SPCK, 1980)

Richard McBrien, *The Church in the Thought of Bishop John Robinson* (London: SCM Press, 1966)

Sallie McFague, *Models of God* (London: SCM Press, 1987)

Alister E. McGrath, *The Making of Modern German Christology: From the Enlightenment to Pannenberg* (Oxford: Basil Blackwell, 1986)

John McIntyre, *The Shape of Christology* (London: SCM Press, 1966)

Jürgen Moltmann, *The Crucified God: The Cross of Christ as the Foundation and Criticism of Christian Theology* (London: SCM Press, 1974)

Jürgen Moltmann, *The Trinity and the Kingdom of God: The Doctrine of God* (London: SCM Press, 1981)

Hugh Montefiore, *The Probability of God* (London: SCM Press, 1985)

Hugh Montefiore (ed.), *Man and Nature* (London: Collins, 1975)

Robert Morgan (ed.), *The Religion of the Incarnation: Anglican Essays in Commemoration of Lux Mundi* (Bristol: Bristol Classical Press, 1989)

Thomas V. Morris, *The Logic of God Incarnate* (Ithaca, NY: Cornell University Press, 1986)

C. F. D. Moule, *The Origin of Christology* (Cambridge: Cambridge University Press, 1977)

C. F. D. Moule (ed.), *G. W. H. Lampe: Christian, Scholar, Churchman. A Memoir by his Friends* (London and Oxford: Mowbray, 1982)

Iris Murdoch, *The Sovereignty of Good* (London: Routledge & Kegan Paul, 1970)

Dennis Nineham, *Explorations in Theology* (London: SCM Press, 1977)

Dennis Nineham, *The Use and Abuse of the Bible: A Study of the Bible in an Age of Rapid Cultural Change* (London: SPCK, 1976)

Dennis Nineham (ed.), *The Church's Use of the Bible* (London: SPCK, 1963)

Dennis Nineham (ed.), *The Gospel of St Mark* (Harmondsworth: Penguin Books, 1963)

Wolfhart Pannenberg, *Jesus – God and Man* (London: SCM Press, 1968)

Arthur Peacocke, *Creation and the World of Science* (Oxford: Oxford University Press, 1979)

Arthur Peacocke, *God and the New Biology* (London: Dent, 1986)

Jaroslav Pelikan, *Jesus through the Centuries: His Place in the History of Culture* (New Haven, Conn., and London: Yale University Press, 1985)

D. Z. Phillips, *Religion without Explanation* (Oxford: Basil Blackwell, 1977)

John Polkinghorne, *One World: The Interaction of Science and Theology* (London: SPCK, 1986)
John Polkinghorne, *Science and Creation: The Search for Understanding* (London: SPCK, 1988)
John Polkinghorne, *Science and Providence: God's Interaction with the World* (London: SPCK, 1989)
William Purcell, *Fisher of Lambeth* (London: Hodder & Stoughton, 1969)
Michael Ramsey, *Image Old and New* (London: SPCK, 1963)
Robert C. Roberts, *Rudolf Bultmann's Theology: A Critical Interpretation* (London: SPCK, 1977)
J. A. T. Robinson, *The Body: A Study in Pauline Theology* (London: SCM Press, 1952)
J. A. T. Robinson, *But That I Can't Believe!* (London: Collins, 1967)
J. A. T. Robinson, *Can We Trust the New Testament?* (London: Mowbray, 1977)
J. A. T. Robinson, *Christian Freedom in a Permissive Society* (London: SCM Press, 1970)
J. A. T. Robinson, *The Difference in Being a Christian Today* (London: Collins, 1971)
J. A. T. Robinson, *Exploration into God* (London: SCM Press, 1967)
J. A. T. Robinson, *Honest to God* (London: SCM Press, 1963)
J. A. T. Robinson, *The Human Face of God* (London: SCM Press, 1973)
J. A. T. Robinson, *In the End God . . . : A Study of the Christian Doctrine of the Last Things* (London: James Clarke, 1950; London: Collins, 1968)
J. A. T. Robinson, *Jesus and His Coming: The Emergence of a Doctrine* (London: SCM Press, 1957)
J. A. T. Robinson, *Liturgy Coming to Life* (London: Mowbray, 1960)
J. A. T. Robinson, *The New Reformation?* (London: SCM Press, 1965)
J. A. T. Robinson, *On Being the Church in the World* (London: SCM Press, 1960; Harmondsworth: Penguin Books, 1969)
J. A. T. Robinson, *The Priority of John*, ed. J. F. Coakley (London: SCM Press, 1985)
J. A. T. Robinson, *Redating the New Testament* (London: SCM Press, 1976)
J. A. T. Robinson, *The Roots of a Radical* (London: SCM Press, 1980)
J. A. T. Robinson, *Truth is Two-Eyed* (London: SCM Press, 1979)
J. A. T. Robinson, *Twelve More New Testament Studies* (London: SCM Press, 1984)
J. A. T. Robinson, *Where Three Ways Meet* (London: SCM Press, 1987)
J. A. T. Robinson, *Wrestling with Romans* (London: SCM Press, 1979)
Richard Robinson, *An Atheist's Values* (Oxford: Oxford University Press, 1964)
Christopher Rowland, *Christian Origins: An Account of the Setting and*

Character of the most Important Messianic Sect of Judaism (London: SPCK, 1985)

Christopher Rowland, *The Open Heaven: A Study of Apocalyptic in Judaism and Early Christianity* (London: SPCK, 1982)

Christopher Rowland, *Radical Christianity: A Reading of Recovery* (Cambridge: Polity Press/Oxford: Basil Blackwell, 1988)

E. P. Sanders, *Jesus and Judaism* (London: SCM Press, 1985)

Edward Schillebeeckx, *Christ: The Christian Experience in the Modern World* (London: SCM Press, 1980)

Edward Schillebeeckx, *Jesus: An Experiment in Christology* (London: Collins, 1979)

Walter Schmithals, *An Introduction to the Theology of Rudolf Bultmann* (London: SCM Press, 1968)

Eduard Schweizer, *Jesus Christ: The Man from Nazareth and the Exalted Lord* (London: SCM Press, 1989)

Graham Shaw, *God in Our Hands* (London: SCM Press, 1987)

Ninian Smart, *Beyond Ideology* (London: Collins, 1982)

Ninian Smart, *The Phenomenon of Christianity* (London: Collins, 1979)

Ninian Smart, *The Religious Experience of Mankind* (London: Collins, 1969)

Ninian Smart, *The World's Religions: Old Traditions and Modern Transformations* (Cambridge: Cambridge University Press, 1989)

Wilfred Cantwell Smith, *Truth and Belief* (Princeton: Princeton University Press, 1979)

Kenneth Surin, *Theology and the Problem of Evil* (Oxford: Basil Blackwell, 1986)

Stewart R. Sutherland, *God, Jesus and Belief: The Legacy of Theism* (Oxford: Basil Blackwell, 1984)

Richard Swinburne, *The Coherence of Theism* (Oxford: Clarendon Press, 1977)

Richard Swinburne, *The Existence of God* (Oxford: Clarendon Press, 1979)

Stephen Sykes, *The Identity of Christianity: Theologians and the Essence of Christianity from Schleiermacher to Barth* (London: SPCK, 1984)

S. W. Sykes and J. P. Clayton (eds), *Christ, Faith and History: Cambridge Studies in Christology* (Cambridge: Cambridge University Press, 1972)

Gerd Theissen, *Biblical Faith: An Evolutionary Approach* (London: SCM Press, 1984)

Robert Towler, *The Need for Certainty: A Sociological Study of Conventional Religion* (London: Routledge & Kegan Paul, 1984)

Lionel Trilling, *The Liberal Imagination* (London: Mercury Books, 1964)

Ernst Troeltsch, *The Absoluteness of Christianity and the History of Religion* (London: SCM Press, 1972)

Matthew Tindal, *Christianity as Old as the Creation or the Gospel a Republication of the Religion of Nature* (1730)

Alec Vidler, *Scenes from a Clerical Life* (London: Collins, 1977)

Alec Vidler, *Twentieth Century Defenders of the Faith: Some Theological Fashions Considered in the Robertson Lectures for 1964* (London: SCM Press, 1965)

Alec Vidler *et al.*, *Objections to Christian Belief* (London: Constable, 1963)

Alec Vidler (ed.), *Soundings: Essays Concerning Christian Understanding* (Cambridge: Cambridge University Press, 1962)

Geoffrey Wainwright (ed.), *Keeping the Faith: Essays to Mark the Centenary of Lux Mundi* (London: SPCK, 1989)

Keith Ward, *The Concept of God* (Oxford: Basil Blackwell, 1974)

Keith Ward, *Holding Fast to God: A Reply to Don Cupitt* (London: SPCK, 1982)

Keith Ward, *Images of Eternity: Concepts of God in Five Religious Traditions* (London: Darton, Longman & Todd, 1987)

Keith Ward, *The Turn of the Tide: Christian Belief in Britain Today* (London: BBC Publications, 1986)

Maurice Wiles, *The Christian Fathers* (London: Hodder & Stoughton, 1966; London: SCM Press, 1977)

Maurice Wiles, *Explorations in Theology* (London: SCM Press, 1979)

Maurice Wiles, *Faith and the Mystery of God* (London: SCM Press, 1982)

Maurice Wiles, *God's Action in the World* (London: SCM Press, 1986)

Maurice Wiles, *The Making of Christian Doctrine: A Study in the Principles of Early Doctrinal Development* (Cambridge: Cambridge University Press, 1967)

Maurice Wiles, *The Remaking of Christian Doctrine: The Hulsean Lectures 1973* (London: SCM Press, 1974)

Maurice Wiles, *What is Theology?* (Oxford: Oxford University Press, 1976)

Maurice Wiles, *Working Papers in Doctrine* (London: SCM Press, 1976)

H. A. Williams, *Some Day I'll Find You* (London: Mitchell Beazley, 1982)

H. A. Williams, *True Resurrection* (London: Mitchell Beazley, 1972; London: Collins, 1983)

H. A. Williams, *The True Wilderness* (London: Constable, 1965; London: Collins, 1976)

Rowan Williams, *Arius: Heresy and Tradition* (London: Darton, Longman & Todd, 1988)

Frances Young, *From Nicaea to Chalcedon: A Guide to the Literature and its Background* (London: SCM Press, 1983)

INDEX

Acts of Apostles, 108, 131, 156, 162, 183, 215
Adam, 21, 100, 146, 235
African religion, 233
Al Ghazzali, 113
Allmen, J. J. von, 282
Alternative Service Book, 42, 182, 263
Altizer, T., 53
Anselm, 18, 49, 274
Antioch, 147
Apollinarius, 104
Aquinas, 49, 113, 131, 243, 308
Arguments for Existence of God, 235
Aristotle, 111
Arius, 104, 143, 147, 184
Armstrong, P., 75
Arnold, M., 6, 96
Athenegoras, 112
Atonement, 17, 21, 100, 139, 146, 204, 220–1, 241, 304–5
Augustine, 215
Avis, P., 281
Ayer, A., 72

Baelz, P., 139, 140
Baillie, D., 143, 160, 166, 241
Baker, J. A., 181–2
Baptism, 41, 85–6, 109, 281–2, 300
Barr, J., 40
Barth, K., 77, 100, 137, 149, 174, 189, 257, 259, 264–5
Bartholomew, D. J., 271
Barton, J., 199, 257, 279, 300
Becket, T., 11

Believing in Church, 262–3, 276
Berlin, I., 300
Biblical authority, 14, 16, 80, 99, 109–10, 112, 257–8, 268, 303–6
Biblical theology, 14–16
Bezzant, J. S., 20–2, 53
Blake, W., 283
Blood-shedding, 304
Body, 40–1
Boethius, 148
Boff, L., 149
Bonhoeffer, D., 50, 51, 54–5, 135
Book of Common Prayer, 14, 17, 21
Bornkamm, G., 145, 188, 294, 299
Bowden, J., 29, 36, 106, 169–90, 255, 291–6
Bradley, F. H., 284
Brown, D., 152–3, 164, 281
Buber, M., 39
Buddhism, 85, 113, 137–8, 215, 220–1, 223, 227–8, 238–9, 244, 249–50, 252–3, 307
Bultmann, R., 49, 50, 65, 84, 158–9, 167, 187–90, 192, 198, 260, 295–6, 301
Burnaby, J., 17, 19
But That I Can't Believe!, 33
Butler, J., 123
Butler, Lord, 34

Cadbury, H. J., 185, 192–3
Cambridge University, 9–12, 15, 41, 48, 56, 259
Camus, A., 117

*Can We Trust the New
  Testament?*, 35, 58
Cappadocian Fathers, 104, 148
Chalcedon, 133, 145–7
'Christ', 156–60, 247, and see
  Messiah
*Christ and the Hiddenness of
  God*, 68–70, 80, 91
Christian Believing, 106, 261–2,
  276
Christian Experience of Trinity,
  141–3
Christian Fathers, 103, 109
Christian Freedom, 55
Christology, 18, 49–50, 102,
  124–68, 247–8, 290–1
Church of England, 13–15, 36–8,
  42, 56, 59, 254, 261–3, 275–8,
  285–6
Church Times, 11, 31, 56, 68, 131
Church's Use of the Bible, 196–7,
  296–7
Clayton, J., 75, 117
Clement of Alexandria, 305
Clement of Rome, 64
Clements, K., 32
Cloud of Unknowing, 246
Coakley, S., 214, 221
Coleridge, S. T., 77, 174
Colonialism, 222
Communicatio idiomatum, 148
Conservative Party, 10
Conservatism in religion, 11–12,
  22–6, 100, 256–7
Constantine, 113
Corinthians, 179, 184
Cowdell, S., 68, 79, 82–3, 85–6
Creed, J. M., 298
Crisis of Moral Authority, 95
Crockford's Clerical Directory, 12
Cultural relativism, 198–200,
  299–302
Cupitt, D., 12, 57, 68–97, 126,
  129, 134, 172, 242, 254–5,
  283–6
Cyprian, 215

Dante, 97
Darwin, C., 96
D'Costa, G., 222, 241
Death and Eternal Life, 223,
  237–9
'Death of God', 9, 88–90, 193,
  278–9
Debate about Christ, 75–6
Deconstructionism, 86
Deism, 29, 119, 123, 274
Derrida, J., 86–7, 268
Descartes, R., 78
Development in theology, 100
Dharma, 213
Difference in Being a Christian,
  56, 59–61
Divorce, 23, 24, 185, 303
Doctrine Commissions, 261–2
Dodd, C. H., 294, 299
Donne, J., 59
Dostoevsky, F., 117
Driver, T., 219, 232
Drury, J., 298
Dumitriu, P., 55, 58
Dunn, J., 152, 180

Eckhart, 14, 41–2, 84, 153
Einstein, A., 272
Eliot, T. S., 108, 284
Encountering Jesus, 241
English religion, 9–15, 46–8, 108,
  257, 275–6
Epistle to Diognetus, 46
Eschatology, 21, 40–1, 43–5,
  186–90, 237–40
Essays and Reviews, 128
Eternal life, 101–2, 163
Ethics, see Morality
Eucharist, 14, 41, 139, 281–2
Evangelicals, 19, 25, 28, 37, 139,
  256, 276
Evans, C. F., 298
Evil, 58–9, 93–4, 116–17, 235–7,
  272, 274, 281, 288–9
Exclusivism, 215–19
Exploration into God, 53–5

Factuality, 79–80, 87–8, 111
Faith and Knowledge, 234–5
Faith and Mystery of God,
    119–20, 122, 162
Farrer, A., 27, 63–4, 115, 135,
    151
Fatherhood of God, 181, 194, 298
Fathers of Church, 102–14, 216
Feminism, 18, 265–71, 285–6,
    292–3
Feuerbach, L., 76
Fisher, G., 14–16, 32
Forrester, 279
Foucault, M., 86–7
Fourth Lateran Council, 215
Francis, 183, 267
Fredricksen, P., 308
Fuller, R. H., 152

Gautama, 138, 213, 227, 238, 259
    and see Buddhism
Germany, 10, 105, 171, 175
Gilkey, L., 223–5
Gnostics, 47, 66, 110
God and the Universe of Faiths,
    228–9, 233
God as Spirit, see Lampe
God, reality of, 17, 18, 26–9,
    48–55, 57, 91–7, 115–16, 138,
    230–1, 265–78, 284
God's Action in World, 115,
    117–18, 120, 145
Godspell, 141
God's Truth, 36, 42, 206
Goulder, M., 126
Gregory Nazianzen, 104
Gregory of Nyssa, 265
Grillmeier, A., 169
Gunton, C., 33, 120–1, 164–5

Habgood, J., 16, 19, 254–5
Hall, R. O., 27
Hamilton, W., 53
Hanson, R. P. C., 147
Hardy, D., 280
Harnack, A. von, 264

Harvey, A., 181, 262–3
Hastings, A., 30, 34
Hebblethwaite, B., 82–3, 87,
    107, 133, 148, 151, 164, 212,
    281
Hebrews, 63–4, 136–7, 153,
    304
Hegel, G. W. F., 96, 215, 283
Hell, 204, 207, 209, 216
Henry II, 11
Hepburn, R. W., 16
Hick, J., 26–9, 117, 126, 128–31,
    145, 212, 216–17, 220–6, 254–5
Hinduism, 215, 217–18, 220,
    238–9, 244–8, 308
Hodgson, L., 103–4, 143, 200,
    206–8
Holding Fast to God, 82, 91–4
Holocaust, 93–4, 308
Holy Spirit, 101, 149
Honest to God, 30–2, 36, 47–52,
    246
Honest to God Debate, 31, 48,
    189–90, 206
Hopkins, G. M., 57
Houlden, L., 11–12, 126
Hulme, T. E., 304
Human Face of God, 33, 35,
    135–8, 160–1, 247
Hume, D., 69, 122
Huxley, J., 161
Hyers, C., 242–3
Hypostasis, 148

Identity of Christianity, 263–5
In Search of Deity, 273–4
In Search of Humanity, 260
In the End God, 35–6, 38–40
Incarnation, 129, 140, 229 and see
    Christology
Incarnation and Myth, 132–5
Inclusivism, 219–25
Inquisition, 10, 152, 226
Interpretation of Religion, 242–5
Irenaeus, 236
Islam, see Muhammad and Quran

James, E., 32
Jantzen, G., 269
Jeffries, R., 54
Jenkins, Daniel, 30
Jenkins, David, 12, 172
Jenson, R., 279
Jerusalem, 63
Jesus and His Coming, 36, 42–5
Jesus and the Gospel of God, 74
Jesus Christ Superstar, 130
Jesus: the Unanswered Questions, 169–90, 291–6
John's gospel, 43, 63–7, 109, 137, 144, 153, 165, 229, 267
John the Baptist, 177
Judaism, 177–80, 188, 220, 233, 308
Julian of Norwich, 270

Kant, I., 146, 283
Kasemann, E., 29
Kasper, W., 159–60, 165
Kaufman, G., 218, 223, 269
Kazantzakis, N., 55
Keats, J., 236, 301
Kee, A., 33, 39
Kierkegaard, S., 39, 92, 284
Kingdom of God, 180 and see Eschatology
King's College, 15
Knitter, P., 212–13, 220, 223–5, 233
Knox, J., 67, 136, 152, 155
Krishna, 111, 246
Kümmel, W. G., 62–3
Küng, H., 217, 250–3, 265

Labour Party, 11
Lady Chatterley's Lover, 32, 38
Lampe, G., 17, 127, 138–41, 143, 146, 148, 153–7, 161–3, 186, 241, 254–5, 261
Lash, N., 133–4
Leach, E., 300
Leap of Reason, 75
Lessing, G. E., 112–13

Lewis, C. S., 14
Lewis, H. D., 167
Liberalism in theology, 25–6, 292
Liberation theology, 130, 266
Life Lines, 76, 78, 81, 85–6, 88
Lightfoot, J. B., 36, 46
Lightfoot, R. H., 297, 301
Liturgical renewal, 14
Liturgy Coming to Life, 41–2
Logos, 66, 154–5, 189, 217
Loisy, A., 264–5, 299
Lonergan, B., 113, 133
Long Legged Fly, 73, 78, 84–5, 89, 95–6
Lord's Prayer, 74, 180
Louth, A., 164, 281
Luckmann, T., 47
Lucretius, 76
Luke's gospel, 63, 156, 298
Luther, M., 136, 274, 308
Lux Mundi, 278–9

McBrien, R., 37, 41
Maccoby, H., 172
McFague, S., 258, 262–71
McGrath, A., 146, 281
McIntyre, A., 48
McIntyre, J., 152
Mackie, J. L., 122
MacKinnon, D., 11, 23
Macquarrie, J., 133, 164, 189, 258, 260–1
Maimonides, 113
Making of Christian Doctrine, 109, 120
Man and Nature, 93
Manson, T. W., 206
Mark's gospel, 62, 136, 200, 302–3
Marxism, 96, 175, 248–9
Mascall, E. L., 131, 144, 146
Matthew's gospel, 215–16
Maurice, F. D., 16
Messiah, 144, 153, 155, 179, 201–4, 210

Metaphysics, 111–13
Miracles, 28, 117–19, 202, 229, 252–3, 272, 287–8
Mitchell, B., 132
Models of God, 265–71
Moltmann, J., 149
Montefiore, C. G., 185, 194, 299
Montefiore, H., 18, 19, 271
Morality, 16, 17, 55, 88–9, 90
Morgan, R., 279
Morris, T., 166–7
Motherhood of God, 18, 270
Moule, C. F. D., 127, 133–5, 152, 164, 199, 300
Muhammad, 227, 229, 252–3, 272
Murdoch, I., 71
Murphy-O'Connor, J., 172
Myth, 111, 124, 129, 213, 277, 309–10

Nanak, 309
Narrative theology, 278
Nature of Christian Belief, 173, 276
Nature of Man, 82
Natural theology, 16–17 and see God
Neill, S., 43
Neoplatonics, 112, 128, 140, 283 and see Platonism
Nestorius, 147, 305
New Christian Ethics, 89–90
New English Bible, 41
New Reformation? 52–3, 355
Newbigin, L., 134–5, 280
Newman, J. H., 96, 105, 174–5, 264
Nicaea, 113–14, 167
Niebuhr, R., 296, 308
Nietzsche, F., 78, 88
Nineham, D., 42, 128, 225, 261, 268, 296–306
Nirvana, 239, 249
Nock, A. D., 128–9

Non-realism, 68, 86–8, 282–4
Norman, E., 172
Norris, R., 280

Objections to Christian Belief, 9
Observer, 31–2, 160
Ogden, S., 247
Oman, J., 276
On Being Church in World, 45–6
O'Neill, J. C., 36
Only Human, 73, 77, 79, 88, 95
Origen, 104
Ousia, 148
Oxford University, 15, 108, 259, 278–9

Panentheism, 55, 275
Pannenberg, W., 145
Pannikar, R., 217, 222–4
Parables, 44, 121, 124, 183, 287
Parousia, 42, 45
Parsons, T., 242
Pascal, B., 76
Paul, 20–1, 40–1, 43, 59, 62–3, 121, 149, 157, 176, 183–4, 215, 293, 305, 308
Peacocke, A., 271
Pelikan, J., 109
Pentecostalism, 139
Perichoresis, 148
Personality in God, 51–5, 94, 246
Philippians, 184
Phillips, D. Z., 116, 284
Philo, 154
Pieris, A., 213
Pius XII, 14
Platonism, 67, 104, 111, 144, 154 and see Neoplatonics
Plotinus, 283
Polkinghorne, J., 258–9
Power, D., 281
Power in Church, 265, 292–3
Prayer, 17–18, 27, 50, 54, 70, 101, 134, 149
Pre-existence of Christ, 101, 135–7, 153–5, 159

Prestige, G. L., 305
Principles of Christian Theology, 260–1
Problems of Religious Pluralism, 220, 224, 228, 230
Purcell, W., 14

Quickswood, Lord, 27
Qumran, 177
Quran, 220, 229

Radicalism in theology, 9–10, 20, 55, 100, 139, 256
Rahner, K., 109, 217, 219–20, 251
Ramsey, I., 133
Ramsey, M., 31
'Reality', 50–2, 224–5, 230–1, 244
Redaction criticism, 183
Redating the New Testament, 34, 62–4
Redeemer, 111, 129, 146, 188
Reincarnation, 231, 238, 252
Remaking of Christian Doctrine, 98–103, 106, 119
Resurrection, 35, 41, 70, 118, 139, 163, 173, 211, 237–8, 289–90
Revelation of John, 45, 63, 67, 187
Roberts, R. C., 159
Robinson, J., 12, 30–61, 84, 125–7, 160–1, 206, 245–8
Robinson, R., 185, 254–5
Roman Catholic Church, see Vatican
Root, H., 15, 17, 19, 254
Roots of a Radical, 36–7
Rowland, C., 187
Ruether, R., 226–7, 270
Runcie, R., 32
Russell, B., 175

Saints, 121, 230–1, 307–8
Salvation, 215–17

Samaritans, 130–1
Samartha, S. J., 217, 219, 228–9
Sanders, E. P., 176–80, 294
Sanders, J. N., 16
Saviour, 227, 268
Schillebeeckx, E., 165, 169, 174–5, 177–8, 184–5
Schmithals, W., 296
Schleiermacher, F., 76–7
Schweitzer, A., 175, 299, 306
Schweizer, E., 26
Science, 16, 87–8, 95–6, 231–2, 258–9, 271–3, 288
Sea of Faith, 68, 72, 76, 79, 87, 95–7
Second Vatican Council, 9, 197, 217
Sexuality, 23–4, 32, 35, 55, 233
Shaw, G., 176
Shiffmann, L., 294
Shinran, 307, 309
Smart, N., 18, 19, 109, 248–50, 255
Smith, M., 172
Smith, W. C., 225, 229
Son of God, 153–5, 309
Son of Man, 44, 144
Soundings, 9–20, 23, 30, 254–5, 278
Southwark diocese, 46–8
Spinoza, B., 116, 153, 275
Stanton, G., 133–6, 259–260
Stockwood, M., 46
Strauss, D. F., 96
Streeter, B. H., 194
Sturdy, J., 34
Suffering of God, 93, 150–1, 240–1, 277
Sufis, 243, 308
Sunday Times, 172
Sunyata, 223, 231
Surin, K., 93
Sutherland, S., 116
Swinburne, R., 88

Sykes, S., 75, 117, 258, 263–5,
278–80
Symbolism, 87, 95

Taking Leave of God, 68, 78, 80,
82–3, 92–3
Taylor, J., 133
Teilhard de Chardin, 54
Temple, W., 143, 276, 279
Teresa, Mother, 183
Tertullian, 245
Thatcher, M., 57
Theissen, G., 122
Thirty-nine Articles, 17
Thomas, M. M., 248
Thou Who Art, 39–40
Tillich, P., 9, 50–1, 53, 84, 187,
270
Tindal, M., 119
Towler, R., 47
Toynbee, P., 160
Transcendence, 16, 33, 49, 84,
92
Trilling, W., 299
Trinity, 104, 137, 141–3, 148–50
Trinity College, 33, 36, 56
Troeltsch, E., 199, 214–15, 264
Truth is Two-eyed, 56, 245–8
Turin Shroud, 35
Tyrrell, G., 74

Unitarians, 103, 131, 140
Universalism, 216, 247–8
Use and Abuse of Bible, 193, 195,
197

Vatican, 139, 250, 264, 292
Vermes, G., 172, 299
Victorians, 96–7
Vidler, A., 9, 14–16, 19, 24–5,
254–5
Vincent de Lérins, 260–1
Virgin birth, 35, 49, 137, 143–4,
159, 173, 261, 287

Wainwright, G., 278, 282
Ward, K., 82–3, 91–2, 113, 151,
166, 259
We Believe in God, 275–8
Weil, S., 279
Wells, G. A., 172
What is Theology?, 172
Where Three Ways Meet, 36–7,
45, 58–9
Who Was Jesus?, 75
Wiles, M., 98–124, 126, 129,
132–3, 144–7, 152, 159–60,
206, 254–5, 266, 272, 280,
286–91
Wilson, Lord, 11, 55
Wisdom in the Old Testament,
154–5
Woods, G., 16, 18, 19
Working Papers in Doctrine,
103–6, 116, 118–19, 144, 152
World Council of Churches, 9, 19
World to Come, The, 72, 75–6,
80, 88–9, 94
Wrestling with Romans, 57

Young, F., 126, 131, 145, 150